D1491413

Social postmodernism defends a postmodern perspective anchored in the politics of the new social movements. The volume preserves the focus on the politics of the body, race, gender, and sexuality as elaborated in postmodern approaches. But these essays push postmodern analysis in a particular direction: toward a social postmodernism which integrates the micro-social concerns of the new social movements with an institutional and cultural analysis in the service of a transformative political vision.

Bringing together authors who have already contributed to debates over theory, politics, and society, *Social postmodernism* explores the territory beyond critical modernism and beyond deconstruction.

Social postmodernism

Cambridge Cultural Social Studies

General editors: JEFFREY C. ALEXANDER, *Department of Sociology, University of California, Los Angeles, and* STEVEN SEIDMAN, *Department of Sociology, University at Albany, State University of New York.*

Editorial Board
JEAN COMAROFF, *Department of Anthropology, University of Chicago*
DONNA HARAWAY, *Department of the History of Consciousness, University of California, Santa Cruz*
MICHELE LAMONT, *Department of Sociology, Princeton University*
THOMAS LAQUEUR, *Department of History, University of California, Berkeley*

Cambridge Cultural Social Studies is a forum for the most original and thoughtful work in cultural social studies. This includes theoretical works focusing on conceptual strategies, empirical studies covering specific topics such as gender, sexuality, politics, economics, social movements, and crime, and studies that address broad themes such as the culture of modernity. While the perspectives of the individual studies will vary, they will all share the same innovative reach and scholarly quality.

Social postmodernism

Beyond identity politics

EDITED BY

Linda Nicholson
University at Albany, State University of New York

and

Steven Seidman
University at Albany, State University of New York

CAMBRIDGE
UNIVERSITY PRESS

Published by the Press Syndicate of the University of Cambridge
The Pitt Building, Trumpington Street, Cambridge CB2 1RP
40 West 20th Street, New York, NY 10011–4211, USA
10 Stamford Road, Oakleigh, Melbourne 3166, Australia

First published 1995

Printed in Great Britain at the University Press, Cambridge

A catalogue record for this book is available from the British Library

Library of Congress cataloguing in publication data
Social postmodernism: beyond identity politics / edited by Linda Nicholson
   and Steven Seidman.
      p.   cm. – (Cambridge cultural social studies)
   ISBN 0 521 47516 3 (hardback) – ISBN 0 521 47571 6 (pbk.)
   1. Sociology – Methodology.   2. Group identity.   3. Political
sociology.   4. Social movements.   5. Postmodernism – Social aspects.
   I. Nicholson, Linda J.   II. Seidman, Steven.   III. Series.
   HM24.S5443   1995
301'.01 – dc20   94-49039CIP

ISBN 0521 47516 3 hardback
ISBN 0521 47571 6 paperback

Contents

Notes on contributors

Kwame Anthony Appiah is Professor of Afro-American Studies at Harvard University. His books include *Assertion and Conditionals, For Truth in Semantics, Necessary Questions*, the novel *Avenging Angel*, and *In My Father's House*.

Stanley Aronowitz is Professor of Sociology and Director of the Cultural Studies Program at the Graduate Center, City University of New York. He is the author of *The Crisis in Historical Materialism, The Politics of Identity*, and *Dead Artists, Live Theories, and Other Cultural Problems*, among other books.

R. W. Connell is Professor of Sociology at the University of California at Santa Cruz. He is the author of thirteen books including *Ruling Class, Ruling Culture, Class Structure in Australian History, Gender and Power, Schools and Social Justice, Rethinking Sex* and the forthcoming, *Masculinities*.

Nancy Fraser is Professor of Political Science in the Graduate Faculty of the New School for Social Research. She is the author of *Unruly Practices: Power, Discourse, and Gender in Contemporary Social Theory*, a co-author of *Feminist Contentions: A Philosophical Exchange*, and the co-editor of *Revaluing French Feminism: Critical Essays on Difference, Culture, and Agency*.

Rosemary Hennessy teaches and writes on postmodern, feminist, and gay and lesbian theory. She works in the English Department of the University at Albany, State University of New York, where she is also affiliated with Women's Studies. She has written *Materialist Feminism and the Politics of Discourse* as well as various essays on feminist and cultural critique.

Chandra Talpade Mohanty is Associate Professor of Women's Studies at Hamilton College. She is co-editor of *Third World Women and the Politics of Feminism* and *Movements, Histories, Identities: Genealogies of Third World Feminism*. She also edits the series, Gender, Culture, and Global Politics, for Garland Publishers. Her recent work focuses on feminist and antiracist pedagogy, and on questions of democracy and social justice in the New World Order.

Chantal Mouffe is the editor of *Gramsci and Marxist Theory*, co-author with Ernesto Laclau of *Hegemony and Socialist Strategy: Towards a Radical Democratic Politics*, and author of *The Return of the Political*.

Linda Nicholson is Professor of Educational Administration and Policy Studies and of Women's Studies at the University at Albany, State University of New York. She is the author of *Gender and History: The Limits of Social Theory in the Age of the Family* and the editor of *Feminism/Postmodernism*. She edits the series Thinking Gender for Routledge.

Cindy Patton is Assistant Professor of English at Temple University. She is the author of *Inventing Aids* and *Last Served? Gendering the HIV Pandemic*.

Shane Phelan teaches political theory at the University of New Mexico. She is the author of *Getting Specific: Postmodern Lesbian Politics* and *Identity Politics: Lesbian Feminism and the Limits of Community*, as well as several articles on feminist theory, Adorno, and Foucault. She is presently co-editing a forthcoming volume, *We Are Everywhere: An Historical Sourcebook in Gay and Lesbian Politics*, and is editing a collection of articles on queer political theory.

Gyan Prakash is Associate Professor of History, Princeton University. He is the author of *Bonded Histories: Genealogies of Labor Servitude in Colonial India*, has recently edited a volume of essays, *After Colonialism: Imperial Histories and Postcolonial Displacements*, and is preparing a book on science and the imagination of modern India.

Ali Rattansi teaches sociology at City University, London. His publications include *Marx and the Division of Labor; Ideology, Method and Marx; Postmodernism and Society* (with Roy Boyne); *Race, Culture and Difference* (with James Donald); *Racism and Antiracism* (with

Peter Braham and Richard Skellington); *Rethinking Radical Education* (with David Reeder); and *Racism, Modernity, and Identity* (with Sallie Westwood). He is a member of the editorial board of the journals *Economy and Society* and *New Formations*.

Steven Seidman is Professor of Sociology at the University at Albany, State University of New York. He is the author of, among other works, *Liberalism and the Origins of European Social Theory, Embattled Eros*, and *Contested Knowledge*. He is, with Jeffrey Alexander, the general editor of the series, Cambridge Cultural Social Studies, and editor of *The Postmodern Turn* and a forthcoming volume, *The Social Construction of Homosexual Desire*.

Iris Marion Young teaches ethics and political philosophy at the University of Pittsburgh in the Graduate School of Public and International Affairs. She is the author of *Throwing Like a Girl and Other Essays in Feminist Philosophy and Social Theory* and *Justice and the Politics of Difference*. She is working on a project about communicative democracy in which she draws on feminist discussions of politics and storytelling and the problems that speaking for others entail.

Acknowledgements

We would like to thank Catherine Max at Cambridge University Press for her support on this project. The secretarial help of Sharon Baumgardner and Eileen Pellegrino has been much appreciated.

This book came out of a long and deep friendship. That friendship has expanded each of our perspectives, enabling us to cross fields of knowledge, political vantage points, and psychological proclivities. The process we have developed over the years in struggling over all kinds of issues made it possible for us to work through whatever differences emerged around the book itself. In fact, our friendship made this collaboration (mostly) fun and for that, and for caring about each other, we would like to thank each other.

The publishers and editors would like to thank the following for permission to reproduce material from their publications: University of Chicago Press for "Interpreting Gender" by Linda Nicholson, from *Signs: Journal of Women in Culture and Society*, 20 (1), for "Gender as Seriality: Thinking About Women as a Social Collective" by Iris Marion Young, from *Signs*, 19 (3), and for "Sex, Lies, and the Public Sphere: Some Reflections on the Confirmation of Clarence Thomas," by Nancy Fraser, from *Critical Inquiry* 18 (Spring 1992); Polity Press for "Feminist Encounters: Locating the Politics of Experience" by Chandra Talpade Mohanty, from Barrett and Phillips (eds.), *Destabilizing Theory* (Cambridge: Polity, 1992); Duke University Press, for "Postcolonial Criticism and Indian Historiography," by Gyan Prakash, from *Social Text* 31/32, vol. 10, nos. 2–3 (Duke University Press, 1992); Oxford University Press for "African Identities" by Kwame Anthony Appiah, from Appiah, *In My Father's House* (New York: Oxford University Press, 1992) and for "Queer Visibility in Commodity Culture" by Rosemary Hennessy, from *Cultural Critique*, 29 (Winter 1994–1995); *Feminists Theorize the Political* (New York: Routledge, 1992); and University of Minnesota Press, for material from chapters 6 and 8 of Shane Phelan's *Getting Specific: Postmodern Lesbian Politics* (Minneapolis, Minn.: University of Minnesota Press, 1995).

Introduction

Linda Nicholson and Steven Seidman

It is perhaps ironic that the very intellectuals thought to have originated postmodern theory – we mean of course Baudrillard, Foucault, and Derrida (Lyotard being the exception) – have refused this characterization of their work. It is again not entirely without paradox that postmodern theory has found its most welcoming reception and home not in France but in the United States – the nation of pragmatism, empiricism, and a much vaunted liberal consensus. And notwithstanding Rorty's liberal pragmatic version of postmodernism, it is among the American left, among neo- and-post-Marxists, feminists, queers, and Third World and postcolonial intellectuals, that postmodernism has been most enthusiastically embraced. Why have Americans, mostly left academic intellectuals but also some outside America (for example, in Britain and Australia) come to advocate a politics and social theory in a postmodern mode?

We think that this is an important question but it cannot be productively engaged by approaching postmodernism in an ahistorical way. Postmodernism is best spoken about in the plural and its meaning best clarified by understanding those who use it in a particular social and discursive setting. So, we submit two stories, our stories, of "why postmodernism." Of course, we know that these are not the whole story or the only ones – indeed they are not even the only stories we could tell but they are, we hope, stories that are suggestive beyond the tales of two left American academic intellectuals.

Why postmodernism: Steve's story

Before I was a postmodernist, I was a Marxist. Why the change? My "conversion" pivoted on my disillusionment with Marxism which

1

broadened into a disenchantment with key aspects of the Western Enlightenment tradition.

Marxism was a natural for me. White, middle class, culturally alienated – a 1960s radical. For me, Marxism was entangled in an oedipal and generational rebellion – against a successful but distant father and against an "affluent" society that promised little more than family, consumerism, and career. Marxism allowed me to stake out a rebellious identity in opposition to the liberalism of my parents and an American national identity. It furnished a standpoint from which to criticize my elders – to expose their hypocrisy by exposing America's social inequalities and its illusions of freedom by appealing to the reign of capital and class. Marxism allowed me a ferocious critique of America and liberal intellectuals that could not be so easily refused as my previously held hippie critique. Moreover, Marx's vision of a fully realized self, especially as elaborated by such neo-Marxist gurus as Erich Fromm and Herbert Marcuse, resonated perfectly with the folk beliefs I absorbed from mainstream and countercultural America. So, I became a Marxist of the Frankfurt School persuasion.

As the 1960s passed into the 1970s, and establishing an academic career moved to the center of my life, my enthusiasm for Marxism waned. Undoubtedly, the failed institutionalization of Marxism in the United States worked against sustaining Marxism in a post-crisis social setting. Moreover, as the heroic days of rebellion passed, and as my education included a serious engagement with classical sociology, my assessment of Marxism proved decidedly mixed. I continued to value Marx's historicist and political critique of ideology and his view of science as in the service of social change. However, I was critical of Marx's collapse of the social into class conflict, which hardly spoke to my radical political impulses which pivoted on issues of the subjective and the cultural, e.g., the body, the psyche, sexuality, and the "spiritual."

By the middle of the 1970s, the spirit of revolution had, for me, given way to a more sobering consideration of political prospects. I thought that progressive social change in the United States pivoted on a liberal–left alliance which went beyond the division between Marxism and liberalism. I imagined that in some of the writings of Durkheim and Weber there was to be found a social liberal ideal that had some kinship with a social democratic reading of Marx. I believed that a reconstruction of European social theory could provide intellectual resources for a social democratic political culture. Although I was questioning Marxism and liberalism, I remained firm in my faith in the Enlightenment – for example, in the link between science, truth, and social progress, in millennial notions of human liberation, in the West as the site of human progress, and in the self as the ultimate ground of knowledge and action.

My belief in the Enlightenment was seriously shaken in the early 1980s. Why? Of course, the succession of Republican administrations dampened my hopes of a liberal–left progressive front. The renewal of Cold War politics under Reagan and the vigor of the new right and neoconservatism further marginalized the left. I, once again, felt like a stranger in America. These developments shaped a context favorable to putting my belief in the Enlightenment into crisis. Personal considerations proved fateful.

As the world left my dreams of change tattered and almost mocked my high-minded European criticalness, my own personal life, despite an academic appointment and higher levels of consumerism, landed me in psychoanalysis. And my analysis brought me face to face with the web of delusions, inner otherness, and just plain psychic craziness that unconsciously drove my life. I initially undertook analysis with the Enlightenment faith that it would replace delusion with reality, opaqueness with scientific insight, unconscious compulsion with deliberate willfulness, and distress with happiness. Wasn't this its promise and indeed the promise of scientific Enlightenment? To be sure, analysis (thankfully) released me from certain inner constraints and did give me an understanding of particular feelings and psychic patterns. Yet, even as my daily life has been less brooding and anguished, my analytical experience contributed to putting my Enlightenment faith into doubt. Analysis revealed a self or "subject" which was de-centered, a psyche populated by multiple, often conflicted identities, selves who were hitherto strange to my conscious life, and a self driven by unconscious desires. Moreover, despite many years of analysis my psyche remained dense and opaque, ruthlessly refusing truth in favor of narratives whose value came to be judged by me – and my analyst – less by their validity than by whether they "worked" or were enabling or hopeful or permitted a provisional psychic coherence. In short, psychoanalysis disposed me to think of subjectivity less in a "modern" language of centered, unified, rational subjects than in a "postmodern" vocabulary of de-centered, multiple selves impelled by unconscious structures. Psychoanalytic understandings looked decidedly less like "science" or "reason" than pragmatic narratives or literary-poetic texts.

My analysis transpired side by side with coming out as gay. I don't of course assume any necessary tie between this event and a postmodern

standpoint. Nevertheless, coming out had for me far-reaching epistemological consequences. While I was already well read in critiques
of scientism, my coming out put me in a daily political relation to science
and, indeed, pressured me to rethink the politics of knowledge beyond
Enlightenment frameworks.

In its servicing of a heterosexist society, science denied me a range of
legal and civil rights; it shaped a context which made me a target of ridi-
cule and violence. It did this by constructing homosexuality as a disease
and as marking a pathological, deviant, morally damaged personage. I
did not conclude that science was an evil social force. I knew that it
could be invoked to justify "normalization." I did conclude, though, that
science is a powerful social force. This power, moreover, lay not only in
its capacity to rationalize the denial of basic civil and social rights and to
enforce social marginalization. More importantly, by virtue of its ties to
institutional practices (e.g., education, medicine, law, government, mass
media, therapeutic regimes), science had the power to inscribe in our
bodies and minds a sexual and social regime. This regime made sexual
object choice into a master category of sexual and social identity and that
purified a heterosexual life while polluting a homosexual one. Science
helped to create a regime of sexual and social order which organizes and
regulates our bodies, desires, identities, and social behavior. Foucault
of course provided the full conceptual articulation of this perspective,
but my personal experience allowed me to hear his arguments about
power/knowledge and the productive and disciplining aspects of power.
It followed that if the regime of sexuality is a disciplinary order, if the
assertion – even affirmatively – of gay identity reinforces this regime,
the Enlightenment project of announcing and liberating the homosexual
is in doubt.

My suspicion toward a Western culture of Enlightenment was further
nourished by internal developments within the gay community during
the 1980s. This was a time of enormous turmoil and division within the
gay movement. The ethnic model of identity that grounded community
and politics was under serious scrutiny. An antigay backlash exposed
the political costs of an insulated community pursuing a single-interest
gay politic. Moreover, voices of difference within the gay movement
threatened to unravel the fragile bonds of solidarity that rested upon the
assertion of a common gay identity. Hitherto excluded segments of the
lesbian and gay community – people of color, sexual rebels, Third World
gays, working-class gays, butches, and fems – protested their silencing
and marginalization by the gay mainstream. They exposed the repressive
politics entailed in asserting a unified gay subject. Rebelling against

the disciplining effects of a politics of identity, a new celebration of multiple, composite identities became the rallying cry of a queer politics of difference. While some saw this as threatening the gains of lesbians and gays, I imagined the new queer politics as potentially recovering the radical impulse of gay liberationism, namely, the ideal of a truly coalitional politic and a politic that goes beyond legitimating homosexual identities to remaking bodies and everyday life. In this regard, I saw the language of postmodernism as resonant with a new queer politics challenging normalization and a routinized politics of respectability.

Why postmodernism: Linda's story

As with Steve, Marxism was for me a means of making sense of many of the political and psychological sentiments which came out of my early years. I was a "red diaper baby" in the sense that my parents gave to me and my brother a strong sense of identification with the underdog and a certain disdain for what they regarded as the shallow and overly consumer-oriented elements of much of American life. My parents' contempt for mainstream American life was also mixed with a not untypical second-generation immigrant desire for their children to succeed, particularly in that arena they viewed with unqualified regard, education. So I became a Marxist academic, using my academic studies both to create a career and refine my understanding of Marxism. In the course of my work in philosophy as an undergraduate and then in the History of Ideas program at Brandeis University, this refinement led to a particular perspective on what was worthwhile in Marx's writings: his critique of capitalism; his vision of a democratic socialist society; and his strong sense of the historicity of all ideas. Against many reigning liberal ideas about "reason" and "objectivity," and in accord with ideas which were beginning to emerge in nascent form in academic and new left culture of the time, Marxism also sensitized me to the power dynamics involved in the production and distribution of knowledges. That sensitivity, and the developing critique of positivism and scientism I was deriving from my studies in the early 1970s, led me to think of the Marxism that saw itself as "a science of society" as not only wrong-headed but as allied with the authoritarianism I identified with the Marxism-Leninism of the Soviet Union and of the Eastern bloc countries. I became, in short, a child of that segment of the new left who thought the words "class" and "Marxism" had political relevance but who also rejected the kind of Marxism associated with the parties of the old left. Not surprisingly, I became attracted to many of the writings of those associated with the

Frankfurt School. In 1973, I found in Jürgen Habermas's *Knowledge and Human Interests* the elegant expression of many of my developing ideas about politics and knowledge. One idea in that book I found particularly compelling was Habermas's way of thinking about the two different Marxes. Habermas drew a distinction between the Marx who provided a powerful historical narrative about the development of capitalism and the Marx who saw himself as providing a philosophical theory about the nature and meaning of human history. I started to think about how this latter Marx, this Marx who thought he could provide a perch upon which to view all of human history, was a Marx who had not taken seriously enough his own ideas about the historicity and power dynamics of the production of ideas.

But in 1973 Marxism was not the only issue on my political and intellectual agenda. Feminism was emerging as a force which both excited me and demanded that I carve some place for it in my intellectual, political, and emotional life. While my Marxist commitments had initially led me to characterize this new movement as a manifestation of "bourgeois" interests, by 1973 such a characterization could no longer fit with the excitement and energy I found from this movement. But, of course, as an academic philosopher I could not just call myself a "feminist." I needed to decide just what kind of feminist I was. I came to describe myself as a "socialist-feminist." In large part this self-description emerged out of my earlier commitment to Marxism. It enabled me to declare myself a feminist while also remaining publicly committed to many of those ideas of Marx's I still found viable: his critique of capitalism, his vision of a future socialist society, and his sense of the historicity of all ideas. But other psychic factors were also at work. As someone who had a deep emotional connection to a father who died when I was just entering adolescence and as one who has always been strongly connected to an older brother, the alternative beckoning theory of radical feminism was never completely attractive. While in the late 1970s I certainly could not use public declarations of allegiances to men to defend any theoretical commitment, I could use the strong sense of historicity I derived from Marx to undermine what I was also seeing as the ahistoricity and lack of attention to differences among women in many radical feminist accounts. Of course at the time I was also being powerfully affected by many of the ideas that were coming out of radical feminism, ideas which were both deepening my commitment to feminism and accentuating my turn away from Marxism. At a certain point, and at least in part because of feminism, I stopped calling myself a Marxist.

It was somewhere in the 1980s, probably through work on my book

Gender and History, that I began to put together theoretically my criticisms of Marxism and of radical feminism. I began to think that what was wrong with both could be expressed in the same terms. Moreover, this common language could also be used to account for each not being able to include what was important in the other. It was Marxism's tendency to see itself as providing a grand theory of history and social organization constituted around such categories as "production" and "labor" which precluded it from adequately theorizing the situation of women. Simultaneously, it was radical feminism's tendency to develop grand theories about "patriarchy" and women which precluded it from seeing differences among women which were, amongst other things, differences of class.

It was around this time that the word "postmodernism" was beginning to enter my intellectual world. It attracted me because it seemed to provide a label by which to name this common problem I saw in Marxism, feminism, and liberal understandings of reason and knowledge: the tendency in elements of all to forget that what they were calling "reason" or "history" or "women" came out of a particular context and were implicated in relations of power. It made sense that liberalism, Marxism, and feminism might suffer from such a common problem. All had emerged within a certain period in Europe and North America where this part of the world had exercised a great amount of power over other parts of the world. As this power was coming into question, so might also the ways of theorizing knowledge which had attended it. The term "postmodern" seemed to provide a name for this break.

Why social postmodernism

We do not think that these two stories exclude other accounts of postmodernism. In particular, we value macrosocial perspectives which, for example, feature the importance of changes in systems of production, technology, and information systems, or perspectives which underscore the importance of deterritorialization or globalization. Yet we are convinced that shifts in left public cultures, in particular, the rise and development of the new social movements and their encounter with Marxist and liberal Enlightenment traditions are one crucial matrix for understanding the formation of postmodern theories in America and perhaps elsewhere. Moreover, we believe that at least certain strains of postmodern thinking are a key resource for rethinking a democratic social theory and politics. While it is understandable that some might be suspicious of perspectives that announce the de-centering of the subject, the end of metanarratives (including Marxism), the interlocking of knowledge and power, and the substitution of a politics of difference for a millennial liberationist politic, we believe that the postmodern turn offers a potentially useful vantage point from which to rethink theory and politics in at least some Western nations.

And yet, we have come to see that while the term "postmodernism" had its benefits, it also had its problems. Some of the problems seemed to us to emerge from those places where postmodernism overlapped with poststructuralism. Such overlaps occurred particularly in relation to thinking about language. For example, as Jean François Lyotard talked about the power dynamics in the play of discourse, so also did Jacques Derrida talk about linguistic and social meaning in relation to the regime of power of "logocentrism." But the concern with undoing reigning beliefs about logocentrism or troubling textual authority on the part of many poststructuralists meant that poststructuralism in particular, but postmodernism also, became significantly associated with a critical mode of analyzing texts. At times, the social was collapsed into the textual, and critique often meant "deconstructing" texts or exposing the instability of those foundational categories and binaries which structured texts and which were said to be carriers of ideological meanings. As important as deconstruction was to politicizing language and knowledge, this "textualizing" turn of the postmodern meant that many of the issues that have been pivotal to social theorists were neglected. In short, the whole field of institutions, social classes, political organizations, political economic processes, and social movements appeared to remain in the hands of Marxists or other theorists whose perspectives were often untouched by postmodern concerns. For Steve Seidman, with his background in social theory, and for Linda Nicholson, with her background in political philosophy, this separation of the "postmodern" and the "social" seemed to mark a wrong turn.

This slippage between postmodern critical analysis and "social" theory seemed to us further accentuated by the nature of postmodernism's critical engagement with the new social movements. For us, and for many others who were also sympathetic to postmodern ideas, the ways that these movements maintained the legacy of modernism was to naturalize or essentialize categories of identity. Thus, Nicholson, as well as other feminists, critiqued those tendencies in feminism which naturalized or essentialized the concept of "woman." Seidman, as well as other gay and lesbian theorists, challenged ahistorical constructions of "the homosexual." Our project was to demonstrate the constructed, historically variable, and varied meanings of such categories, that is, to "genealogize" or "deconstruct" these categories. But many such attempts also seemed to us to turn away from "the social." By focusing on what was wrong in the understanding of specific categories of identity, our attention remained fixed on the individual categories themselves. We were paying little attention to the ways in which the genealogies we and others were constructing intertwined with each other. Many of us had abandoned broader, systematic, and integrating perspectives on social processes and dynamics. Postmodern critique narrowed into a critique of representations or knowledges, leaving relatively unattended their social and historical contexts.

narrowing

But one of the serious causes of the turn from the social appeared to us as the pronounced negative or critical aspect of much postmodern theorizing. It is difficult to focus on the interrelation of social patterns when one is fixed on avoiding totalizing or essentializing analyses. This negative bent of much postmodern intellectual work was quickly perceived by its critics and soon became described as a sign not only of its theoretical weakness but also of its political weakness. Postmodernism, it was claimed, could show only what was wrong: it could provide no positive directions either intellectually or politically. After all, was it not impossible to generate strong political movements while also deconstructing the categories such movements were based upon?

✳ t
(t) problem

In this volume, we wish to show that it is possible for postmodern thinkers to focus on institutions as well as texts, to think about the interrelations of social patterns without being essentializing or totalizing, and to create constructive as well as deconstructive analyses of the social. The positive possibilities of postmodern theorizing can be matched, we believe, by constructive ideas about political action. Such ideas may seriously challenge and expand our ideas about how political change can take place. But, to transform present understandings of "the political" is not equivalent to abandoning politics altogether. Rather, through the following essays we hope to begin the process of imagining what "postmodern" social analysis can be and of how "postmodern" political action can be understood.

the HOPE for POMO

Critiques of identity

This volume begins this task by looking at the critique postmodernism has made of identity politics. As the three essays in the first section show, the critique is a complex one. Those who reject the postmodern turn often equate the postmodern or poststructural term "deconstruction" with the ordinary-language term "destruction." But the postmodern move to "deconstruct" does not translate into a move to destroy or abandon. Rather, as Linda Nicholson demonstrates in her opening essay "Interpreting Gender," a feminist deconstructive analysis of the concept of "gender" does not mean eliminating it. Rather, it entails a critical examination of its history to see what baggage the term carries from that history and the political effects of that baggage. It means "redeploying" the meaning of the term so that feminists can accomplish their political ends without encountering some of the difficulties past uses of the term have generated.

Nicholson argues that even after the development of the concept of "gender," many feminists continued to hold onto the idea that the male/female distinction is rooted in some fundamental features of biology. "Gender" was introduced to undermine widely held beliefs in the biological basis of many of the traits associated with women and men, beliefs expressed through the concept of "sex." However, insofar as "gender" was understood to supplement rather than supplant "sex," the idea of some biological basis of the male/female distinction remained. The conjunction of "gender" and "sex" was made possible by what Nicholson describes as an implicit "coat-rack" understanding of human identity: where biological givens distinguishing women and men constitute the basic "rack" upon which different societies "throw" different interpretations, the latter constituting "gender." Nicholson argues that this understanding of human identity articulates a particular worldview developed in the early modern period in Western Europe and North America where biology rather than the Bible came to be seen as the "cause" or "basis" of socially given distinctions. While this transformation had many manifestations, including the development of the biologically based concept of "race," in relation to the male/female distinction, it generated an understanding of differences between women and men both as more rigidly binary than had previously been the case and as the direct manifestation of the "facts" of biology. While the feminist introduction of the concept of "gender" represented a move to get beyond this worldview, keeping "sex" as a supplementary term has prevented feminists from wholly doing so. Nicholson depicts this limited transcendence in feminist theory by pointing to what she describes as "biological foundationalism." While the latter is not equivalent to "biological determinism," it shares with the latter the ideas that certain givens of biology exist cross-culturally and are always potential contributors to the social understanding of the male/female distinction.

Nicholson claims that it is this idea that there are certain cross-cultural

givens of biology, albeit always subject to possibly diverse social interpretations, which provided the theoretical grounds for the elaboration
of "difference feminism," that is, that feminism which stressed the
similarities among women and their differences from men. "Difference
feminism," however, has been most at fault in ignoring differences
among women. Nicholson argues that adequately to get beyond this erasure of differences requires that we get beyond biological foundationalism
as well. Doing so means abandoning the idea of differences as that which
supplements certain basic similarities. It means coming to see differences
as that which "go all the way down" affecting the very criteria of what it
means to be a man or a woman in diverse societies. This does not mean
abandoning attention to the body; instead, it means seeing the meaning
given to the body and how this meaning is related to the male/female
distinction as historically variable. This way of thinking about the "body"
supports an understanding of the term "woman" not as reflective of
some one determinate meaning, but rather as reflective of a diverse set
of meanings related through a complex set of "family resemblances."

While Nicholson's essay focuses on the grounding of "woman" in
biology as a contributor to essentialist tendencies within feminism,
Chandra Talpade Mohanty's "Feminist Encounters: Locating the Politics
of Experience" focuses on essentialism itself and its relation to politics.
Even in the absence of "biological foundationalism," "essential" or
"unitary" characteristics can be attributed to the category of "woman."
For example, it could be argued that while the meaning of "woman"
is completely socially constructed, this construction has been similar in
central ways throughout a long span of human history. Mohanty's essay
elaborates many of the problems inherent in such an essential or unitary
understanding of "woman."

Most basically, such an assumption erases social, historical differences
among women, differences which are those of power. Using Robin
Morgan's essay, "Planetary Feminism: The Politics of the 21st Century"
as an example, Mohanty illustrates how this kind of assumption affects
such an erasure. It does so by placing women outside history and,
as related, by employing a problematic, individualized conception of
experience.

Mohanty argues that Morgan, by eliding the difference between
history as a written record and history as a course of events, depicts
"history" as a male construction. Consequently, women are portrayed
as having no part in history and as ahistorically endowed with certain
traits, for example, as being "truth tellers." Such a depiction ignores the
ways in which women have been differently situated in history and in

the ways such differences have affected both the lives they have lived and the truth and power of the stories they have told.

Allied to this depiction of women as outside history is a conception of women's experience as given and individual. There is in Morgan's essay, according to Mohanty, no sense of experience as socially constructed in accord with different historical contexts.

The *experience* of struggle is thus defined as both personal and ahistorical. In other words, the political is *limited to* the personal and all conflicts among and within women are flattened. If sisterhood itself is defined on the basis of personal intentions, attitudes, or desires, conflict is also automatically constructed on only the psychological level. Experience is thus written in as simultaneously individual (that is, located in the individual body/psyche of wom*a*n) and general (located in wom*e*n as a preconstituted collective).

Mohanty draws on Bernice Johnson Reagon's "Coalition Politics: Turning the Century" to generate ideas about identity and politics which are different from those of Morgan. Particularly, Mohanty points to Reagon's idea of political struggle as being based on a recognition of difference rather than on imputed commonalities in experience. This idea of political struggle opposes metaphors of "coalition" to metaphors of "home." Whereas the latter suggested criteria of unity separating those on the inside from those on the outside, the former suggest constructed and contingent comings together which can coexist with differences. In short, it represents a notion of political struggle where alliances are made around explicit goals rather than presumed on the basis of imputed commonalities. It represents "sisterhood" as that which needs to be achieved rather than that which can be assumed.

While the first two essays in this volume focus on problems in feminism as a site of identity politics, similar kinds of problems have been found in many post-1960s social struggles, in those of the gay and lesbian movement, and in struggles by African-Americans in the United States and in nationalist and postcolonial struggles around the world. The essay by Gyan Prakash provides a framework for understanding the genesis of such problems. In "Postcolonial Criticism and Indian Historiography," as Prakash makes explicit, oppositional discourses emerge within a complex relationship to the discourses of domination they seek to overthrow.

Focusing on Marxism as an example of this point, Prakash shows how this discourse can be seen as a continuation of the very territorial imperialism it sought to overthrow. By employing a unified concept of "capitalism" and by making this concept foundational to the analysis of all those societies which have been affected by it, Marxism effectively homogenized the histories of these societies.

In fact, like many other nineteenth-century European ideas, the staging of the Eurocentric mode-of-production narrative as History should be seen as an analogue of nineteenth-century territorial imperialism. From this point of view, Marx's ideas on changeless India – theorized, for example in his concept of the "Asiatic mode of production" – appear not so much mistaken as the discursive form produced by the universalization of Europe, by its appropriation of the absolute other into a domesticated other.

The point here is not to abandon an analysis of capitalism nor to stop using the concept of "class" but to understand how the dynamics of capitalism and class intersect with other determinations. By doing so, it becomes possible to recognize "the irreducible heterogeneity of metropolitan capital with the colonial subaltern" and consequently to extricate Marxism from the imperialistic elements of its nineteenth-century Western European heritage.

However, a word of caution is in order. As Prakash emphasizes, the idea here is not to idealize heterogeneity per se. It is not to emphasize difference for the sake of difference nor to include a list of determinations, such as those of gender, race, ethnicity, etc., for the sake of some current ideal of what is politically appropriate. Rather, it is to recognize that all categories of analysis – even those used in the service of political opposition – are the affects of specific relations of power. In the case of postcolonial discourse this means recognizing that an emphasis on difference emerges from the ambivalence produced in the very enunciation of colonial discourses. As colonial discourses asserted unchanging identities both to the colonizer and colonized, they also acknowledged differences and potential disruptions to these forms of identity. They thus created the very stress points which their critics can employ against them. Consequently, the lesson here is not some absolute celebration of difference but a sensitivity to the relations of power which make a focus on difference both possible and an effective tool of subversion.

If the above essays begin to show some of the complexities involved in the critique of identity politics, the essays in the second section illustrate the limits of some versions of this critique.

Critiques of the deconstruction of identity

As the above comments make clear, we see the force of at least some critiques of identity politics as both theoretical and political.

Nicholson's, Mohanty's, and Prakash's essays underscore the theoretical and political gains of a critique of identity, for example as creating a space for imagining the possibility of a coalitional politics of difference and a reflexive critique of power/knowledge regimes. Although such critiques of identity have been productive, especially as they have leaned on postmodern or poststructural conceptual strategies, others have revealed certain stress points. This section reviews some of these tensions.

Kwame Anthony Appiah's essay "African Identities" illustrates the need to preserve the deconstructive critique of identity and yet retain some kind of politic of identity. Appiah comments on the personal and political impulses behind his theoretical reckoning with questions of identity and politics. As the son of an African father and a European mother, and as someone who grew up in both Ghana and Britain and who now lives in the United States, Appiah was personally troubled by the way individual and national identity has been framed by the African/European binary. This binary leaves no "home" or coherent cultural space for Appiah's own experience. Deconstructing such unitary, totalizing identities as "African" and "European" was integral to his own personal struggle for psychological and cultural coherence. The African/European binary was disturbing for political reasons as well. It interferes with the effectiveness of a Pan-African antiracist movement. On the one hand, the construction of an "African identity" is inevitably normative and exclusionary; it has the effect of impeding African solidarity and mobilization. On the other hand, this binary obstructs the formation of alliances with Americans and Europeans committed to antiracist struggle. Appiah believes that only the deconstruction of essentialized group identities and totalizing binaries makes possible the kinds of coalition building and political mobilization strategies that can create an effective Pan-African movement.

Deconstructing the notion of a unitary, essentially fixed African identity is pivotal then to his political project. Appiah considers three key strategies that have given cultural and intellectual currency to an essentialized, totalizing concept of group identity. A racial strategy appeals to a common biological foundation; an historical strategy invokes a shared history; a metaphysical strategy imagines a unique common culture or African spirit. Appiah exposes the inconsistencies and conceptual flaws of each strategy as well as underscoring the undesirable moral and political consequences of an essentialist concept of African identity.

Does criticizing a unitary essentializing approach to African identity mean abandoning identity categories and politics? No. Recall that Appiah wishes to defend the conceptual and political possibilities of a Pan-African antiracist movement. Toward this goal, Appiah proposes to substitute for an essentialized group identity a concept of identity that insists upon its irreducibly heterogeneous, plural, changeable, and ultimately chosen and "fictitious" character. Although African peoples and cultures are quite different, even contradictory, within the continent and across the diaspora, the idea of an African identity and movement continues to be invented and given personal and social force through myths and political organizations. Such a social fact cannot be denied or devalued simply because it is not true or real in some fundamental philosophical sense. African identities are very real in their personal and social effect and in their political consequences. Appiah believes that we can and should defend such socially constructed realities but always with an eye to their strategic social and political gains. We should never, however, surrender our criticalness toward constructions which essentialize and totalize group identities.

Appiah engages then in a deconstructive critique of group identity and politics in the style of poststructural critics. Nevertheless, he gestures toward the limits of such a deconstructive strategy in two ways. First, he argues that it is not enough to point to the general instability, heterogeneity, and exclusionary character of identity categories. We need to analyze simultaneously the precise historical context and the economic, political, and cultural forces which are intertwined with identity categories and politics. "Identities are complex and multiple and grow out of a history of changing responses to economic, political, and cultural forces, almost always in opposition to other identities." For example, Appiah notes that the three central ethnic identities of modern Nigerian political life – Hausa-Fulani, Yoruba, Igbo – materialized in the transition from colonial to postcolonial status.

David Laitin has pointed out that "the idea that there was a single Hausa-Fulani tribe . . . was largely a political claim of the NPC [Northern Peoples' Congress] in their battle against the South," while "many elders intimately involved in rural Yoruba society today recall that, as late as the 1930s, 'Yoruba' was not a common form of political identification." . . . [And as] Johannes Fabian has observed, the powerful Lingala- and Swahili-speaking identities of modern Zaire exist "because spheres of political and economic interest were established before the Belgians took full control, and continued to inform relations between regions under colonial rule." Modern Ghana witnesses the development of an Akan identity, as speakers of the three major regional dialects of Twi – Asante, Fante, Akuapem – organize themselves into a corporation against an (equally novel) Ewe unity.

Departing from the deconstructive critiques of many poststructuralists, Appiah advises intellectuals to analyze identity formations and movements in their precise sociohistorical context and in relation to institutional and political forces.

In a second departure, Appiah argues that whereas many postmodern analysts approach identities only as disciplinary, constraining structures, he underscores the affirmative political possibilities of identity-based movements. For example, "[b]ecause the value of identities is thus relative, we must argue for and against them case by case. And given the current situation in Africa, I think it remains clear that another Pan-Africanism – . . . *not* the project of a racialized Negro nationalism – however false or muddled its theoretical roots, can be a progressive force." This would entail building alliances among, say, African-Americans, African-Caribbeans, African-Latins, and continental Africans to struggle against racism and to intervene into various regional conflicts. Such a Pan-African movement, finally, is not a mere idea but articulates concrete developments, for example, common problems due to a similar positioning in a world economy, common discourses, or symbolic resources, and the existence of already regional Pan-African organizations such as the African Development Bank or the African caucuses serving in the UN or the World Bank.

A similar impulse, both appreciative of the deconstruction of identity and yet aiming to expose its theoretical and political limits, is central to Steve Seidman's and Rosemary Hennessy's essays – both of which address the theoretical and political significance of queer theory and politics. If decolonialization and the subsequent resurgence of racially based nationalist movements were a key juncture in shaping the rise of a deconstructive-styled race theory, the feeble efforts at coalition building in the 1970s exposed in the antigay backlash and the explicit assimilationism of gay politics in the context of AIDS and the renewal of HIV radicalism, shaped the context of the "postmodern" turn in queer theory.

In Seidman's essay, "Deconstructing Queer Theory or the Under-Theorization of the Social and the Ethical," mainstream lesbian and gay theory and politics is distinguished from queer theory. The former is characterized by the ethnic modeling of homosexuality. Homosexuals are seen as forming an ethnic minority with their own distinctive identities, cultures, and political interests. Gay theory analyzes the formation of homosexual identities and their functioning as the foundations for community development and politics. Such minoritizing concepts of homosexuality are viewed as part of the consolidation of affirmative lesbian and gay identities in the 1970s. Seidman argues that minoritizing approaches have been valuable in legitimating homosexuality in American culture and serving as symbolic resources for the successful community-building efforts of the 1970s and 1980s.

And, yet, the limits of the ethnic nationalist model became apparent in the failure of the lesbian and gay movement effectively to form coalitions to respond to the antigay backlash and the AIDS crisis. Similarly, internal solidarity was unraveling with as much intensity as the antigay backlash. The growing discontent within the lesbian and gay mainstream for its excluding and marginalizing of segments of the community who were different, for example, not white or not middle class or involved in nonconventional sexual or gender practices – a discontent exhibited in the sex and race debates – exposed the limits of a minority model of gay identity and politics.

The deconstructive turn that characterizes much so-called queer theory is, at once, a response to the crisis of a minority model, and an effort to imagine an alternative model of homosexual theory and politics. In the former role, Seidman insists on the considerable social and political importance of queer theory. It exposes the assertion of a unitary gay or lesbian identity anchored in a common experience or set of values as normative and having disciplinary effects. In this regard, queer theory does not so much press to abandon identity categories but rethinks them as open to conflicting and multiple meanings and as always interlocking with categories of gender, race, class, and so on. This theoretical move makes possible newly imagined composite or hybrid and fluid identities which, in turn, facilitate both coalition building and a politics of difference.

Queer theory does more than rethink categories and strategies of identity and politics. It shifts the very center of theorizing homosexuality.

Queer theorists argue that homosexuality should not be treated as an issue of the lives and fate of a social minority . . . [They] urge an epistemological shift. They propose to focus on a cultural level . . . Specifically, their object of analysis is the hetero/homosexual opposition. This is understood as a category of knowledge, a way of defining and organizing selves, desires, behaviors, and social relations. Through the articulation of this hetero/homosexual figure in texts and social practices . . . it contributes to producing mutually exclusive heterosexualized and homosexualized subjects and social worlds.

Queer theory shifts the center of analysis from viewing homosexuality as a minority identity to a cultural figure. The hetero/homo binary is imagined, parallel to the masculine/feminine trope, as a symbolic code structured into the texts of daily life, from popular culture (e.g., television sitcoms or popular songs) to disciplinary knowledges, law, therapeutic practices, criminal justice, and state policies. It frames the way we know and organize personal and social experience, with the effect of reproducing heteronormativity. Queer theory aims to expose the operation of the hetero/homo code in the center of society and to contribute to destabilizing its operation. Queer theory aspires to imagine a sexual and social regime beyond the hetero/homo code and beyond heteronormativity – a regime organized around the tolerance, indeed the celebration, of social differences.

Seidman interprets queer theory as marking a valuable shift in lesbian and gay thinking. It opens up the possibility of gay theory as a general social theory and critique, not just a theory of a social minority. Similarly, it opens up the possibility of a politics beyond minority rights and representation to a politics contesting normative heterosexuality and, indeed, contesting a sexual and social regime organized around hetero/-homosexuality as master categories of desire, identity, and social life. While appreciating its theoretical and political gains, Seidman criticizes queer theory for its failure to go beyond its "critique of knowledge" to a critique of the social conditions which make such hetero/homo knowledges possible. In a series of critical readings of queer theorists, Seidman tries to show that while each theorist deconstructs identities and dominant sexual knowledges, each fails to provide an account of the social conditions making such a critique and oppositional politics possible. Similarly, while these queer theorists tie their critical theory to a politics of difference against the normalizing politics of mainstream straight and gay America, none of them articulates the ethical standpoint that guides their ideas and that might give coherence to their view of social difference.

Queer theory was made possible by particular social conditions, even if queer theorists have not analyzed them. For example, Seidman emphasizes changes in the feminist and gay movements in response to both internal and external developments. In particular, Seidman points to the fact that queer theory formed in the university which, in the past few decades, has become arguably the major site in the production and legitimation of knowledges. This explains, in part, the shape of queer theory and its importance – as a participant in the struggle over power/-knowledge regimes as they are centered or originate in the academe.

Queer theory has only recently exploded onto the public scene. Inevitably, it is becoming the site of important critical disputes over the meaning of queer and, more generally, over the project of a gay theory and politic. Rosemary Hennessy's "Queer Visibility in Commodity Culture" suggests a somewhat different social account and interpretation, though her essay parallels Seidman's general point that queer theory has failed to articulate its cultural critique into a social critique.

Hennessy appreciates the renewal of radical social criticism intended by queer theory, in particular, its aim to trace the operation of heterosexuality in daily life and its insistence on the socially constructed, politically produced character of desire and sexual identities. Yet it is less queer theory's failure to realize its radical project that she criticizes than a kind of "false consciousness" that attends to queer theory. Despite its radical intentions, the structure of queer theory never really escapes a certain middle-class or "bourgeois individualism." Class is the absent reflexive moment in queer theory. Unfortunately, says Hennessy, it is indicative of the general abandonment of materialism and, therewith, queer theory surrenders its warrant as a serious critical social theory.

For Hennessy, queer theory arises and never gets beyond a preoccupation with analyzing and problematizing subjectivity and cultural representations. Whether it is queer theory's deconstruction of the gay or lesbian subject or Queer Nation's "visibility" actions, it is the surface of society – the realm of subjectivity, cultural image, or social appearance – that is the object of analysis or political intervention. Like Seidman, Hennessy criticizes queer theory and politics for neglecting the relation between identity and symbolic politics and the sociohistorical conditions making queer subjects and visibility possible. However, for Hennessy, it is a specific articulation of the social that drives her critique. Queer theory has failed to incorporate in any serious way a materialist theory of society – that is, a framework which links identity to class, capitalism, and patriarchy.

In a series of critical readings of Judith Butler, Diana Fuss, and Teresa de Lauretis, Hennessy proposes that these theorists never go beyond a critical discursive analysis of questions of subjectivity, identity, and representation. Where, Hennessy asks, are the efforts to articulate discursive orders with the sexual division of labor or multinational corporate economies or patriarchy? Without such efforts to link questions of identity to institutional contexts and interlocking systems of domination, queer theory resembles those Western avant-garde movements, from Dadaism to the Situationists, whose "radical" cultural project of

compliance
w/
consumer Kism

aestheticizing daily life or performatively parodying "the natural," fit all too well within consumer capitalism.

Many of the aesthetic features of the avant-garde reverberate in this more worldly [queer] "social postmodernism": a tendency toward formalist modes of reading, a focus on performance and aesthetic experimentation, an idealist retreat to mythic/psychic spirituality, and the disparity between a professed agenda for broad social change and a practice focused exclusively on cultural politics. One way to begin to understand this gravitation toward cultural politics . . . is to consider it in relation to the more general aestheticization of everyday life in consumer capitalism.

The aestheticization of daily life is part of the saturation of the everyday with the commodity as a carrier of images, signs, and meanings. Many of these meanings focus on fashioning or stylizing the self and everyday reality, suggesting a highly voluntaristic and protean concept of subjectivity not unlike that of queer theory. This fetishizing of appearance and an active subjectivity conceals and legitimates the underlying social relations of class and gender domination that remain at the core of capitalist patriarchy. By remaining at the level of "the sphere of circulation" or the play of images, discourses, and subjectivity, queer theory and politics engage in a form of "opposition" that ironically perpetuates the illusion of freedom in commodity culture while concealing the material reality of domination and oppression. Thus the new queer visibility in the mass media is less a serious challenge to heteronormativity or a sign of a new acceptance of queers than a recognition of new market strategies and sites to be colonized by capital. Queer visibility has not contested heteronormativity or patriarchy or capitalism but perhaps is indicative of a new type of capitalist integration and political neutralization of queer people. Only by exposing the middle-class status of much queer theory and politics, says Hennessy, can we hope to revive a truly critical historical materialist queer theory and politics.

The essays in parts I and II cohere around a dual impulse: first, to take seriously but not uncritically the assertion of identity as a basis of political mobilization. We cannot ignore that identity-based movements in the United States and elsewhere have become pivotal agents of change and political contestation. And yet, we cannot ignore that identity can be a fulcrum for both coalitionally based movements and narrow single-interest group movements. The "postmodern" turn is intended to articulate identity politics in a way that pressures it to move in the former direction. Second, these essays have maintained that the framing of identities must be attentive to the historical context in which they are a part and articulated in relation to the social forces –

int.

potential
and
dangers of
identity
based
politics

classes, institutions, status groups, social processes such as globalization or commodification – which give coherence to questions of identity. In the next section, we introduce a series of essays which explore possible social articulations of postmodern analysis and critique.

Postmodern approaches to the social

The question thus becomes: how do we generate ways of understanding identity as central to personal and group formation while avoiding essentialism? And, how do we articulate identity so that it can be understood in relation to sociohistorical dynamics? The contributors to part III address these questions by formulating postmodern approaches to the social.

[margin handwriting: identity w/o essentialism; identity w/ sociohistorical detail?]

Iris Marion Young begins with the dilemma that the use of identity categories raises: how can we use group labels without attributing to them any essential characteristics? On the one hand, we need group labels. Social analyses which are not merely accounts of individual intentions and actions must speak in the language of groups. On the other hand, group labels suggest common characteristics, a suggestion negated by the often amorphous criteria defining group membership. In reference to the category of "woman," this dilemma has given rise to the suggestion that we think of this category only as designating political affiliation. But, according to Young, this suggestion will not work. The identification of "woman" with a self-conscious political movement seems to designate arbitrarily what, from the vantage point of common sense, seems merely a specific group of women. Moreover, it also appears to restrict in a disciplinary way who gets to be counted as a "woman."

Borrowing Sartre's concept of seriality, Young proposes an alternative way out of the dilemma. Whereas the idea of a "group" suggests shared characteristics, a series has no such determining characteristics; its vaguer and more amorphous unity is derived only from its shared passive relationship to a specific material milieu. This milieu both constrains and enables individual actions but neither defines nor determines them. Thus the series lacks defining attributes or characteristics: *[margin handwriting: ?]*

Membership in serial collectives define an individual's being, in a sense – one "is" a farmer, or a commuter, or a radio listener, and so on, together in series with others similarly positioned. But the definition is anonymous, and the unity of the series is amorphous, without determinate limits, attributes, or intentions. Sartre calls it a unity "in flight," a collective gathering that slips away at the edges, whose qualities and characteristics are impossible to pin down because they are an inert result of the confluence of actions. There is no concept of the series, no specific set of attributes that form the sufficient conditions for membership in it.

In relation to gender, bodies constitute one of the types of "practico-inert" objects that position individuals as women or men. But bodies themselves gain their meaning through specific structural arrangements. And Young claims that it is the set of meanings, rules, and practices that comprise institutionalized heterosexuality which form the material milieu enabling the differentiation of female from male bodies. But bodies are only one of the types of "practico-inert" objects that position women as gendered beings. Also involved are such other "materialized historical products" as pronouns, verbal and visual representations, clothes, tools, spaces, etc., which Young claims are themselves structured in relation to gender through the sexual division of labor. While some sexual division of labor and the system of institutionalized heterosexuality set the parameters for the series "woman," because the specific content of both varies historically and because in any given context neither determines what it means to be a woman, the series "woman" exists without defining characteristics.

In short, Young responds to the dilemma of identity by proposing a conceptual strategy which avoids both nominalism and essentialism. In the concept of the "series," Young suggests a way of conceptualizing group identity which allows for a conception of "the social" where patterns can be described but which are fluid in nature.

Whereas Young argues for a new analytical approach to social groups, other contributors to this section rearticulate "the social" more by emphasizing the historicity of the categories by which social life is constituted. They argue that particular categories of identity must be understood within the context of a given historical setting. This move is intended to avoid certain poststructuralist analyses which theorize identity in relation to ahistorical theories of language or of psychoanalysis. Instead the coherence of identity categories becomes a "social" issue requiring attention to the specific sociohistorical context such categories emerge out of and help shape.

This type of focus is pivotal in the essay by Cindy Patton where the political context of identity categories, as used by theorists and political agents, is examined in some detail. In "Refiguring Social Space," Patton argues that it was a particular set of social and historical circumstances which made the postulation of social identity a useful mechanism for making political claims. However, those circumstances have changed, requiring the reassessment of identity politics.

Patton's essay provides a novel analysis of the historical rise of identity politics and of the present circumstances which challenge its utility. She points to the emergence of identity politics out of the space provided by the civil rights movement. As the civil rights movement transformed the African-American population from a group to a claimant for political rights, so the later women's and gay and lesbian movements used the concept of civil rights to make a similar move. "Civil rights was no longer a compensatory, temporary conduit designed to incorporate a class of bodies viewed as historically always present but excluded as subjects, but an open door that permitted more bodies to make different claims to subject status." By employing the concept of civil rights as a means to make claims on the body politic, feminists and gays and lesbians could, to use the language of Bourdieu, transform social into political capital. This move, while reaping important results, also generated its own reactions. One of the consequences of situating civil rights as an open door was the suggestion of an endless proliferation of identities, all of which could make social claims for rights and representation. The new right has seized on this political logic. In response, it has reconfigured "civil rights" as that which belongs properly to "true Americans," identifying the claims of the excluded as requests for "special privileges." Social space became redefined from an expanding sphere open to new configurations to a bounded sphere identified with the family and those operating by the values the new right has associated with it. This bounded sphere became depicted as the space of a beleaguered minority threatened by the increasing claims of "special interests." The new right has thus worked to reconstitute the social whole in a binary mode which differentiates an "us" who truly belong from a "them" who threaten to engulf and destroy.

One of the benefits of Patton's analysis is that it enables us to understand the advantages and disadvantages of identity politics in historically specific ways. As she emphasizes, identity politics has reaped important political rewards. However, that success rested on a very particular and not necessarily enduring sociohistorical context. "The difficulty with 'identity politics' is not so much that we mistakenly 'believed' in our self-namings but that we believed in the promise of inalienable rights, rights which would accrue once our status as political subjects was secured." The task facing us today, accordingly, may involve less the question of defending or rejecting identity politics than it is in figuring out how to generate its positive possibilities in an environment where civil rights has a different meaning than in an earlier time.

Patton's essay underlines the point that categories of analysis are social constructs whose meanings and consequences shift in different contexts. The essay by Ali Rattansi, "Just Framing: Ethnicities and Racisms in a 'Postmodern' Framework," elaborates this point in relation to the concepts of racism and ethnicity. Rattansi rejects definitions of racism or ethnicity that ignore the myriad of differences among racial and ethnic categorizations. Concepts of race and ethnicity vary not only in relation to the degree of centrality of biology but also in relation to their intersection with concepts of nationality, sexual difference, and class. Nor, Rattansi claims, does the language of cultural difference even have any "necessary political belonging," being employed as means for political resistance as well as for projects of domination.

The point to be deduced from such an argument, however, is not merely to urge complexity, to add more differentiations to the theorist's understanding of race or of other categorizations of social life. Rather, what emerges from Rattansi's essay, as well as from Patton's, is a new understanding of the social world and consequently of the categories which the social theorist can best employ to depict it. This is an understanding of social reality as itself being continually reshaped by the changing categories social actors use to understand themselves, others, and the spaces they share.

A "postmodern" framing conceptualizes *ethnicity* as part of a *cultural politics of representation*, involving processes of "self-identification" as well as formation by disciplinary agencies such as the state and including the involvement of the social sciences, given their incorporation in the categorization and redistributive activities of the state and campaigning organizations.

Social life becomes no longer, as it tended to be in much modern social theory, a relatively static field, understandable through the use of abstract categories. Rather, it becomes a field continually in shift where the very categories actors are using to depict it are productive of the shifts themselves. Following this understanding, the social theorist becomes, with the social worker, the state agent, the journalist, and the protester, one more social actor in the process of social production.

Therefore, as the above essays reveal, a postmodern social analysis involves the rethinking of the very nature of the basic categories through which the social whole is viewed and constituted. Such a postmodern approach rejects an understanding of such categories as the family, the state, the individual, and the homosexual as "natural." This move de-essentializes such categories by placing them within specific historical and political contexts. It thus avoids the essentialist disposition of some modern modes of understanding; it also avoids those poststructuralist arguments which often ignore the institutional context of discursive practices.

Fraser

A "social postmodern" turn is evident in Nancy Fraser's "Politics, Culture, and the Public Sphere: Toward a Postmodern Conception." Fraser aims to retrieve the concept of the public sphere from modern discourses. She claims that this concept is a useful one, enabling us to situate discourse in institutionalized settings. It thus provides an alternative to those kinds of theoretical approaches which "dissociate cultural studies from critical social theory." The problem, however, is the way in which modern theory has tended to employ this concept. Such theory has often been organized around three prevailing assumptions: that democratic public spaces can exist without social equality; that a multiplicity of competing publics are necessarily a threat to democracy; and that public discourse need be about the common good.

Fraser questions all of these assumptions and their usefulness for a concept of the public sphere. Instead she develops a postliberal, *arg* postmodern conception of the public which recognizes the necessity of social equality for political democracy; which accepts the idea that a multiplicity of counterpublics may at times expand democratic, discursive space; and which includes rather than excludes interests that have been understood as "private."

In elaborating the point of the admissibility of "private" issues into public debate, Fraser takes on the broad question of how we understand the concept of "public" and the counterconcept of "private." She argues that these concepts do not designate naturally given or preexisting social spheres. "[R]ather, they are cultural classifications and rhetorical labels. In political discourse, they are frequently deployed to delegitimate some interests, views, and topics and to valorize others."

Fraser develops this argument by focusing on the confirmation process of Associate Supreme Court Justice Clarence Thomas. Here she emphasizes that a central element in the struggle was contesting battles over where the line between public and private was to be drawn. These battles were staged differently and had different consequences for Clarence Thomas and Anita Hill. While Thomas' prior sexual habits were successfully defended as "off-limits to public debate," this claim was not achieved on behalf of Anita Hill. These different consequences point to the need for understanding publicity not only as a cultural categorization emerging out of particular political struggles, but also as a multivalent one, having, as a consequence of such struggles, different meanings for different groups.

Such a conception takes as its starting point the multivalent, contested character of the categories of privacy and publicity with their gendered and racialized subtexts. It acknowledges that in highly stratified late capitalist societies, not everyone stands in the same relation to privacy and publicity; some have more power than others to draw and defend the line.

In short, "publicity" like "identity" must be viewed as a cultural construction whose deployment must be assessed in relation to a particular context. At issue in the use of both the categories of "identity" and "publicity," as well as other categories of social life, is the question of "for whom" and "in relation to what specific consequences."

Postmodernism, therefore, (does not) represent an abandonment of "the social." Rather, it represents new ways of conceptualizing it. A postmodern conceptualization deviates from a modern one in understanding the categories by which social life is organized as historically emergent rather than naturally given, as multivalent rather than unified in meaning, and as the frequent result and possible present instrument in struggles of power. Whereas in the context of modernist understandings, a negative or "deconstructionist" emphasis may have been and still is necessary, such an emphasis need not be either all that a postmodern approach includes nor understood as that which is removed from institutional social analysis. As the essays in this section illustrate, postmodern approaches can be seen not as those which avoid the social but rather as those which reinterpret its meaning.

Postmodern approaches to the political

If postmodern thinkers are now feeling pressed to articulate a concept of the social that goes beyond textual meanings or sign systems, perhaps this is so, in part, because of their perception of a narrow identity-based politics and an exclusively discursively based theory. In addition, we would like to think that, at least for many parts of the world, we are leaving a period of social and political conservatism. We hope that many of the events in the last decade or so, such as the end of the Soviet empire and of apartheid in South Africa or the revival of radical social activism in the United States (e.g., ACT-UP or Queer Nation) open new possibilities for democratic social change. If we are right, there will be a heightened demand for theories which focus on social institutions and processes such as changes in the public sphere, nationalism, social *admits to neglect of this topic!*

movements, information systems, and the globalization of capital. Once again, social theory and politics might go hand in hand. But what would a postmodern politics look like?

Some critics of the postmodern turn have called into question the very idea of a postmodern politics. They argue that a theoretical perspective which announces the "death of the subject" or refuses a concept of the self as unified or coherent surrenders any basis for political mobilization. In "Feminism, Citizenship, and Radical Democratic Politics," Chantal Mouffe addresses this critique directly.

Mouffe

Many feminists believe that, without seeing women as a coherent identity, we cannot ground the possibility of a feminist political movement in which women could unite as women in order to formulate and pursue specific feminist aims. Contrary to that view, I will argue that, for those feminists who are committed to a radical democratic politics, the deconstruction of essential identities should be seen as the necessary condition for an adequate understanding of the variety of social relations where the principles of liberty and equality should apply.

Mouffe disputes the feminist view which assumes that only a concept of woman as a coherent identity makes feminist politics possible. To be sure, essentialist constructions of womanhood make possible certain kinds of feminist struggles, for example, a liberal feminism which asserts demands for women's equal rights or a radical feminism which might promote a distinctively feminine concept of citizenship or politics. However, Mouffe argues that the de-centering of the unity of the category of "woman" encourages a "radical democratic politics."

How? and what are the drawbacks?

If feminists conceive of women as a distinct unitary group grounded in some presumed common experiences or values, politics is imagined as articulating these shared ways of being or thinking. Thus, if women's experiences are seen as similar to men's, feminist politics may well center on demands for equal opportunities, representations, and rights for women. If, on the other hand, women's experience is imagined as different in some fundamental way from men's, feminist politics may focus on asserting and legitimating women's uniquely feminine values. The limits of a feminist epistemology grounded in a concept of essential female identity are that it cannot give expression to all of women's experiences, i.e., it is normative and exclusionary. The limits of a feminist politics grounded in a notion of unitary gender identity are that it weakens coalition-building efforts and surrenders to a single-interest group politic of either assimilationism or separatism. In both cases, coalitional politics is either abandoned or rendered feeble. Moreover,

limits essential ♀ identity

such a feminist politic does not challenge the dominant masculine liberal model of citizenship and politics.

By contrast, Mouffe argues, if feminists approach identities as always multiple or, to use Mouffe's poststructural language, as always framed in discourses and practices in multiple, sometimes contradictory ways – e.g., simultaneously gender-subordinate but racially dominant – we can imagine a feminist politics that is part of a broader radical democratic project. How so? If we cannot separate gender identity easily, if at all, from racial, sexual, national, or class positioning, then "women" as a category cannot be thought apart from these other social identities. There would be no separate, independent "women's" experience that could be marked off and presumed as the ground of feminist politics. Rather, "women's" interests would be viewed as always inflected by particular race, class, sexual, or national concerns. There is no "woman" in general, only women who simultaneously occupy particular race, class, sexual, or national social positions. This deconstruction of identity politics suggests a new approach to politics: less a politics organized exclusively around separate identities than a politics organized around specific issues, struggles, goals, and broad democratic principles which bring together interested parties.

What does such a concept of radical democratic politics mean for feminism? It does not mean abandoning a concept of "women" or gender-based politics. We can reject a notion of gender identity as a common essence while retaining a nonessentialist framing of women. "The absence of a female essential identity and of a pregiven unity . . . does not preclude the construction of multiple forms of unity and common action. As the result of the construction of nodal points, partial fixations can take place and precarious forms of identification can be established around the category 'women' that provide the basis for a feminist identity and a feminist struggle." Such struggles, however, would not be focused exclusively on gender since gender is viewed as interlocking with class, sexuality, race, nationality, and so on. Mouffe's idea of democratic politics aspires to recover an expansive transformative political vision in the tradition of Western Marxism while recognizing that individuals will continue to organize under the identities of women, gay, black, or working class. Her model of politics suggests that alliances between selves differently positioned will be promoted by viewing identities as multiple and interlocking and by a more issues-centered, coalitional politics. Moreover, in a suggestive proposal, Mouffe offers as a common bond uniting such a democratic project the notion of a collective political identity based on the principle of "liberty and equality for all."

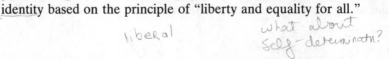

Indicative perhaps of a new sense of democratic prospects in the United States and elsewhere, theorists and activists are exploring the contours of a positive progressive politics. This is what we find exciting and hopeful about Mouffe's proposal for a radical democratic politics. She begins to imagine such a politics without appealing to essentialized identities or the evolutionary theory of Marxism. This same project informs Shane Phelan's "A Space for Justice: Lesbians and Democratic Politics."

but shed/n give e's!

Phelan considers the prospects of a lesbian democratic politics that no longer trades on the essentialism of lesbian-feminism and is impatient with the refusal of poststructuralist queer theory to go beyond deconstructive critique. She sketches some of the conceptual underpinnings of a postmodern lesbian politics.

Drawing on the poststructural critique of essential identities and the parallel critique by people of color, Phelan describes a conceptual strategy to make coherent a (postmodern) coalitional politics. Given the diversity of lesbians' lives and values, the appeal to a common experience and interest cannot ground lesbian politics. If the assumption of a common lesbian experience is made problematic, so too is the idea of a common lesbian interest and therefore the very foundation of "modern" lesbian politics. In other words, Phelan aims to trouble what she perceives as the operative logic in contemporary lesbian politics: an assumed homology between experience, interest, identity, and politics. Although such a lesbian politics has been historically important, serious limitations have been attached to it. In particular, coalition building is seriously weakened as alliances appear as the stringing together of separate identity-based groups – women, lesbians, gay men, blacks, Latinos and Latinas – around a particular struggle. Such coalitions are temporary and unified only by a utilitarian calculus which assumes that groups support each other with the expectation of a future payback.

why?

isn't this what Mouffe proposes!

However, if we assume that identities are multiple, unstable, and interlocking, the logic of identity politics is made problematic. Although such arguments evoke fears of the unraveling of sexual politics, Phelan sees productive possibilities. Central to her proposal is the suggestion to approach the concept of "lesbian interest" not as grounded in common experiences or shared values but as an expression of a demand for public recognition and inclusion advanced by lesbians making claims as citizens.

values ? Jus. citizenship (?)

The formal claim of an interest – say as a lesbian – does not yet commit a lesbian to a particular desire or need. It establishes lesbianism as a relevant political identity from which to proceed. This provides the space to articulate a "lesbian good" without predetermining what that good will be. It also opens the *int.*

category of "lesbian" to negotiation – claiming lesbianism as a relevant identity cannot simply avoid "common sense" notions of what such an identity is, but it need not rest with those notions either. The identity itself becomes open to politics.

what does this mean?

Phelan wishes to view the assertion of lesbian identity, in part, as a civic act. In this formulation, the concept of lesbian interest loses any essentializing connotations and instead suggests a public political identity. The advantage of this formulation of lesbian interest is that it does not render it exclusive or captive to narrow concerns but allows an assertion of lesbian interest to attach to a wide range of social and political issues and struggles. For example, from this perspective Phelan imagines lesbians articulating an "interest" in decent, affordable housing. This would not be seen as an issue for all lesbians or as one grounded in anything defining of a lesbian. Moreover, it would not be an exclusively lesbian issue but would be an issue potentially for all individuals for whom the lack of decent, affordable housing is a concern. Lesbians would need to work on housing issues along with many nonlesbians and would do so by articulating their unique housing concerns, just as those positioned in unique class or racial terms would clarify their specific concerns.

Recognizing the multiplicity of lesbian experiences, interests, and therefore political identities does not mean surrendering all claims to commonality. Phelan sees the reframing of lesbian identity as a political demand for recognition and participation as equal citizens as providing a kind of unifying political force. The focus on social issues, specific goals, and coalitional struggles based on affinities of interest means that public officials will be pressured to take as seriously the lives and issues of lesbians as they would other citizens. The concept of citizenship and political identity provides a unifying reference for lesbians without repressing their differences. Like Mouffe, Phelan imagines a lesbian politic as part of a broader politics. "In the end, our goal should be to articulate a lesbian agenda as part of a radical democratic creed shared across sexualities and other differences."

?

Phelan sees in Queer Nation a movement with a decidedly postmodern temper. In its politics against normalization and its assertion of a hybrid, composite identity based on loose affinities of interests and aims, Queer Nation suggests a postmodern movement. However, whereas Queer Nation is somewhat compromised by a nationalist strain, Stanley Aronowitz argues that no such nationalism characterizes ACT-UP, perhaps a better exemplar of a postmodern social movement today.

nationalism automatically retrograde?

In "Against the Liberal State: ACT-UP and the Emergence of

Postmodern Politics," Aronowitz suggests that the political logic and success of ACT-UP mark a shift to a postmodern political culture. Modern liberal politics has been organized around the logic of electoral, majoritarian rule. Citizens elect representatives and expect them to enact social policy which reflects majority electoral sentiment. The mobilization of electoral majorities which elect public officials legitimates public representatives and their legislation. This liberal political logic is now in doubt.

In contrast to the leading premise of modern politics, namely, that the legitimacy of the liberal state is guaranteed by electoral majorities, ACT-UP tacitly challenges the *ethical* legitimacy of the majority – just as business interests have buried the majority interest in areas such as tax policy, national health care, and environmental protection. Although ACT-UP eschews doctrinal pronouncements, it insists on and seeks to impose a *substantive* rather than procedural criterion upon claims to representation. If the majority accepts or otherwise acquiesces to the institutionalized homophobia of the state . . . citizens are under no obligation to obey the law and rules of conduct prescribed in its name.

On the one hand, liberal majoritarian politics is threatened by business interests which increasingly dictate public policy – demanding tax breaks or deferment of public investment – by its threat to relocate or significantly reduce their present investments. This capturing of public policy by corporate interest is evident in urban policies across the country. On the other hand, movements such as ACT-UP are similarly placing liberal politics in doubt by their ability to shape public policy through successful social and media, not electoral, mobilization. Both of these developments suggest, says Aronowitz, that the legitimacy of public policies are increasingly grounded not in majority rule, whose legitimacy is established by electoral procedures, but in the ability of groups to impose a substantive standard upon claims to representation or to win public support for their particular substantive interests. The indeterminate relation between elections and public policy spells a potential crisis of modern liberal politics and a shift to a postmodern politics where power is responsive to substantive concerns and where the media becomes a key site for political mobilization. Aronowitz suggests that these developments have ambivalent moral implications. If business-driven policies underscore illiberal possibilities, ACT-UP suggests the democratic potential of a postmodern political culture.

The future of American politics significantly depends upon the out-come of the struggles of contemporary social movements. In this regard, Aronowitz perceives in ACT-UP radical democratic social possibilities.

Whereas the history of many progressive social movements in postwar America has been either to become part of the Democratic Party as a pressure group (e.g., labor), thereby losing much of their radical democratic force, or to become part of the state in the form of a service agency (Gay Men's Health Crisis), thereby becoming part of the politics of management, ACT-UP has not – yet – surrendered its politics of protest and radical confrontation. This movement continues to engage in direct-action practices, refuses to bow to economically driven public policy, and has not reduced politics to electoral practices. ACT-UP demands shared power, input into decision-making processes, and asserts that substantive criteria should guide public policy. Indeed, in its organizational structure, for example, its rejection of a bureaucratic centralized mode of decision making, its engagement with the politics of science, its de-centralized, voluntary, action-oriented style of practice, and its demand to be involved in institutional decision making, even in "expert" realms (e.g., medicine and science), ACT-UP exemplifies a radical democratic styling of a postmodern politic.

Whether the argument for a postmodern politics takes the form of Mouffe's call for a deconstruction of essentialized identities or Phelan's rethinking of identity and interest, or Aronowitz's advocacy of social movements as carriers of substantive reason, there is unanimity on one overriding point that we feel should be underlined: a postmodern politics is conceived as radically democratic. A postmodern politics suggests less an abandonment of modern values (e.g., liberty, equality, citizenship, autonomy, public participation) than an effort to preserve these values by rethinking the premises of modern culture and politics. Nor in these versions of postmodern politics is there a refusal to articulate common grounds or unifying points in politics. Rather, these proposals criticize efforts to deduce such commonality from some general principle or to ground them in a quasi-transcendental foundational philosophy or a philosophical anthropology. This articulation of the premises and goals of a postmodern political project is reaffirmed in R. W. Connell's "Democracies of Pleasure: Thoughts on the Goals of Radical Sexual Politics."

Connell suggests that "postmodernity" means the end of the politics of sexual liberation. This is so because postmodern perspectives deconstruct the very idea of a sexuality to be liberated. "There is no thing there to liberate." This does not mean sexual politics must surrender a political direction or positive project. In this regard, Connell is critical of efforts to substitute a politics of discursive and body play for a liberatory sexual politics. Connell advocates a return to strong

[handwritten margin notes: "a pomo politics is...", "so all commonalities are contingent?", "Connell", "thank-you!"]

social approaches to analyzing sexuality and a sexual politics tied to social structural change.

Criticizing liberationist sexual politics by deconstructing sexuality has led some poststructuralists into an exclusively discursive sex theory and playful sexual politic. With regard to the former, Connell wishes to preserve the deconstructive turn which denaturalizes the body and desire but he aims to avoid an exclusively discourse-centered approach to "sexuality." He urges instead that the body and desire be approached not only in relation to discourse but also in relation to institutions and organizations such as the state, families, the church, or the corporation. In place of discourse as the site of sexual analysis, he proposes the guiding idea of "sexual social relations." From this sociological standpoint, "sexuality" can be analyzed in terms of the creation of and struggles around hierarchies of power and legitimation, inequalities in desires, behaviors, and relations, and issues of constraint and scarcity. Sexual practices should be studied, he concludes, like any other social practice, in terms of questions of power, inequality, legitimacy, domination, scarcity, and so on.

Deploying the concept of sexual social relations, Connell frames sexual politics in terms similar to other spheres of politics. "To understand sexuality neither as nature nor discourse, but as a sphere of social practices that constitute social relations, helps clarify the goal of sexual politics." If the goal is not the liberation of sexuality, it is, he says, the liberation of people, and sexual politics means freeing people from unnecessary constraints and inequities in the realm of the body and desire. "It is meaningful to speak of 'sexual liberation' where oppression is accomplished in the sexual social relations between groups of people. What 'liberation' then means is that the oppressed gain power over their own lives, power that was formerly exercised by other groups." In other words, sexual politics is not all that different from gender, race, or class politics: it is about equality, empowerment, and democratization through altering sexual social relations, i.e., changes in social institutions. The goal of sexual liberation is not the end of repression or the end of the social structuring of desire, but the democratization of sexual social relations. "This means a search for equality and empowerment across the whole social terrain of the body-reflexive practices relating to erotic pleasure and reproduction." Democracies of pleasure involve sexual resource sharing, shared decision making, equitable distribution of knowledge, and social respect; like any process of democratization, sexual democracy entails social structural changes, e.g., changes in schools, AIDS policies, and mass media.

Social postmodernism: a language of radical democratic theory and politics

As a way of thinking about knowledge, self, society, and politics, postmodernism has roots in the struggles over social life that have been at the center of many Western societies in the past few decades. We should not forget that deconstruction made its appearance as part of the revolts against the disciplinary, normalized order of French society in the late 1960s. Similarly, the articulation of self-conscious postmodern social theories in the United States emerged in relation to developments in the new social movements, especially in the 1980s and 1990s. With regard to the latter, the postmodern turn is closely connected to the failure of the new social movements to forge coalitions in the face of a well-organized backlash against progressive democratic change. Simultaneously, the surfacing of voices of difference within the movements was pivotal in facilitating the deconstruction of essentialized identities and advocating a radical cultural politics of difference.

Many of us who have adopted a postmodern perspective have drawn positively on such critical traditions as Marxism, feminism, or gay liberationism. However, we have also believed that such radical "modernist" theories frequently have absorbed the assumptions of the society they criticized, limiting their contemporary oppositional force. We believe that to preserve a democratic critical tradition requires a radical rethinking of the premises and language of social knowledge and politics. We have sought to refashion the political culture of the left so that intellectuals could speak to the multiplicity of oppositional movements, be attentive to their specific struggles, be coalitional, and affirm strategies and social goals that valued difference. For us, and many contributors to this volume, the best available language was, and perhaps remains, that of postmodernism.

But, as the essays in this volume argue, this involves a postmodern perspective of a certain type, one which attends to histories, institutions, and social processes. In this regard, we have sought to overcome the limits of those "poststructuralist" or "deconstructionist" approaches which have failed to articulate the interconnections between oppositional movements, refused to state a positive, transformative social and political project, and neglected the institutional, social structural contexts of discursive, textual meanings. This does not mean, however, that a poststructural strain of critical social analysis which has relied heavily on deconstructing texts has not been very important in pressuring a critical reflexivity regarding knowledge, society, and politics. The problematizing of essentialized identities, the de-centering of the subject and society, the re-centering of the social around analyzing power/knowledge regimes, are major resources for critical analysis and a democratic politics. In contrast to many of its detractors, we believe that deconstruction makes possible a politics of coalition building, a cultural politics of social tolerance and difference, a critical politics of knowledge, and an affirmation of particular, local struggles without disavowing the possibilities of broader forms of social solidarity and political mobilization. The critique of deconstruction, therefore, should not lead to its abandonment but to its absorption in a "social postmodernism," as at least one strategy for imagining a democratic social theory and politics as we approach the end of the second millennium.

hopeful view of deconstruction

Social postmodernism makes the case for a type of social thinking which integrates deconstruction while simultaneously incorporating some of the analytically synthesizing and expansive political hopes of the modernist tradition of social theorizing. We think this move might be productive for generating conceptual and political strategies that can continue to expose inequalities, oppressions, forms of social injustice, and sites of conflict and change in societies that mix modern and postmodern features.

Mo + po

This volume is at best suggestive of one direction for theory and politics. Indeed, there is hardly unity among those who mark out the terrain of "social postmodernism" beyond the need to move beyond the current impasse in theory and politics. Nevertheless, we hope that this volume suggests at least one possible move beyond the antinomy of "radical modernism" (Marxism, feminism, Afrocentrism, gay liberationism) and postmodern deconstruction: a theoretical perspective which refashions both into a new language of radical democratic theory and politics.

PART I

Critiques of identity

1

Interpreting gender

Linda Nicholson

"Gender" is a strange word within feminism. While many of us assume
it has a clear and commonly understood meaning, it is actually used in
at least two very different and, indeed, somewhat contradictory ways.
On the one hand, "gender" was developed and is still often used as a
contrast term to "sex," to depict that which is socially constructed as
opposed to that which is biologically given. On this usage, "gender" is
typically thought to refer to personality traits and behavior in distinction
from the body. Here, gender and sex are understood as distinct. On the
other hand, "gender" has increasingly become used to refer to any social
construction having to do with the male/female distinction, including
those constructions that separate "female" bodies from "male" bodies.
This latter usage emerged when many came to realize that society shapes
not only personality and behavior; it also shapes the ways in which
the body appears. But if the body is itself always seen through social
interpretation, then sex is not something that is separate from gender
but is, rather, that which is subsumable under it. Joan Scott provides
an eloquent description of this second understanding of "gender" where
the subsumption of sex under gender is made clear: "It follows then
that gender is the social organization of sexual difference. But this does
not mean that gender reflects or implements fixed and natural physical
differences between women and men; rather gender is the knowledge
that establishes meanings for bodily differences . . . We cannot see
sexual differences except as a function of our knowledge about the
body and that knowledge is not 'pure,' cannot be isolated from its
implication in a broad range of discursive contexts" (1988, 2). I want to
argue that while this second understanding of gender has become more
dominant within feminist discourse, the legacy of the first survives, in
certain subtle but important respects, even within the thinking of many
of those who would endorse the second. This legacy not only casts the

39

relation between these two senses of "gender" as more complex than the above either/or portrayal, but it also generates obstacles in our abilities to theorize about differences among women.

The first of these two senses of gender has its roots in the coming together of two ideas important within modern Western thought: the material basis of self-identity and the social constitution of human character. By the time of the emergence of the "second wave" of feminism in the late 1960s, one legacy of the first idea was the notion, dominant in most industrialized societies, that the male/female distinction was caused by and expressed, in most essential respects, "the facts of biology." This conception was reflected in the fact that the word most commonly used to depict this distinction, "sex," was a word with strong biological associations. Early second-wave feminists correctly saw this idea as conceptually underpinning sexism in general. Because of its implicit claim that differences between women and men are rooted in biology, the concept of sex suggested the immutability of such differences and of the hopelessness of change. To undermine the power of this concept, feminists of the late 1960s drew on the idea of the social constitution of human character. Within English-speaking countries, this was done by extending the meaning of the term "gender." Prior to the late 1960s, gender was a term that had primarily been used to refer to the difference between feminine and masculine forms within language. As such, it conveyed strong associations about the role of society in distinguishing that which is coded male from that which is coded female. Feminists extended the meaning of the term to refer now also to differences between women and men in general.

But most interesting is that "gender" at that time was generally not seen as a replacement for "sex," but was viewed, rather, as a means to undermine the encompassing pretensions of sex. Most feminists during the late 1960s and early 1970s accepted the premise that there existed real biological phenomena differentiating women and men used in all societies in similar ways to generate a male/female distinction. What was new in the idea they advanced was only that many of the differences associated with women and men were neither of this type nor the direct effects of such. Thus "gender" was introduced as a concept to supplement "sex," not to replace it. Moreover, "gender" was not only viewed as not replacing "sex" but "sex" seemed essential in elaborating the very meaning of "gender." In her important article, "The Traffic in Women," for instance, Gayle Rubin introduced the phrase "the sex/gender system" and defined it as "the set of arrangements upon which a society transforms biological sexuality into products of human activity, and in which these transformed sexual needs are satisfied" (1975, 159). Here, the biological is being assumed as the basis upon which cultural meanings are constructed. Thus, at the very moment the influence of the biological is being undermined, it is also being invoked.

Rubin's position in this essay is not idiosyncratic. Rather, it reflects an important feature of much twentieth-century thinking about "socialization." Many of those who accept the idea that character is socially formed and thus reject the idea that it emanates from biology do not necessarily reject the idea that biology is the site of character formation. In other words, they still view the physiological self as the "given" upon which specific characteristics are "superimposed"; it provides the location for establishing where specific social influences are to go. The feminist acceptance of such views meant that sex still retained an important role: it provided the site upon which gender was thought to be constructed.

Such a conception of the relationship between biology and socialization makes possible what can be described as a "coat-rack" view of self-identity. Here the body is viewed as a type of rack upon which differing cultural artifacts, specifically those of personality and behavior, are thrown or superimposed. One crucial advantage of such a position for feminists was that it enabled them to postulate both commonalities and differences among women. If one thought of the body as the common rack upon which different societies impose different norms of personality and behavior, then one could explain both how some of those norms might be the same in different societies and how some others might be different. The shape of the rack itself could make certain demands as to what got tossed upon it without being determinative, in a sense reminiscent of biological determinism. As such a position would construe cross-cultural commonalities in personality and behavior as the result of a social reaction to the givens of biology, biology here does not "determine" such commonalities in any strict sense of that term. One could still envision a future in which a particular society could react to such demands in very different ways than in the past. Thus, such a coat-rack view of the relationship between biology and society enabled many feminists to maintain the claim often associated with biological determinism – that the constancies of nature are responsible for certain social constancies – without having to accept one of the crucial disadvantages of such a position from a feminist perspective – that such social constancies cannot be transformed. Moreover, such a view also enabled feminists to assert differences among women as well as similarities. The claim that some of what is thrown upon the rack is similar across cultures – as a response to certain features of the rack itself – is compatible with the claim that some other things thrown upon it are also different.

But what is interesting is that many who would endorse the understanding of sex identity as socially constructed still think of it as a cross-cultural phenomenon. They do so, I would claim, because they think of it as the cross-culturally similar social response to some "deeper" level of biological commonality, represented in the material "givens" of the body, i.e., that women have vaginas and men have penises. Thus many feminists increasingly have thought of sex identity both as a social construction and as common across cultures. Linking this position and one that thinks of sex as independent of gender is the idea that distinctions of nature, at some basic level, ground or manifest themselves in human identity. I label this common idea "biological foundationalism." In relation to the male/female distinction, it expresses itself in the claim that distinctions of nature, at some basic level, manifest themselves in or ground sex identity, a cross-culturally common set of criteria for distinguishing women and men.

Biological foundationalism and the coat-rack view of identity in general stand in the way of our truly understanding differences among women, differences among men, and differences regarding who gets counted as either. Through the belief that sex identity represents that which is common across cultures, we frequently have falsely generalized matters specific to modern Western culture or to certain groups within it. It has been difficult to identify such faulty generalizations as such because of the alliance of biological foundationalism with some form or other of social constructionism. Feminists have long come to see how claims about the biological causes of personality and behavior falsely generalize socially specific features of human personality and behavior onto all human societies. But biological foundationalism is not equivalent to biological determinism; all of its forms, though some more extensively so than others, include some element of social constructionism. Thus, even the earliest feminist position that construes sex as independent of gender, in using the term "gender" at all, allows for some social input into the construction of character. Moreover, any position that recognizes at least some of what is associated with the male/female distinction as a social response, tends to theorize some difference in how societies interpret this distinction. Such difference is sometimes allowed through the assumption of a past or future society that has responded or will respond to the givens of biology in different kinds of ways than has been true for most human societies. For example, sometimes the argument that the generalization being expressed is only true for "patriarchal societies" is given as a disclaimer against overgeneralization. But typically, no precise criteria are offered to let us know where the boundaries of "patriarchal" societies fall. Thus, what looks like an historical claim functions primarily to jettison the demand for historical reference. Moreover, even if one accepts the reference to patriarchy as entailing reference to any society where some form of sexism exists, such a disclaimer precludes investigation into the different ways the body might be interpreted differently even among such societies. Other problems attend the postulation of differences coexisting with similarities. Such theories are dualistic regarding differences, both allowing for differences, and also presuming commonalities. But the problem with such a dualistic type of approach is that it generates what Elizabeth Spelman describes as an additive type of analysis. "In sum," she elaborates, "according to an additive analysis of sexism and racism, all women are oppressed by sexism; some women are further oppressed by racism. Such an analysis distorts Black women's experiences of oppression by failing to note important differences between the contexts in which Black women and white women experience sexism. The additive analysis also suggests that a woman's racial identity can be 'subtracted' from her combined sexual and racial identity" (Spelman 1988, 128). In other words, a dualistic approach obscures the possibility that what we are describing as commonalities may also be interlaced with differences.

In short, it is not enough to claim that the body always comes to us through social interpretation, i.e., that sex is subsumable under gender. We must also come to accept explicitly one of the implications of this idea, that we cannot look to the body to ground cross-cultural claims about the male/female distinction. The human population differs within itself not only in social expectations regarding how we think, feel, and act but also in the ways in which the body is viewed and the relationship between such views and expectations concerning how we think, feel, and act. In short, we need to understand social variations in the male/female distinction as related to differences that go "all the way down," that is, as tied not just to the limited phenomena many of us associate with gender (i.e., to cultural stereotypes of personality and behavior), but also to culturally various understandings of the body, and to what it means to be a woman and a man. In this alternative view the body does not disappear from feminist theory. Rather, it becomes a variable rather than a constant, no longer able to ground claims about the male/female distinction across large sweeps of human history but still there as always a potentially important element in how the male/female distinction gets played out in any specific society.

Historical context

The tendency to think of sex identity as given, as basic and common cross-culturally, is a very powerful one. If we can see it as historically rooted, as the product of a belief system specific to modern Western societies, we can appreciate the deep diversity in the forms through which the male/female distinction has been and can come to be understood.

European-based societies from the seventeenth through the nineteenth centuries increasingly came to think about people as matter in motion, as physical beings ultimately distinguishable from others by reference to the spatial and temporal coordinates we occupy. This meant a tendency to think about human beings in increasingly "thing-like" terms, that is, as both similar to the objects around us – because composed of the same substance, "matter" – and as separate from such objects and from each other – because of the distinctive spatial and temporal coordinates which each self occupies.[1]

But it is not only that the language of space and time became increasingly central as a means for providing identity to the self. The growing dominance of a materialist metaphysics also meant an increasing tendency to understand the "nature" of things in terms of the specific configurations of matter they embodied. The import of this for emerging views of self-identity was a growing tendency to understand the "nature" of human selves in terms of the specific configurations of matter that they embodied. Thus the material or physical features of the body increasingly took on the role of providing testimony to the "nature" of the self it housed.

In the late twentieth century, we associate the body's increasing role in providing testimony to the nature of the self it houses with an increasing belief in biological determinism. During the seventeenth and eighteenth centuries, however, a growing sense of the self as natural or material conjoined two emphases that only in later centuries would be viewed as antithetical: a heightened consciousness of the body as a source of knowledge about the self, and a sense of the self as shaped by the external world. A heightened consciousness of the self as bodily can be illustrated by the kinds of issues seventeenth- and eighteenth-century theorists increasingly thought relevant to attend to. Thus, for example, while an early seventeenth-century patriarchalist such as Sir Robert Filmer might use the Bible to justify women's subordination to men, the later natural-law theorist John Locke would cite differences in male and female bodies to accomplish a related goal (Locke 1965, 364). But "nature" for natural-law theorists such as Locke did not mean just the body in distinction from other kinds of phenomena. It could also refer to the external influences provided by vision or education. Thus, while Locke might point to differences in women's and men's bodies to make a point, he could also in his writings on education view the minds of girls and boys as malleable in relation to the specific external influences they were subject to. In short, "materialism" at this point in history combines the seeds of what were later to become two very different and opposing traditions. As Ludmilla Jordanova notes:

> It had become clear by the end of the eighteenth century that living things and their environment were continually interacting and changing each other in the process . . . The customs and habits of day-to-day life such as diet, exercise and occupation, as well as more general social forces such as mode of government, were taken to have profound effects on all aspects of people's lives . . . The foundation to this was a naturalistic conceptual framework for understanding the physiological, mental and social aspects of human beings in a coordinated way. This framework underlay the relationship between nature, culture and gender in the period.   (1989, 25–26)

As Jordanova points out, this tendency to view the bodily and the cultural as interrelated is expressed in the use of such eighteenth-century "bridging" concepts as temperament, habit, constitution, and sensibility (1989, 27).

Yet to say that a growing focus on the materiality of the self during the seventeenth and eighteenth centuries did not translate simply into biological determinism does not negate the point that the body was increasingly emerging as a source of knowledge about the self in contrast to older theological views. And one way in which this focus on the body began to shift understandings of self-identity is that the body increasingly began to be employed as a resource for attesting to the differentiated nature of human beings, such as on the basis of race. As many commentators have pointed out, race was first employed as a means of categorizing human bodies in the late seventeenth century, and it was only then and in the eighteenth century with such publications as the influential *Natural System* by Carolus Linnaeus (1759) and Friedrich Blumenbach's *Lunité du Genre Humain, et de ses Varieties* (On the natural varieties of mankind, 1804), that there began to be made what were taken to be authoritative racial divisions of human beings.[2] This does not mean that physical differences between, for example, Africans and Europeans were not noted by Europeans prior to the eighteenth century. They certainly were noted and used to justify slavery. But, as Winthrop Jordan points out, physical differences were only one group of such differences; that Africans engaged in "strange" social practices and were "heathens," i.e., not Christians, also provided justification in the European mind for the practice of taking Africans as slaves (1968, 3–98). Moreover, to note a physical difference, or even to attribute moral and political significance to it, is not the same as using it to "explain" basic divisions among the human population as the concept of race increasingly did from the late eighteenth century on.

The sexed body

The above example of race illustrates how the growing dominance of a materialist metaphysics did not mean the construction of new social distinctions *ex nihilo* but rather the elaboration and "explanation" of previously existing ones. To be sure, such new "explanations" also entailed transformations in the very meaning of the distinctions themselves. Such is the case in the modern Western understanding of the male/female distinction. Although the growth of a materialistic metaphysics obviously did not create this distinction, it did entail changes in the importance of physical characteristics and in their role: from signaling this distinction to explaining it. At the time such a metaphysics was increasingly taking hold, other social changes were also occurring, such as a growing separation of a domestic and public sphere, that increasingly gave support to the biological explanation of the male/female distinction as a binary one.

Thomas Laqueur, in his study of medical literature on the body from the Greeks through the eighteenth century, identifies a significant shift in the eighteenth century from a "one-sex" view of the body to a "two-sex" view. In the earlier view, the female body was seen as a lesser version of the male body "along a vertical axis of infinite gradations," whereas in the later view the female body becomes "an altogether different creature along a horizontal axis whose middle ground was largely empty" (Laqueur 1990, 148).

That in the earlier view physical differences between the sexes are viewed as differences of degree rather than of kind manifests itself in a variety of ways. Whereas we, for example, view female sexual organs as different organs from those of men, and by their difference signifying the distinction of women *from* men, in the earlier view these organs were viewed as less-developed versions of male organs. Thus, in the old view, the female vagina and cervix did not constitute something distinct from the male penis; rather, together, they constituted a less-developed version of it. Similarly, in the old view, the process of menstruation did not describe a process distinctive to women's lives but was seen as just one more instance of the tendency of human bodies to bleed, the orifice from which the blood emerged being perceived as not very significant. Bleeding itself was viewed as one way bodies in general got rid of an excess of nutriments. Since men were thought to be cooler beings than women, they were thought to be less likely to possess such a surplus and hence less likely to possess a need to bleed (Laqueur 1990, 36–37). Similarly, Laqueur points to Galen's argument that women must produce semen, since otherwise Galen asks, there would be no reason for them to possess testicles, which they clearly do (1990, 35–36). In short, the organs, processes, and fluids we think of as distinctive to male and female bodies were rather thought of as convertible within a "generic corporeal economy of fluids and organs" (Laqueur 1990, 40). As Laqueur demonstrates, this "generic corporeal economy of fluids and organs" began to give way to a new "two-sex" view: "Organs that had shared a name – ovaries and testicles – were now linguistically distinguished. Organs that had not been distinguished by a name of their own – the vagina, for example – were given one. Structures that had been thought common to man and woman – the skeleton and the nervous system – were differentiated so as to correspond to the cultural male and female" (Laqueur 1990, 35).

Another manifestation of this new "two-sex" view was the delegitimation of the concept of hermaphroditism. As Michel Foucault points out, in the eighteenth century, hermaphroditism became a shrinking concept. Foucault notes that during this century the hermaphrodite of previous centuries became the "pseudo-hermaphrodite" whose "true" sexual identity only required sufficiently expert diagnosis:

Biological theories of sexuality, juridical conceptions of the individual, forms of administrative control in modern nations, led little by little to rejecting the idea of a mixture of the two sexes in a single body, and consequently to limiting the free choice of indeterminate individuals. Henceforth, everybody was to have one and only one sex. Everybody was to have his or her primary, profound, determined and determining sexual identity; as for the elements of the other sex that might appear, they could only be accidental, superficial, or even quite simply illusory. From the medical point of view, this meant that when confronted with a hermaphrodite, the doctor was no longer concerned with recognizing the presence of the two sexes, juxtaposed or intermingled, or with knowing which of the two prevailed over the other, but rather with deciphering the true sex that was hidden beneath ambiguous appearances.   (Foucault 1980, vii)

These new ways of thinking about the relation between female and male bodies are related to a variety of cultural changes. As many commentators on the history of the family and of gender have pointed out, one important consequence of emerging industrialization and growing urbanization was an increasing differentiation of domestic and non-domestic life, associated respectively with women and men.[3] But these new ways of thinking about the male and female body also can be related to the increased tendency, discussed above, for the body to serve as the source of information about the self and thus to serve as the source of information about one's identity as male or female. As Laqueur points out, it is not as though, in the older view, physical differences between women and men were not assumed; they were. Such differences, however, were seen as being the logical expression of a certain cosmological order governed by difference, hierarchy, interrelation – as "markers" of the male/female distinction rather than as its basis or "cause" (Laqueur 1990, 151–52).

When the Bible or Aristotle is the source of authority about how the relationship between women and men is to be understood, any asserted differences between women and men are to be justified primarily through reference to these texts. When, however, the texts of Aristotle and the Bible lose their authority, nature and the body become the means for grounding any perceived distinction between women and men. This means that to the extent there is a perceived need for the male/female distinction to be constituted as a deep and significant one, the body must "speak" this distinction loudly, that is, in every aspect of its being. The consequence is a two-sex view of the body.

Sex and gender

This concept of sex identity as a sharply differentiated male and female self rooted in a deeply differentiated body was dominant in most industrialized countries at the time of the emergence of second-wave feminism. But there were also ideas around at the time that feminists could draw upon to begin to challenge it. The growth of a materialistic metaphysics in early modern Western societies was never uncontested; many cultural and intellectual movements throughout Western modernity have striven to prove the distinctiveness of human existence in relation to the rest of the physical world.[4] Some of these movements, particularly those grounded in religion, have continued to stress a religious, rather than physiological, grounding of the male/female distinction. Moreover, even from within this metaphysics there emerged perspectives that challenged a biologically grounded concept of sex identity. In the nineteenth century, one theorist who maintained a strong materialism while also elaborating with great theoretical sophistication the idea of the social constitution of human character was Karl Marx. He, along with many other nineteenth- and twentieth-century thinkers, contributed to a way of thinking about human character that acknowledged the deep importance of society in constituting such character that second-wave feminists could draw on. Although the challenge to this concept of sex identity has been extensive in second-wave writings, it has also been incomplete. Still maintained is the idea that there exist some physiological givens that are used similarly in all cultures to distinguish women and men and that at least partially account for certain commonalities in the norms of male and female personality and behavior. This position, which I have labeled "biological foundationalism," has enabled many feminists explicitly to reject biological determinism while holding onto one of its features: the presumption of commonalities across cultures.

What I am calling "biological foundationalism" is best understood as representing a continuum of positions bounded on one side by a strict biological determinism and on the other side by the position I would like feminists to endorse: that biology cannot be used to ground claims about "women" or "men" transculturally. One advantage of depicting biological foundationalism as representative of a range of positions is that it counters a common contemporary tendency to think of social constructionist positions as all alike in the role that biology plays within them. Thus, feminists have frequently assumed that as long as one acknowledged any distance at all from biological determinism, one thereby avoided all of the problems associated with this position. But I want to claim that the issue is more relative: that feminist positions have exhibited more or less distance from biological determinism and, to the degree that they have done so, have exhibited more or less of the problems associated with that position, specifically its tendency to generate faulty generalizations that represent projections from the theorist's own cultural context.

Let me elaborate this point by using my earlier "coat-rack" metaphor. All those positions I am labeling biological foundationalist assume that there exists a common biological rack that all societies must respond to in some way or other in elaborating the distinction between male and female. If one were a strict biological determinist, the rack alone would constitute this distinction. But given that all biological foundationalists are social constructionists in some form or another, all assume some social reaction to the rack as partly constitutive of the male/female distinction. But there are various ways of conceptualizing such reactions or conceptualizing "what gets thrown upon the rack." One could think of what is thrown upon the rack as significantly similar across most societies as a direct response to the givens of the rack. Alternatively, one could think of what is thrown upon the rack as mostly different in different cultures, with what is shared representing only a minimal common response to the givens of the rack. Finally, of course, one could give up the idea of the rack altogether. Here biology, rather than being construed as that which all societies share in common, would be viewed as a culturally specific set of ideas that might or might not be translatable into somewhat related ideas in other societies, but even when translatable could not be assumed to shape in cross-culturally similar ways each society's understanding of the male/female distinction.

To show how various forms of biological foundationalism have surfaced in second-wave theory, let me begin with the writings of two thinkers who represent a position close to one end of this continuum. Both of the following theorists are explicitly social constructionist. Yet both use the body to generate or justify generalizations about women across cultural contexts in a way which is not significantly different from biological determinism.

The first writer I would like to turn to is Robin Morgan in her introduction to *Sisterhood is Global*, "Planetary Feminism: The politics of the 21st century."[5] In this essay, Morgan is explicit about the many ways women's lives vary across culture, race, nationality, etc. She also believes, however, that certain commonalities exist amongst women. As she makes clear, such commonalities are for her not determined by biology but are rather "the result of a common condition which, despite variations in degree, is experienced by all human beings who are born female" (Morgan 1984, 4). While she never explicitly defines this common condition, she comes closest to doing so in the following passage: "To many feminist theorists, the patriarchal control of women's bodies as the means of reproduction is the crux of the dilemma . . . The tragedy within the tragedy is that because we are regarded primarily as reproductive beings rather than full human beings, we are viewed in a (male-defined) sexual context, with the consequent epidemic of rape, sexual harassment, forced prostitution, and sexual traffick in women, with transacted marriage, institutionalized family structures, and the denial of individual women's own sexual expression" (Morgan 1984, 6–8).

Passages such as these suggest that there is something about women's bodies, specifically our reproductive capacities, that, while not necessarily resulting in a particular social outcome, nevertheless sets the stage for a certain range of male reactions across cultures that are common enough in nature to establish a certain commonality in women's experience as victims of such reactions. Again, this commonality in female bodies does not determine this range of reactions, in the sense that in all cultural contexts such a commonality would generate a reaction that was of this type, but this commonality nevertheless does lead to this kind of reaction across many contexts. The difference between this type of a position and biological determinism is very slight. As I noted, biological determinism is commonly thought to apply only to contexts where a phenomenon is not affected by any variations in cultural context. Because Morgan is allowing that some variations in cultural context could affect the reaction, she is not here being a strict biological determinist. But because she believes that this commonality in female bodies does lead to a common type of reaction across a wide range of diverse cultural contexts, there is, in reality, only a small space that separates her position from that of a strict biological determinism. When we see that within a theory biology can have a more or less determining influence, so can we also see that one can be more or less a social constructionist.

Another writer who explicitly rejects biological determinism but whose position also ends up being functionally very close to it is Janice Raymond. In *A Passion for Friends*, Raymond explicitly rejects the view that biology is the cause of women's uniqueness. "Women have no biological edge on the more humane qualities of human existence," she claims, "nor does women's uniqueness proceed from any biological differences from men. Rather, just as any cultural context distinguishes one group from another, women's 'otherness' proceeds from women's culture" (Raymond 1986, 21). This position is also present in Raymond's earlier book, *The Transsexual Empire* (1979). What is very interesting about *The Transsexual Empire*, however, is that much of the argument here, as was the case with Morgan's argument, rests on the assumption of an extremely invariant relationship between biology and character, though an invariance that is not of the usual biological determinist kind. In this work, Raymond is extremely critical of transsexuality in general, of what she labels the "female-to-constructed male" in particular, and most especially of those "female-to-constructed males" who call themselves "lesbian-feminists." While many of Raymond's criticisms stem from the convincing position that modern medicine is not the most appropriate arena for challenging existing gender norms, other parts of her criticism emerge from certain assumptions about an invariant relationship between biology and character. Specifically, Raymond doubts the veracity of claims on the part of any biological male to have "a female within him": "The androgynous man and the transsexually constructed lesbian-feminist deceive women in much the same way, for they lead women into believing that they are truly one of us – this time not only one in behavior but one in spirit and conviction" (1979, 100).

For Raymond *all* women differ in certain important respects from *all* men. This is not because the biologies of either directly determine a certain character. Rather, she believes that the possession of a particular kind of genitals, i.e., those labeled "female," generates certain kinds of reactions from others that are different in kind from the reactions generated by the possession of those kinds of genitals labeled "male." The commonality among these reactions and their differences from those experienced by those with male genitals are sufficient to ensure that no one born with male genitals can claim enough in common with those born with female genitals to warrant the label "female." Thus she claims: "We know that we are women who are born with female chromosomes and anatomy, and that whether or not we were socialized to be so-called normal women, patriarchy has treated and will treat us like women. Transsexuals have not had this same history. No man can have the history of being born and located in this culture as a woman. He can have the history of *wishing* to be a woman and of *acting* like a woman, but this gender experience is that of a transsexual, not of a woman" (Raymond 1979, 114).

Raymond qualifies her claims in this passage to those living within patriarchal societies. But across such societies Raymond is assuming enough of a homogeneity of reaction that biology, for all intents and purposes, becomes a "determinant" of character. To be sure, biology does not here directly generate character. But because it here invariably leads to certain common reactions, which also invariably have a specific effect on character, it becomes in effect a cause of character. Like Morgan, Raymond is not claiming that biology generates specific consequences independent of culture. For both, however, variability within and amongst societies becomes so muted in relation to a certain class of issues that culture becomes, in relation to these issues, a vanishing variable. The invocation of culture does, of course, allow these theorists to postulate differences existing side by side with the commonalities and also leaves open the possibility of a distant society where biology might not have such effects. But in neither case does it interfere with the power of biological givens to generate important commonalities among women across a wide span of human history.

I have focused on the writings of Robin Morgan and Janice Raymond in the above for the purpose of illustration. The type of "biological foundationalism" exemplified in their writings is not at all unique to these two writers but represents, I believe, a major tendency within second-wave theory, particularly in that tendency known as radical feminism. This, of course, is not surprising. Since the early 1970s, radical feminists have tended to be in the vanguard of those who have stressed the similarities among women and their differences from men. But it is difficult justifying such claims without invoking biology in some way or other. During the 1970s, many radical feminists explicitly endorsed biological determinism.[6] Biological determinism became, however, increasingly distasteful among feminists for a variety of reasons. Not only did it possess an unpleasant association with antifeminism, but it also seemed to disallow differences among women and – in the absence of feminist biological warfare – seemed to negate any hopes for change. The task became that of creating theory that allowed for differences among women, made at least theoretically possible the idea of a future without sexism, and yet that also justified cross-cultural claims about women. Some version of a strong form of biological foundationalism became the answer for many radical feminists.

While radical feminist writings are a rich source of strong forms of biological foundationalism, they are not the only source of biological foundationalism in general. Even theories that pay more attention to cultural history and diversity than do those of many radical feminists often rely on some use of biological foundationalism to make critical moves. Beginning in the 1970s and early 1980s, much of second-wave feminism in general began to move in the direction of stressing similarities among women and their differences from men, changing from what Iris Young has called a humanistic stance to a more gynocentric one (1985, 173–83). The enormous attention given at this time to books such as Carol Gilligan's *In a Different Voice* (1983) and Nancy Chodorow's *The Reproduction of Mothering* (1978) can be said to follow from the usefulness of the former in elaborating difference between women and men and of the latter in accounting for it. While both of these works strikingly exemplify a difference perspective, neither fits easily into the category of radical feminism. Yet in both of these works, as well as in others of this period that also emphasize difference, such as in those of such French feminists as Luce Irigiray, there is an interesting overlap with perspectives embodied in much radical feminist analysis. Specifically, these works claim a strong correlation between people with certain biological characteristics and people with certain character traits. To be sure, in a work such as Chodorow's *Reproduction of Mothering*, such claims are built upon a rich and complex story about culture: about how the possession of certain kinds of genitals gets one placed in a particular psycho-social dynamic only in specific types of circumstances and only insofar as those genitals possess certain kinds of meanings. Nevertheless, I would still describe a work such as *The Reproduction of Mothering* as biologically foundationalist. I do so because its complex and sophisticated story of child development, as a story supposedly applicable to a wide range of cultures, rests on the assumption that the possession of certain kinds of genitals does possess a common enough meaning across this range of cultures to make possible the postulation of a fundamentally homogeneous set of stories about child development. To assume that the cultural construction of the body serves as an unchanging variable across sweeps of human history and combines with other relatively static aspects of culture to create certain commonalities in personality formation across such history suffices, in my account, to indicate some version of biological foundationalism.

A problem running throughout the above theories, a problem that many commentators have pointed out, is that "a feminism of difference" tends to be "a feminism of uniformity." To say that "women are different from men in such and such ways" is to say that women *are* "such and such." But inevitably characterizations of women's "nature" or "essence" – even if this is described as a socially constructed "nature" or "essence" – tend to reflect the perspective of those making the characterizations. And as those who have the power to make such characterizations in contemporary European-based societies tend to be white, heterosexual, and from the professional class, such characterizations tend to reflect the biases of those from these groups. It was thus not surprising that the gynocentric move of the 1970s soon gave way to outcries from women of color, lesbians, and those of working-class backgrounds that the stories being told did not reflect their experiences. Thus, Chodorow was soon critiqued for elaborating a basically heterosexual story and she, Gilligan, and radical feminists such as Mary Daly have been accused of speaking primarily from a white, Western, middle-class perspective.[7]

My argument is that in all those cases where feminist theory makes generalizations across large sweeps of history, what is being assumed is common perspectives throughout such history about the meaning and import of female and male bodies. Many writers have pointed out how in these types of theories the specific content of the claim tends to reflect the culture of the theorist making the generalization. But also being borrowed from the theorist's cultural context is a specific understanding of bodies. This understanding is then assumed to underlie a story of character development or societal reaction applicable across an indefinitely vague span of time. The methodological move here is not different from that employed by biological determinists: the assumed "givenness" and commonality of nature across cultures is being drawn on to give credibility to the generality of the specific claim. In short, it is not only that certain specific ideas about women and men – that women are relational, nurturing, and caring while men are aggressive and combative – are being falsely generalized, but that also being falsely generalized, and indeed making these further generalizations about character possible, are certain specific assumptions about the body and its relation to character – that there are commonalities in the distinctive givens of the body that generate commonalities in the classification of human beings across cultures and in the reactions by others to those so classified. The problems associated with "a feminism of difference" are both reflected in and made possible by "biological foundationalism."

But the rejoinder might be made that what my argument is failing to allow for is that in many historical contexts people have interpreted the body in relatively similar ways and this common interpretation has led to certain cross-cultural commonalities in the treatment of women. True, it might be the case that some feminist scholarship falsely assumed the generalizability of some specific character traits found in contemporary middle-class Western life, i.e., that women are more nurturant than men. But it has not generally been problematic to assume, for contemporary Western societies as well as for most others, that the possession of one of two possible kinds of bodies does lead to the labeling of some people as women and others as men and that this labeling bears *some* common characteristics with *some* common effects.

This is a powerful response, but, I would claim, one that derives its power from a subtle misreading about how gender operates cross-culturally. Most societies known to Western scholarship do appear to have some kind of a male/female distinction. Moreover, most appear to relate this distinction to some kind of bodily distinction between women and men. From such observations it is very tempting to move to the above claims. I would argue, however, that such a move is faulty. And the reason is that "some kind of male/female distinction" and "some kind of bodily distinction" include a wide range of possible subtle differences in the meaning of the male/female distinction and of how the bodily distinction works in relationship to it. Because these differences may be subtle, they are not necessarily the kinds of things that contemporary Western feminists will first see when they look at premodern European cultures or cultures not dominated by the influence of modern Europe. But subtle differences around such issues may contain important consequences in the very deep sense of what it means to be a man or a woman. For example, certain Native American societies that have understood identity more in relation to spiritual forces than has been true of modern European-based societies have also allowed for some of those with male genitals to understand themselves and be understood by others as half-man/half-woman in ways that have not been possible within those European-based societies. Within these latter societies, the body has been interpreted as such an important signifier of identity that someone with female genitals has also not been thought ever to occupy legitimately the role of "husband," whereas in many African societies this is not the case. In short, while all of these societies certainly possess some kind of male/female distinction and also relate this distinction in some important way or another to the body, subtle differences in how the body itself is viewed may contain some very basic implications for what it means to be male or female and, consequently, produce important differences in the degree and ways in which sexism operates. In short, such subtle differences in the ways in which the body itself is read may relate to differences in what it means to be a man or woman that "go all the way down."[8]

But this point may be established not only by looking at the relation between contemporary Western societies and certain "exotic" others. Even within contemporary European-based societies we can detect important tensions and conflicts in the meaning of the body and in how the body relates to male and female identity. While certainly these are societies that, over the last several centuries, have operated with a strongly binary male/female distinction and have based this distinction on an attributed binary biology, they have also been societies that, in varying degrees, have also articulated notions of the self that deny differences among women and men, and not just as a consequence of 1960s feminism. In part, this denial of differences is manifest in the degree to which the belief that women and men are fundamentally the same is also a part of the hegemonic belief system of the societies in which many of us operate and has been available for feminists to draw on as an attack upon differences. Indeed, it is at least partly as a consequence of a general cultural tendency in some European-based societies to disassociate somewhat biology and character that feminism itself was made possible. One of the weaknesses of a difference-based feminism is that it cannot account for the phenomenon of such societies having produced feminists – that is, beings whose genitals, by virtue of the account, should have made us completely feminine but whose actual political skills and/or presence in such previously male-dominated institutions as the academy must indicate some masculine socialization. Moreover, it seems inadequate to conceptualize such socialization as merely an "add-on" to certain "basic" commonalities. In short, it is because of a certain prior disassociation of biology and socialization that, at a very basic level, many of us are who we are.

In short, a feminism of difference and the biological foundationalism on which it rests contain, in contemporary European-based societies, elements of both truth and falsity. Because these are societies that to a significant degree perceive female and male genitals as binary and also link character to such genitals, people born with "male" genitals are likely to be different in many important respects from people born with "female" genitals as a consequence of "possessing" such genitals. A feminism of difference and the biological foundationalism on which it rests, however, are also false not only because of the failure of both positions to recognize the historicity of their own insights but also because neither allows for the ways in which even within contemporary European-based societies the belief system their insights reflect possesses a multitude of cracks and fissures. Thus, a feminism of difference can provide no insight into those of us whose psyches are the manifestation of such cracks. Take, for example, those who are born with "male" genitals yet think of themselves as female. Raymond in *The Transsexual Empire* claims that "male-to-constructed females" are motivated by the desire to seize control, at least symbolically, of women's power to reproduce (1979, 28–29). She also claims that "female-to-constructed males" are motivated by the desire to seize the general power given to men, that is, are "male-identified" to the extreme (Raymond 1979, xxiii–xxv). Assuming for the sake of discussion that such accounts are valid, they still leave unanswered such questions as why particular women are so male-identified, or why only some men wish to seize symbolic control of women's power to reproduce or do it in this particular way. Any appeals to "false consciousness," like their earlier Marxist counterparts, merely place the lack of an answer at a deeper level, as again no account is made why some and not others succumb to "false consciousness."[9] Thus, even to the extent that the culture itself links gender to biology, a feminist analysis that follows this approach is unable to account for those who deviate.

Because a feminism of difference is both true and false within the societies in which many of us operate, the process of endorsing or rejecting it is similar to looking at those pictures in psychology textbooks where one moment the picture looks like the head of a rabbit and the next moment looks like the head of a duck. Within each "view," features stand out that had previously been hidden, and the momentary interpretation feels like the only possible one. Much of the power of books such as Chodorow's *Reproduction of Mothering* and Gilligan's *In a Different Voice* lay in the fact that they generated radically new ways of viewing social relations. The problem, however, is that these new ways of configuring reality, while truly powerful, also missed so much. Like a lens that only illuminates certain aspects of what we see by shadowing others, these visions kept from sight the many contexts where we as women and men deviate from the generalizations these analyses generated, either because the cultural contexts of our childhoods were not ones where these generalizations were encompassing or because the specific psychic dynamics of our individual childhoods undermined any simple internalization of these generalizations. Thus, from within the perspective of a feminism of difference it became impossible for women to acknowledge both the ways in which the generalizations generated from the analyses poorly captured their own notions of masculinity and femininity and also, even when they did, how their own psyches might embody masculine traits. Any acknowledgement of this latter deviation seemed to make one's membership in the feminist community particularly suspect.

This last point illuminates what is often forgotten in debates about the truth of such generalizations: since evidence can be accumulated both for their truth and their falsity, their endorsement or rejection is not a consequence of a dispassionate weighing of the "evidence." Rather, it is our disparate needs, both individual and collective, that push those of us who are women to see ourselves more or less like other women and different from men. At a collective level, the need to see ourselves as very much like each other and different from men made a lot of things possible at a certain moment in history. Most importantly, it enabled us to uncover sexism in its depth and pervasiveness and to build communities of women organized around its eradication. It also contained some major weaknesses, however, most notably its tendency to eradicate differences among women. The question facing feminism today is whether we can generate new visions of gender that retain what has been positive in "a feminism of difference" while eliminating what has been negative.

How then do we interpret "woman"?

Within contemporary European-based societies there is a strong tendency to think in either/or ways regarding generalities: either there are commonalities that tie us all together *or* we are all just individuals. A large part of the appeal of theories that supported "a feminism of difference" was that they generated strong ammunition against the common societal tendency to dismiss the import of gender, to claim that feminism is not necessary since "we are all just individuals." A feminism of difference uncovered many important social patterns of gender, patterns that enabled many women to understand their circumstances in social rather than idiosyncratic terms.

My argument against a feminism of difference does not mean that we should stop searching for such patterns. It is rather that we should understand them in different and more complex terms than we have tended to do, particularly that we should become more attentive to the historicity of any patterns we uncover. As we search for that which is socially shared, we need to be searching simultaneously for the places where such patterns break down. My argument thus points to the replacement of claims about women as such or even women in patriarchal societies with claims about women in particular contexts.[10]

The idea that we can make claims about women that span large historical stretches has been facilitated by the idea that there is something common to the category of "woman" across such historical stretches: that all share, at some basic level, certain features of biology. Thus what I have called biological foundationalism gives content to the claim that there exists some common criteria defining what it means to be a woman. For political purposes such criteria are thought to enable us to differentiate enemy from ally and to provide the basis for feminism's political program. Thus, there will be many who view my attack on "biological foundationalism" as an attack on feminism itself: if we do not possess some common criteria providing meaning to the word "woman," how can we generate a politics around this term? Does not feminist politics require that the category "woman" have some determinate meaning?

To counter this idea that feminist politics requires that "woman" possess some determinate meaning, I would like to borrow some ideas about language from Ludwig Wittgenstein. In arguing against a philosophy of language that claimed that meaning in general entailed

such determinacy, Wittgenstein pointed to the word "game". He argued
that it is impossible to come up with any one feature which is common
to everything which is called a "game":

> For if you look at them [the proceedings that we call "games"] you will not
> see something that is common to *all*, but similarities, relationships, and a
> whole series of them at that . . . Look for example at board-games, with
> their multifarious relationships. Now pass to card-games; here you find many
> correspondences with the first group but many common features drop out,
> and others appear. When we pass next to ball-games, much that is common
> is retained, but much is lost . . . And the result of this examination is: we see
> a complicated network of similarities overlapping and criss-crossing: sometimes
> overall similarities, sometimes similarities of detail.
>
> (Wittgenstein 1953, 31e–32e)

Thus, the meaning of "game" is revealed not through the determination
of some specific characteristic, or set of such, but through the elaboration of a complex network of characteristics, with different elements
of this network being present in different cases. Wittgenstein used the
phrase "family relationships" to describe such a network, since members
of a family may resemble one another without necessarily sharing any
one specific feature in common. Another metaphor that suggests the
same point is that of a tapestry unified by overlapping threads of color
but where no one particular color is found throughout the whole.[11]

I want to suggest that we think of the meaning of "woman" in the same
way that Wittgenstein suggested we think about the meaning of "game,"
as a word whose meaning is not found through the elucidation of some
specific characteristic but is found through the elaboration of a complex
network of characteristics. This suggestion certainly allows for the fact
that there might be some characteristics – such as possessing a vagina
and being over a certain age – that play a dominant role within such a
network over long periods of time. It also allows for the fact that the
word may be used in contexts where such characteristics are not present,
for example, in English-speaking countries prior to the adoption of the
concept of "vagina," or in contemporary English-speaking societies to
refer to those who do not have vaginas but who still feel themselves to
be women, i.e., to transsexuals before a medical operation. Moreover,
if our frame of reference is not only the English term "woman" but also
all those words into which "woman" is translatable, then such a mode of
thinking about the meaning of "woman" becomes even more helpful.

Conceptualizing "woman" in this way is helpful mostly because of its
non-arrogant stance towards meaning. As I mentioned, such a way of
thinking about the meaning of "woman" and of its non-English cognates

does not reject the idea that over stretches of history there will be patterns. To give up on the idea that "woman" has one clearly specifiable meaning does not entail that it has no meaning. Rather, this way of thinking about meaning works upon the assumption that such patterns are found within history and must be documented as such. We cannot presuppose that the meaning dominant in contemporary, industrialized Western societies must be true everywhere or across stretches with indeterminate boundaries. Thus, such a stance does not reject the idea that the "two-sex" body has played an important role in structuring the male/female distinction and thus the meaning of "woman" over a certain portion of human history. But it does demand that we be clear about what exact portion that is and even within it, what are the contexts in which it does not apply. Moreover, because such a stance recognizes that the meaning of "woman" has changed over time, it also recognizes that those presently advocating nontraditional understandings of it, such as transsexuals, cannot be dismissed merely on the grounds that their interpretations contradict standard patterns. Janice Raymond claims that no one born without a vagina can claim to have had comparable experiences to those born with one. My question is: how can she know this? How can she know, for example, that some people's parents were not operating with a greater slippage between biology and character than is true for many in contemporary industrialized societies and thus really did provide to their children with "male" genitals experiences comparable to those born with vaginas? Historical change is made possible by some people having experiences that really are different from those that have predominated in the past.

Thus I am advocating that we think about the meaning of "woman" as illustrating a map of intersecting similarities and differences. Within such a map, the body does not disappear but rather becomes an historically specific variable whose meaning and import is recognized as potentially different in different historical contexts. Such a suggestion, in assuming that meaning is found rather than presupposed, also suggests that the search itself is not a research/political project that an individual scholar will be able to accomplish alone in her study. Rather, it implies an understanding of such a project as necessarily a collective effort undertaken by many in dialogue.

Moreover, as both the above references to transsexuals and my earlier discussion of commonality among women and difference with men should indicate, it is a mistake to think of such a search as an "objective" task undertaken by scholars motivated only by the disinterested pursuit of truth. What we see and feel as commonalities and differences will at least partially depend on our diverse psychic needs and political goals. To clarify the meaning of a word where ambiguity exists and where diverse consequences follow from diverse clarifications is itself a political act. Thus, the clarification of the meaning of many concepts in our language, such as "mother," "education," "science," "democracy," while often portrayed as merely descriptive acts, are, in actuality, stipulative. With a word as emotionally charged as "woman," where so much hangs on how its meaning is elaborated, any claim about such must be viewed as a political intervention.

But if elaborating the meaning of "woman" represents an ongoing task and an ongoing political struggle, does this not undermine the project of feminist politics? If those who call themselves feminists cannot even decide upon who "women" are, how can political demands be enacted in the name of women? Does not feminism require the very presupposition of unity around meaning that I am saying we cannot possess?

To respond to these concerns, let me suggest a slightly different way of understanding feminist politics than has often been taken for granted. Normally when we think of "coalition politics," we think of groups with clearly defined interests coming together on a temporary basis for purposes of mutual enhancement. In such a view, coalition politics is something that feminists enter into with "others." But we could think about coalition politics as not something merely external to feminist politics but as that which is also internal to it. This means that we think about feminist politics as the coming together of those who want to work around the needs of women where such a concept is not understood as necessarily singular in meaning or commonly agreed upon. The coalition politics of such a movement would be formulated in the same way as coalition politics in general are formulated, as either comprised of lists of demands that take care of the diverse needs of the groups constituting the coalition, as comprised of demands articulated at a certain abstract level to include diversity, or as comprised of specific demands that diverse groups temporarily unite around. Indeed, I would claim that such strategies are those that feminists have increasingly adopted over the past twenty-five-year period. Thus white feminists started talking about reproductive rights instead of abortion on demand when it became clear that many women of color saw access to prenatal care or freedom from involuntary sterilization as at least as relevant to their lives, if not more so, than access to abortion. In other words, feminist politics of the past twenty-five years have already increasingly been exhibiting internal coalitional strategies. Why cannot our theorization of "woman" reflect such a politics?

This type of politics does not demand that "woman" possess a singular meaning. Moreover, even when feminist politics does claim to speak on behalf of some one understanding of "woman," can it not explicitly acknowledge such an understanding as political and thus provisional, as open to whatever challenges others might want to put forth? In other words, can we not be clear that any claims we make on behalf of women or women's interests are stipulative rather than descriptive, as much based on an understanding of what we want women to be as on any collective survey as to how those who call themselves women perceive themselves? Acknowledging the political character of such claims means, of course, abandoning the hope that it is easy determining whose definition of women or women's interests one might want to include in one's own claims. But, I would argue, that determination has never been easy. Feminists speaking in the name of women have often ignored the claims of right-wing women as they have also taken on certain ideals about women's interests from the male left. That white feminists in the United States have increasingly felt it necessary to take seriously the demands of women of color and not the demands of white, conservative women is not because the former possess vaginas that the latter do not but because the ideals expressed by many of the former more closely conform to many of their own than do those of the conservative women. Maybe it is time that we explicitly acknowledge that our claims about women are not based on some given reality but emerge from our own places within history and culture; they are political acts that reflect the contexts we emerge out of and the futures we would like to see.

Notes

This essay has a long and complex genealogy. For this reason I cannot begin to thank all of the people who have read or heard some part of the present essay and contributed to the birth of the present version. Many, many people will find much of this familiar. A few special thanks are, however, necessary. I would like to thank the Duke–UNC-Chapel Hill Center for Research on Women for providing me with a Rockefeller Foundation Humanist-in-Residence Fellowship for 1991–92. That fellowship, combined with a University at Albany, State University of New York, sabbatical gave me a year to think about many of the ideas in this essay. I also want to thank Steve Seidman for reading every draft and for intervening in the development of this essay at several crucial points.

1. While the growth of a materialist metaphysics may have contributed to the growth of that strong sense of individualism that many writers have linked to modern Western conceptions of the self, it would be a mistake to see such individualism merely as a result of the growth of such a metaphysics.

Some writers, such as Charles Taylor, have pointed to an emerging sense of "inwardness," one aspect of such an individualism, as early as in the writings of Augustine. See Taylor 1990, 127–42. And, according to Colin Morris, such a turn to a language of inwardness represents a widespread twelfth-century phenomenon. A decline of this tendency in the middle of the twelfth century was followed by its gradual resurfacing, culminating in the late fifteenth-century Italian Renaissance (Morris 1972). Moreover, even in the period after the emergence of a materialistic metaphysics, other social transformations have contributed to the development of such a sense of individualism differently amongst different social groups.

2. For discussions of this point see: Winthrop Jordan 1968; Cornell West 1988; Lucius Outlaw 1990; and Michael Banton and Jonathan Harwood, 1975.

3. Laqueur also claims that the binarism of the new view was a consequence of these social structural transformations in the lives of women and men. See Laqueur 1990, 193–243.

4. Any elaboration of this opposition requires a book-length discussion. That a full-scale materialism was not easily endorsed in the very early period is most obviously indicated in the dualism of one of the most outspoken advocates of such a materialism, Rene Descartes. But the "Cambridge Platonists," who were sympathetic to some version of materialism, thought Descartes' position was much too radical. For an informative discussion of religious tensions around the adoption of materialism through the modern period, see John Hedley Brooke 1991. In the late nineteenth century, other, non-religious arguments emerged against the utility of scientific modes of explanation in accounting for human behavior and social laws. This movement was most pronounced in Germany and received a full elaboration in the writings of Wilhelm Dilthey.

5. It was as a consequence of reading Chandra Talpade Mohanty's very insightful discussion of Robin Morgan's introduction to *Sisterhood is Global* that I thought of looking to Morgan's essay as a useful exemplar of biological foundationalism. See Chandra Talpade Mohanty 1992. I see the intent of Mohanty's analysis very much overlapping with mine though there are differences in the specific form of each.

6. One radical feminist theorist who explicitly endorses biological determinism in the late 1970s is Mary Daly. In a 1979 interview in the feminist journal *off our backs*, Daly responded to the question whether men's problems are rooted in biology with the response that she was inclined to think they were. This interview was brought to my attention by Carol Anne Douglas 1990. For other instances of this tendency within radical feminist theory during the 1970s, see Alison Jaggar 1983.

7. Judith Lorber, in faulting Chodorow's work for not paying enough attention to social structural issues, explicitly raised questions about the class biases of *The Reproduction of Mothering*. Her more general points, however, would apply to issues of race as well. See her contribution to the critical symposium

on *The Reproduction of Mothering* in *Signs* 1981. Elizabeth Spelman focuses on the ways in which Chodorow's account insufficiently addresses issues of race and class in *Inessential Woman* 1988. Adrienne Rich has noted the lacuna in Chodorow's analysis regarding lesbianism in "Compulsory Heterosexuality and Lesbian Existence," *Signs* 1980. Audre Lorde has raised issues of racism in relation to Mary Daly's *Gyn/Ecology* in "An Open Letter to Mary Daly," in Cherrie Moraga and Gloria Anzaldua, eds., *This Bridge Called My Back: Writings by Radical Women of Color* 1981. Spelman also looks at the ways in which Mary Daly's analysis tends to separate sexism and racism and make the latter secondary to the former in *Inessential Woman*. The separatism of radical lesbian-feminism has been criticized as ignoring issues of race. See, for example, the Combahee River Collective's "Black Feminist Statement" (1981) in *This Bridge Called My Back*. The class and race biases of Gilligan's work have been pointed to by John Broughton in "Women's Rationality and Men's Virtues," *Social Research* 1983. I also develop this issue in my article in that same volume, "Women, Morality, and History."

8. On the ways in which the Native American berdache undermine European notions of gender see Walter L. Williams 1986 and Harriet Whitehead 1981. For a very useful discussion of the phenomenon of female husbands see Ifi Amadiume 1987. Igor Kopytoff 1990 provides an extremely provocative discussion of the relation between the phenomenon of female husbands and broader issues concerning the nature of self-identity.

9. This general weakness in arguments that employ the concept of "false consciousness" was suggested to me in another context by Marcia Lind.

10. Of course, the demand for particularity is always relative. As such, any demand for particularity cannot be interpreted in absolutist terms but only as that we move more in such a direction.

11. The tapestry metaphor was first used in an article I co-authored with Nancy Fraser to provide a model for how we think about feminist theory in general. See Nancy Fraser and Linda Nicholson 1990.

References

Amadiume, Ifi. 1987. *Male Daughters, Female Husbands: Gender and Sex in an African Society*. Atlantic Highlands, N.J.: Zed Books.

Banton, Michael and Jonathan Harwood. 1975. *The Race Concept*. New York: Praeger.

Brooke, John Hedley. 1991. *Science and Religion: Some Historical Perspectives*. Cambridge: Cambridge University Press.

Broughton, John. 1983. "Women's Rationality and Men's Virtues." *Social Research*, 50(3): 597–642.

Chodorow, Nancy. 1978. *The Reproduction of Mothering: Psychoanalysis and the Sociology of Gender*. Berkeley: University of California Press.

Combahee River Collective. 1981. "Black Feminist Statement." In *This Bridge Called My Back: Writings by Radical Women of Color*, ed. Cherrie Moraga and Gloria Anzaldua, 210–18. Watertown, Mass.: Persephone Press.

Daly, Mary. 1979. "Interview." *off our backs*, 9(5): 23.

Douglas, Carol Anne. 1990. *Love and Politics: Radical Feminist and Lesbian Theories*. San Francisco: ism Press.

Foucault, Michel. 1980. *Herculine Barbin*, trans. Richard McDougall. New York: Pantheon.

Fraser, Nancy and Linda Nicholson. 1990. "Social Criticism Without Philosophy: An Encounter Between Feminism and Postmodernism." In *Feminism/Postmodernism*, ed. Linda Nicholson, 19–38. New York: Routledge.

Gilligan, Carol. 1983. *In a Different Voice: Psychological Theory and Women's Development*. Cambridge, Mass.: Harvard University Press.

Jaggar, Alison. 1983. *Feminist Politics and Human Nature*. Totowa, N. J.: Rowman and Allanheld.

Jordan, Winthrop. 1968. *White Over Black: American Attitudes Toward the Negro*, 1550–1812. Chapel Hill, N. C.: University of North Carolina Press.

Jordanova, Ludmilla. 1989. *Sexual Visions: Images of Gender in Science and Medicine Between the Eighteenth and Twentieth Centuries*. Madison, Wis.: University of Wisconsin Press.

Kopytoff, Igor. 1990. "Women's Roles and Existential Identities." In *Beyond the Second Sex: New Directions in the Anthropology of Gender*, ed. Peggy Reeves Sanday and Ruth Gallagher Goodenough, 77–98. Philadelphia, Pa.: University of Pennsylvania Press.

Laqueur, Thomas. 1990. *Making Sex: Body and Gender from the Greeks to Freud*. Cambridge, Mass.: Harvard University Press.

Locke, John. 1965. *Two Treatises of Government*, ed. and with introduction by Peter Laslett. New York: New American Library.

Lorber, Judith. 1981. "Critical Symposium on *The Reproduction of Mothering*." *Signs: Journal of Women in Culture and Society*, 6(3): 482–86.

Lorde, Audre. 1981. "An Open Letter to Mary Daly." In *This Bridge Called My Back: Writings by Radical Women of Color*, ed. Cherrie Moraga and Gloria Anzaldua, 94–97. Watertown, Mass.: Persephone Press.

Mohanty, Chandra Talpade. 1992. "Feminist Encounters: Locating the

Politics of Experience." In *Destabilizing Theory*, ed. Michele Barrett and Anne Phillips, 74–92. Cambridge, England: Polity Press.

Morgan, Robin. 1984. Introduction to "Planetary Feminism: The Politics of the 21st Century." In *Sisterhood is Global: The International Women's Movement Anthology*, ed. Robin Morgan, 1–37. Garden City, New York: Doubleday.

Morris, Colin. 1972. *The Discovery of the Individual*. London: SPCK.

Nicholson, Linda. 1983. "Women, Morality and History." *Social Research*, 50(3): 514–36.

Outlaw, Lucius. 1990. "Toward a Critical Theory of Race." In *The Anatomy of Racism*, ed. David Theo Goldberg, 58–82. Minneapolis, Minn.: University of Minnesota Press.

Raymond, Janice. 1979. *The Transsexual Empire: The Making of the She-Male*. Boston: Beacon Press.

　　1986. *A Passion for Friends: Towards a Philosophy of Female Affection*. Boston: Beacon Press.

Rich, Adrienne. 1980. "Compulsory Heterosexuality and Lesbian Existence." *Signs: Journal of Women in Culture and Society*, 5(4): 631–60.

Rubin, Gayle. 1975. "The Traffic in Women." In *Toward an Anthropology of Women*, ed. Rayna R. Reiter, 157–210. New York: Monthly Review Press.

Scott, Joan. 1988. *Gender and the Politics of History*. New York: Columbia University Press.

Spelman, Elizabeth. 1988. *Inessential Woman: Problems of Exclusion in Feminist Thought*. Boston: Beacon Press.

Taylor, Charles. 1989. *Sources of the Self: The Making of the Modern Identity*. Cambridge: Harvard University Press.

West, Cornell. 1988. *Prophetic Fragments*. Grand Rapids, Mich.: William B. Erdmans and Trenton, N. J.: Africa World.

Whitehead, Harriet. 1981. "The Bow and the Burden Strap: A New Look at Institutionalized Homosexuality in Native North America." In *Sexual Meanings: The Cultural Construction of Gender and Sexuality*, ed. Sherry B. Ortner and Harriet Whitehead, 80–115. Cambridge: Cambridge University Press.

Williams, Walter L. 1986. *The Spirit and the Flesh: Sexual Diversity in American Indian Culture*. Boston: Beacon Press.

Wittgenstein, Ludwig. 1953. *Philosophical Investigations*, trans. G. E. M. Anscombe. New York: Macmillan.

Young, Iris Marion. 1985. "Humanism, Gynocentrism and Feminist Politics." *Hypatia: A Journal of Feminist Philosophy*, 3, a special issue of *Women's Studies International Forum*, 8(3): 173–83.

2

Feminist encounters: locating the politics of experience

Chandra Talpade Mohanty

Feminist and antiracist struggles in the 1990s face some of the same urgent questions encountered in the 1970s. After two decades of engagement in feminist political activism and scholarship in a variety of sociopolitical and geographical locations, questions of difference (sex, race, class, nation), experience, and history remain at the center of feminist analysis. Only, at least in the US academy, feminists no longer have to contend as they did in the 1970s with phallocentric denials of the legitimacy of gender as a category of analysis. Instead, the crucial questions in the 1990s concern the construction, examination, and, most significantly, the institutionalization of difference *within* feminist discourses. It is this institutionalization of difference that concerns me here. Specifically, I ask the following question: how does the politics of location in the contemporary United States determine and produce experience and difference as analytical and political categories in feminist "cross-cultural" work? By the term "politics of location" I refer to the historical, geographical, cultural, psychic, and imaginative boundaries which provide the ground for political definition and self-definition for contemporary US feminists.[1]

Since the 1970s, there have been key paradigm shifts in Western feminist theory. These shifts can be traced to political, historical, methodological, and philosophical developments in our understanding of questions of power, struggle, and social transformation. Feminists have drawn on decolonization movements around the world, on movements for racial equality, on peasant struggles, and on gay and lesbian movements, as well as on the methodologies of Marxism, psychoanalysis, deconstruction, and poststructuralism to situate our thinking in the 1990s. While these developments have often led to progressive, indeed radical, analyses of sexual difference, the focus on questions of subjectivity and identity which is a hallmark of contemporary feminist theory has also had some problematic effects in the area of race and Third World/ postcolonial studies. One problematic effect of the postmodern critique of essentialist notions of identity has been the dissolution of the category of race – however, this is often accomplished at the expense of a recognition of racism. Another effect has been the generation of discourses of diversity and pluralism which are grounded in an apolitical, often individualized identity politics.[2] Here, questions of *historical interconnection* are transformed into questions of discrete and separate histories (or even herstories) and into questions of identity politics.[3] While I cannot deal with such effects in detail here, I work through them in a limited way by suggesting the importance of analyzing and theorizing difference in the context of feminist cross-cultural work. Through this theorization of experience, I suggest that historicizing and locating political agency is a necessary alternative to formulations of the "universality" of gendered oppression and struggles. This universality of gender oppression is problematic, based as it is on the assumption that the categories of race and class have to be invisible for gender to be visible. In the 1990s, the challenges posed by black and Third World feminists can point the way towards a more precise, transformative feminist politics. Thus, the juncture of feminist and antiracist/Third World/postcolonial studies is of great significance, materially as well as methodologically.[4]

Feminist analyses which attempt to cross national, racial, and ethnic boundaries produce and reproduce difference in particular ways. This codification of difference occurs through the naturalization of analytic categories which are supposed to have cross-cultural validity. I attempt an analysis of two recent feminist texts which address the turn of the century directly. Both texts also foreground analytic categories which address questions of cross-cultural, cross-national differences among women. Robin Morgan's "Planetary Feminism: The Politics of the 21st Century" and Bernice Johnson Reagon's "Coalition Politics: Turning the Century" are both *movement* texts and are written for diverse mass audiences. Morgan's essay forms the introduction to her 1984 book, *Sisterhood is Global: The International Women's Movement Anthology*, while Reagon's piece was first given as a talk at the West Coast Women's Music Festival in 1981, and has since been published in Barbara Smith's 1983 anthology, *Home Girls: A Black Feminist Anthology*.[5] Both essays construct contesting notions of experience, difference, and struggle within and across cultural boundaries. I stage an encounter between these texts because they represent for me, despite their differences from each other, an alternative presence

– a thought, an idea, a record of activism and struggle – which can help me both locate and position myself in relation to "history." Through this presence, and with these texts, I can hope to approach the end of the century and not be overwhelmed.

The status of "female" or "woman/women's" experience has always been a central concern in feminist discourse. After all, it is on the basis of shared experience that feminists of different political persuasions have argued for unity or identity among women. Teresa de Lauretis, in fact, gives this question a sort of foundational status: "The relation of experience to discourse, finally, is what is at issue in the definition of feminism" (1986, 5.) Feminist discourses, critical and liberatory in intent, are not thereby exempt from inscription in their internal power relations. Thus, the recent definition, classification, and assimilation of categories of experientially based notions of "woman" (or analogously, in some analyses, "lesbian") to forge political unity require our attention and careful analysis. Gender is *produced* as well as uncovered in feminist discourse, and definitions of experience, with attendant notions of unity and difference, form the very basis of this production. For instance, gender inscribed within a purely male/female framework reinforces what Monique Wittig has called the heterosexual contract.[6] Here difference is constructed along male/female lines, and it is being female (as opposed to male) which is at the center of the analysis. Identity is seen as either male or female. A similar definition of experience can also be used to craft lesbian identity. Katie King's analysis indicates this:

The construction of political identity in terms of lesbianism as a magical sign forms the pattern into which the feminist taxonomic identities of recent years attempt to assimilate themselves . . . Identifying with lesbianism falsely implies that one knows all about heterosexism and homophobia magically through identity or association. The "experience" of lesbianism is offered as salvation from the individual practice of heterosexism and homophobia and the source of intuitive institutional and structural understanding of them. The power of lesbianism as a privileged signifier makes analysis of heterosexism and homophobia difficult since it obscures the need for counter-intuitive challenges to ideology.
(1986, 85)

King's analysis calls into question the authority and presence of "experience" in constructing lesbian identity. She criticizes feminist analyses in which difference is inscribed simply within a lesbian/heterosexual framework, with "experience" functioning as an unexamined, catch-all category. This is similar to the female/male framework Wittig calls attention to, for although the terms of the equation are different, the status and definition of "experience" are the same. The politics of being "woman" or "lesbian" are deduced from the *experience* of being woman or lesbian. Being female is thus seen as *naturally* related to being feminist, where the experience of being female transforms us into feminists through osmosis. Feminism is not defined as a highly contested political terrain; it is the mere effect of being female.[7] This is what one might call the feminist osmosis thesis: females are feminists by association and identification with the experiences which constitute us as female.

The problem is, however, that we cannot avoid the challenge of *theorizing* experience. For most of us would not want to ignore the range and scope of the feminist political arena, one characterized quite succinctly by de Lauretis: "feminism defines itself as a political instance, not merely a sexual politics but a politics of everyday life, which later . . . enters the public sphere of expression and creative practice, displacing aesthetic hierarchies and generic categories, and . . . thus establishes the semiotic ground for a different production of reference and meaning" (1986, 10). It is this recognition that leads me to an analysis of the status of experience and difference, and the relation of this to political praxis in Morgan's and Reagon's texts.

"A place on the map is also a place in history"[8]

The last decade has witnessed the publication of numerous feminist writings on what is generally referred to as an international women's movement, and we have its concrete embodiment in *Sisterhood is Global*, a text which in fact describes itself as "*The* international women's movement anthology." There is considerable difference between international feminist networks organized around specific issues like sex tourism and multinational exploitation of women's work, and the notion of *an* international women's movement which, as I attempt to demonstrate, implicitly *assumes* global or universal sisterhood. But it is best to begin by recognizing the significance and value of the publication of an anthology such as this. The value of documenting the indigenous histories of women's struggles is unquestionable. Morgan states that the book took twelve years in conception and development, five years in actual work, and innumerable hours in networking and fundraising. It is obvious that without Morgan's vision and perseverance this anthology would not have been published. The range of writing represented is truly impressive. At a time when most of the globe seems to be taken over by religious fundamentalism and big business, and the colonization of space takes precedence over survival concerns, an anthology that documents women's organized resistances has significant value in helping us envision a better future. In fact, it is because I recognize the value and importance of this anthology that I am concerned about the political implications of Morgan's framework for cross-cultural comparison. Thus my comments and criticisms are intended to encourage a greater internal self-consciousness within feminist politics and writing, not to lay blame or induce guilt.

Universal sisterhood is produced in Morgan's text through specific assumptions about women as a cross-culturally singular, homogeneous group with the same interests, perspectives, and goals and similar experiences. Morgan's definitions of "women's experience" and history lead to a particular self-presentation of Western women, a specific codification of differences among women, and eventually to what I consider to be problematic suggestions for political strategy.[9] Since feminist discourse is productive of analytic categories and strategic decisions which have material effects, the construction of the category of universal sisterhood in a text which is widely read deserves attention. In addition, *Sisterhood is Global* is still the only text which proclaims itself as the anthology of *the* international women's movement. It has had world-wide distribution, and Morgan herself has earned the respect of feminists everywhere. And since authority is always charged with responsibility, the discursive production and dissemination of notions of universal sisterhood are together a significant political event which perhaps solicits its own analysis.

Morgan's explicit intent is "to further the dialogue between and solidarity of women everywhere" (1984, 8). This is a valid and admirable project to the extent that one is willing to assume, if not the reality, then at least the possibility, of universal sisterhood on the basis of shared good will. But the moment we attempt to articulate the operation of contemporary imperialism with the notion of an international women's movement based on global sisterhood, the awkward political implications of Morgan's task become clear. Her particular notion of universal sisterhood seems predicated on the erasure of the history and effects of contemporary imperialism. Robin Morgan seems to situate *all* women (including herself) outside contemporary world history, leading to what I see as her ultimate suggestion that transcendence rather than engagement is the model for future social change. And this, I think, is a model which can have dangerous implications for women who do not and cannot speak from a location of white, Western, middle-class privilege. A place on the map (New York city) is, after all, also a locatable place in history.

What is the relation between experience and politics in Morgan's text? In "Planetary Feminism" the category of "women's experience" is constructed within two parameters: woman as victim, and woman as truth-teller. Morgan suggests that it is not mystical or biological commonalities which characterize women across cultures and histories, but rather a common condition and world view:

The quality of feminist political philosophy (in all its myriad forms) makes possible a totally new way of viewing international affairs, one less concerned with diplomatic postures and abstractions, but focused instead on concrete, *unifying* realities of priority importance to the survival and betterment of living beings. For example, the historical, cross-cultural opposition women express to war and our healthy skepticism of certain technological advances (by which most men seem overly impressed at first and disillusioned at last) are only two instances of shared attitudes among women which seem basic to a common world view. Nor is there anything mystical or biologically deterministic about this commonality. It is the result of a *common condition* which, despite variations in degree, is experienced by all human beings who are born female.   (1984, 4)

This may be convincing up to a point, but the political analysis that underlies this characterization of the commonality among women is shaky at best. At various points in the essay, this "common condition" that women share is referred to as the suffering inflicted by a universal "patriarchal mentality" (1984, 1), women's opposition to male power and androcentrism, and the experience of rape, battery, labor, and childbirth. For Morgan, the magnitude of suffering experienced by most of the women in the world leads to their potential power as a world political force, a force constituted in opposition to Big Brother in the United States, Western and Eastern Europe, China, Africa, the Middle East, and Latin America. The assertion that women constitute a potential world political force is suggestive; however, Big Brother is *not exactly the same* even in, say, the United States and Latin America. Despite the similarity of power interests and location, the two contexts present significant differences in the manifestations of power and hence of the possibility of struggles against it. I part company with Morgan when she seems to believe that Big Brother is the same the world over because "he" simply represents male interests, notwithstanding particular imperial histories or the role of monopoly capital in different countries.

In Morgan's analysis, women are unified by their shared perspective (for example, opposition to war), shared goals (betterment of human beings), and shared experience of oppression. Here the homogeneity of women as a group is produced not on the basis of biological essentials (Morgan offers a rich, layered critique of biological materialism), but rather through the psychologization of complex and contradictory historical and cultural realities. This leads in turn to the assumption of women as a unified group on the basis of secondary sociological universals. What binds women together is an ahistorical notion of the sameness of their oppression and, consequently, the sameness of their struggles. Therefore in Morgan's text cross-cultural comparisons are based on the assumption of the singularity and homogeneity of women as a *group*. This homogeneity of women as a group, is, in turn, predicated on a definition of the *experience of oppression* where difference can only be understood as male/female. Morgan assumes universal sisterhood on the basis of women's shared opposition to androcentrism, an opposition which, according to her, grows directly out of women's shared status as its victims. The analytic elision between the *experience* of oppression and the *opposition* to it illustrates an aspect of what I referred to earlier as the feminist osmosis thesis: being female and being feminist are one and the same; we are *all* oppressed and hence we *all* resist. Politics and ideology as self-conscious struggles and choices necessarily get written out of such an analysis.

Assumptions pertaining to the relation of experience to history are evident in Morgan's discussion of another aspect of women's experience: woman as truth-teller. According to her, women speak of the "real" unsullied by "rhetoric" or "diplomatic abstractions." They, as opposed to men (also a coherent singular group in this analytic economy), are authentic human beings whose "freedom of choice" has been taken away from them: "Our emphasis is on the individual voice of a woman speaking not as an official representative of her country, but rather as a truth-teller, with an emphasis on reality as opposed to rhetoric" (Morgan 1984, xvi). In addition, Morgan asserts that women social scientists are "freer of androcentric bias" and "more likely to elicit more trust and . . . more honest responses from female respondents of their studies" (1984, xvii). There is an argument to be made for women interviewing women, but I do not think this is it. The assumptions underlying these state-ments indicate to me that Morgan thinks women have some kind of privileged access to the "real," the "truth," and can elicit "trust" from other women purely on the basis of their being not-male. There is a problematic conflation here of the biological and the psychological with the discursive and the ideological. "Women" are collapsed into the "suppressed feminine" and men into the dominant ideology.

These oppositions are possible only because Morgan implicitly erases from her account the possibility that women might have *acted*, that they were anything but pure victims. For Morgan, history is a male construction; what women need is herstory, separate and outside of his-story. The writing of history (the discursive and the representational) is confused with women as historical actors. The fact that women are representationally absent from his-story does not mean that they are/were not significant social actors in history. However, Morgan's focus on herstory as separate and outside history not only hands over all of world history to the boys, but potentially suggests that women have been universally duped, not allowed to "tell the truth," and robbed of all *agency*. The implication of this is that women as a group seem to have forfeited any kind of material referentiality.

What, then, does this analysis suggest about the status of experience in this text? In Morgan's account, women have a sort of cross-cultural coherence as distinct from men. The status or position of women is assumed to be self-evident. However, this focus on the position of women whereby women are seen as a coherent group in *all* contexts, regardless of class or ethnicity, structures the world in ultimately Manichean terms, where women are always seen in opposition to men, patriarchy is always essentially the invariable phenomenon of male domination, and the religious, legal, economic, and familial systems are implicitly assumed to be constructed by men. Here, men and women are seen as whole groups with *already constituted* experiences as groups, and questions of history, conflict, and difference are formulated from what can only be this privileged location of knowledge.

I am bothered, then, by the fact that Morgan can see contemporary imperialism only in terms of a "patriarchal mentality" which is enforced by men as a *group*. Women across class, race, and national boundaries are participants to the extent that we are "caught up in political webs not of our making which we are powerless to unravel" (Morgan 1984, 25). Since women as a unified group are seen as unimplicated in the process of history and contemporary imperialism, the logical strategic response for Morgan appears to be political transcendence: "To fight back in solidarity, however, as a real political force requires that women transcend the patriarchal barriers of class and race, and furthermore, transcend even the solutions the Big Brothers propose to the problems they themselves created" (1984, 18). Morgan's emphasis on women's transcendence is evident in her discussions of (1) women's deep opposition to nationalism as practiced in patriarchal society, and (2) women's involvement in peace and disarmament movements across the world, because, in her opinion, they desire peace (as opposed to men who cause war). Thus, the concrete reality of women's involvement in peace movements is substituted by an abstract "desire" for peace which is supposed to transcend race, class, and national conflicts among women. Tangible responsibility and credit for organizing peace movements is replaced by an essentialist and psychological unifying desire. The problem is that in this case women are not seen as political agents; they are merely allowed to be well intentioned. Although Morgan does offer some specific suggestions for political strategy which require resisting "the system," her fundamental suggestion is that women transcend the left, the right, and the center, the law of the father, God, and the system. Since women have been analytically constituted outside real politics or history, progress for them can only be seen in terms of transcendence.

The *experience* of struggle is thus defined as both personal and ahistorical. In other words, the political is *limited to* the personal and all conflicts among and within women are flattened. If sisterhood itself is defined on the basis of personal intentions, attitudes, or desires, conflict is also automatically constructed on only the psychological level. Experience is thus written in as simultaneously individual (that is, located in the individual body/psyche of wom*a*n) and general (located in wom*e*n as a preconstituted collective). There seem to be two problems with this definition. First, experience is seen as being immediately accessible, understood, and named. The complex relationships between behavior and its representation are either ignored or made irrelevant; experience is collapsed into discourse and vice versa. Second, since experience has a fundamentally psychological status, questions of history and collectivity are formulated on the level of attitude and intention. In effect, the sociality of collective struggles is understood in terms of something like individual–group relations, relations which are common-sensically seen as detached from history. If the assumption of the *sameness* of experience is what ties woman (individual) to women (group), regardless of class, race, nation, and sexualities, the notion of experience is anchored firmly in the notion of the individual self, a determined and specifiable constituent of European modernity. However, this notion of the individual needs to be self-consciously historicized if as feminists we wish to go beyond the limited bourgeois ideology of individualism, especially as we attempt to understand what cross-cultural sisterhood might be made to mean.

Towards the end of "Planetary Feminism" Morgan talks about feminist diplomacy:

What if feminist diplomacy turned out to be simply another form of the feminist aphorism "the personal is political"? Danda writes here of her own feminist epiphany, Amanda of her moments of despair, La Silenciada of personally bearing witness to the death of a revolution's ideals. Tinne confides her fears, Nawal addresses us in a voice direct from prison, Hilkla tells us about her family and childhood; Ama Ata confesses the anguish of the woman artist, Stella shares her mourning with us, Mahnaz communicates her grief and her hope, Nell her daring balance of irony and lyricism, Paola the story of her origins and girlhood. Manjula isn't afraid to speak of pain, Corrine traces her own political evolution along-side that of her movement. Maria de Lourdes declares the personal and the political inseparable. Motlalepula still remembers the burning of a particular maroon dress, Ingrid and Renate invite us into their private correspondence, Marielouise opens herself in a poem, Elena appeals personally to us for help, Gwendoline testifies about her private life as a public figure . . .

And do we not, after all, recognize one another?   (1984, 35–36)

It is this passage more than any other that encapsulates Morgan's individualized and essentially equalizing notion of universal sisterhood, and its corresponding political implications. The lyricism, the use of first names (the one and only time this is done), and the insistence that we must easily "recognize one another" indicate what is left unsaid: we must identify with *all* women. But it is difficult to imagine such a generalized identification predicated on the commonality of women's interests and goals across very real divisive class and ethnic lines – especially, for example, in the context of the mass proletarianization of Third World women by corporate capital based in the United States, Europe, and Japan.

Universal sisterhood, defined as the transcendence of the "male" world, thus ends up being a middle-class, psychologized notion which effectively erases material and ideological power differences within and among groups of women, especially between First and Third World women (and, paradoxically, removes us all as actors from history and politics). It is in this erasure of difference as inequality and dependence that the privilege of Morgan's political "location" might be visible. Ultimately in this reductive utopian vision, men *participate* in politics while women can only hope to *transcend* it. Morgan's notion of universal sisterhood *does* construct a unity. However, for me, the real challenge arises in being able to craft a notion of political unity without relying on the logic of appropriation and incorporation and, just as significantly, a denial of *agency*. For me the unity of women is best understood not as *given*, on the basis of a natural/psychological commonality; it is something that has to be worked for, struggled toward – *in history*. What we need to do is articulate ways in which the historical forms of oppression relate to the category "women," and not to try to deduce one from the other. In other words, it is Morgan's formulation of the relation of synchronous, alternative histories (herstories) to a diachronic, dominant historical narrative (History) that is problematic. One of the tasks of feminist analysis is uncovering alternative, nonidentical histories which challenge and disrupt the spatial and temporal location of a hegemonic history. However, sometimes attempts to uncover and locate alternative histories code these very histories as either totally dependent on and determined by a dominant narrative, or as isolated and autonomous narratives, untouched in their essence by the dominant figurations. In these rewritings, what is lost is the recognition that it is the very co-implication of histories with History which helps us situate and understand oppositional agency. In Morgan's text, it is the move to characterize alternative herstories as separate and different from history that results in a denial of feminist agency. And it is this potential repositioning of the relation of oppositional histories/spaces to a dominant historical narrative that I find valuable in Reagon's discussion of coalition politics.

"It ain't home no more": rethinking unity

While Morgan uses the notion of sisterhood to construct a cross-cultural unity of women and speaks of "planetary feminism as the politics of the 21st century," Bernice Johnson Reagon uses *coalition* as the basis to talk about the cross-cultural commonality of struggles, identifying *survival*, rather than *shared oppression*, as the ground for coalition. She begins with this valuable political reminder: "You don't go into coalition because you *like* it. The only reason you would consider trying to team up with somebody who could possibly kill you, is because that's the only way you can figure you can stay alive" (Reagon 1983, 357).

The governing metaphor Reagon uses to speak of coalition, difference, and struggle is that of a "barred room." However, whereas Morgan's barred room might be owned and controlled by the Big Brothers in different countries, Reagon's internal critique of the contemporary left focuses on the barred rooms constructed by oppositional political movements such as feminist, civil rights, gay and lesbian, and Chicano/a political organizations. She maintains that these barred rooms may provide a "nurturing space" for a little while, but they ultimately provide an illusion of community based on isolation and the freezing of difference. Thus, while sameness of experience, oppression, culture, etc., may be adequate to construct this space, the moment we "get ready to clean house" this very sameness in community is exposed as having been built on a debilitating ossification of difference.

Reagon is concerned with differences *within* political struggles, and the negative effects, in the long run, of a nurturing, "nationalist" perspective: "At a certain stage nationalism is crucial to a people if you are going to ever impact as a group in your own interest. Nationalism at another point becomes reactionary because it is totally inadequate for surviving in the world with many peoples" (1983, 358). This is similar to Gramsci's analysis of oppositional political strategy in terms of the difference between wars of maneuver (separation and consolidation) and wars of position (reentry into the mainstream in order to challenge it on its own terms). Reagon's insistence on breaking out of barred rooms and struggling for coalition is a recognition of the importance – indeed the inevitable necessity – of wars of position. It is based, I think, on a recognition of the need to resist the imperatives of an expansionist US state, and of imperial History. It is also, however, a recognition of the limits of identity politics. For once you open the door and let others in, "the room don't feel like the room no more. And it ain't home no more" (Reagon 1983, 359).

The relation of coalition to home is a central metaphor for Reagon. She speaks of coalition as opposed, by definition, to home.[10] In fact, the confusion of home with coalition is what concerns her as an urgent problem, and it is here that the status of experience in her text becomes clear. She criticizes the idea of enforcing "women-only" or "woman-identified" space by using an "in-house" definition of woman. What concerns her is not a sameness which allows us to identify with each other as women, but the exclusions particular normative definitions of "woman" enforce. It is the exercise of violence in creating a legitimate *inside* and an illegitimate *outside* in the name of identity that is significant to her – or, in other words, the exercise of violence when unity or coalition is confused with home and used to enforce a premature sisterhood or solidarity. According to her this "comes from taking a word like 'women' and using it as a code" (Reagon 1983, 360). The experience of being woman can create an illusory unity, for it is not the experience of being woman, but the meanings attached to gender, race, class, and age at various historical moments that is of strategic significance.

Thus, by calling into question the term "woman" as the automatic basis of unity, Reagon would want to splinter the notion of experience suggested by Morgan. Her critique of nationalist and culturalist positions, which after an initial necessary period of consolidation work in harmful and exclusionary ways, provides us with a fundamentally political analytic space for an understanding of experience. By always insisting on an analysis of the operations and effects of power in our attempts to create alternative communities, Reagon foregrounds our *strategic* locations and positionings. Instead of separating experience and politics and basing the latter on the former, she emphasizes the politics that always define and inform experience (in particular, in left, antiracist, and feminist communities). By examining the differences and potential divisions *within* political subjects as well as collectives, Reagon offers an implicit critique of totalizing theories of history and social change. She underscores the significance of the traditions of political struggle, what she calls an "old-age perspective" – and this is, I would add, a global perspective. What is significant, however, is that the global is forged on the basis of memories and counternarratives, not on an ahistorical universalism. For Reagon, global, old-age perspectives are founded on humility, the gradual chipping away of our assumed, often ethnocentric centers of self/other definitions.

Thus, her particular location and political priorities lead her to emphasize a politics of engagement (a war of position), and to interrogate totalizing notions of difference and the identification of exclusive spaces as "homes." Perhaps it is partly also her insistence on the urgency and difficult nature of political struggle that leads Reagon to talk about difference in terms of racism, while Morgan often formulates difference in terms of cultural pluralism. This is Reagon's way of "throwing yourself into the next century":

Most of us think that the space we live in is the most important space there is, and that the condition we find ourselves in is the condition that must be changed or else. That is only partially the case. If you analyze the situation properly, you will know that there might be a few things you can do in your personal, individual interest so that you can experience and enjoy change. But most of the things that you do, if you do them right, are for people who live long after you are forgotten. That will happen if you give it away . . . The only way you can take yourself seriously is if you can throw yourself into the next period beyond your little meager human-body-mouth-talking all the time.   (1983, 365)

We take ourselves seriously only when we go "beyond" ourselves, valuing not just the plurality of the differences among us but also the massive presence of the Difference that our recent planetary history has installed. This "Difference" is what we see only through the lenses of our present moment, our present struggles.

I have looked at two recent feminist texts and argued that feminist discourse must be self-conscious in its production of notions of experience and difference. The rationale for staging an encounter between the two texts, written by a white and black activist respectively, was not to identify "good" and "bad" feminist texts. Instead, I was interested in foregrounding questions of cross-cultural analysis which permeate "movement" or popular (not just academic) feminist texts, and in indicating the significance of a politics of location in the United States of the 1980s and the 1990s. Instead of privileging a certain limited version of identity politics, it is the current *intersection* of antiracist, anti-imperialist, and gay and lesbian struggles which we need to understand to map the ground for feminist political strategy and critical analysis.[11] A reading of these texts also opens up for me a temporality of *struggle*, which disrupts and challenges the logic of linearity, development, and progress which are the hallmarks of European modernity.

But why focus on a temporality of struggle? And how do I define *my* place on the map? For me, the notion of a temporality of struggle defies and subverts the logic of European modernity and the "law of identical temporality." It suggests an insistent, simultaneous, non-synchronous process characterized by multiple locations, rather than a search for origins and endings which, as Adrienne Rich says, "seems a way of stopping time in its tracks" (1986, 227). The year 2000 is the end of the Christian millennium, and Christianity is certainly an indelible part of postcolonial history. But we cannot afford to forget those alternative, resistant spaces occupied by oppositional histories and memories. By not insisting on *a* history or *a* geography but focusing on a temporality of struggle, I create the historical ground from which I can define myself in the United States of the 1990s, a place from which I can speak to the future – not the end of an era but the promise of many.

The United States of the 1990s: a geopolitical power seemingly unbounded in its effects, peopled with "natives" struggling for land and legal rights, and "immigrants" with their own histories and memories. Alicia Dujovne Ortiz writes about Buenos Aires as "the very image of expansiveness" (1986–87, 76). This is also how I visualize the United States of the 1990s. Ortiz writes of Buenos Aires:

A city without doors. Or rather, a port city, a gateway which never closes. I have always been astonished by those great cities of the world which have such precise boundaries that one can say exactly where they end. Buenos Aires has no end. One wants to ring it with a beltway, as if to point an index finger, trembling with uncertainty, and say: "You end there. Up to this point you are you. Beyond that, God alone knows!" . . . a city that is impossible to limit with the eye or the mind. So, what does it mean to say that one is a native of Buenos Aires? To belong to Buenos Aires, to be *Porteno* – to come from this Port? What does this mean? What or who can we hang onto? Usually we cling to history or geography. In this case, what are we to do? Here geography is merely an abstract line that marks the separation of the earth and sky. (1986–87, 76)

If the logic of imperialism and the logic of modernity share a notion of time, they also share a notion of space as territory. In the North America of the 1990s geography seems more and more like "an abstract line that marks the separation of the earth and sky." Witness the contemporary struggle for control over oil in the name of "democracy and freedom" in Saudi Arabia. Even the boundaries between space and outer space are not binding any more. In this expansive and expanding continent, how does one locate oneself? And what does location as I have inherited it have to do with self-conscious, strategic location as I choose it now?

A National Public Radio news broadcast announces that all immigrants to the United States now have to undergo mandatory AIDS testing. I am reminded very sharply of my immigrant status in this country, of my plastic identification card which is proof of my legitimate location in the United States. But location, for feminists, necessarily implies self- as well as collective definition, since meanings of the self are inextricably bound up with our understanding of collectives as social agents. For me, a comparative reading of Morgan's and Reagon's documents of activism precipitates the recognition that experience of the self, which is often discontinuous and fragmented, must be historicized before it can be generalized into a collective vision. In other words, experience must be historically interpreted and theorized if it is to become the basis of feminist solidarity and struggle, and it is at this moment that an understanding of the politics of location proves crucial.

In this country I am, for instance, subject to a number of legal/ political definitions: "postcolonial," "immigrant," "Third World." These definitions, while in no way comprehensive, do trace an analytic and political space from which I can insist on a temporality of struggle. Movement *between* cultures, languages, and complex configurations of meaning and power have always been the territory of the colonized. It is this *process*, what Caren Kaplan in her discussion of the reading and writing of home/exile has called "a continual reterritorialization, with the proviso that one moves on" (1986–87, 98), that I am calling a temporality of struggle. It is this process, this reterritorialization through struggle, that allows me a paradoxical continuity of self, mapping and transforming my political location. It suggests a particular notion of political agency, since my location forces and enables specific modes of reading and knowing the dominant. The struggles I choose to engage in are then an intensification of these modes of knowing – an engagement on a different level of knowledge. There is, quite simply, no transcendental location possible in the United States of the 1990s.

I have argued for a politics of engagement rather than a politics of transcendence, for the present and the future. I *know* – in my own non-synchronous temporality – that by the year 2000 apartheid will be discussed as a nightmarish chapter in black South Africa's history, the resistance to and victory over the efforts of the US government and multinational mining conglomerates to relocate the Navajo and Hopi reservations from Big Mountain, Arizona, will be written into elementary-school textbooks, and the Palestinian homeland will no longer be referred to as the "Middle East question" – it will be a reality. But that is my preferred history: what I hope and struggle for, I garner as *my* knowledge, create it as the place from where I seek to know. After all, it is the way in which I understand, define, and engage in feminist, anti-imperialist, and antiracist collectives and movements that anchors my belief in the future and in the efficacy of struggles for social change.

Notes

1. I am indebted to Adrienne Rich's essay, "Notes Toward a Politics of Location (1984)," for the notion of the "politics of location" (Rich 1986, 210–31). In a number of essays in this collection, Rich writes eloquently and provocatively about the politics of her own location as a white, Jewish, lesbian-feminist in North America. See especially "North American Tunnel Vision (1983)" and "Blood, Bread, and Poetry: The Location of the Poet (1984)" in Rich 1986.

   While I attempt to modify and extend Rich's notion, I share her sense of urgency as she asks feminists to reexamine the politics of location in North America:

   > A natural extension of all this seemed to me the need to examine not only racial and ethnic identity, but location in the United States of North America. As a feminist in the United States it seemed necessary to examine how we participate in mainstream North American cultural chauvinism, the sometimes unconscious belief that white North Americans possess a superior right to judge, select, and ransack other cultures, that we are more "advanced" than other peoples of this hemisphere . . . It was not enough to say "As a woman I have no country; as a woman my country is the whole world." Magnificent as that vision may be, we can't explode into breadth without a conscious grasp on the particular and concrete meaning of our location here and now, in the United States of America.   (Rich 1986, 162)

2. I address one version of this, the management of race and cultural pluralism in the US academy, in some depth, in my essay "On Race and Voice: Challenges for Liberal Education in the 1990s" (Chandra Talpade Mohanty 1989–90).
3. Two recent essays develop the point I am trying to suggest here. Jenny Bourne identifies the problems with most forms of contemporary identity politics which equalize notions of oppression, thereby writing out of the picture any analysis of structural exploitation or domination. See her 1987 "Jewish Feminism and Identity Politics."

   In a similar vein, S. P. Mohanty uses the opposition between "History" and "histories" to criticize an implicit assumption in contemporary cultural theory that pluralism is an adequate substitute for political analyses of dependent relationships and larger historical configuration. For Mohanty, the ultimate target is the cultural and historical *relativism* which he identifies as the unexamined philosophical "dogma" underlying political celebrations of pure difference. This is how he characterizes the initial issues involved:

   > Plurality [is] thus a political ideal as much as it [is] a methodological slogan. But . . . a nagging question [remains]: How do we negotiate between my history and yours? How would it be possible for us to recover our commonality, not the humanist myth of our shared human attributes which are meant to distinguish us all from animals, but more significantly, the imbrication of our various pasts and presents, the ineluctable relationships of shared and contested meanings, values, material resources? It is necessary to assert our dense particularities, our lived and imagined differences. But could we afford to leave unexamined the question of how our differences are intertwined and indeed hierarchically organized? Could we, in other words, really *afford* to have entirely different histories, to see ourselves as living – and having lived – in entirely heterogeneous and discrete spaces?
   >
   > (S. P. Mohanty 1989, 13)

4. For instance, some of the questions which arise in feminist analyses and politics which are situated at the juncture of studies of race, colonialism, and Third World political economy pertain to the systemic production, constitution, operation, and reproduction of the institutional manifestations of power. How does power operate in the constitution of gendered and racial subjects? How do we talk about contemporary political praxis, collective consciousness, and collective struggle in the context of an analysis of power? Other questions concern the discursive codifications of sexual politics and the corresponding feminist political strategies these codifications engender. Why is sexual politics defined around particular issues? One might examine the cultural and historical processes and conditions under which sexuality is constructed during conditions of war. One might also ask under what historical conditions sexuality is defined as sexual violence, and investigate the emergence of gay and

lesbian sexual identities. The discursive organization of these questions is significant because they help to chart and shape collective resistance. Some of these questions are addressed by contributors in a collection of essays I have co-edited with Ann Russo and Lourdes Torres, entitled *Third World Women and the Politics of Feminism* (Mohanty, Russo, and Torres 1991).

5. See Robin Morgan, "Planetary Feminism: The Politics of the 21st Century" (Morgan 1984, 1–37); I also refer to the "Prefatory Note and Methodology" section (Morgan 1984, xiii–xxiii) in this essay. See also Reagon 1983.

6. Monique Wittig develops this idea in "The Straight Mind" (Wittig 1980, 103).

7. Linda Gordon discusses this relation of female to feminist in "What's New in Women's History" (Gordon 1986).

8. See Rich 1986, 212.

9. Elsewhere I have attempted a detailed analysis of some recent Western feminist social science texts about the Third World. Focusing on works which have appeared in an influential series published by Zed Press of London, I examine this discursive construction of women in the Third World and the resultant Western feminist self-representations. See Chandra Talpade Mohanty 1988.

10. For an extensive discussion of the appeal and contradictions of notions of home and identity in contemporary feminist politics see Martin and Mohanty 1986.

11. For a rich and informative account of contemporary racial politics in the United States, see Omi and Winant 1986. Surprisingly, this text erases gender and gay politics altogether, leading me to wonder how we can talk about the "racial state" without addressing questions of gender and sexual politics. A good companion text which in fact emphasizes such questions is Anzaldua and Moraga 1983. Another, more contemporary text which continues some of the discussions in *This Bridge Called My Back*, also edited by Gloria Anzaldua, is *Making Face, Making Soul, Haciendo Caras, Creative and Critical Perspectives by Women of Color* (Anzaldua 1990).

References

Anzaldua, G. 1990. *Making Face, Making Soul, Haciendo Caras, Creative and Critical Perspectives by Women of Color*. San Francisco: Aunt Lute.

Anzaldua, G., and C. Moraga, eds. 1983. *This Bridge Called My Back: Writings by Radical Women of Color*. New York: Kitchen Table, Women of Color Press.

Bourne, Jenny. 1987. "Jewish Feminism and Identity Politics." *Race and Class*, 29: 1–24.

De Lauretis, Teresa, ed. 1986. *Feminist Studies/Critical Studies*. Bloomington, Ind.: Indiana University Press.

Gordon, Linda. 1986. "What's New in Women's History." In *Feminist Studies/Critical Studies*, ed. Teresa de Lauretis, 20–31. Bloomington, Ind.: Indiana University Press.

Kaplan, Caren. 1986–87. "The Poetics of Displacement in *Buenos Aires*." *Discourse*, 8: 94–102.

King, Katie. 1986. "The Situation of Lesbianism as Feminism's Magical Sign: Contests for Meaning and the US Women's Movement, 1968–1972." *Communication*, 9: 65–91.

Martin, Biddy and Chandra Talpade Mohanty. 1986. "Feminist Politics: What's Home Got to Do with It?" In *Feminist Studies/Critical Studies*, ed. Teresa de Lauretis, 191–212. Bloomington, Ind.: Indiana University Press.

Mohanty, Chandra Talpade. 1988. "Under Western Eyes: Feminist Scholarship and Colonial Discourses." *Feminist Review*, 30: 61–88.

1989–90. "On Race and Voice: Challenges for Liberal Education in the 1990s." *Cultural Critique*, 14: 179–208.

Mohanty, Chandra Talpade, Ann Russo, and Lourdes Torres. 1991. *Third World Women and the Politics of Feminism*. Bloomington, Ind., and Indianapolis, Ind.: Indiana University Press.

Mohanty, S. P. 1989. "Us and Them: On the Philosophical Bases of Political Criticism." *Yale Journal of Criticism*, 2: 1–31.

Morgan, Robin. 1984. *Sisterhood is Global: The International Women's Movement Anthology*. New York: Anchor Press/Doubleday.

Omi, Michael, and Howard Winant. 1986. *Racial Formation in the United States: From the 1960s to the 1980s*. New York: Routledge.

Ortiz, Alicia Dujovne. 1986–87. "*Buenos Aires* (An Excerpt)." *Discourse*, 8: 73–83.

Reagon, Bernice Johnson. 1983. "Coalition Politics: Turning the Century." In *Home Girls: A Black Feminist Anthology*, ed. Barbara Smith, 356–68. New York: Kitchen Table, Women of Color Press.

Rich, Adrienne. 1986. *Blood, Bread, and Poetry: Selected Prose 1979–1985*. New York: W. W. Norton and Co.

Smith, Barbara, ed. 1983. *Home Girls: A Black Feminist Anthology*. New York: Kitchen Table, Women of Color Press.

Wittig, Monique. 1980. "The Straight Mind." *Feminist Issues*, 1: 103–10.

3

Postcolonial criticism and Indian historiography

Gyan Prakash

One of the distinct effects of the recent emergence of postcolonial criticism has been to force a radical rethinking and reformulation of forms of knowledge and social identities authored and authorized by colonialism and Western domination. For this reason, it has also created a ferment in the field of knowledge. This is not to say that colonialism and its legacies remained unquestioned until recently: nationalism and Marxism come immediately to mind as powerful challenges to colonialism. But both of these operated with master-narratives that put Europe at its center. Thus, when nationalism, reversing Orientalist thought, attributed agency and history to the subjected nation, it also staked a claim to the order of Reason and Progress instituted by colonialism; and when Marxists pilloried colonialism, their criticism was framed by a universalist mode-of-production narrative. Recent postcolonial criticism, on the other hand, seeks to undo the Eurocentrism produced by the institution of the West's trajectory, its appropriation of the other as History. It does so, however, with the acute realization that postcoloniality is not born and nurtured in a panoptic distance from history. The postcolonial exists as an aftermath, as an after – after being worked over by colonialism.[1] Criticism formed in this process of the enunciation of discourses of domination occupies a space that is neither inside nor outside the history of Western domination but in a tangential relation to it. This is what Homi Bhabha (1989) calls an in-between, hybrid position of practice and negotiation, or what Gayatri Chakravorty Spivak (1990) terms catachresis; "reversing, displacing, and seizing the apparatus of value-coding." In the rest of this essay, I describe this catachrestic reinscription and the anxieties it provokes in the field of Indian historiography where postcolonial criticism has made a particularly notable appearance.

The ambivalence of postcolonial criticism

A prominent example of recent postcolonial criticism consists of the writings in several volumes of *Subaltern Studies* (edited and theorized most extensively by Ranajit Guha) which challenge existing historiography as elitist and advance in its place a subaltern perspective.[2] A collective of historians writing from India, Britain, and Australia, the *Subaltern Studies* scholars use the perspective of the subaltern to combat fiercely the persistence of colonialist knowledge in nationalist and mode-of-production narratives. It is important to note that their project is derived from Marxism, or from the failure of the realization of the Marxist collective consciousness. For it is this failure of the subaltern to act as a class-conscious worker that provides the basis for representing the subaltern as resistant to the appropriation by colonial and nationalist elites, or to various programs of modernity. The subaltern is a figure produced by historical discourses of domination, but it nevertheless provides a mode of reading history different from those inscribed in elite accounts. Reading colonial and nationalist archives against their grain and focusing on their blind-spots, silences, and anxieties, these historians seek to uncover the subaltern's myths, cults, ideologies, and revolts that colonial and nationalist elites sought to appropriate and conventional historiography has laid to waste by the deadly weapon of cause and effect. Ranajit Guha's *Elementary Aspects of Peasant Insurgency* (1983) is a powerful example of this scholarship which seeks to recover the peasant from elite projects and positivist historiography. In this wide-ranging study full of brilliant insights and methodological innovation, Guha provides a fascinating account of the peasant's insurgent consciousness, rumors, mythic visions, religiosity, and bonds of community. From Guha's account, the subaltern emerges with forms of sociality and political community at odds with nation and class, and in defiance of the models of rationality and social action that conventional historiography uses. Guha argues persuasively that such models are elitist insofar as they deny the subaltern's autonomous consciousness, and are drawn from colonial and liberal-nationalist projects of appropriating the subaltern. Brilliantly deconstructive though such readings of the colonial-nationalist archives were, the early phase of the *Subaltern Studies* was marked by a desire to retrieve the autonomous will and consciousness of the subaltern. This is no longer the case in more recent writings, but even in earlier writings the desire to recover the subaltern's autonomy is repeatedly frustrated because sub-alterity, by definition, signifies the impossibility of autonomy.

The concept of a subaltern history, derived from its simultaneous possibility and impossibility in discourses of domination, exemplifies the ambivalence of postcolonial criticism: formed in history, it reinscribes and displaces the record of that history by reading its archives differently from its constitution (in Spivak's sense of catachresis). This ambivalent criticism is observable also in writings, that, with a somewhat different focus than the *Subaltern Studies*, subject forms of knowledge, culture, and "traditions," canonized by colonial and Western discourses, to searching scrutiny and radical reinscription. Examinations of the nineteenth-century reformist attempts to suppress and outlaw the practices of widow sacrifice (*sati*), for example, rearticulate them by revealing that colonial rulers and Indian male reformers formulated and used gendered ideas to enforce new forms of domination even as they questioned the burning of widows; studies of criminality point to power relations at work in classifying and acting upon "criminal tribes" even as threats to life and property were countered; and enquiries into labor servitude depict how the free/unfree opposition concealed the operation of power in the installation of free labor as the natural human condition while it provided a vantage-point for challenging certain forms of corporeal domination.[3] The aim of such studies is not to unmask dominant discourses but to explore their fault-lines in order to provide different accounts, to describe histories revealed in the cracks of the colonial archaeology of knowledge.

In part, the critical gaze that these studies direct at the archaeology of knowledge enshrined in the West arises from the fact that most of them are being written in the First World academy where the power of hegemonic discourses about India is so palpable. This is not to say that the reach of these discourses does not extend beyond metropolitan centers; but outside the First World, in India itself, the power of Western discourses operates through its authorization and deployment by the nation-state – the ideologies of modernization and instrumentalist science are so deeply sedimented in the national body politic that they neither manifest themselves nor function exclusively as forms of imperial power (Mani 1989). In the West, on the other hand, the production and distribution of Orientalist concepts continue to play a vital role in projecting the First World as the radiating center around which others are arranged. It is for this reason that postcolonial criticisms produced in the metropolitan academy evince certain affinities with deconstructive critiques of the West.[4] In this respect, both Michel Foucault's and Jacques Derrida's critiques of Western thought intersect with postcolonial criticism – Foucault, because his account of the genealogies of the West provides a powerful critique of the rule of modernity that the colonies experienced in a peculiar form. Derrida's relevance is not obvious but is no less important because, exposing how structures of signification effect their closures through a strategy of opposition and hierarchization that edit, suppress, and marginalize everything that upsets founding values, he provides a way to undo the implacable oppositions of colonial thought – East/West, traditional/modern, primitive/civilized. If these oppositions, as Derrida's analysis of the metaphysics of presence shows, aim relentlessly to suppress the other as an inferior, as a supplement, their structures of signification can also be rearticulated differently.

Metaphysics – the white mythology which reassembles and reflects the culture of the West: the white man takes his own mythology, Indo-European mythology, his own *logos*, that is, the *mythos* of his idiom, for the universal form that he must still wish to call Reason . . . White mythology – metaphysics has erased within itself the fabulous scene that has produced it, the scene that nevertheless remains active and stirring, inscribed in white ink, an invisible design covered over in the palimpsest.   (Derrida 1982, 213)

If the production of white mythology has nevertheless left "an invisible design covered over in the palimpsest," the structure of signification, of *différance*, can be rearticulated differently than that which produced the West as Reason. For postcolonial theorists, the value of Derrida's insight lies in the disclosure that the politics displacing other claims to the margins can be undone by rearticulating the structure of differences that existing foundations seek to suppress and that strategies for challenging the authority and power derived from various foundational myths (History as the march of Man, of Reason, Progress, Modes-of-Production) lie inside, not outside, the ambivalence that these myths seek to suppress. From this point of view, critical work seeks its basis not without but within the fissures of dominant structures. Or, as Spivak puts it, the deconstructive philosophical position (or postcolonial criticism) consists in saying an "impossible 'no' to a structure, which one critiques, yet inhabits intimately" (1990a, 28).

For an example of this deconstructive strategy that rearticulates a structure that one inhabits intimately, let us turn to archival documents dealing with the abolition of *sati*, or Hindu widow sacrifice in the early nineteenth century. The historian encounters these as records documenting the contests between the British "civilizing mission" and Hindu heathenism, between modernity and tradition; and of previous readings about the beginning of the emancipation of Hindu women and about the birth of modern India. This is so because, as Lata Mani has shown (1987), the very existence of these documents has a history involving the fixing of women as the site for the colonial and the indigenous male elite's constructions of authoritative Hindu traditions. The accumulated sources on *sati* – whether or not the burning of widows was sanctioned by Hindu codes, did women go willingly or not to the funeral pyre, on what grounds could the immolation of women be abolished – come to us marked by early nineteenth-century colonial and indigenous/patriarchal discourses. And just as the early nineteenth-century encounter between colonial and indigenous elites and textual sources was resonant with colonial-patriarchal voices, the historian's confrontation today with sources on *sati* cannot escape the echo of that previous rendezvous. In repeating that encounter, how does the historian today *not replicate* the early nineteenth-century staging of *sati* as a contest between tradition and modernity (or different visions of tradition), between the slavery of women and efforts towards their emancipation, between barbaric Hindu practices and the British civilizing mission? Mani accomplishes this task brilliantly by showing that the opposing arguments were founded on the fabrication of the law-giving scriptural tradition as the origin of Hindu customs: both those who supported and those who opposed *sati* sought the authority of textual origins for their beliefs. During the debate, however, the whole history of the fabrication of origins was effaced, as was the collusion between indigenous patriarchy and colonial power in constructing the origins for and against *sati*. Consequently, as Spivak states starkly, the debate left no room for the woman's enunciatory position. Caught in the contest over whether traditions did or did not sanction *sati* and over whether the woman self-immolated willingly or not, the colonized subaltern woman disappeared: she was literally extinguished for her dead husband in the indigenous patriarchal discourse, or offered the disfiguring choice of the Western notion of the sovereign, individual will.[5] The problem here is not one of sources (the absence of women's testimony), but that the very staging of the debate left no place for the widow's enunciatory position: she is left no position from which she can speak. Spivak makes this silencing of the woman speak of the limits of historical knowledge, but the critic can do so because the colonial archive comes with a pregnant silence.[6]

Spivak very correctly marks the silencing of the subaltern woman as the point at which the interpreter must acknowledge the limits of historical understanding; it is impossible to retrieve the woman's voice when she was not given a subject-position from which to speak. But this refusal to retrieve the woman's voice because it would involve the conceit that the interpreter speaks for her does not disable understanding; rather, Spivak manages to reinscribe the colonial and indigenous patriarchal archive when she shows that the tradition-versus-modernization story was told by obliterating the colonized women's subject-position. Here, the interpreter's recognition of the limit of historical knowledge does not disable criticism but enables the critic to mark the space of the silenced subaltern as *aporetic*. The recognition of the subaltern as the limit of knowledge, in turn, resists a paternalist "recovery" of the subaltern's voice and frustrates our repetition of the imperialist attempt to speak for the colonized subaltern woman. This argument appears to run counter to the radical historian's use of the historiographical convention of retrieval to recover the histories of the traditionally ignored – women, workers, peasants, and minorities. Spivak's point, however, is not that such retrievals should not be undertaken, but that they mark the point of the subaltern's silencing in history. The project of retrieval begins at the point of the subaltern's erasure; its very possibility is also a sign of its impossibility, and represents the intervention of the historian-critic whose discourse must be interrogated persistently and whose appropriation of the other should be guarded against vigilantly (Young 1990, 164–65).

Capitalism and colonialism

These directions of postcolonial criticism make it a disturbing and ambivalent practice, perched between traditional historiography and its failures, between the elite and the subaltern, within the folds of dominant discourses and seeking to rearticulate their pregnant silence – outlining "an invisible design covered over in the palimpsest." How do these strategies fare when compared with a powerful tradition of historiography of India that seeks to encompass its colonial history in the larger narrative of the development of capitalism? Does not the concern with rearticulating colonial discourses necessarily neglect the story of capitalist exploitation and imperialist profits?

Elsewhere, I have argued that we cannot thematize Indian history in terms of the development of capitalism and simultaneously contest capitalism's homogenization of the contemporary world. Critical history cannot simply document the process by which capitalism becomes dominant, for that amounts to repeating the history we seek to displace; instead, criticism must reveal the difference that capitalism either represents as the particular form of its universal existence or sketches only in relation to itself (Prakash 1990b). This argument has drawn the criticism that my position commits me to view capitalism as a "disposable fiction," and reveals a simplistic understanding of the relationship between capitalism and heterogeneity. It is suggested that we recognize the structure of domination as a totality (capitalism) which alone provides the basis for understanding the sources of historical oppression and formulating critical emancipatory positions.[7]

Does a refusal to thematize modern Indian history in terms of the development of capitalism amount to saying that capitalism is a "disposable fiction," and that class relations are illusory? Not at all. My point is that making capitalism the foundational theme amounts to homogenizing the histories that remain heterogenous with it. It is one thing to say that the establishment of capitalist relations has been one of the major features in India's recent history but quite another to regard it as the foundation of colonialism. It is one thing to say that class relations affected a range of power relations in India – involving the caste system, patriarchy, ethnic oppression, Hindu–Muslim conflicts – and quite another to oppose the latter as "forms" assumed by the former. The issue here is not that of one factor versus several; rather, it is that, as class is inevitably articulated with other determinations, power exists in a form of relationality in which the dominance of one is never complete. For example, although colonial rule in India constructed the labor force according to the economy of the free/unfree opposition, this domestication of otherness (of "Hindu" and "Islamic" forms of "slavery") as unfreedom also left "an invisible design covered over in the palimpsest."[8] It is precisely by highlighting the "invisible design" that capitalism's attempts either to subsume different structures or to polarize them can be shown as incompletely successful. Only then can we, as critics, examine the fault-lines of this discourse, and make visible the ambivalence and alterity present in the constitution of capitalism as a foundational theme. This means listening attentively when the culture and history that the critic inhabits make capitalism name and speak for histories that remained discrepant with it. To the extent that these discrepancies are made to speak in the language of capitalism – as "precapitalist" peasants, "unfree laborers," "irrational" peasants – its "foundational" status is not a "disposable fiction." But it is equally true that in domesticating all the wholly other subject-positions as self-consolidating otherness (*pre*capitalist, *un*free laborers, *ir*rational peasant), capitalism is also caught in a structure of ambivalence it cannot master. This is why study after study show that capitalism in the Third World, not just in India, was crucially "distorted," "impure," mixed with "precapitalist survivals." To think of the incompleteness and failures of capitalist modernity in the Third World in critical terms, therefore, requires that we reinscribe the binary form in which capitalism's partial success is portrayed, that we render visible processes and forms that its oppositional logic can appropriate only violently and incompletely. Of course, historians cannot recover what was suppressed, but they can critically confront the effects of that silencing, capitalism's foundational status, by writing histories of irretrievable subject-positions, by sketching the traces of figures that come to us only as disfigurations. Again, not to restore the "original" figures, but to find the limit of foundations in shadows that the disfigurations themselves outline.

To write of histories at the point of capitalism's "distorted" and "impure" development in India does not amount to disregarding class or abandoning Marxism. At issue here is the irreducible heterogeneity of metropolitan capital with the colonial subaltern, a heterogeneity that an unexamined Eurocentric Marxism would have us overlook. I am not suggesting that acknowledging Marx's Eurocentrism requires abandoning Marxism altogether. But students of Indian history, who know only too well the Eurocentricity of Marx's memorable formulation that the British conquest introduced a history-less India to History, cannot now regard the mode-of-production story as a normative universal. In fact, like many other nineteenth-century European ideas, the staging of the Eurocentric mode-of-production narrative as History should be seen as an analogue of nineteenth-century territorial imperialism. From this point of view, Marx's ideas on changeless India – theorized, for example, in his concept of the "Asiatic mode of production" – appear not so much mistaken as the discursive form produced by the universalization of Europe, by its appropriation of the absolute other into a domesticated other. Such a historicization of the Eurocentrism in nineteenth-century Marxism enables us to understand the collusion of capitalism and colonialism, and to undo the effect of that collusion's imperative to interpret Third World histories in terms of capital's logic. To suggest that we reinscribe the effects of capitalism's foundational status by writing about histories that remained heterogeneous with the logic of capital, therefore, is not to abandon Marxism but to extricate the class analysis from its nineteenth-century heritage, acknowledging that its critique of capitalism was both enabled and disabled by its historicity as a European discourse.

The alternative would have us view colonialism as *reducible* to the development of capitalism in Britain and in India. The conflation of the metropolitan proletariat with the colonized subaltern that this produces amounts to a homogenization of irreducible difference. Of course, it could be argued that capitalism, rather than homogenizing difference, is perfectly capable of utilizing and generating heterogeneity. But the notion that capitalism is a founding source responsible for originating and encompassing difference amounts to appropriating heterogeneity as a self-consolidating difference, that is, refracting "what might have been the absolutely Other into a domesticated Other . . ." (Spivak 1985b, 253). This assimilation of difference into identity becomes inevitable when capitalism is made to stand for History; the heterogeneity of histories of the colonized subaltern with those of the metropolitan proletariat is then effaced, and absolute otherness is appropriated into self-consolidating difference.

The issue of the heterogeneity of social identities and cultural forms raised by the relationship of colonialism to capitalism is not one that can be resolved easily by the extension of the race-class-gender formula; the question of colonial difference is not one of the adequacy of a single factor (class) versus multiple factors, nor are we constrained to choose forms of sociality other than class. What is at issue in the articulation of class with race, caste, gender, nation, ethnicity, and religion is that these categories were not equal; woman as a category was not equal to worker; being an upper-caste Hindu was not a form of sociality equal with citizenship in the nation-state that the nationalists struggled to achieve. Thus, the concept of multiple selves, incorporating a variety of social identities and so popular with the contemporary liberal multiculturalists, cannot be adequate for conceiving colonial difference. Instead, we have to think of the specificity of colonial difference as class overwriting race and gender, of nation overinscribing class, ethnicity, and religion, and so forth – an imbalanced process, but nevertheless a process that can be rearticulated differently. This is the concept of heterogeneity and cultural difference as it emerges from postcoloniality.

The question of heterogeneity

The postcolonial disruption of master narratives authorized by imperialism produces an insistence on the heterogeneity of colonial histories that is often mistaken for the postmodern pastiche. Though the present currency of such concepts as de-centered subjects and parodic texts may provide a receptive and appropriative frame for postcolonial criticism, its emphasis on heterogeneity neither aims to celebrate the polyphony of native voices nor does it spring forth from superior value placed on multiplicity. Rather, it arises from the recognition that the *functioning* of colonial power was heterogeneous with its founding oppositions. Not only were colonies the dark underside, the recalcitrant supplement that subverted the self-same concepts of Modernity, Civilization, Reason, and Progress with which the West wrapped itself, but the very enunciation of colonial discourses was ambivalent. Thus, the postcolonial insistence on heterogeneity emanates from the insight that colonial discourses operated as the structure of *writing*; and that the structure of their enunciation remained heterogeneous with the binary oppositions that colonialism instituted in ordering the discursive field to serve unequal power relations. Homi Bhabha's analysis of colonial mimicry outlines the postcolonial critic's distinct notion of difference.

Writing of the stereotypes and pseudoscientific theories that were commonly used in colonial discourse, Bhabha suggests that these were attempts to normalize the ambivalence produced in the contradictory enunciation of colonial discourses. This ambivalence arose from the "tension between the synchronic panoptical vision of domination – the demand for identity, stasis – and the counter-pressure of the diachrony of history – change, difference" (Bhabha 1985a, 126). Under these opposing pressures, the colonial discourse was caught up in conflict, split between "what is always 'in place,' already known, and something that must be anxiously repeated . . . as if the essential duplicity of the Asiatic or the bestial sexual license of the African that needs no proof, can never really, in discourse, be proved" (Bhabha 1983, 18). If, on the one hand, the colonial discourse asserted that the colonizers and the colonized were fixed, unchanging identities, the repetition of this assertion, on the other hand, meant that discourse was forced constantly to reconstitute and refigure this fixity; consequently, the discourse was split between proclaiming the unchangeability of colonial subjects and acknowledging their changing character by having to re-form and reconstitute subjects. If it created the colonizer/colonized opposition, it also produced figures and processes that its structure of power relations could not easily accommodate (Bhabha 1983, 23–25). Bhabha traces an example of such an ambivalent functioning of discourse in the construction of the colonial stereotype of mimicmen applied to English-speaking Indians. He argues that if the British portrayal of the resemblance of Anglicized Indians with Englishmen as mimicry was a "strategy of reform, regulation, and discipline, which 'appropriates' the Other," the stereotype of mimicry was also the mark of a recalcitrant difference, "a *difference that is almost the same, but not quite*" (Bhabha 1985a, 126). If the colonial discourse produced a "reformed" other

– the Anglicized Indian (the infamous "Babu") who resembled the English – the strategy of assimilation acknowledged a recalcitrant difference: the Anglicized Indian was a brown Englishman, at best – "not white/not quite." To be sure, the acknowledgement of recalcitrant difference took the racist form of Macaulay's notorious formulation that these mimicmen were to be "Indian in blood and color, but English in taste, in opinions, in morals, and in intellect." But the use of racism also signifies a heterogeneity that could not be appropriated. Bhabha fastens on this blind-spot of the discourse to show that the flat assertion of stereotypes was also the moment of fear and anxiety in the discourse because the recalcitrant difference of the re-formed Babu turned mimicry into mockery; confronted with Englishness in the brown figure of the Indian, the authority of self-ness was put under profound stress.

Bhabha's analysis of colonial discourse at the point of its stress departs from the strategy of reversal practiced by previous criticism. For, at these moments of indeterminacy, when the discourse can be seen to veer away from the implacable logic of oppositionality, the critic can intervene, and, using historical work as a license for a strategy of critical reading, renegotiate the terms of the discourse. The cultural difference that emerges from the renegotiation of the discourse is not polymorphous diversity released from the straitjacket of binary oppositions; instead, it is a heterogeneity that the existing dichotomies themselves make simultaneously possible and impossible. Bhabha (1985b) reads this heterogeneity in the native rewriting of the colonial text, in those "hybrid" moments when the colonized produce not a copy of the original but misappropriate it, thereby reformulating the master text, exposing its ambivalence, and denying its authority. From this point of view, categories of racial, class, ethnic, gender, and national difference arise not as the result of a well-intentioned liberal gesture but as social identifications formed at the point of colonialism's conflictual and contingent mode of functioning.

History and colonialism arose together in India. As India was introduced to history, it was also stripped of a meaningful past; it became a history-less society brought into the age of History. The flawed nature of history's birth in India was not lost on the nationalists who pressed the nation-state's claim to the age of history, and Marxists struggled against capital's collusion with colonialism to make the worker the agent of history. Consequently, history, flawed at birth, has lived an embattled life in India. These constitute the point of departure for postcolonial criticism.[9] For postcolonial historiography, the embattled and anxious enunciation of history as a form of being and knowledge provides the opportunity to seize and reinscribe it catachrestically, not to restore lost forms of telling and knowing but to pick apart the disjunctive moments of discourses authorized by colonialism and authenticated by the nation-state and rearticulate them in another – third – form of writing history. It is from the "scene that nevertheless remains active and stirring, inscribed in white ink, an invisible design covered over in the palimpsest" that the colonial and the subaltern supplement reinscribes and revises the narratives of the modern, the West, and Man – white mythology.

Notes

1. Gayatri Chakravorty Spivak speaks of postcoloniality in similar terms: "We are always *after* the empire of reason, our claims to it always short of adequate" [emphasis in original] (Spivak 1990b, 228).
2. The writings of this group include Guha 1981–89; Guha 1983; Chatterjee 1986; and Chakrabarty 1989.
3. See Das 1986 and Mani 1987. For criminality, see Nigam 1990. For the discourse of freedom see Prakash 1990a.
4. On poststructuralism, postcolonial criticism, and the critique of the West, see Young 1990.
5. See Spivak 1988, in particular 299–307.
6. For a similar argument about the colonized woman caught between indigenous patriarchy and the politics of archival production, see also Spivak 1985a.
7. See O'Hanlon and Washbrook 1992, and my reply, Prakash 1992, from which this essay draws.
8. For a study of the process of this covering over in the context of "unfree" laborers, see Prakash 1990a. Dirks 1987, similarly, traces the marks of a relationship between caste and power in the process that hollowed out the political space in a south Indian kingdom and filled it with colonial power.
9. For a related argument, see Chakrabarty 1991.

References

Bhabha, Homi. 1983. "The Other Question" *Screen*, 24(6): 18–36.
    1985a. "Of Mimicry and Man: The Ambivalence of Colonial Discourse." *October*, 34 (Fall): 71–80.
    1985b. "Signs Taken for Wonders: Questions of Ambivalence and

Authority Under a Tree Outside Delhi, May 1817." *Critical Inquiry*, 12(1): 144–65.

1989. "The Commitment to Theory." In *Questions of the Third Cinema*, ed. J. Pines and P. Willemen, 112–31. London: BFI Publishing.

Chakrabarty, Dipesh. 1989. *Rethinking Working-Class History: Bengal 1890–1940*. Princeton, N. J.: Princeton University Press.

1991. "History as Critique and Critique(s) of History." *Economic and Political Weekly*, 26(37): 2162–66.

Chatterjee, Partha. 1986. *Nationalist Thought and the Colonial World: A Derivative Discourse?* London: Zed Books.

Das, Veena. 1986. "Gender Studies, Cross-Cultural Comparison, and the Colonial Organization of Knowledge." *Berkshire Review*, 21.

Derrida, Jacques. 1982. *Margins of Philosophy*, trans. Alan Bass. Chicago: University of Chicago Press.

Dirks, Nicholas. 1987. *The Hollow Crown: Ethnohistory of an Indian Kingdom*. Cambridge: Cambridge University Press.

Guha, Ranajit. 1983. *Elementary Aspects of Peasant Insurgency in Colonial India*. Delhi: Oxford University Press.

Guha, Ranajit, ed. 1981–89. *Subaltern Studies*, vols. I–VI. Delhi: Oxford University Press.

Mani, Lata. 1987. "Contentious Traditions: The Debate on Sati in Colonial India." *Cultural Critique*, 7: 119–56.

1989. "Multiple Mediations: Feminist Scholarship in the Age of Multinational Reception." *Inscriptions*, 5: 1–23.

Nigam, Sanjay. 1990. "Disciplining and Policing the 'Criminals by Birth,'" pts. I and II. *Indian Economic and Social History Review*, 27(2): 131–64, and 27(3): 257–87.

O'Hanlon, Rosalind, and David Washbrook. 1992. "After Orientalism: Culture, Criticism, and Politics in the Third World." *Comparative Studies in Society and History*, 34(1): 141–67.

Prakash, Gyan. 1990a. *Bonded Histories: Genealogies of Labor Servitude in Colonial India*. Cambridge: Cambridge University Press.

1990b. "Writing Post-Orientalist Histories of the Third World: Perspectives from Indian Historiography." *Comparative Studies in Society and History*, 32(2): 383–408.

1992. "Can the Subaltern Ride? A Reply to O'Hanlon and Washbrook." *Comparative Studies in Society and History*, 34(1): 168–84.

Spivak, Gayatri Chakravorty. 1985a. "The Rani of Sirmur: An Essay in the Reading of the Archives." *History and Theory*, 24(3): 247–72.

1985b. "Three Women's Texts and a Critique of Imperialism." *Critical Inquiry*, 12(1): 243–61.

1988. "Can the Subaltern Speak?" In *Marxism and Interpretation of Culture*, ed. Cary Nelson and Lawrence Grossberg, 271–313. Urbana, Ill.: University of Illinois Press.

1990a. "The Making of Americans, the Teaching of English, the Future of Colonial Studies." *New Literary History*, 21(4).

1990b. "Poststructuralism, Marginality, Postcoloniality and Value." In *Literary Theory Today*, ed. Peter Collier and Helga Geyer-Ryan. London: Polity Press.

Young, Robert. 1990. *White Mythologies: Writing History and the West.* London: Routledge.

PART II

Critiques of the deconstruction of identity

4

African identities

Kwame Anthony Appiah

> It is, of course, true that the African identity is still in the making.
> There isn't a final identity that is African. But, at the same time, there
> *is* an identity coming into existence. And it has a certain context and
> a certain meaning. Because if somebody meets me, say, in a shop in
> Cambridge, he says "Are you from Africa?" Which means that Africa
> means something to some people. Each of these tags has a meaning,
> and a penalty and a responsibility.[1]   Chinua Achebe

The cultural life of most of black Africa remained largely unaffected by
European ideas until the last years of the nineteenth century, and most
cultures began our own century with ways of life formed very little
by direct contact with Europe. Direct trade with Europeans – and
especially the slave trade – had structured the economies of many of
the states of the West African coast and its hinterland from the middle
of the seventeenth century onward, replacing the extensive gold trade
that had existed at least since the Carthaginian empire in the second
century BCE. By the early nineteenth century, as the slave trade went
into decline, palm nut and groundnut oils had become major exports
to Europe, and these were followed later by cocoa and coffee. But
the direct colonization of the region began in earnest only in the later
nineteenth century, and European administration of the whole of West
Africa was only accomplished – after much resistance – when the Sokoto
caliphate was conquered in 1903.

On the Indian Ocean, the eastward trade, which sent gold and slaves
to Arabia, and exchanged spices, incense, ivory, coconut oil, timber,
grain, and pig iron for Indian silk and fine textiles, and pottery and
porcelain from Persia and China, had dominated the economies of the
East African littoral until the coming of the Portuguese disrupted the
trade in the late fifteenth century. From then on European trade became
increasingly predominant, but in the middle of the nineteenth century
the major economic force in the region was the Arab Omanis, who had

captured Mombasa from the Portuguese more than a century earlier. Using slave labor from the African mainland, the Omanis developed the profitable clove trade of Zanzibar, making it, by the 1860s, the world's major producer. But in most of East Africa, as in the West, extended direct contact with Europeans was a late nineteenth-century phenomenon, and colonization occurred essentially only after 1885.

In the south of the continent, in the areas where Bantu-speaking people predominate, few cultures had had any contact with Europeans before 1900. By the end of the century the region had adopted many new crops for the world economy; imports of firearms, manufactured in the newly industrialized West, had created a new political order, based often on force; and European missionaries and explorers – of whom David Livingstone was, for Westerners, the epitome – had traveled almost everywhere in the region. The administration of southern Africa from Europe was established in law only by the end, in 1902, of the Boer War.

Not surprisingly, then, European cultural influence in Africa before the twentieth century was extremely limited. Deliberate attempts at change (through missionary activity or the establishment of Western schools) and unintended influence (through contact with explorers and colonizers in the interior, and trading posts on the coasts) produced small enclaves of Europeanized Africans. But the major cultural impact of Europe is largely a product of the period since World War I.

To understand the variety of Africa's contemporary cultures, therefore, we need, first, to recall the variety of precolonial cultures. Differences in colonial experience have also played their part in shaping the continent's diversities, but even identical colonial policies identically implemented working on the very different cultural materials would surely have produced widely varying results.

No doubt we can find generalizations at a certain abstract level that hold true of most of black Africa before European conquest. It is a familiar idea in African historiography that Africa was the last continent in the Old World with an "uncaptured" peasantry, largely able to use land without the supervision of feudal overlords and able, if they chose, to market their products through a complex system of trading networks.[2] While European ruling classes were living off the surplus of peasants and the newly developing industrial working class, African rulers were essentially living off taxes on trade. But if we could have traveled through Africa's many cultures in those years – from the small groups of Bushman hunter-gatherers, with their Stone Age materials, to the Hausa kingdoms, rich in worked metal – we should have felt in every place profoundly different impulses, ideas, and forms of life. To speak of an African identity in the nineteenth century – if an identity is a coalescence of mutually responsive (if sometimes conflicting) modes of conduct, habits of thought, and patterns of evaluation; in short, a coherent kind of human social psychology – would have been "to give to aery nothing a local habitation and a name."

Yet there is no doubt that now, a century later, an African identity is coming into being. I have argued throughout these essays that this identity is a new thing; that it is the product of a history, some of whose moments I have sketched; and that the bases through which so far it has largely been theorized – race, a common historical experience, a shared metaphysics – presuppose falsehoods too serious for us to ignore.

Every human identity is constructed, historical; every one has its share of false presuppositions, of the errors and inaccuracies that courtesy calls "myth," religion "heresy," and science "magic." Invented histories, invented biologies, invented cultural affinities come with every identity; each is a kind of role that has to be scripted, structured by conventions of narrative to which the world never quite manages to conform.

Often those who say this – who deny the biological reality of races or the literal truth of our national fictions – are treated by nationalists and "race men" as if they are proposing genocide or the destruction of nations, as if in saying that there is literally no Negro race, one was obliterating all those who claim to be Negroes, in doubting the story of Okomfo Anokye, one is repudiating the Asante nation. This is an unhelpful hyperbole, but it is certainly true that there must be contexts in which a statement of these truths is politically inopportune. I am enough of a scholar to feel drawn to truth telling, *ruat caelum*; enough of a political animal to recognize that there are places where the truth does more harm than good.

But, so far as I can see, we do not have to choose between these impulses: there is no reason to believe that racism is always – or even usually – advanced by denying the existence of races; and, though there is some reason to suspect that those who resist legal remedies for the history of racism might use the nonexistence of races to argue in the United States, for example, against affirmative action, that strategy is, as a matter of logic, easily opposed. For, as Tvetzan Todorov (1986) reminds us, the existence of racism does not require the existence of races. And, we can add, nations are real enough, however invented their traditions.[3]

To raise the issue of whether these truths are truths to be uttered is to be forced, however, to face squarely the real political question: the question, itself, as old as political philosophy, of when we should endorse the ennobling lie. In the real world of practical politics, of everyday alliances and popular mobilizations, a rejection of races and nations in theory can be part of a program for coherent political practice, only if we can show more than that the black race – or the Shona tribe or any of the other modes of self-invention that Africa has inherited – fit the common pattern of relying on less than the literal truth. We would need to show not that race and national history are falsehoods but they are useless falsehoods at best or – at worst – dangerous ones: that another set of stories will build us identities through which we can make more productive alliances.

The problem, of course, is that group identity seems to work only – or, at least, to work best – when it is seen by its members as natural, as "real." Pan-Africanism, black solidarity, can be an important force with real political benefits, but it doesn't work without its attendant mystifications. (Nor, to turn to the other obvious exemplum, is feminism without its occasional risks and mystifications either.) Recognizing the constructedness of the history of identities has seemed to many incompatible with taking these new identities with the seriousness they have for those who invent – or, as they would no doubt rather say, discover – and possess them.[4] In sum, the demands of agency seem always – in the real world of politics – to *entail a misrecognition of its genesis*; you cannot build alliances without mystifications and mythologies. And this chapter is an exploration of ways in which Pan-African solidarity can be appropriated by those of us whose positions as intellectuals – as searchers after truth – make it impossible for us to live through the falsehoods of race and tribe and nation, whose understanding of history makes us skeptical that nationalism and racial solidarity can do the good that they can do without the attendant evils of racism – and other particularisms; without the warring of nations.

Where are we to start? I have argued often in these pages against the forms of racism implicit in much talk of Pan-Africanism.

But these objections to a biologically rooted conception of race may still seem all too theoretical: if Africans can get together around the idea of the "black person," if they can create through this notion productive alliances with African-Americans and people of African descent in Europe and the Caribbean, surely these theoretical objections should pale in the light of the practical value of these alliances. But there is every reason to doubt that they can. Within Africa – in the OAU, in the

Sudan, in Mauritania[5] – racialization has produced arbitrary boundaries (—)
and exacerbated tensions; in the diaspora alliances with other peoples of
color, qua victims of racism – people of south Asian descent in Britain,
Hispanics in the United States, "Arabs" in France, Turks in Germany –
have proved essential.

In short, I think it is clear enough that a biologically rooted conception
of race is both dangerous in practice and misleading in theory: African
unity, African identity, need securer foundations than race.   arg.

The passage from Achebe with which I began this chapter continues
in these words: "All these tags, unfortunately for the black man, are
tags of disability." But it seems to me that they are not so much labels
of disability as disabling labels; which is, in essence, my complaint
against Africa as a racial mythology – the Africa of Crummell and
DuBois (from the New World) and of the *bolekaja* critics (from the
Old); against Africa as a shared metaphysics – the Africa of Soyinka;
against Africa as a fancied past of shared glories – the Africa of Diop
and the "Egyptianists."

Each of these complaints can be summarized in a paragraph.

"Race" disables us because it proposes as a basis for common action   *very nice*
the illusion that black (and white and yellow) people are fundamentally
allied by nature and, thus, without effort; it leaves us unprepared,   *ie*
therefore, to handle the "intraracial" conflicts that arise from the very   *inter-ethnic*
different situations of black (and white and yellow) people in different   *war in*
parts of the economy and of the world.   *Rwanda*
                                                                              ie.
The African metaphysics of Soyinka disables because it founds our   *class*
unity in gods who have not served us well in our dealings with the world   *divisions*
– Soyinka never defends the "African world" against Wiredu's charge
that since people die daily in Ghana because they prefer traditional
herbal remedies to Western medicines, "any inclination to glorify the
unanalytical [i.e., the traditional] cast of mind is not just retrograde; it
is tragic." Soyinka has proved the Yoruba pantheon a powerful literary
resource, but he cannot explain why Christianity and Islam have so
widely displaced the old gods, or why an image of the West has so
powerful a hold on the contemporary Yoruba imagination; nor can his
mythmaking offer us the resources for creating economies and polities
adequate to our various places in the world.

And the Egyptianists – like all who have chosen to root Africa's
modern identity in an imaginary history – require us to see the past as
the moment of wholeness and unity; tie us to the values and beliefs of
the past; and thus divert us (this critique is as old as Césaire's appraisal

of Tempels) from the problems of the present and the hopes of the future.

If an African identity is to empower us, so it seems to me, what is required is not so much that we throw out falsehood but that we acknowledge first of all that race and history and metaphysics do not enforce an identity: that we can choose, within broad limits set by ecological, political, and economic realities what it will mean to be African in the coming years.

I do not want to be misunderstood. We are Africans already. And we can give numerous examples from multiple domains of what our being African means. We have, for example, in the OAU and the African Development Bank, and in such regional organizations as SADDC and ECOWAS, as well as in the African caucuses of the agencies of the UN and the World Bank, African institutions. At the Olympics and the Commonwealth Games, athletes from African countries are seen as Africans by the world – and, perhaps, more importantly, by each other. Being African already has "a certain context and a certain meaning."

But, as Achebe suggests, that meaning is not always one we can be happy with, and that identity is one we must continue to reshape. And in thinking about how we are to reshape it, we would do well to remember that the African identity is, for its bearers, only one among many. Like all identities, institutionalized before anyone has permanently fixed a single meaning for them – like the German identity at the beginning of this century, or the American in the later eighteenth century, or the Indian identity at independence so few years ago – being African is, for its bearers, one among other salient modes of being, all of which have to be constantly fought for and rethought. And indeed, in Africa, it is another of these identities that provides one of the most useful models for such rethinking; it is a model that draws on other identities central to contemporary life in the subcontinent, namely, the constantly shifting redefinition of "tribal" identities to meet the economic and political exigencies of the modern world.

Once more, let me quote Achebe:

The duration of awareness, of consciousness of an identity, has really very little to do with how deep it is. You can suddenly become aware of an identity which you have been suffereing from for a long time without knowing. For instance, take the Igbo people. In my area, historically, they did not see themselves as Igbo. They saw themselves as people from this village or that village. In fact in some place "Igbo" was a word of abuse; they were the "other" people, down in the bush. And yet, after the experience of the Biafran War, during a period of two years, it became a very powerful consciousness. But it was *real* all the time. They all spoke the same language, called "Igbo," even though they were not using that identity in any way. But the moment came when this identity became very, very powerful . . . and over a very short period.

A short period it was, and also a tragic one. The Nigerian civil war defined an Igbo identity: it did so in complex ways, which grew out of the development of a common Igbo identity in colonial Nigeria, an identity that created the Igbo traders in the cities of northern Nigeria as an identifiable object of assault in the period that led up to the invention of Biafra.

Recognizing Igbo identity as a new thing is not a way of privileging other Nigerian identities: each of the three central ethnic identities of modern political life – Hausa-Fulani, Yoruba, Igbo – is a product of the rough-and-tumble of the transition through colonial to postcolonial status. David Laitin has pointed out that "the idea that there was a single Hausa-Fulani tribe . . . was largely a political claim of the NPC [Northern Peoples' Congress] in their battle against the South," while "many elders intimately involved in rural Yoruba society today recall that, as late as the 1930s, 'Yoruba' was not a common form of political identification" (1986, 7–8). Nnamdi Azikiwe – one of the key figures in the construction of Nigerian nationalism – was extremely popular (as Laitin also points out) in Yoruba Lagos, where "he edited his nationalist newspaper, the *West African Pilot*. It was only subsequent events that led him to be defined in Nigeria as an *Igbo* leader" (Laitin 1986, 7–8). Yet Nigerian politics – and the more everyday economy of ordinary personal relations – is oriented along such axes, and only very occasionally does the fact float into view that even these three problematic identities account for at most seven out of ten Nigerians.

And the story is repeated, even in places where it was not drawn in lines of blood. As Johannes Fabian has observed, the powerful Lingala- and Swahili-speaking identities of modern Zaire exist "because spheres of political and economic interest were established before the Belgians took full control, and continued to inform relations between regions under colonial rule."[6] Modern Ghana witnesses the development of an Akan identity, as speakers of the three major regional dialects of Twi – Asante, Fante, Akuapem – organize themselves into a corporation against an (equally novel) Ewe unity.[7]

When it is not the "tribe" that is invested with new uses and meanings, it is religion. Yet the idea that Nigeria is composed of a Muslim North, a Christian South, and a mosaic of "pagan" holdovers is as inaccurate as the picture of three historic tribal identities. Two out of every five southern Yoruba people are Muslim, and, as Laitin, tell us:

Many northern groups, especially in what are today Benue, Plateau, Gongola, and Kwara states, are largely Christian. When the leaders of Biafra tried to convince the world that they were oppressed by northern Muslims, ignorant foreigners (including the pope) believed them. But the Nigerian army . . . was led by a northern Christian.[8]

It is as useless here as with race to point out in each case that the tribe or the religion is, like all social identities, based on an idealizing fiction, for life in Nigeria or in Zaire has come to be lived through that idealization: the Igbo identity is real because Nigerians believe in it, the Shona identity because Zimbabweans have given it meaning. The rhetoric of a Muslim North and a Christian South structured political discussions in the period before Nigerian independence. But it was equally important in the debates about instituting a Muslim Court of Appeals in the Draft Constitution of 1976, and it could be found, for example, in many an article in the Nigerian press as electoral registration for a new civilian era began in July 1989.

There are, I think, three crucial lessons to be learned from these cases. First, that identities are complex and multiple and grow out of a history of changing responses to economic, political and cultural forces, almost always in opposition to other identities. Second, that they flourish despite what I earlier called our "misrecognition" of their origins; despite, that is, their roots in myths and in lies. And third, that there is, in consequence, no large place for reason in the construction – as opposed to the study and the management – of identities. One temptation, then, for those who see the centrality of these fictions in our lives, is to leave reason behind: to celebrate and endorse those identities that seem at the moment to offer the best hope of advancing our other goals, and to keep silence about the lies and the myths. But, as I said earlier, intellectuals do not easily neglect the truth, and, all things considered, our societies profit, in my view, from the institutionalization of this imperative in the academy. So it is important for us to continue trying to tell our truths. But the facts I have been rehearsing should imbue us all with a strong sense of the marginality of such work to the central issue of the resistance to racism and ethnic violence – and to sexism, and to the other structures of difference that shape the world of power; they should force upon us the clear realization that the real battle is not being fought in the academy. Every time I read another report in the newspapers of an African disaster – a famine in Ethiopia, a war in Namibia, ethnic conflict in Burundi – I wonder how much good it does to correct the theories with which these evils are bound up; the solution is food, or mediation, or some other more material, more practical step. And yet, as I have tried to argue in this book, the shape of modern Africa (the shape of our world) is in large part the product, often the unintended and unanticipated product, of theories; even the most vulgar of Marxists will have to admit that economic interests operate *through* ideologies. We cannot change the world simply by evidence and reasoning, but we surely cannot change it without them either.

beautiful!

What we in the academy *can* contribute – even if only slowly and marginally – is a disruption of the discourse of "racial" and "tribal" differences. For, in my perfectly unoriginal opinion, the inscription of difference in Africa today plays into the hands of the very exploiters whose shackles we are trying to escape. "Race" in Europe and "tribe" in Africa are central to the way in which the objective interests of the worst-off are distorted. The analogous point for African-Americans was recognized long ago by DuBois.[9] DuBois argued in *Black Reconstruction* that racist ideology had essentially blocked the formation of a significant labor movement in the United States, for such a movement would have required the collaboration of the 9 million ex-slave and white peasant workers of the South (Robinson 1983, 313). It is, in other words, because the categories of difference often cut across our economic interests that they operate to blind us to them. What binds the middle-class African-American to his dark-skinned fellow citizens downtown is not economic interest but racism and the cultural products of resistance to it that are shared across (most of) African-American culture.

true

It seems to me that we learn from this case what John Thompson has argued recently, in a powerful but appreciative critique of Pierre Bourdieu: namely, that it may be a mistake to think that social reproduction – the processes by which societies maintain themselves over time – presupposes "some sort of consensus with regard to dominant values or norms." Rather, the stability of today's industrialized society may require "a pervasive *fragmentation* of the social order and a proliferation of divisions between its members." For it is precisely this fragmentation that prevents oppositional attitudes from generating "a coherent alternative view which would provide a basis for political action."

N

int.

Divisions are ramified along the lines of gender, race, qualifications and so on, forming barriers which obstruct the development of movements which could threaten the *status quo*. The reproduction of the social order may depend less upon a consensus with regard to dominant values or norms than upon a *lack of consensus* at the very point where oppositional attitudes could be translated into political action.[10]

Thompson allows us to see that within contemporary industrial societies an identification of oneself as an African, above all else, allows the fact one is, say, not an Asian, to be used against one; in this setting – as we see in South Africa – a racialized conception of one's identity is retrogressive. To argue this way is to presuppose that the political meanings of identities are historically and geographically relative. So it is quite consistent with this claim to hold, as I do, that in constructing alliances *across* states – and especially in the Third World – a Pan-African identity, which allows African-Americans, African-Caribbeans, and African-Latins to ally with continental Africans, drawing on the cultural resources of the black Atlantic world, may serve useful purposes. Resistance to a self-isolating black nationalism *within* Britain or France or the United States is thus theoretically consistent with Pan-Africanism as an international project.

Because the value of identities is thus relative, we must argue for and against them case by case. And given the current situation in Africa, I think it remains clear that another Pan-Africanism – the project of a continental fraternity and sorority, *not* the project of a racialized Negro nationalism – however false or muddled its theoretical roots, can be a progressive force. It is as fellow Africans that Ghanaian diplomats (my father among them) interceded between the warring nationalist parties in Rhodesia under UDI; as fellow Africans that OAU teams can mediate regional conflicts; as fellow Africans that the human rights assessors organized under the Banjul Declaration can intercede for citizens of African states against the excesses of our governments. If there is, as I have suggested, hope, too, for the Pan-Africanism of an African diaspora once it, too, is released from bondage to racial ideologies (alongside the many bases of alliance available to Africa's peoples in their political and cultural struggles), it is crucial that we recognize the independence, once "Negro" nationalism is gone, of the Pan-Africanism of the diaspora and the Pan-Africanism of the continent. It is, I believe, in the exploration of these issues, these possibilities, that the future of an intellectually reinvigorated Pan-Africanism lies.

Finally, I would like to suggest that it is really unsurprising that a continental identity is coming into cultural and institutional reality through regional and subregional organizations. We share a continent and its ecological problems; we share a relation of dependency to the world economy; we share the problem of racism in the way the industrialized world thinks of us (and let me include here, explicitly, both "Negro" Africa and the "Maghrib"); we share the possibilities of the development of regional markets and local circuits of production; and our intellectuals participate, through the shared contingencies of our various histories, in a common discourse whose outlines I have tried to limn in this book.

"ɔdɛnkyɛm nwu nsuo-ase mma yɛmmɛfrɛ kwakuo sɛ ɔbɛyɛ no ayie," goes an Akan proverb: "The crocodile does not die under the water so that we can call the monkey to celebrate its funeral." Each of us, the proverb can be used to say, belongs to a group with its own customs. To accept that Africa can be in these ways a usable identity is not to forget that all of us belong to multifarious communities with their local customs; it is not to dream of a single African state and to forget the complexly different trajectories of the continent's so many languages and cultures. "African solidarity" can surely be a vital and enabling rallying cry; but in this world of genders, ethnicities, and classes, of families, religions, and nations, it is as well to remember that there are times when Africa is not the banner we need.

Notes

1. Achebe, Interview.
2. See, for example, Robert Harms *Times Literary Supplement*, 29 November 1985.
3. You don't have to believe in witchcraft, after all, to believe that women were persecuted as witches in colonial Massachusetts.
4. Gayatri Spivak recognizes these problems when she speaks of "strategic" essentialisms (1988, 205).
5. The violence between Senegalese and Mauritanians in the spring of 1989 can only be understood when we recall that the legal abolition of racial slavery of "Negroes," owned by "Moorish" masters, occurred in the early 1980s.
6. This passage continues: "Increasingly also Lingala and Swahili came to divide functions between them. Lingala served the military and much of the administration in the capital of the lower Congo; Swahili became the language of the workers in the mines of Katanga. This created cultural connotations which began to emerge very early and which remained prevalent in Mobutu's Zaire. From the point of view of Katanga/Shaba, Lingala has been the undignified jargon of unproductive soldiers, government clerks, entertainers, and, recently, of a power clique, all of them designated as

batoka chini, people from down-river, i.e. from Kinshasa. Swahili as spoken in Katanga was a symbol of regionalism, even for those colonials who spoke it badly": Fabian 1986, 42–43. The dominance of Swahili in certain areas is already itself a colonial product (Fabian 1986, 6).

7. Similarly, Shona and Ndebele identities in modern Zimbabwe became associated with political parties at independence, even though Shona-speaking peoples had spent much of the late precolonial period in military confrontations with each other.

8. Laitin (1986, 8). I need hardly add that religious identities are equally salient and equally mythological in Lebanon or in Ireland.

9. That "race" operates this way has been clear to many other African-Americans: so, for example, it shows up in a fictional context as a central theme of George Schuyler's *Black No More*; see, for example, 59. DuBois (as usual) provides – in *Black Reconstruction* – a body of evidence that remains relevant. As Cedric J. Robinson writes, "Once the industrial class emerged as dominant in the nation, it possessed not only its own basis of power and the social relations historically related to that power, but it also had available to it the instruments of repression created by the now subordinate Southern ruling class. In its struggle with labour, it could activate racism to divide the labour movement into antagonistic forces. Moreover, the permutations of the instrument appeared endless: Black against white; Anglo-Saxon against southern and eastern European; domestic against immigrant; proletariat against share-cropper; white American against Asian, Black, Latin American, etc." Robinson, 1983, 286.

10. Thompson 1984, 62–63. Again and again, in American labor history, we can document the ways in which conflicts organized around a racial or ethnic group identity can be captured by the logic of the existing order. The financial support that black churches in Detroit received from the Ford Motor Company in the 1930s was only a particularly dramatic example of a widespread phenomenon: corporate manipulation of racial difference in an effort to defeat labor solidarity. See, for example, Olson 1969; Gordon, et al., 1982, 141–43; and Jameson, 1981, 54.

References

DuBois, W. E. B. 1935. *Black Reconstruction*. New York: Russel and Russel.

Fabian, Johannes. 1986. *Language and Colonial Power*. Cambridge: Cambridge University Press.

Gordon, David M., et al. 1982. *Segmented Work, Divided Workers*. Cambridge: Cambridge University Press.

Jameson, Fredric. 1981. *The Political Unconscious*. Ithaca, N.Y.: Cornell University Press.

Laitin, David. 1986. *Hegemony and Culture: Politics and Religious Change Among the Yoruba.* New York: Columbia University Press.

Olson, James S. 1969. "Race, Class and Progress: Black Leadership and Industrial Unionism, 1936–1945." In *Black Labor in America*, ed. M. Cantor. Westport, Conn.: Negro Universities Press.

Robinson, Cedric J. 1983. *Black Marxism: The Making of the Black Radical Tradition.* London: Zed Books.

Schuyler, George. 1931. *Black No More.* New York: Negro Universities Press.

Spivak, Gayatri Chakravorty. 1988. *In Other Worlds.* New York: Routledge.

Thompson, John B. 1984. *Studies in the Theory of Ideology.* Berkeley: University of California Press.

Todorov, Tzvetan. 1986. "'Race,' Writing and Culture." In *"Race," Writing, and Difference*, ed. Henry Louis Gates, Jr. Chicago: University of Chicago Press.

5

Deconstructing queer theory or the under-theorization of the social and the ethical

Steven Seidman

From at least the early 1950s through the mid-1970s, the idea was widespread in American society that what was called homosexuality was a phenomenon with a uniform essential meaning across histories. Both mainstream America and the homosexual mainstream assumed that homosexuality marks out a common human identity. Public dispute has centered on the moral significance of this presumed natural fact. Whereas the post-World War II scientific, medical, and legal establishment routinely figured homosexuality as signaling a psychologically abnormal, morally inferior, and socially deviant human type, homophile groups and their supporters defended the "normality" of "the homosexual." Even the mainstream lesbian and gay movements of the 1970s primarily contested stereotypes of homosexuality, not the notion that "the homosexual" is a distinct human type. Public struggles easily folded into friend-versus-foe of the homosexual.

Since the late 1970s, the terms of the struggle over "homosexuality" have changed dramatically. The assumption that "homosexuality" is a uniform, identical condition has given way to the notion that the meaning of same-sex sexual desire varies considerably within and across societies (e.g., by class, race, ethnicity, or subcultural identity). By the early 1980s, it had become conventional wisdom among many intellectuals at least that the meaning and therefore the experience of same-sex sexuality articulates a social and historical, not a natural and universal, logic.

One consequence of the "constructionist" questioning of "essentialism" has been the loss of innocence within the gay community. The presumption of a lesbian and gay community unified by a common baseline of experience and interest has been placed into seemingly permanent doubt. The struggle over homosexuality has been grudgingly acknowledged to be a struggle among lesbian, gay, bisexual, and queer individuals and groups who hold to different, sometimes conflicting, social interests, values, and political agendas. A new cynicism has crept into lesbian and gay intellectual culture. Representations of homosexuality produced within these subcultures evoke similar suspicions with regard to their disciplining role and their regulatory power effects as representations issuing from a heterosexist cultural mainstream. No discourse or representation of homosexuality, no matter how sincerely it speaks in the name of liberation, can escape the suspicion that it exhibits particular social interests and entails definite political effects. All images of homosexuality have, to use Foucault's term, power/knowledge effects or are perceived as productive of social hierarchies. The simple polarity between friend and foe of homosexuality has given way to a multivocal cultural clash that is so disconcerting to some intellectuals that they have retreated into the presumed certainties of a naturalistic ontology, e.g., the gay brain.

I write in 1993 with a sense of the end of an era. The sex and race debates exposed deep and bitter divisions among lesbians and gay men; AIDS has threatened the very desires by which many of us have defined and organized ourselves into a community with the spectre of disease and death; a relentless politic of coming out, being out, and outing, has failed to deliver on its promise of liberation from fear and prejudice; the growing crisis of lesbian-feminism and the dubious gains of the gay mainstream surrendering to a single-interest group politic of assimilationism suggest the exhaustion of the dominant templates of lesbian and gay politics. Solidarity built around the assumption of a common identity and agenda has given way to social division; multiple voices, often speaking past one another, have replaced a defiant monotone which drowned out dissonant voices in favor of an illusory but exalted unity.

If we are witnessing the passing of an era, it is, in no small part, because of the discrediting of the idea of a unitary, common sexual identity. The troubling of identity was instigated initially in the sex and race debates. Sex rebels protesting the consolidation of a gay and lesbian-feminist sexual ethic, and the resounding public voices of people of color contesting the writing of the lesbian and gay subject as a white, middle-class figure, were crucial discursive junctures in the growing sense of crisis in the lesbian and gay mainstream. I view the assertion of a queer politics and theory as both a response to, and further instigation of, this crisis. Although many meanings circulate under this sign, queer suggests a positioning as oppositional to both the heterosexual and homosexual mainstream. I take the critique of "the homosexual subject," perhaps the grounding idea of modern Western images of homosexuality, as central to queer interventions. Both queer theory and politics intend to expose and disturb the normalizing politics of identity as practiced in the straight and lesbian and gay mainstream; whereas queer politics mobilizes against all normalized hierarchies, queer theory put into permanent crisis the identity-based theory and discourses that have served as the unquestioned foundation of lesbian and gay life. Queers disrupt and subvert in the name of a politic of difference which moves back and forth between anarchism and a radical democratic pluralism. My focus will be on the theory side of queer interventions.

Queer theory represents a powerful force in rethinking homosexuality as a culture and politics. It might seem odd to think of mostly academic theorists as shaping a movement of cultural change. Yet their placement in prestigious universities, their growing prominence in gay intellectual culture, and their influence in the radical politics of Queer Nation and HIV/AIDS activism suggests that they have become an important force shaping lesbian and gay culture and politics. Indicative of their social influence is their critical reception from old-guard humanistic intellectual elites. For example, Jeff Escoffier (1990) registers concern about the depoliticization of gay intellectuals as they are converted to deconstruction. Similarly, in a brief review of the 1991 lesbian and gay studies conference, Simon Watney (1992) criticizes queer theory for marginalizing AIDS politics in favor of the high ground of theory. In *Lingua franca*, Daniel Harris (1991) attacks deconstruction for trivializing AIDS politics by single-mindedly focusing on media criticism. These criticisms evidence a cultural clash among elites who represent divergent intellectual and political standpoints. Such cultural collisions should not be discounted as mere ideological obfuscation. Cultural elites produce representations and discourses which shape images of self and community, social norms, and political strategies. Although news reporters, novelists, artists, and film makers may have access to more people, academic intellectuals influence these media and cultural elite directly and exert a broad public influence through teaching and writing. Just as an earlier generation of liberationist theorists shaped gay cultural and political life, today it is a new movement, a generation of queer theorists, who are shaping lesbian and gay intellectual culture.

To grasp the social and political significance of queer theory, I wish to situate it historically. I sketch the historical contours of the development of lesbian and gay intellectual culture from the early 1970s to the present. This sketch is intended to be merely suggestive. This is followed by a characterization of the basic ideas of queer theory and its social and political meaning. Finally, I expose its own silences while appreciating its important connection to a politics of knowledge.

I. Situating post-Stonewall gay intellectual culture

A first phase of lesbian and gay intellectual culture spanned roughly the years between 1968 and 1975. In 1968, there was only the beginnings of a gay community and that only in a few major urban areas. A lesbian and gay cultural apparatus, if one can speak of that in 1968, was the product of a previous generation which organized around the Mattachine Society and the Daughters of Bilitis. Reflecting the local and clandestine character of these organizations, there were no national public lesbian- or gay-identified newspapers, magazines, or presses; no institutionalized gay art or theatre, and only a few gay-identified writers who mostly wrote in isolation. Homosexual theory moved back and forth between a view of homosexuality as a secondary psychological disorder characteristic of a segment of the population and a normal desire present in varying degrees in the human population. The beginnings of a theory of homosexuality as an oppressed minority was voiced by radicals such as Harry Hay but largely ignored. Gay politics was overwhelmingly oriented to civil rights with the aim of social assimilation (D'Emilio 1983).

[margin note: Phase 1]

A lesbian and gay liberationist movement emerged in response both to the forced heterosexualization of society and to the assimilationist politics of the homophile movement (Adam 1987; Altman 1982; Faderman 1991). At its cultural forefront were mostly young, educated, white individuals who identified themselves as gay liberationists or lesbian-feminists. They criticized the heterosexism and sexism of the social mainstream. Inspired by the new left and feminism, they substituted a transformative politics for the politics of assimilationism of the Mattachine Society and the Daughters of Bilitis. Liberationist thinking exhibited several major strains. For example, homosexuality was often viewed as a natural, universal condition. Protest was aimed at the pathologizing of homosexuality. Homosexuality was being reclaimed as natural, normal, and good without challenging a sexual regime organized around hetero/homosexuality. However, some liberationists struggled against a system of mutually exclusive sexual and gender roles; they envisioned an androgynous, polymorphous ideal of humanity

[margin note: N identity politics organized around a valid strategic purpose: 1 acceptance!]

liberated from the roles of heterosexual/homosexual and man/woman and from a narrow genital-centered sexuality. Other liberationists, especially lesbian-feminists and the "radical fairie movement," assumed and celebrated the differences between heterosexuals and homosexuals; radically nationalistic, they aimed to build a new community and culture. Some proposed a separatist agenda while others appealed to liberal pluralistic images of the American mosaic.

By the early 1970s, we can observe the beginnings of a lesbian and gay national cultural apparatus. Liberationists were pivotal in shaping this intellectual culture. They published journals, magazines, newsletters, and newspapers; national publications cropped up circulating lesbian and gay art, literature, and theory. Although many lesbian- and gay-identified intellectuals had ties to academia – indeed many were graduate students or professors – their writings were squarely anchored in movement culture and politics. In part, this position reflected their weak ties to academia (as junior faculty in a fiercely hostile setting) and their strong ties (e.g., through self-definition and community affiliation) to the evolving movement. With their primary personal and social roots in the movement, gay liberationists and lesbian-feminists were able to merge the roles of intellectual and activist (e.g., Altman 1971; Bunch 1975). The style and language of their writing is indicative of the interests of movement activists, e.g., critiques that typically took the form of short essays, poems, pamphlets, manifestoes, memoirs, short stories, and autobiographical statements rather than analytical or theoretically oriented books. Their work appeared in inexpensive newsletters, newspapers, pamphlets, or books and anthologies written for general public consumption. In short, in the early years of gay liberation and lesbian-feminism, lesbian/gay intellectual culture was firmly rooted in movement concerns and public struggles. Liberationists were, if you will, public intellectuals, spokespersons for a social movement and community-in-the-making.

A second phase of lesbian and gay culture spans roughly the mid-1970s to the mid-1980s. This was a period of community building and the political maturation of the lesbian and gay movements. A fully elaborated and institutionalized gay community dotted the social landscape of virtually all major cities across the United States. A pivotal part of this social development was the creation of a national, public lesbian and gay cultural apparatus that included newspapers, periodicals, gay national presses, and artistic and literary associations. A national gay and lesbian culture existed for the first time in the United States by the mid-1980s.

Although gay liberationists were pivotal in this community-building effort, their ideas and agenda were marginalized in the new lesbian and gay mainstream. Liberationist visions of creating a new humanity gave way to ethnic nationalist models of identity and single-interest group politics inspired by either a liberal assimilationist ideal or, in the case of lesbian-feminism, a separatist ideological agenda. Being lesbian and gay was celebrated, often as a natural, unchangeable condition, or, among lesbian-feminists, as a political choice.

A new intelligentsia appeared. With the institutionalization of lesbian/ gay communities across the nation, a new stratum of lesbian- and gay-identified cultural workers (e.g., writers, news reporters, artists, and knowledge producers) could be supported by newspapers, magazines, book publishers, and theatres. Moreover, the expanded tolerance for homosexuality in the mainstream United States allowed for the rise of a new stratum of gay academic intellectuals who made homosexuality into the topic of their research and theorizing. Many of these academics had roots in gay liberationism or lesbian-feminist communities. They were, in general, critical of the view of homosexuality as a transhistorical condition. They disputed attempts to frame homosexual identity as a fixed, universally identical phenomenon without, however, breaking away from identity politics. They approached homosexuality in social and historical terms. In particular, the merging of homosexuality and identity was analyzed as a recent Western historical event, not a natural, universal condition.

Unlike a previous generation of lesbian- and gay-identified intellectuals, this generation (e.g., Weeks 1977; D'Emilio 1983; Boswell 1980; Faderman 1981) were much more academically anchored. Mostly historians, they often were tenured faculty; they wrote for academic journals or published books in university presses; they were the first generation of intellectuals who could succeed in academia despite assuming a lesbian or gay identity. Although many of these intellectuals were academics, their work was not divorced from movement culture and politics. In part, this unity reflects the fact that as historians they generally wrote in a style broadly accessible to the lay community, even as they aimed for recognition by their colleagues. Moreover, many had a history of social activism and were politically and socially integrated into lesbian and gay life; these lay communities were a chief audience for this new intelligentsia. Perhaps most importantly, their work, which focused on the social formation of a homosexual identity and community, reinforced the heightened minoritization of lesbian and gay life in the late 1970s. Thus, although many of these intellectuals wrote as academics seeking collegial status, their strong ties to the history and current politics of the movement, and their identification with disciplines that valued public education, allowed them to merge the roles of academic and public intellectual.

[handwritten: Phase 3]

The third phase of an evolving lesbian/gay intellectual culture spans the period between roughly the mid-1980s and the present. Community building continued as the lesbian and gay communities assumed the form of fully institutionalized subcultures. Moreover, while the previous period witnessed dramatic social and political successes, a drive to become mainstream dominated movement politics in this period. Indeed, the antigay backlash of the late 1970s through the early 1980s might be read as evidence of the very success of mainstreaming. Mainstreaming is evident in the marketing of blatantly gay-identified fashion; in the inclusion of gays in the Rainbow Coalition as an integral partner; in the diminished danger social and cultural elites felt in being associated publicly with lesbian and gay causes. Perhaps the most dramatic illustration of mainstreaming occurred in the realm of intellectual culture. Mainstream high-brow journals, magazines, and presses opened up to lesbian- and gay-identified writers, especially in academically oriented publishing. Journals such as *October*, *Social Text*, *Socialist Review*, *Radical America*, *South Atlantic Quarterly*, *differences*, *Oxford Review*, and *Raritan* have published major statements on lesbian/gay themes. Important presses, from Routledge and Beacon to university presses such as Chicago, Columbia, Duke, Minnesota, and Indiana, have developed strong lists in lesbian and gay studies. Gay studies degree programs and research centers are being established in major universities.

The mainstreaming of lesbian and gay intellectual culture means that the university has become a chief site for the production of lesbian and gay discourses. To be sure, discourses of same-sex experiences continue to be produced by nonacademic cultural workers, e.g., film makers, journalists, novelists, poets, essayists, pornographers, political activists, and writers. Yet is increasingly gay-identified academics who are controlling the production of lesbian and gay knowledges. And while this development suggests that lesbians and gay men will have a voice in the struggles over the production and circulation of knowledge, it [handwritten: // mvmt. wli feminism!] also means that gay intellectual culture is now more divided than ever between an academic and nonacademic sector. Moreover, as the gap widens between an academically dominated discourse of homosexuality and everyday gay culture, there is the distinct possibility that gay theory and politics will have only a feeble connection. As theorists and activists are socially positioned differently, as they speak in different languages to divergent publics, their relations may be strained and weak; for example, theorists might invoke activists for political correctness while activists appeal to theory for cultural respectability.

The third phase has seen the rise of a new force in lesbian and gay intellectual culture: queer theory. An older intellectual elite of self-taught interpreters of lesbian and gay life (e.g., Katz 1976; Martin and Lyon 1972; Rich 1980) and professional historians and social scientists (e.g., D'Emilio 1983; Trumbach 1977; Weeks 1977; Smith-Rosenberg 1975), whose roots and chief public were the lesbian and gay community, are losing ground in the struggle over defining knowledges of "homosexuality" to a new cultural elite of academics who increasingly deploy the sign of queer to describe or position their approach. The most conspicuous strain of queer theory draws heavily on French poststructural theory and the critical method of deconstruction. Producers of queer theory are integrated into academia more completely than previous generations who produced gay knowledges; they are mostly English professors who pursue collegial status as well as recognition from the lesbian and gay nonacademic cultural elite, e.g., public writers, editors of magazines and newspapers, commercial publishers, and political elites. Queer theorists have often come of age during a period of the renewed activism of HIV/AIDS politics and share a spirit of the renewal of transformative politics with groups like ACT-UP or Queer Nation. Queer theory is profoundly shaping gay intellectual culture, at least that segment previously controlled by independent scholars, academic historians, and social scientists.

Queer theorists are positioned to become a substantial force in shaping lesbian and gay intellectual culture. Frequently unified by generation and by academic affiliation, sharing a culture based on common conceptual and linguistic practices, and capturing the spirit of discontent toward both the straight mainstream and the lesbian and gay mainstream, queer theory is an important social force in the making of gay intellectual culture and politics in the 1990s. I wish to contribute to understanding and assessing this cultural movement.

II. Deconstructing gay identity: queer theory and the politics of knowledge

Despite an antigay backlash, the lesbian and gay movement made giant steps towards community building and social mainstreaming in the 1980s. In urban centers across the United States the lesbian and gay community staked out a public territorial, institutional, cultural, and political identity. From this social base, lesbians and gay men campaigned, with a great deal of success, for social inclusion, as evidenced by civil rights legislation, political representation, legal reform, and the appearance of affirmative media representations.

Social success may, ironically, have allowed for hitherto-muted differences to surface publicly. Differences that were submerged for the sake of solidarity against a heterosexist mainstream erupted into public view. In particular, clashes over sexuality and race served as key sites for differences to coalesce socially. Local skirmishes over sexual ethics and political priorities escalated into a general war over the social coherence and desirability of asserting a lesbian and gay identity (Seidman 1993).

The dominant ethnic nationalist model of identity and politics was criticized for exhibiting white, middle-class, hetero-imitative values and liberal political interests. On the political front, parallel criticisms of the lesbian and gay mainstream surfaced among HIV/AIDS activists (e.g., ACT-UP) and Queer Nation activists who positioned themselves in opposition to the normalizing, disciplining cultural politics of the lesbian and gay social center. They challenged the very basis of mainstream gay politics: a politics organized on the premise of a unified subject. By calling themselves queer, and by organizing around broad issues of controlling the body or access to health care, a new post-identity cultural political force coalesced in the 1980s. On the intellectual front, a wave of lesbian- and gay-identified people of color and sex radicals attacked the unitary gay identity construction as normative and as a disciplining force which excludes and marginalizes many desires, acts, and identities of lesbian- and gay-identified individuals. They evolved various alternative proposals for rethinking identity and politics, for example, the notion of interlocking subject positions and sites of oppression and resistance. Nevertheless, it has been the movement of queer theorists, drawing on French poststructuralism, who have theoretically articulated this challenge to identity politics and whose ideas have moved into the center of lesbian and gay intellectual culture.

Poststructural theory frames literary criticism less as a matter of defining or contesting a canon, engaging in a dialogue on presumably universal questions of literary form, or as delineating the formal structures of a text, than as a type of social analysis. Literary texts are viewed as social and political practices, as organized by social and cultural codes, and indeed as social forces that structure identities, social norms, and power relations. In particular, texts are viewed as organized around foundational symbolic figures such as masculine/feminine or heterosexual/homosexual. Such binary oppositions are understood as categories of knowledge; they structure the way we think and organize experience. These linguistic and discursive meanings contribute to the making of social hierarchies. Deconstruction aims to disturb or displace the power of these hierarchies by showing their arbitrary, social, and political character. Deconstruction may be described as a cultural politics of knowledge. It is this rendering of literary analysis into social analysis, of textual critique into social critique, of readings into a political practice, of politics into the politics of knowledge, that makes deconstruction and the queer theory inspired by it an important movement of theory and politics.

Who are the queer theorists? Some names may serve as initial markers: Eve Sedgwick (1990), Diana Fuss (1991), Judith Butler (1990, 1991), Lee Edelman (1994), Michael Moon (1991), Teresa de Lauretis (1991), Thomas Yingling (1990), and D. A. Miller (1991). Key texts include Sedgwick's *Epistemology of the Closet* (1990), Butler's *Gender Trouble* (1990), and Diana Fuss's *Essentially Speaking* (1989). A central statement is the anthology, *Inside/Out: Lesbian Theories, Gay Theories*, edited by Diana Fuss (1991). Let me be clear. I am not speaking of an intellectually and politically unified cultural movement. Queer theorists are a diverse lot exhibiting important disagreements and divergences. Nevertheless, they share certain broad commitments – in particular, they draw heavily on French poststructural theory and deconstruction as a method of literary and social critique; they deploy in key ways psychoanalytic categories and perspectives; they favor a de-centering or deconstructive strategy that retreats from positive programmatic social and political proposals; they imagine the social as a text to be interpreted and criticized towards the aim of contesting dominant knowledges and social hierarchies.

I intend to sketch what I take to be the dominant intellectual and political impulse of queer theory. I do not intend to provide detailed analyses of key texts. My aim is to make the project of a particularly influential cultural movement intelligible and to begin to assess its importance. In the remainder of this section, I wish to state, as clearly as I can, the guiding impulse and core ideas of this body of work.

Homosexual theory – whether essentialist or constructionist – has favored a view of homosexuality as a condition of a social minority. Although essentialist and constructionist perspectives may assume that homoeroticism is a universal experience, both viewpoints simultaneously aim to account for the making of a homosexual social minority. For example, an essentialist position might hold that only some individuals are exclusively or primarily homosexual. Holding to this assumption, the analyst might proceed to explain how this homosexual population has come to speak for itself as a social minority. A social constructionist position might assume that, though same-sex experiences are a universal condition, only some individuals in some societies organize their lives around homoeroticism. A social analyst who assumes constructionist premises may wish to trace the social factors which have transformed this universal homoerotic desire into a homosexual identity. Despite differences between so-called essentialist and constructionist assumptions regarding same-sex experience, lesbian and gay analysts have been preoccupied with explaining the social forces creating a self-conscious homosexual minority. Both essentialist and social constructionist versions of lesbian/gay theory in the 1970s and 1980s have related stories of the coming of age of a collective homosexual subject.

Queer theorists have criticized the view of homosexuality as a property of an individual or group, whether that identity is explained as natural or social in origin. They argue that this perspective leaves in place the heterosexual/homosexual binary as a master framework for constructing the self, sexual knowledge, and social institutions. A theoretical and political project which aims exclusively to normalize homosexuality and to legitimate homosexuality as a social minority does not challenge a social regime which perpetuates the production of subjects and social worlds organized and regulated by the heterosexual/homosexual binary. Minoritizing epistemological strategies stabilizes a power/knowledge regime which defines bodies, desires, behaviors, and social relations in binary terms according to a fixed hetero/homo sexual preference. Such linguistic and discursive binary figures inevitably get framed in hierarchical terms, thus reinforcing a politics of exclusion and domination. Moreover, in such a regime homosexual politics is pressured to move between two limited options: the liberal struggle to legitimate homosexuality in order to maximize a politics of inclusion and the separatist struggle to assert difference on behalf of a politics of ethnic nationalism.

To date, the dominant logic of lesbian and gay politics has been that of battling heteronormativity toward the end of legitimating homosexuality. As important as that project is, queer theorists have exposed its limits. A binary sex system, whether compulsively heterosexual or not, creates rigid psychological and social boundaries that inevitably give rise to systems of dominance and hierarchy – certain feelings, desires, acts, identities, and social formations are excluded, marginalized, and made inferior. To the extent that individuals feel compelled to define themselves as hetero-or-homosexual, they erect boundaries and protective identities which are self-limiting and socially controlling. Moreover, identity constructions developed on the basis of an exclusively hetero- or-homo desire are inherently unstable; the assertion of one identity category presupposes, incites, and excludes its opposite. The declaration of heterosexual selfhood elicits its opposite, indeed needs the homosexual in order to be coherent and bounded. In fact, the very consciousness of the homosexual other cannot but elicit suspicions of homosexual desire in oneself and others across the range of daily same-sex interactions, friendships, dreams, fantasies, and public images. Heterosexuality and homosexuality belong together as an unstable coupling, simultaneously mutually productive and subverting.

Beyond producing a series of psychological, social, and political oppositions and instabilities, a binary sexual regime places serious limits on sexual theory and politics. To the extent that sexual (and self) identity is defined by sexual orientation equated with gender preference, a vast range of desires, acts, and social relations are never made into an object of theory and politics. To equate sexual liberation with heterosexual and homosexual legitimation presupposes an extremely reductive notion of "the sexual" since it leaves out of consideration any explicit concern with the body, sensual stimulation, and sex acts and relations other than in terms of gender preference. Implicit in the texts of the queer theorists is the claim that the mainstream focus on legitimating a homo-sexual preference and identity betrays middle-class, conventional intimate values. By focusing politics exclusively on legitimating same-sex gender choice, the lesbian and gay movement leaves politically uncontested a range of particular sexual and intimate values that may be marginalized or devalued in other respects. In other words, the gay mainstream takes for granted the normative status of long-term monogamous, adult-to-adult, intraracial, intragenerational, romantic sexual and intimate values. If a person's sexual orientation involves, say, same-sex S/M or interracial or commercial sex, s/he would be resistant to reducing the politics of sexual orientation to gender preference and the legitimation of a homosexual identity. The gay mainstream, including gay theory, is criticized as a disciplining, normative force, one unwittingly reinforcing dynamics of exclusion and hierarchy.

Queer theorists argue that homosexuality should not be treated as an issue of the lives and fate of a social minority. Implicit in this approach is the notion that the identity of the individual is the ultimate foundation for gay theory and politics. The gay community and its politics is imagined as the summation and mobilization of individuals who are self-defined as gay or lesbian. Queer critics urge an epistemological shift. They propose to focus on a cultural level. Their field of analysis is linguistic or discursive structures and, in principle, their institutional settings. Specifically, their object of analysis is the hetero/homosexual opposition. This is understood as a category of knowledge, a way of defining and organizing selves, desires, behaviors, and social relations. Through the articulation of this hetero/homosexual figure in texts and social practices (e.g., therapeutic regimes or marital customs and laws), it contributes to producing mutually exclusive heterosexualized and homosexualized subjects and social worlds. Just as feminists claim to have discovered a gender code (the masculine/feminine binary) which shapes the texture of personal and public life, a parallel claim is made for the hetero/homosexual figure. Queer interventions urge a shift from a framing of the question of homosexuality in terms of personal identity and the politics of homosexual oppression and liberation to imagining homosexuality in relation to the cultural politics of knowledge. In this regard, queer theory places the question of homosexuality at the center of society and social analysis. Queer theory is less a matter of explaining the repression or expression of a homosexual minority than an analysis of the hetero/homosexual figure as a power/knowledge regime that shapes the ordering of desires, behaviors, and social institutions, and social relations – in a word, the constitution of the self and society.

The shift from approaching homosexuality as an issue of individual identity (its repression, expression, and liberation) to viewing it as a cultural figure or category of knowledge is the central claim of Eve Sedgwick's *Epistemology of the Closet* (1990). Her opening paragraph announces a framing of homosexuality in terms of a cultural politic of knowledge.

> *Epistemology of the Closet* proposes that many of the major nodes of thought and knowledge in twentieth-century Western culture as a whole are structured – indeed, fractured – by a chronic, now endemic crisis of homo/heterosexual definition . . . The book will argue that an understanding of virtually any aspect of modern Western culture must be, not merely incomplete, but damaged in its central substance to the degree that it does not incorporate a critical analysis of modern homo/heterosexual definition.
>   (Sedgwick 1990, 1)

From the turn of the [nineteenth] century "every given person . . . was now considered necessarily assignable . . . to a homo-or-a-heterosexuality, a binarized identity . . . It was this new development that left no space in the culture exempt from the potent incoherences of homo/-heterosexual definition" (Sedgwick 1990, 2). The homo/heterosexual definition is said to shape the culture of society, not just individual identities and behaviors. It does so, moreover, not only by imposing sexual definitions on bodies, actions, and social relations, but, perhaps more significantly, by shaping broad categories of thought and culture whose thematic focus is not always explicitly sexual.

> I think that a whole cluster of the most crucial sites for the contestation of meaning in twentieth-century western culture are consequently and quite indelibly marked with the historical specificity of homo-social/heterosexual definition . . . Among those sites are . . . the pairings secrecy/disclosure and private/public. Along with and sometimes through these epistemologically charged pairings, condensed in the figures of "the closet" and "coming out," this very specific crisis of definition has then ineffaceably marked other pairings as basic to modern cultural organization as masculine/feminine, majority/minority, innocence/initiation, natural/ artificial, new/old, growth/decadence, urbane/provincial, health/illness, same/different, cognition/paranoia, art/kitsch, sincerity/sentimentality, and voluntarity/addiction. So pervasive has the suffusing stain of homo/heterosexual crisis been that to discuss any of these indices in any context, in the absence of an antihomophobic analysis, must perhaps be to perpetuate unknowingly compulsions implicit in each.
>
> (Sedgwick 1990, 72)

Sedgwick insists that these categories of knowledge are unstable. Modern Western sexual definitions move between contradictory positions. For example homosexuality may be viewed as specific to a minority of the human population (i.e., some individuals are exclusively homosexual) or understood as universal (i.e., all people are thought to have homosexual desires). The instability of the homo/hetero sexual definition makes it a favorable site for deconstructive analysis. "One main strand of argument in this book is deconstructive . . . The analytic move it makes is to demonstrate that categories presented in a culture as symmetrical binary oppositions – heterosexual/homosexual, in this case – actually subsist in a more unsettled and dynamic tacit relation" (Sedgwick 1990, 9–10). Sedgwick wishes to reveal the instability of this symbolic trope and to disrupt its hierarchical structuring for the purpose of displacing or neutralizing its social force.

In the collection *Inside/Out* (Fuss 1991), the figuring of society as a social text and of social analysis into deconstructive analysis is made into the programmatic center of queer theory. Departing from Sedgwick, who attends exclusively to the canonized texts of academic "high" culture, the contributors to this volume deploy a deconstructive critical method on the "texts" of popular culture, e.g., Alfred Hitchcock's film *Rope* (Miller 1991), the 1963 horror movie, *The Haunting* (White 1991), or popular representations of Rock Hudson (Meyer 1991).

In her introduction to *Inside/Out* (1991) and in *Essentially Speaking* (1989), Diana Fuss sketches a framework for a deconstructive or queer cultural politic of knowledge. She contrasts conventional approaches to identity which view it as a property of an object with a poststructural approach which defines identity as a discursive relational figure. "Deconstruction dislocates the understanding of identity as self-presence and offers, instead, a view of identity as difference. To the extent that identity always contains the specter of non-identity within it, the subject is always divided and identity is always purchased at the price of the exclusion of the Other, the repression or repudiation of non-identity" (Fuss 1989, 103). In other words, persons or objects acquire identities only in contrast to what they are not. The affirmation of an identity entails the production and exclusion of that which is different or the creation of otherness. This otherness, though, is never truly excluded or silenced; it is present in identity and haunts it as its limit or impossibility.

Fuss applies this deconstructive approach to the hetero/homosexual figure:

> The philosophical opposition between "heterosexual" and "homosexual" . . . has always been constructed on the foundations of another related opposition: the couple "inside" and "outside." The metaphysics of identity that has governed discussions of sexual behavior and libidinal object choice has, until now, depended on the structural symmetry of these seemingly functional distinctions and the inevitability of a symbolic order based on a logic of limits, margins, borders, and boundaries. Many of the current efforts in lesbian and gay theory, which this volume seeks to showcase, have begun the difficult but urgent textual work necessary to call into question the stability and ineradicability of the hetero/homo hierarchy, suggesting that new (and old) sexual possibilities are no longer thinkable in terms of a simple inside/outside dialectic. But how, exactly, do we bring the hetero/homo opposition to the point of collapse?
>
> (1991, 1)

The point of departure for queer theory is not the figure of homosexual repression and the struggle for personal and collective expression or the making of homosexual/gay/lesbian identities but the hetero/homosexual discursive or epistemological figure. The question of its origin is less compelling than a description of its social textual efficacy. Thus, virtually every essay in *Inside/Out* searches out this symbolic figure in a wide range of publicly circulating social texts. To the extent that Fuss's introduction is intent on making the case for shifting theory away from its present grounding in identity concepts to a cultural or epistemological centering, she intends to underscore, and indeed contribute to, the destabilizing of the hetero/homo code and the limits of a politics organized around the affirmation of a homo-sexual identity. She rehearses the standard deconstructive critique: the hetero/homo code creates hierarchies of insides and outsides. A politics organized around an affirmative homo-sexual identity reinforces this code and creates its own inside/outside hierarchy.

Deconstructive analysis aims to expose the limits and instabilities of a binary identity figure. "Sexual identities are rarely secure. Heterosexuality can never fully ignore the close psychical proximity of its terrifying (homo) sexual other, any more than homosexuality can entirely escape the equally insistent social pressures of (hetero) sexual conformity. Each is haunted by the other . . ." (Fuss 1991, 4). Deconstructive analysis reveals that the hetero/homo presuppose each other, each is elicited by the other, contained, as it were, in the other, which ultimately accounts for the extreme defensiveness, the hardening of each into a bounded, self-protective hardcore and, at the same time, the opposite tendency toward confusion and collapse. "The fear of the homo, which continually rubs up against the hetero (tribadic-style), concentrates and codifies the very real possibility and ever-present threat of a collapse of boundaries, an effacing of limits, and a radical confusion of identities" (Fuss 1991, 6). The collapse of this binary identity figure as a cultural social force and as a framework of opposition politics as identity politics is the aim of the deconstructive project. Fuss advocates a politics of ~Subversion~ cultural subversion. "What is called for is nothing less than an insistent and intrepid disorganization of the very structures which produce this inescapable logic" (1991, 6).

III. The limits of queer textualism

From the beginning of the homophile movement in the 1950s through ~politics~ gay liberationism and the ethnic nationalism of the 1980s, lesbian and ~of i~ gay theory in the United States has been wedded to a particular metanarrative. This has been a story of the formation of a homosexual subject and its mobilization to challenge a heteronormative society. Gay theory has been linked to what I wish to call a "politics of interest." This refers to a politics organized around the claims for rights and social, cultural, and political representation by a homosexual subject. In the early homophile quest for tolerance, in the gay liberationist project of liberating the homosexual self, or in the ethnic nationalist assertion of equal rights and representation, the gay movement has been wedded to a politics of interest.

Queer theory has proposed an alternative to, or supplement of, the paradigm of an identity-based politics of interest. Abandoning the homosexual subject as the foundation of theory and politics, queer critics take the hetero/homosexual discursive figure as its object of knowledge and critique. This binary is said to function as a central category of knowledge which structures broad fields of Western culture and social conventions. Queer social analysts expose the ways this epistemological figure functions in Western culture and social practices. The hetero/homosexual definition serves as a sort of global framework within which bodies, desires, identities, behaviors, and social relations are constituted and regulated.

Queer theorists, or at least one prominent strain, may be described as proposing a cultural "politics of knowledge." Their aim is to trace the ways the hetero/homo figure structures discourses and representations which are at the center of Western societies. They aim to make gay theory central to social theory or cultural criticism, rather than approach it as a minority discourse. Paralleling the Marxist or feminist claims about the bourgeois/proletariat and masculine/feminine oppositions, queer analysts claim for the hetero/homo binary the status of a master category of social analysis. They wish to contest this structure of knowledge and cultural paradigm. They intend to subvert the hetero/homo hierarchy not with the goal of celebrating the equality or superiority of homosexuality nor with the hope of liberating a homosexual subject. Rather, the deconstructive project of queer theory and politics aims at neutralizing and displacing the social force of this cultural figure. But by what means and to what end?

As I consider the politics of queer theory, I will register some reservations. We have seen that, as I read this intervention, queer social critics are clear about their aim and strategy: they wish to trace the cultural operation of the hetero/homo hierarchical figure with the aim of reversing and disturbing its infectious and pervasive social power. But how? What force is claimed for deconstructive critique and what is its ethical and political standpoint?

Fuss insists that the aim of queer analysis is to "question the stability and ineradicability of the hetero/homo hierarchy [and to bring] the hetero/homo opposition to the point of collapse" (1991, 1). But how? Fuss calls for an "analysis interminable, a responsibility to exert sustained pressure from/on the margins to reshape and to reorient the field of sexual difference to include sexual differences" (1991, 6). Fuss does not assume that this "analysis interminable" is sufficient to subvert the hetero/homo hierarchy. Cultural critique must be wedded to a politics of interest. Fuss assumes that only social agents challenging institutional arrangements and relations of power can effect a major cultural and social change. However, she also believes that current social movements such as the lesbian and gay and women's movements are organized around the assertion of unitary, essentialized identities which perpetuate and stabilize the hetero/homo figure. This is her dilemma: the very subjects positioned to trouble the hetero/homo hierarchy are invested in it. Deconstructive critique cannot disavow identity, as it is the very subjects who claim identities as man, woman lesbian, and gay who are the only agents of change. Thus, the queer project aims to deconstruct and refigure identities as multiple and fluid with the hope that "such a view of identity as unstable and potentially disruptive . . . could in the end produce a more mature identity politics . . . [and] stable political subjects" (Fuss 1989, 104). Unfortunately, there is no analysis of what such subjects might look like or what configuration of interests and social will might propel them to instigate the kinds of changes Fuss wishes. Indeed, there is no account of the social conditions (e.g., changes in the economy or state or class, gender, or racial formation) that make her own critique of identity politics possible. What social forces are producing this political and discursive pressuring on the center? This under-theorization of the social is even clearer in Eve Sedgwick.

Sedgwick is no idealist. She is keenly aware of the limits of deconstructive analysis. Sedgwick holds that "there is reason to believe that the oppressive sexual system of the past hundred years was if anything born and bred . . . in the briar patch of the most notorious and repeated decenterings and exposures" (1990, 10). The staying power of the hetero/homo figure rests, in no small part, on the fact that it has been rearticulated in a dense cultural network of normative definitions and binaries such as secrecy/disclosure, knowledge/ignorance, private/public, natural/artificial, wholeness/decadence, domestic/foreign, urbane/provincial, health/illness, and sincerity/sentimentality. In other words, the hetero/homo figure is woven into the core cultural premises and understandings of Western societies. At one level, Sedgwick's project is to identify the ways the hetero/homo definition has been sustained by being written into the cultural organization of Western societies. Here we may raise an initial concern about the politics of knowledge. If the exposure of the instabilities and contradictions of the hetero/-homo structuring of Western cultural configurations does not effectively displace or de-center this figure, deconstructive critique would seem to have surrendered much, if not all, political force. Sedgwick seems to be acknowledging that the social force of the deconstructive critique is contingent upon its being connected to a politics of interest. However, the only politics of interest she alludes to is the varied movements of homosexual politics, which assume the validity of the hetero/homo figure while challenging its particular hierarchical ordering. It would seem that the logical move for Sedgwick is to link cultural to social analysis and to couple a deconstructive critique of knowledge to a constructive politics of interest. Unfortunately, Sedgwick's analysis remains at the level of the critique of knowledge and the de-centering of cultural meanings, an intervention which by her own account has been going on for a century. This uncoupling of cultural from social analysis is a departure from at least the original intention of Derrida, who insisted on linking discursive meanings to their institutional settings and thereby connecting deconstructive to institutional critique. "What is somewhat hastily called deconstruction is not . . . a specialized set of discursive procedures . . . [but] a way of taking a position, in its work of analysis, concerning the political and institutional structures that make possible and govern our practices . . . Precisely because it is never concerned only with signified content, deconstruction should not be separable from this politico-institutional problematic" (Derrida, quoted in Culler 1982, 156). Queer theory has largely abandoned institutional analysis. In Sedgwick, the hetero/homo definition functions as an autonomous cultural logic, prolifically generating categories and fields of knowledge. These cultural meanings are never linked to social structural arrangements or processes such as nationalism, colonialism, globalization, or dynamics of class or family formation or popular social movements. Lacking an understanding of the ways cultural meanings are interlaced with social forces, especially in light of Sedgwick's analysis of the productive and infectious character of the hetero/homo figure, greatly weakens the political force of her analysis.

Queer theory is a response to the hierarchies of sexual and homosexual politics. No less than liberationist or lesbian-feminist theory, queer analysis is responding to the damaged lives and suffering engendered in a compulsively heterosexual society. The former approach homosexual politics by asserting a homosexual subject struggling for liberation against oppression. By contrast, queer theorists approach homosexual politics in relation to a power/knowledge regime organized around the hetero/homo hierarchical figure which is said to function as a master framework for the constitution and ordering of fields of knowledge and cultural understandings which shape the making of subjectivities, social relations, and social norms. I perceive a parallel with many feminist discourses in the 1980s. In the face of the staying power of male domination and resistance to change, many feminists in the 1980s turned away from learning theory and sex-role theory to psychoanalytic theory and to a quasi-naturalistic gynocentric or cultural feminism. Queer theory suggests a deep cultural logic to explain the staying power of heterosexism. The roots of heterosexism are not socialization, prejudice, tradition, or scapegoating, but a basic way of organizing knowledges and fields of daily life which are deeply articulated in the core social practices of Western societies.

Queer theory analyzes homosexuality as part of a power/knowledge regime rather than as a minority social identity. It hopes to contribute to destabilizing this regime, to disrupt its foundational cultural status. But to what end? What is the ethical and political standpoint of queer theory?

The deconstructive critique of the hetero/homo hierarchical figure is tied to a politics of difference. Its goal is to release possibilities for bodily, sexual, and social experiences which are submerged or marginalized by the dominant regime. Queer theory's social hope is allied to proliferating forms of personal and social difference. The queer politics of difference is, I believe, different in important respects from the assertion of difference that surfaced in the race and sex debates. In the latter case, the assertion of difference often remained tied to a politics of identity; the aim was to validate marginalized subjects and communities. For example, the cultural criticism of people of color did not deconstruct or contest identity categories but sought to multiply identity political standpoints. Deconstructive queer theorists affirm the surfacing of new subject voices but are critical of its identity political grounding in the name of a more insistent politics of difference. Despite its critique of methodological individualism or the view of the individual as the source and center of knowledge, society, and history, much queer theory, at least its deconstructive currents, is wedded to a social vision whose ultimate value lies in promoting individuality and tolerance of difference; where queer theory does not edge into an anarchistic social ideal it gestures towards a democratic pluralistic ideal.

The tie between queer theory and a politics of difference needs to be at least provisionally queried. What kind of politics is this and what kinds of differences are intended and with what ethical force? Unfortunately, we must proceed obliquely since queer theorists have not directly engaged such questions. Consider Eve Sedgwick. If one of her aims is to explain the persistence of compulsive heterosexuality by reference to the hetero/homo figure as productive of cultural fields of knowledge, her other aim is to expose the ways a multitude of desires have been muted, marginalized, and depoliticized by this power/knowledge regime. Sedgwick exposes the monumental constriction involved in defining sexual orientation primarily by gender preference. Revealing the immense condensation entailed in rendering the gender of sexual-object choice into a master category defining sexual and social identity is a main pivot of her work.

Historically, the framing of *Epistemology of the Closet* begins with a puzzle. It is a rather amazing fact that, of the many dimensions along which the genital activity of one person can be differentiated from that of another (dimensions that include preference for certain acts, certain zones or sensations, certain physical types, a certain frequency, certain symbolic investments, certain relations of age or power, a certain species, a certain number of participants, etc. etc. etc.), precisely one, the gender of object choice, emerged from the turn of the century, and has remained, as the dimension denoted by the now ubiquitous category of "sexual orientation" . . . *Epistemology of the Closet* does not have an explanation to offer for this sudden, radical condensation of sexual categories; instead, . . . the book explores its unpredictably varied and acute implications and consequences.   (Sedgwick 1990, 8–9)

As hetero/homosexuality become master categories of a sexual regime, as sexual desires, identities, and politics are comprehended by the hetero/homo object choice, a whole series of possible sites of individuation, identity, pleasure, social definition, and politics (e.g., sex act, number of partners, time, place, technique) are suppressed or depoliticized. The moral and political force of Sedgwick's critique of the hetero/homo figure, as I read her, draws on the cultural capital of a politics of sexual difference. Against the sexual and social condensation of the hetero/homo power/knowledge regime, Sedgwick implicitly appeals to an order of sexual difference. This is a social ideal where desires, pleasures, bodies, social relations, and sexualities multiply and proliferate. But what would such an order of difference look like? What ethical guidelines would permit such sexual innovation while being attentive to considerations of power and legitimate normative regulation? Not all self and social expressions would be tolerated; we cannot evade the need for a sexual ethic and regulation, including structures of discipline and moral hierarchy. What would such a normative order look like? Sedgwick's silence on these matters is, I think, indicative of a refusal on the part of many queer theorists to articulate their own ethical and political standpoint and to imagine a constructive social project.

In *Gender Trouble* (1990) and elsewhere (1991), Judith Butler proposes a variant of deconstructive analysis but one which gestures

Butler

towards a constructive politics. Butler's focus is a system of compulsive heterosexuality which is said to contribute to the formation of a bipolar sex/gender system. In this power/knowledge regime, a rigid natural order is posited that assumes a causality that proceeds from a bipolar sexed subject (male or female), to gender bipolarity (men and women), and to a heteronormative sexuality. Butler aims to show that instead of a natural sex/gender system underwriting heterosexuality, the latter is the unconscious compulsion behind figuring a natural, dichotomous sex/gender system as an order of truth. In a deconstructive move, Butler aims to trouble this power/knowledge regime by suggesting that this presumed order of nature is a contingent, politically enacted social order. To illustrate this point, she analyzes drag as a practice which disturbs the sex/gender/sexuality system by presumably exhibiting the performative character of sex and gender and its fluid relation to sexuality. Butler is not suggesting drag or a performative politics as an alternative to the politics of interest; rather she is proposing, as I read her, that the current Western sex/gender/compulsively heterosexual system is maintained, in part, because it functions as a configuration of knowledge. This power/knowledge regime needs to be exposed as social and political; drag or performative disruptions are practical counterparts, as it were, of deconstructive critique. They do not replace the politics of interest but supplement it.

political role of drag

For Butler, deconstructive analysis takes aim at a system of compulsive heterosexuality which is said to underpin the production of bipolar sexed and gendered subjects. Her critique aims to undermine this sex/gender/sexual order for the purpose of ending the compulsion to enact a rigid bipolar gender identity and conform to a narrow heterosexuality. Butler's critique is inspired by an ideal of difference – by the possibilities of a social space where selves can fashion bodies, gender identities, and sexualities without the normative constraints of compulsive heterosexuality and bipolar gender norms. In this regard, drag serves as more than an exemplar of cultural politics; it prefigures a social ideal – of a porous, fluid social terrain that celebrates individuality and difference. Her appeal to difference, however, lacks an ethical reflection. For example, which differences are permissible and what norms would guide such judgements? Moreover, I detect in Butler the suggestion of a post-identity order as part of a social ideal characterized by minimal disciplinary and constraining structures. But what would such an order look like? What concept of self or subject is imaginable in the absence of a strong identity concept? Moreover, are not such identities productive of rich experiences, subjective stability, and social bonds?

but also involves shaping of natural body

Difference

If self identities were not regulatory, what structures would serve to organize subjectivities?

IV. The university and the politics of knowledge

Deconstruction originated in France in the late 1960s. A reaction to both structuralism and the social rebellions issuing from new oppositional subjects (e.g., prisoners, students, cultural workers, women), deconstruction exhibited the spirit of rebellion of a post-Marxian left. It advocated a politics of negative dialectics, of permanent resistance to established orders and hierarchies. Animating the spirit of May 1968 was a politics of difference, a vaguely anarchistic, aestheticized ideal of fashioning a social space of minimal constraint and maximum individuality and tolerance of difference. However, deconstruction presupposed subjects with bounded identities who conformed to normative orders which made discipline and political mobilization possible as a condition of their own critique and a transformative politics. Moreover, deconstructive critics have been notorious in refusing to articulate the ethical standpoint of their critique and politics making them vulnerable to charges of nihilism or opportunism. As we have seen, many of the same limitations are evident in queer theory.

Queer theory originated in the United States, amongst mostly English and Humanities professors in the 1980s. It would be a mistake, however, to dismiss queer theory as merely academic. Its roots are, in part, the renewed activism of the 1980s associated with HIV/AIDS activism and the confrontational, direct-action, anti-identity politics of Queer Nation. Moreover, I wish to suggest that much queer theory can be viewed as a response to the development in the postwar United States of the university as a chief site in the production and validation of knowledge. The university and its disciplinary knowledges have become a major terrain of social conflict as knowledge is viewed as a key social power. Knowledges were of course politicized in the social rebellions of the 1960s. For example, feminists criticized the social sciences for producing knowledges which constructed and positioned women as different, inferior, and socially subordinate to men. In the 1980s, debates over canons and multiculturalism have rendered the sphere of knowledge a key arena of politics. Accordingly, the housing of queer theory in the university should not, as some critics fear, be interpreted as necessarily depoliticizing theory. To the contrary, its academic positioning makes a cultural politics of disciplinary knowledges possible. Such a politics is important precisely because such knowledges are a major social force shaping subjects and social practices. Although we need to interrogate the politics of knowledge in terms of how it articulates with a politics of interest, it would be a mistake to dismiss its key role in social struggles in Western postmodernity.

The persuasive force of the queer project depends on the extent to which one assumes that the dominant models of lesbian and gay politics presuppose the hetero/homo binary. Queer interventions aim to expose their unconscious complicity in reproducing a heteronormative order and an order that condenses sexual freedom to legitimating same-sex gender preference. Yet queer theorists have often surrendered to a narrow culturalism or textualism; they have not articulated their critique of knowledge with a critique of the social conditions productive of such textual figures; they have not provided an account of the social conditions of their own critique. The "social" is often narrowed into categories of knowledge and culture while the latter is itself often reduced to linguistic, discursive binary figures. The "historical" is similarly reduced to an undifferentiated space, e.g., the modern West or the period 1880–1980 in modern Western societies. Finally, the ethical standpoint of their own discourses is veiled. Queer critics have refused to give social and moral articulation to the key concepts of difference as they invoke it to critique the compulsiveness to identity in modern Western societies. If we are to recover a fuller social critical perspective and a transformative political vision, one fruitful direction is to articulate a politics of knowledge with an institutional social analysis that does not disavow a willingness to spell out its own ethical standpoint.

References

I wish to thank Linda Nicholson and the "Theory and Cultural Studies" sociology group of the Northeast (especially Charles Lemert, Patricia Clough, Ron Lembo, and Roz Bologh) for their helpful comments on earlier drafts.

Adam, Barry. 1987. *The Rise of a Gay and Lesbian Movement*. Boston: Twayne.
Altman, Dennis. 1971. *Homosexual: Oppression and Liberation*. New York: Avon Books.
   1982. *The Homosexualization of America*. Boston: Beacon Press.
Boswell, John. 1980. *Christianity, Social Tolerance, and Homosexuality*. Chicago: University of Chicago Press.

Bunch, Charlotte. 1975. "Lesbians in Revolt." In *Lesbianism and the Women's Movement*, ed. Charlotte Bunch and Nancy Myron. Baltimore, Md.: Diana Press.

Butler, Judith. 1990. *Gender Trouble: Feminism and the Subversion of Identity*. New York: Routledge.

— 1991. "Imitation and Gender Subordination." In *Inside/Out*, ed. Diana Fuss, 13–31. New York: Routledge.

Culler, Jonathan. 1982. *On Deconstruction*. Ithaca, N. Y.: Cornell University Press.

D'Emilio, John. 1983. *Sexual Politics, Sexual Communities*. Chicago: University of Chicago Press.

De Lauretis, Teresa. 1991. "Queer Theory and Lesbian and Gay Sexualities: An Introduction." *differences*, 3: iii–xviii.

Edelman, Lee. 1994. *Homographesis*. New York: Routledge.

Escoffier, Jeffrey. 1990. "Inside the Ivory Closet." *Out/Look*, 10 (Fall): 40–48.

Faderman, Lillian. 1981. *Surpassing the Love of Men*. New York: William Morrow and Co.

— 1991. *Odd Girls, Twilight Lovers*. New York: Columbia University Press.

Fuss, Diana. 1989. *Essentially Speaking*. New York: Routledge.

— 1991. "Inside/Out." In *Inside/Out: Lesbian Theories, Gay Theories*, ed. Diana Fuss, 1–10. New York: Routledge.

Harris, Daniel. 1991. "AIDS and Theory: Has Academic Theory Turned AIDS into Meta-Death." *Lingua franca*, (June): 16–19.

Katz, Jonathan Ned. 1976. *Gay American History*. New York: Thomas Y. Crowell.

Martin, Del, and Phyllis Lyon. 1972. *Lesbian Woman*. New York: Bantam.

Meyer, Richard. 1991. "Rock Hudson's Body." In *Inside/Out*, ed. Diana Fuss, 259–88. New York: Routledge.

Miller, D. A. 1991. "Anal Rope." In *Inside/Out*, ed. Diana Fuss, 119–41. New York: Routledge.

Moon, Michael. 1991. *Disseminating Whitman*. Cambridge: Harvard University Press.

Rich, Adrienne. 1980. "Compulsory Heterosexuality and Lesbian Existence." *Signs*, 5 (Summer): 631–60.

Sedgwick, Eve. 1990. *Epistemology of the Closet*. Berkeley: University of California Press.

Seidman, Steven. 1993. "Identity and Politics in a Gay 'Postmodern' Culture: Some Historical and Conceptual Notes." In *Fear of a*

Queer Planet, ed. Michael Warner, 105–42. Minneapolis, Minn.: University of Minnesota Press.

Smith-Rosenberg, Carroll. 1975. "The Female World of Love and Ritual: Relations Between Women in Nineteenth-Century America." *Signs*, 1 (Autumn): 1–29.

Trumbach, Randolph. 1977. "London's Sodomites: Homosexual Behavior and Western Culture in the Eighteenth Century." *Journal of Social History*, 11: 1–33.

Watney, Simon. 1992. "Lesbian and Gay Studies in the Age of AIDS." *NYQ* (March): 42–43, 72–73.

Weeks, Jeffrey. 1977. *Coming Out*. London: Quartet Books.

Yingling, Thomas. 1990. *Hart Crane and the Homosexual Text*. Chicago: University of Chicago Press.

6

Queer visibility in commodity culture

Rosemary Hennessy

For a lesbian and gay political project that has had to combat the heteronormative tyranny of the empirical in order to claim a public existence at all, how visibility is conceptualized matters. Like "queer," "visibility" is a struggle term in gay and lesbian circles now – for some simply a matter of display, for others the effect of discourses or of complex social conditions. In the essay that follows I will try to show that for those of us caught up in the circuits of late capitalist consumption, the visibility of sexual identity is often a matter of commodification, a process that invariably depends on the lives and labor of invisible others.

This argument needs to be prefaced, however, with several acknowledgements and qualifications. First of all, the increasing cultural representation of homosexual concerns as well as the recent queering of sex gender identities undoubtedly have had important positive effects. Cultural visibility can prepare the ground for gay civil rights protection; affirmative images of lesbians and gays in the mainstream media, like the growing legitimation of lesbian and gay studies in the academy, can be empowering for those of us who have lived most of our lives with no validation at all from the dominant culture. These changes in lesbian and gay visibility are in great measure the effect of the relentless organizing efforts of lesbians and gay men. In the past decade alone groups like the National Gay and Lesbian Task Force, the Human Rights Campaign Fund, GLADD, and ACT-UP have fought ardently against the cultural abjection and civic eradication of homosexuals. Like other gay and lesbian academics now who are able to teach and write more safely about our history, I am deeply indebted to those who have risked their lives and careers on the front lines to make gay and lesbian studies a viable and legitimate intellectual concern. Without their efforts my work would not be possible.

But the new degree of homosexual visibility in the United States
and the very existence of a queer counterdiscourse also need to be   KiSM
considered critically in relation to capital's insidious and relentless
expansion. Not only is much recent gay visibility aimed at producing
new and potentially lucrative markets, but as in most marketing strategies, money, not liberation, is the bottom line.[1] In her analysis of ✳
the commodification of lesbians, Danae Clark has observed that the
intensified marketing of lesbian images is less indicative of a growing
acceptance of homosexuality than of capitalism's appropriation of gay
"styles" for mainstream audiences. Visibility in commodity culture is
in this sense a limited victory for gays who are welcome to be visible
as consumer subjects but not as social subjects (Clark 1991, 192). The
increasing circulation of gay and lesbian images in consumer culture has
the effect of consolidating an imaginary, class-specific gay subjectivity for   *class-*
both straight and gay audiences. This process is not limited to the spheres   *specific gay*
of knowledge promoted by popular culture and retail advertising but   *subjectivity*
also infiltrates the production of subjectivities in academic and activist
work.

Because so much of lesbian and gay studies and queer theory has   *sexuality*
all but ignored the historical relationship between (homo)sexuality and   ⬍
capitalism, however, one of the dangers of an analysis that sets out   KiSM
to address the connection between the processes of commodification
and the formation of lesbian and gay identities is that it risks being
misread. Drawing attention to the operations of commodity capitalism
on lesbian, gay, and queer knowledges can be misconstrued to mean –
as I certainly do not – that the material processes of commodification
are only economic, that they are all determining, and impossible to
oppose. As I understand it, the materiality of social life consists of an
ensemble of human practices whose complex interdeterminate relations
to one another vary historically. These practices include economic divisions of labor and wealth, political arrangements of state and nation,
and ideological organizations of meaning-making and value. Although
capitalism is a mode of production characterized by the economic
practice of extracting surplus value through commodity exchange, the
processes of commodification pervade all social structures. In certain
social formations under late capitalism, information has become so
much the structure in dominance that language, discourse, or cultural
practice is often taken to be the only arena of social life. The challenge
for social theory now is to queer-y the reigning Foucauldian materialism
that reduces the social to culture or discourse and to refute misreadings
of postmodern historical materialism as advocating a return to economic

determinism. To examine the historical relations between homosexuality and commodification as they operate at all levels of capitalist societies does not mean dismissing the materiality of discourse and the ways culture constructs subjectivities, reproduces power relations, and foments resistance – quite the contrary. Postmodern historical materialist critiques of sexuality are postmodern to the extent that they participate in postmodernity's historical and critical remapping of social relations, but at the same time they maintain that sexuality is a material practice that shapes and is shaped by social totalities like capitalism, patriarchy, and imperialism as they manifest themselves differently across social formations and within specific historical conjunctures. As social practice, sexuality includes lesbian, gay, and queer resistance movements that have built social and political networks, often by way of capitalist commercial venues. That academic gay studies and queer theory have not very rigorously enquired into the relations between sexuality and capitalism is indicative of the retreat from historical materialism in social and cultural theory in the past decade. But I think it also suggests the particular class interests that have increasingly come to define lesbian and gay studies.

Although I have been using the words "queer" and "lesbian and gay" as if they were interchangeable, these are in fact contentious terms, signifying identity and political struggle from very different starting points. The now more traditional phrase "lesbian and gay" assumes a polarized division between hetero- and homo-sexuality and signals discrete and asymmetrically gendered identities. The more fluid and ambiguous term "queer" has recently begun to displace "lesbian and gay" in several areas of urban industrialized culture – under the signature of "queer theory" in the realm of cultural studies, in avant-garde gay and lesbian subcultures, and in new forms of radical sexual political activism. Lending a new elasticity to the categories "lesbian and gay," queer embraces the proliferation of sexualities (bisexual, transvestite, and pre- and post-op transsexual, to name a few) and the compounding of outcast positions along racial, ethnic, and class as well as sexual lines – none of which is acknowledged by the neat binary division between hetero and homosexual. In other words, "queer" not only troubles the gender asymmetry implied by the phrase "lesbian and gay," but potentially includes "deviants" and "perverts" who may traverse or confuse hetero/homo divisions and exceed or complicate conventional delineations of sexual identity and normative practice. "Queer" often professes to define a critical standpoint that makes visible how heteronormative attempts to fix sexual identities tend to

(margin handwritten notes) def. POMO historical materialism

fail often because they are overdetermined by other issues and conflicts
– over race or national identity, for example. To the extent that queer
tends to advance a subjectivity that is primarily sexual, it can threaten
to erase the intersections of sexuality with class as well as the gender
and racial histories that still situate queer men and women differently.
In this respect queer is, as Judith Butler indicates, a "site of collective
contestation" (1993, 228) that is only partially adequate to the collectivity
it historically represents.

note limitations of queer (N)

While in this essay I may string together the terms "lesbian and
gay" and "queer," then, this is not in order to conflate them but to
indicate that both expressions are being used to name homosexual
identities now, even if in contesting ways. To the extent that my
analysis focuses primarily on "queer" issues this is because they are
increasingly shaping postmodern reconfigurations of gay and lesbian
cultural study and politics. Even though many formulations of queer
theory and identity are to my mind limited, it does not follow that the
viability of "queer" as a sign of collective history and action is to be
dismissed. Instead I would argue for a renarration of queer critique as
enquiry into the ensemble of social processes – systems of exploitation
and regimes of state and cultural power – through which sexualities are
produced. I agree with Butler that the two dimensions of queering –
the historical enquiry into the formation of homosexualities it signifies
and the deformative and misappropriative power the term enjoys –
are both constitutive (Butler 1993, 229). But I would add that these
dimensions of queer praxis need to be marshaled as forces for collective
and transformative social intervention.

arg – renarration of queer critique (N)

Queer theory and/as politics

Most well known in political circles from the activities of Queer
Nation, "queer" has recently begun to circulate more widely in public
and academic writings, the sign of an unsettling critical confrontation
with heteronormativity, a distinctly postmodern rescripting of identity,
politics, and cultural critique. Although queer academic theory and
queer street politics have their discrete features and histories, both
participate in the general transformation of identities occurring in
Western democracies now as new conceptions of cultural representation
are being tested against the political and economic arrangements of a
"New World Order" – postcolonial, post-Cold War, postindustrial. The
emergence of queer counterdiscourses has been enabled by postmodern
reconfigurations of subjectivity as more flexible and ambivalent and by

shifting political pressures within the gay community. Among them are the new forms of political alliance between gay men and lesbians yielded by activist responses to the spectacle and devastation of AIDS and to a lesser extent by challenges to gay politics from radical race movements in the 1970s and 1980s. In troubling the traditional gay-versus-straight classification, "queer" draws upon postmodern critiques of identity as stable, coherent, and embodied. Queer knowledges upset traditional identity politics by foregrounding the ways contested issues of sexuality involve concerns that, as Michael Warner puts it, are not captured by the languages designed to name them (1993, xv). By targeting heteronormativity rather than heterosexuality, queer theory and activism also acknowledge that heterosexuality is an institution that organizes more than just the sexual: it is socially pervasive, underlying myriad taken-for-granted norms that shape what can be seen, said, and valued. Adopting the term that has been used to cast out and exclude sexual deviants is a gesture of rebellion against the pressure to be invisible or apologetically different. It is an "in-your-face" rejection of the "proper" response to heteronormativity from a stance that purports to be both antiassimilationist and antiseparatist. Like lesbian-feminism and the gay liberation movement, the queer critique of heteronormativity is intensely and aggressively concerned with issues of visibility. Chants like "We're here, we're queer, get used to it" and actions like Queers Bash Back, Queer Nights Out, Queer Kiss-Ins and Mall Zaps are aimed at making visible those identities that the ubiquitous heteronormative culture would erase. Politically the aim of queer visibility actions is not to include queers in the cultural dominant but continually to pressure and disclose the heteronormative.

Although their often distinct institutional positions situate queer theorists and activists differently in relation to the professional managerial class and the regimes of power/knowledge they help organize, ideologically these contrasts are less neat than is often acknowledged. Both queer activists and theorists employ some of the same counterdiscourses to expand and complicate the parameters of sexuality; both set out to challenge empiricist notions of identity as grounded in an embodied or empirical visibility; and both recast identity as a version of performance: as drag, masquerade, or signifying play. Across the promotion of more permeable and fluid identities in both queer theory and activism, however, visibility is still fetishized to the extent that it conceals the social relations new urban gay and queer identities depend on. The watchwords of queer praxis in both arenas are "make trouble and have fun" (Berube and Escoffier 1991, 15). But often trouble-making takes the form of a cultural politics that relies on concepts of the social, of resistance, and of pleasure that keep invisible the violent social relations new urban identities depend on.

In order to examine some of these concepts and their consequences I want to look more closely at academic and activist knowledges, beginning with three academic theorists whose writings are shaping the new queer theory and whose reputations now rest on their work in this area: Judith Butler, Diana Fuss, and Teresa de Lauretis. All three articulate a version of cultural studies with loose affiliations to poststructuralism. All three offer critiques of heteronormativity that, to paraphrase de Lauretis, are interested in altering the standard of vision, the frame of reference of visibility, of what can be seen and known (1991, 224). And all three are concerned to varying degrees with the invisibility of lesbians in culture.

Judith Butler's *Gender Trouble* (1990a) offers one of the most incisive and widely read critiques of heterosexuality. Against what she calls "the metaphysics of substance" or empiricist and humanist conceptions of the subject, Butler launches a rearticulation of gender identity aimed at making visible the ways in which the fiction of a coherent person depends on a heterosexual matrix. How we see sex and gender is for Butler a function of discourses which set the limits to our ways of seeing. From Butler's postmodern vantage point, the seeming internal coherence of the person is not natural but rather the consequence of certain regulatory practices which "govern culturally intelligible notions of identity" (1990a, 16–17). Identity, then, is not a matter of a person's experience, self-expression, or visible features but of "socially instituted and maintained norms of intelligibility." Intelligible genders are those that inaugurate and maintain "relations of coherence and continuity among sex, gender, sexual practice and desire." In this sense gender intelligibility depends on certain presuppositions which the dominant knowledges safeguard or keep invisible. Chief among them is the heterosexual "matrix of intelligibility" that produces "discrete and asymmetrical oppositions between 'masculine' and 'feminine,' where these are understood to be expressive attributes of 'male' and 'female.'" All sexual practices in which gender does not follow from sex, and desire does not follow from either sex or gender thereby become either invisible or perverse (Butler 1990a, 17).

Despite the efforts to safeguard these presuppositions, the fiction of a coherent identity is inevitably vulnerable to exposure as a representation, and it is the deliberate enactment of this fiction as a fiction, and not some utopian sexuality outside or free from heterosexual constructs, that for Butler serves as the site of resistance to heterosexuality. She argues that if sex is released from its naturalized meanings it can make gender trouble – subverting and displacing reified notions of gender that support heterosexual power. This process can only occur *within* the terms set by the culture, however, through parodic repetitions like drag that expose the heterosexual matrix as a fabrication and sex as "a performatively enacted signification" (Butler 1990a, 33). Drag for Butler is not merely a matter of clothing or cross-dressing. It is a discursive practice that discloses the fabrication of identity through parodic repetitions of the heterosexual gender system. As parody, drag belies the myth of a stable self preexisting cultural codes or signifying systems. Against the dominant reading of drag as a failed imitation of the "real thing," Butler posits it as a subversive act. By turning a supposed "bad copy" of heterosexuality (butch and femme, for example) against a way of thinking that posits heterosexuality as the "real thing," drag exposes this pseudo-original as itself a "copy" or representation. It follows for Butler that lesbian or gay identity is inevitably drag, a performance that plays up the indeterminacy of identity and for this reason can be seized upon for political resistance.[2]

According to Butler, then, visibility is not a matter of detecting or displaying empirical bodies but of knowledges – discourses, significations, modes of intelligibility – by which identity is constituted. In this sense her work is clearly a postmodern critique of identity, identity politics, and positivist notions of the visible. Her analysis of sexuality and gender undoubtedly has a strong social dimension: she speaks to and out of feminism and understands the processes that construct sexuality and gender as political. For Butler heterosexuality is a regime of power and discipline that affects people's lives. But her reconceptualization of the experiential and embodied self as only a *discursive* construct is a strategy that safeguards some presuppositions of its own.

One such presupposition is that the social is equivalent to the cultural. Throughout her work, Butler's approach to the problem of identity begins with the premise that identity is only a matter of representation, of the discourses by which subjects come to be established. This notion of the discursively constructed subject is heavily indebted to Foucault, and it is Foucault's problematic concept of materialism and of discursive practices that troubles Butler's analysis as well. While Foucault understands the materiality of the social to be comprised of both discursive and nondiscursive practices, he never explains the material connection between them. Furthermore, most of his attention is invariably devoted to discursive practices.[3] This social logic of non-correspondence appears in Butler's analysis, too, and is most explicit in her explanation of materialism in *Bodies That Matter* (1993). In her own words, this new book is a "poststructuralist rewriting of discursive performativity as it operates in the materialization of sex" (Butler 1993, 12). This poststructuralist reading of materiality begins with the premise that matter is never simply given but always materialized. But what constitutes this materializing is one domain of social production only – the regulatory practices, norms, and discourses that constitute ideology (Butler 1993, 10). Butler's version of materiality is directed against notions of the body and of sex common among constructionists who still maintain them to be in some ways "matter" in the sense of a constitutive "outside" that exceeds the boundaries of discourse. But by explaining materiality so exclusively in terms of discursive practices, Butler effectively conflates the materiality of the social into culture. While she frequently refers to heterosexuality as an institution or a norm, she never explains the material differences or relations between institutions and normative discourses. Are they one and the same? Do institutions like the family, the military, or schools organize and rely on more than discourses: aspects of life like labor and wealth, or social resources like health and health care, the distribution of food and shelter? All of these aspects of social life are, of course, discursively mediated and regulated, but at the same time their materiality is not simply discursive.

I am not disputing that the insidious dictates of heterosexuality operate through the discourses of culture, but surely they organize and help shape other features of social life as well. While political and economic practices are always made intelligible and shaped by our ways of making sense of them, reducing materiality to discourse alone has the effect of obscuring much of social life. The ways of making sense of sexuality that are dispersed through institutions like the military, churches, or the media also depend on and condition divisions of labor and are affected by the operations of particular state and national formations. The proposal to lift the ban on gays in the US military, for instance, threatens to disclose the fiction of heterosexual coherence. But the discourses of identity and sexual citizenship that organize this proposal have only become possible under certain historical conditions, among them changes in the place of the United States in global politics after the Cold War and in the sexual division of labor that has enabled a more flexible patriarchal gender ideology in multinational capitalist economies.

Given Butler's reduction of the social to discourses, it is not surprising that she understands history in very local, limited terms, a feature of her work that is in keeping with its poststructuralist roots. For example, at one point she admits that gender parody in itself is not subversive, rather its meaning depends on "a context and reception in which subversive confusions can be fostered" (Butler 1990a, 139). She quickly passes over the problem of historical "context" (it appears in one of her frequent series of rhetorical questions). But it is, I think, a crucial issue for queer politics now. What does it mean to say that what can be seen as parodic and what gender parody makes visible depend on a context in which subversive confusions can be fostered? What exactly is meant by "context" here?

As Butler uses it, context would seem to be a crucial feature of the meaning-making process: its contingent foundation serves as a backdrop of sorts linking one discursive practice – drag, for example – to others; through these links, presumably, meaning is produced. But considering historical context is quite different from historicizing. Historicizing does not establish connections only in this local scene of reception – between one discursive practice and another – nor does it leave unaddressed the relationship between the discursive and the nondiscursive. Historicizing starts by acknowledging that the continuation of social life depends on its (re)production in various spheres. As a mode of reading, it traces connections between and among these spheres at several levels of analysis – connecting particular conjunctural arrangements in a social formation to more far-reaching ones. To historicize the meaning of drag among the urban middle class in the United States at the turn of the twenty-first century would be to link it as a discursive practice to the social relations that make it possible and in so doing situate practices specific to a particular social formation in the United States within the larger frame of late capitalism's geopolitics and multinational economy. Butler's presupposed concept of the social displaces analysis of social totalities like capitalism and patriarchy, however, in favor of an exclusive emphasis on the specific and the local (à la Foucault). In so doing she confines history to a very limited frame whose unspoken "context" has a very specific address: the new bourgeois professional class.

This historical address is most evident in her earlier conceptions of drag as subversive political practice. For Butler, drag challenges the notion of identity implicit in "coming out," the act of making visible one's homosexuality. In her essay "Imitation and Gender Insubordination" (1991), she argues that coming out is a process one can never completely achieve. No homosexual is ever entirely "out" because identity, always undermined by the disruptive operations of the unconscious and of signification, can never be fully disclosed. This means that any avowal of the "fact" of one's homosexual (or heterosexual) identity is itself a fiction. Performative activities like drag play up the precarious fabrication of a coherent and internal sexual identity by putting on display the made-up (in)congruity of sex, gender, and desire. In her essay, "Performative Acts and Gender Constitution" (1990b), Butler acknowledges these social limitations on signification – "one is compelled to live in a world in which genders constitute univocal signifiers, in which gender is stabilized, polarized, rendered discrete and intractable" and where performing one's gender wrong initiates a set of punishments (1990b, 279). But here, as elsewhere, the critical force of Butler's commentary denaturalizes reified versions of sexuality by addressing them as discursively constructed rather than considering why they are historically secured as they are. Even though Butler concedes that the subversiveness of gender parody depends on the historical context in which it is received, most of her earlier analysis assumes that *anyone* might participate in exposing the fiction of sexual identity.

But of course, they cannot. One reason is that, unfortunately, societies are still organized so that meaning is taken to be anchored in referents or signifieds; "lesbian" and "gay" are often read as referring to authentic identities, either benign or malevolent perversions of a naturalized norm. To date, the indeterminate meanings Butler assigns these words are not shared by all. Gay bashings, at times with murderous outcomes, indicate that the insistence of the signified in the symbolic order continues to organize social life, as does the military's latest "don't ask, don't tell" policy. And in both cases the disclosure of the identity "homosexual" has definite consequences for people's lives. A book like Leslie Feinberg's *Stone Butch Blues* (1993) or a film like Jennie Livingston's *Paris Is Burning*, both of which document the ways "gender parody" often blurs into "passing," each demonstrates the powerful hold on lesbian and gay imaginations of the notion that sex should align with gender. For many lesbians and gays who have not had the social resources or mobility to insulate themselves from heteronormativity's insistence that sex equals gender, drag has been not so much playful subversion as a painful yearning for authenticity, occasionally with brutally violent results.

In *Bodies That Matter* (1993) Butler addresses some of the ways Livingston's documentary of the Harlem balls in *Paris Is Burning* tests her own earlier arguments on performative subversion and the contextual boundaries of drag. As Butler reads their representation in *Paris Is Burning*, drag balls are highly qualified social practices that can both denaturalize and re-idealize gender norms. Furthermore, the murder of Venus Xtravaganza by one of her clients (for whom the discovery that Venus had male genitals is perhaps not at all a playful subversion of gender identity) dramatizes the limits of gender parody. In other words, as she puts it, "there is passing and then there is passing" (Butler 1993, 130). Unlike Willie Ninja who "makes it" as a gay man into the mainstream of celebrity glamor, Venus is ultimately treated the way women of color are treated. Butler's reading of the film acknowledges the insistence of the signified in the symbolic order – Venus dies, she tells us, because the possibilities for resignifying sex and race which the drag balls represent are eradicated by the symbolic. Her death "testifies to a tragic misreading of the social map of power" (Butler 1993, 131) and suggests that the resignification of the symbolic order along with the phantasmic idealizations that drag enacts do have their refusals and their consequences.

There are moments in this essay when Butler hints that the social map of power, while discursive, also includes more than the symbolic order – for example, when she refers to the situation of the numbers of poor black women that the balls' idealizations deny, or when she indicates that the balls' phantasmic excess constitutes the site of women "not only as marketable goods within an erotic economy of exchange, but as goods which, as it were, are also privileged consumers with access to wealth and social privilege and protection" (Butler 1993, 132). But for the most part, here, too, the materiality of social life is ultimately and insistently confined to the ideological. While she makes use of concepts like "ideology" and "hegemony" in this essay conceptually to relate discourse, subjectivity, and power, the systemic connections among ideology, state, and labor in the historical materialist theories of Althusser and Gramsci are dropped out. The result is that important links among social contradictions that materially affect people's lives – uneven and complex though they may be – remain unexplained. I am thinking here especially of connections between the continual effort (and failure) of the heterosexual imaginary to police identities and the racialized gendered division of labor Butler alludes to earlier.

To sum up, my reading of Butler's work suggests several points about the materiality of sexuality that are politically important to queer theory and politics. First of all, if the materiality of social life is taken to be an ensemble of economic, political, and ideological production, we can still acknowledge that the coherent sex/gender identities heterosexuality secures may be fabrications always in need of repair, but their fragility can be seen not as the property of some restlessness in language itself but as the effect of social struggle. Second, the meanings that are taken to be "real" are so because they help secure a certain social order, an order that is naturalized as the way things are or should be and that "illegitimate" meanings to some degree threaten. Because it is the social order – the distribution of wealth, of resources, and power – that is at stake in the struggle over meanings, a politics that contests the prevailing constructions of sexual identity and that aims to disrupt the regimes they support will need to address more than discourse. Third, the naturalized version of sexual identity that currently dominates in the United States as well as the oppositional versions that contest it are conditioned by more than just their local contexts of reception. Any specific situation is made possible and affected by dimensions of social life that exceed it. A social practice like drag, then, needs to be analyzed at several levels: in terms of the conjunctural situation – whether you are looking at what drag means when walking a ball in Harlem or turning a trick in the Village, performing in a Hasty Pudding revue at Harvard or hoping to pass in Pocatello; in terms of its place in the social formation – whether this local scene occurs in an urban or rural area, in the United States, Germany, Nicaragua, or India, at the turn of the twentieth or of the twenty-first century; and in terms of the global relations that this situation is tied to – how even the option of drag as a flexible sexual identity depends on the availability not only of certain discourses of sexuality, aesthetics, style, and glamor but also of a circuit of commodity production, exchange, and consumption specific to industrialized economies. Recognizing that signs are sites of social struggle, then, ultimately leads us to enquire into the social conditions that enable and perhaps even foster the slipping and sliding of signification. Is the subversiveness of a self-consciously performative identity like drag at risk if we enquire into certain other social relations – the relations of labor, for instance – that help enable it? What is the consequence of a theory that does not allow this kind of question?

I want to suggest that one consequence is the risk of promoting an updated, postmodern, reinscription of the bourgeois subject's fetishized identity. Alienation of any aspect of human life from the network of social relations that make it possible constitutes the very basis of fetishization. By limiting her conception of the social to the discursive, Butler unhinges identity from the other material relations that shape it. Her performative identity recasts bourgeois humanist individuality as a more fluid and indeterminate series of subversive bodily acts, but this postmodern subject is severed from the collective historical processes and struggles through which identities are produced and circulate. Moreover, in confining her analysis of the inflection of sexuality by racial, national, or class difference to specific historical contexts, she forecloses the possibility of marshaling collectivities for social transformation across differences in historical positioning.

This postmodern fetishizing of sexual identity also characterizes the recent essays of Diana Fuss and Teresa de Lauretis. While their projects are distinct and differently nuanced, they share an ideological affiliation in that the subjects their work constructs are in many ways much the same. Unlike Butler, both Fuss and de Lauretis reference commodity culture in the cultural forms their essays target – advertising and film – and, significantly, de Lauretis occasionally explicitly mentions the commodity. For some readers Fuss's emphatic psychoanalytic approach and de Lauretis's more insistently political feminist analysis might seem to distinguish their theoretical frameworks both from Butler's and from one another's. But it is precisely these differences that I want to question.

In "Fashion and the Homospectatorial Look" (1992) Diana Fuss is concerned with relations of looking that structure fashion photography, in particular the tension between the ideological project to invite viewers to identify with properly heterosexual positions and the surface structure of the fashion photo which presents eroticized images of the female body for consumption by a female audience (1992, 713). Her essay sets out to decode this tension, which Fuss formulates in terms of the "restless operations of identification" (1992, 716). Drawing primarily on psychoanalytic theories of subjectivity (Freud, Lacan, Kristeva), Fuss explains this restlessness of identity as an effect of the subject's entry into the symbolic and its subjugation to the law of the father, a law which mitigates against return to an always irretrievable presymbolic unity. Fuss argues that by persistently representing the female body "in pieces" (showing only a woman's legs, hands, arms, face . . .), fashion photography reminds the woman spectator of her fetishization. But unlike Marx who takes fetishization to be the concealment of a postive network of social relations, Fuss understands fetishization as Freud does, that is, as a lack (castration). For Freud fetishization is the effect of a failed resolution to the Oedipal romance whereby the child disavows his knowledge that the mother does not have a penis by substituting other body parts (a leg, a hand, a foot) for it. Through their fixation on women's body parts, Fuss argues, fashion photos dramatize the role woman plays in the disavowal of the mother's castration, at the same time the fragmented body serves as substitute for the missing maternal phallus (1992, 720). Fashion fetishism is in this sense an effort to compensate for the "divisions and separations upon which subjectivity is based" (Fuss 1992, 721). At the same time, it also points to some of the mechanisms of primary identification, in particular the "fundamental female homosexuality in the daughter's pre-Oedipal identification with the mother" (Fuss 1992, 721). The fascination of fashion photography with repeated close-ups of a woman's face, Fuss argues, entails the ambivalent disavowal – denial and recognition – of the source of pain and pleasure invoked by the potential restitution of this lost object for an always imperfectly Oedipalized woman.

The Freudian concept of the fetish Fuss appropriates might be read as itself a symptom of capitalism's fetishizing of social relations in that it condenses into the nuclear family circle and onto a psychically charged object – the phallus – the more extensive network of historical and social relations the bourgeois family and the father's position within it entail.[4] Fuss fetishizes identity in the sense that she imagines it only in terms of atomized parts of social life – a class-specific formation of the family and the processes of signification in the sphere of cultural representation. Her concepts of vision and the look participate in this economy of fetishization in that visibility is divorced from the *social* relations that make it possible and understood to be only a matter of *cultural* construction: "If subjects look differently," she asserts, "it is only the enculturating mechanisms of the look that instantiate and regulate these differences in the first place" (Fuss 1992, 736–37).

Like Butler's theory, her analysis is not aimed at claiming lesbian or gay identity as a resistant state of being in its own right, but instead sets out to queer-y the dominant sexual symbolic order by exposing the ways it is continually disrupted by the homospectatorial gaze. Heterosexuality is not an original or pure identity; its coherence is only secured by at once calling attention to and disavowing its "abject, interiorized, and ghostly other, homosexuality" (Fuss 1992, 732). For her, too, identity is postmodern in its incoherence and social in its constructedness, but because it is consistently framed in terms of the individual psyche and its history, the subject for Fuss is ultimately an updated version of the bourgeois individual. This individual, moreover, constitutes the historical frame for the images of fashion photography that "tell us as much about the subject's current history as they do about her already shadowy prehistory, perhaps even more" (Fuss 1992, 734). The "perhaps even more" is significant here because it is this individualized "prehistory," a story of lost origins and mother–daughter bonds, that Fuss emphasizes. Indeed it constitutes the basis for the homospectatorial look. Although she insists that the lesbian looks coded by fashion photography "radically de-essentialize conventional notions of identity" (Fuss 1992, 736), contradictorily, an essentially gendered and embodied spectatorial encounter between infant and mother anchors the "history" that constitutes the fashion text's foundational reference point. If history is localized in Judith Butler's queer theory, then, it is even more narrowly circumscribed in Fuss's reading of fashion ads, where it is reduced to an individual's presocial relationship to the mythic mother's face (Fuss 1992, 722).

Locating the basis for identity in a space/time outside history – in memories of an archaic choric union between mother and child – has the effect of masquerading bourgeois individualism's universal subject – with all of the political baggage it carries – in postmodern drag. Like Butler, Fuss admits history makes a difference to meaning: "more work needs to be done on how spectators from different gendered, racial, ethnic, economic, national and historical backgrounds might appropriate or resist these images" (Fuss 1992, 736). But the recognition of sexuality's differential historical context so late in her essay echoes the familiar liberal gesture. Premised on a notion of history as "background," this assertion thematizes difference by encapsulating the subject in individualized cultural slots, while the social struggles over difference that foment the "restless operations of identity" remain safely out of view.

Teresa de Lauretis's essay "Film and the Visible," originally presented at the 1991 conference How Do I Look: Queer Film and Video shares many of the features of Butler's and Fuss's analyses. While she, too, draws upon psychoanalysis as well as a loosely Foucauldian analytic, her work is, I think, generally taken to be more "social" in its approach, and she at times situates it as such against a more textual analysis. Her purported objective in this essay is indeed "not to do a textual analysis" but to "put into discourse" the terms of an autonomous form of lesbian sexuality and desire in relation to film. While there are films about lesbians that may offer positive images, she argues, they do not necessarily produce new ways of seeing or new inscriptions of the lesbian subject (de Lauretis 1991, 224). De Lauretis presents Sheila McLaughlin's film *She Must Be Seeing Things* as an exemplary alternative because it offers spectators a new position for looking – the place of a woman who desires another woman. While the effort to articulate the dynamics of a specifically lesbian sexuality links de Lauretis's work with Diana Fuss's essay, unlike Fuss, she renounces formulations of lesbian sexuality founded in the mother–child dyad. At the same time, for de Lauretis lesbian sexuality is neither contingent with heterosexual female sexuality nor independent of the Oedipal fantasy structure. However, the presuppositions on which these two assertions rest belie her antitextualist stance and link her "new subjectivity" with other fetishized queer identities in the poststructuralist strand of cultural studies.

De Lauretis reads McLaughlin's film as a tale of two women who are lovers and image makers. One (Jo) literally makes movies and the other (Agatha) does so more figuratively in the fantasies she fabricates about her lover. The film demonstrates the ways a pervasive heterosexuality structures the relations of looking for both women; at the same time, the two women's butch/femme role-playing flaunts its (in)congruence with heterosexual positions by marking these roles *as* performances. De Lauretis contends that this role-playing is always at one remove from the heterosexual paradigm, and it is the space of this "remove" that constitutes for her the "excess" of the lesbian subject position. As in Butler's similar argument about performative identities, however, lesbian excess is fundamentally and exclusively a matter of cultural representation. This partial frame of reference for the social is compounded by de Lauretis's reading of Jo's film-within-the-film as a lesbian revision of the psychoanalytic Oedipal drama. Although she reads the interpolated film as a skewed rewriting of the primal scene from the perspective of a woman desiring another woman, de Lauretis's endorsement of this origin story has the effect of equating generic lesbian identity with a very specific bourgeois construction, founded in highly individualized notions of fantasy, eroticism, scopophilia, and romance.

That the narrow limits of her conception of the subject are ultimately the effect of the historical position from which she is reading comes clear in the audience discussion of her essay included in the collection. The first question from the audience addresses a gap in de Lauretis's text – one might even call it an "excess" – that is, her erasure of the film's treatment of racial difference. Her response to this question reveals the fascination with form that underlies de Lauretis's way of reading. Although she may seem more "social" in her orientation, like Fuss and Butler, she, too, fetishizes meaning by cutting it off from the social and historical forces that make texts intelligible. In defense of her omission of any discussion of race, de Lauretis argues that she has "concluded that the film *intentionally focuses on other aspects of their relationship* [emphasis added]" (1991, 268). Despite her initial disclaimers to the contrary, meaning for de Lauretis here seems to be firmly rooted in the text. Indeed throughout the essay she defines the "new position of seeing" McLaughlin's film offers the viewer by reference to the various textual devices that comprise it – the film's reframing of the Oedipal scenario, its structuring of the spectator's look, its title, and its campy use of masquerade, cross-dressing, and Hollywood spectacle.

The audience's insistent return to the problem of racial difference can be read as resistance both to this formalist approach to visibility and to the generic lesbian subject it offers.

While de Lauretis insists that race "is not represented as an issue in this film" (1991, 268), clearly for her audience this is not the case. Their questions suggest the need for another way of understanding meaning, not as textual but as historical – the effect of the ways of knowing that spectators/readers bring to a text, ways of making sense that are enabled and conditioned by their different social positions. For some viewers this film may not deal with Freud or Oedipus, show Agatha sharing a common fantasy with Jo, or any number of the things de Lauretis sees in it, but it may deal with a black Latina who is also a lesbian and a lawyer in love with a white woman. The "visibility" of these issues is not a matter of what is empirically "there" or of what the film intends, but of the frames of knowing that make certain meanings "seeable." From this vantage point, a text's very limited "dealing" or "not dealing" with a particular social category can be used to make available another possible telling of its tale, one that might begin to enquire into the historical limits of any particular construction of social reality.[5] At the very least the problem of Agatha as a Brazilian Latina pressures de Lauretis's closing assertion that *She Must Be Seeing Things* "locates itself historically and politically in the North American lesbian community" (1991, 263).

In another essay, "Sexual Indifference and Lesbian Representation,"[6] de Lauretis acknowledges that lesbian identity is affected by the operation of "interlocking systems of gender, sexual, racial, class and other, more local categories of social stratification" (1993, 148). However, the conception of the social hinted at here and the notion of community it entails are somewhat different from those offered above. For in this essay de Lauretis uses Audre Lorde's image of the "house of difference" ("our place was the very house of difference rather than the security of any one particular difference") to define a social life that is not pluralistic, and a community that is not confined to North America, but (in de Lauretis's words) "at once global and local – global in its inclusive and macro-political strategies, and local in its specific, micro-political practices" (1993, 148). If taken seriously, the social and historical frame to which de Lauretis alludes briefly here would radically recast the fetishized conception of identity that leads her to suggest that in order to address the issue of race we would need to "see a film made by or about lesbians of color" (1993, 269). But even in her allusion to a more systemic mode of reading the connection between sexuality and divisions of labor remains entirely invisible, an excess whose traces are hinted only in passing references to the commodity. What would it mean to understand the formation of queer identities in a social logic that did not suppress this other story?

While queer theorists generally have not elaborated the answer, two of de Lauretis's brief remarks on commodification provide glimpses of this unexplored way of seeing. One of them appears in a fleeting comment on Jill Dolan's contention that "desire is not necessarily a fixed, male-owned commodity, but can be exchanged, with a much different meaning, between women," an assertion de Lauretis reads as either "the ultimate camp representation" or "rather disturbing. For unfortunately – or fortunately as the case may be – commodity exchange does have the same meaning between women as between men by definition – that is by Marx's definition of the structure of capital" (1993, 152). The other appears in her argument that the critique of heterosexuality in films like *The Kiss of the Spider Woman* and *The Color Purple* is "suppressed and rendered invisible by the film's compliance with the apparatus of commercial cinema and its institutional drive to, precisely, commodity exchange" (de Lauretis 1993, 153). Both of these remarks suggest an order of (in)visibility that queer theory's critique of heterosexuality does not explore. What is the connection between the ways commodity exchange renders certain social relations (in)visible and the way of looking that structure heteronormativity or even queer theory? Do fetishized versions of identity in queer theory comply with the institutional drive to commodity exchange in the academy?

Queer nationalism: the avant-garde goes SHOPping

If academic queer theory for the most part ignores the relationship between sexuality and commodification, groups like Queer Nation do not. Founded in New York city in 1990 by a small group of activists frustrated by ACT-UP's exclusive focus on AIDS, Queer Nation has grown into a loosely organized collection of local chapters stretching across the United States.[7] The list of affinity groups comprising Queer Nation is too long and too variable to list here; included among them are the Suburban Homosexual Outreach Program (SHOP), Queers Undertaking Exquisite and Symbolic Transformation (QUEST), and United Colors which focuses on the experiences of queers of color.[8] Queer Nation is less committed to ACT-UP's strategies of direct action through civil disobedience than to creating awareness and increasing queer visibility. Often representing their tactics as explicitly postmodern, Queer Nation shares many of the presuppositions of queer theory:

deconstructing the homo/hetero binary in favor of a more indeterminate sexual identity; targeting a pervasive heteronormativity by miming it with a campy inflection; employing a performative politics that associates identity less with interiority than with the public spectacle of consumer culture.

The signifier "nation" signals a commitment to disrupting the often invisible links between nationhood and public sexual discourse as well as transforming the public spaces in which a (hetero) sexualized national imaginary is constructed in people's everyday lives – in shopping malls, bars, advertising, and the media. In seizing the public space as a "zone of political pedagogy," Queer Nation, like ACT-UP, advances some useful ways of thinking about pedagogy as a public political practice.[9] My concern here, however, is with how their antiassimilationist politics understands and makes use of the commodity as part of a campaign for gay visibility.

For Queer Nation, visibility is a crucial requirement if gays are to have a safe public existence. To this end they reterritorialize various public spaces through an assortment of strategies like the policing of neighbourhoods by Pink Panthers dressed in "Bash Back" T-shirts or Queer Nights Out and Kiss-Ins where groups of gay couples invade straight bars or other public spaces and scandalously make out (Berlant and Freeman 1992, 160–63). In its most "postmodern moments" Queer Nation uses the hyperspaces of commodity consumption as sites for political intervention. Queer Nation is not interested in marketing positive images of gays and lesbians so much as inhabiting and subverting consumer pleasure in commodities in order to "reveal to the consumer desires he/she didn't know he/she had" (Berlant and Freeman 1992, 164). Tactics like producing Queer Bart Simpson T-shirts or rewriting the trademarks of corporations that appropriate gay street styles (changing the "p" in GAP ads to "y") are meant to demonstrate "that the commodity is a central means by which individuals tap into the collective experience of public desire" and to disrupt the heterosexual presupposition on which that desire rests (Berlant and Freeman 1992, 164). To this end, the Queer Shopping Network of New York and the Suburban Homosexual Outreach Program (SHOP) of San Francisco stage mall visibility actions. By parading into suburban shopping spaces dressed in full gay regalia, holding hands, or handing out flyers, they insert gay spectacle into the centers of straight consumption. Berlant and Freeman argue that the queer mall spectacle addresses "the consumer's own 'perverse' desire to experience a different body and offers *itself* as the most stylish of the many attitudes on sale at the mall" (1992, 164).

If in postmodern consumer culture the commodity is a central means by which desire is organized, how are Queer Nation's visibility actions disrupting this process? I want to suggest that while Queer Nation's tactics attend to the commodity, the framework in which the commodity is understood is similar to the informing framework of much queer theory. It is, in short, a cultural one in which the commodity is reduced to an ideological icon. Like queer theory, Queer Nation tends to focus so exclusively on the construction of meanings, on forging an oppositional practice that "disrupts the *semiotic* boundaries between gay and straight [emphasis added]" (Berlant and Freeman 1992, 168), that social change is reduced to the arena of cultural representation. Condensed into a cultural signifier, the commodity remains securely fetishized. Infusing consumer space with a gay sensibility may queer-y commodities, but "making queer good by making goods queer" (Berlant and Freeman 1992, 168) is hardly antiassimilationist politics! If the aim of mall visibility actions is to make the pleasures of consumption available to gays, too, and to commodify queer identity as "the most stylish of the many attitudes on sale at the mall," then inclusion seems to be precisely the point. Disclosing the invisible heterosexual meanings invested in commodities, I am suggesting, is a very limited strategy of resistance, one that ultimately nourishes the commodity's gravitation toward the new, the exotic, the spectacular.

As in queer theory, many of the activities of Queer Nation take visibility at face value and in so doing short-circuit the historicity of visibility concealed in the logic of the commodity. In *Capital* Marx demonstrates that this sort of "oversight" is very much a part of the commodity's secret and its magic: "A commodity appears at first sight an extremely obvious, trivial thing. But its analysis brings out that it is a very strange thing, abounding in metaphysical subtleties and theological niceties." Marx's "analysis" of the commodity explains this "first sight" as a fiction, not in the sense that it is false or merely a copy of a copy but in the sense that it confuses the seeable with the visible. The visible for Marx is not an empirical but an historical effect. Indeed, it might be said that much of Marx's critique of the commodity redefines the nature of vision by establishing the connection between visibility and history.[10] In *Capital* Marx demonstrates that the value of a commodity is material, not in the sense of its being made of physical matter but in the sense that it is socially produced through human labor and the extraction of surplus value in exchange. Although the value of commodities is materially embodied in them, it is not visible in the objects themselves as a physical property. The illusion that value resides in objects rather than in the social relations between individuals and objects Marx calls commodity fetishism. When the commodity is fetishized, the labor that has gone into its production is rendered invisible. Commodity fetishism entails the misrecognition of a structural effect as an immediate property of one of its elements, as if this property belonged to it outside of its relation to other elements (Zizek 1989, 24). This fetishizing is enhanced and encourged under late capitalism when the spheres of commodity production and consumption are so often widely separated.

Any argument for the continued pertinence of Marx's theory of the commodity risks being misread as a reductive "return" to orthodox Marxism. While a more extensive engagement with contemporary rewritings of Marxian commodity theory, Baudrillard especially, is necessary to forestall such a misreading, they are beyond the scope of this essay. Certainly Marx was not theorizing commodity fetishism from the vantage point of late capitalism's flexible production and burgeoning information technologies and their effects on identities and cultures. Nonetheless, because his reading of the commodity invites us to begin by seeing consciousness, state, and political economy as interlinked historical and material forces by which social life is made and remade, it is to my mind a more politically useful critical framework for understanding and combating the commodification of identities than a political economy of the sign. When the commodity is dealt with merely as a matter of signification, meaning, or identities, only one of the elements of its production – the process of image-making it relies on – is made visible. The exploitation of human labor on which the commodity's appearance as an object depends remains out of sight. Changing the Bart Simpson logo on a T-shirt to "Queer Bart" may disrupt normative conceptions of sexuality that infuse the circulation of commodities in consumer culture, but it offers a very limited view of the social relations commodities rely on, and to this extent it reinforces their fetishization.

Queer-y-ing the avant-grade

Some of the problems in queer theory and politics I address above are reminiscent of the contradictions that have punctuated the history of the avant-grade in the West over the past hundred years. It is a history worth examining because the modes of reading in cultural studies and queer intellectual activity now are in the process of repeating it. The genealogy of the concept of the avant-garde in radical political thought dates from the 1790s when it signaled the progressive romantic notion of art as an instrument for social revolution (Calinescue 1987). Early twentieth-century avant-garde movements, provoked by the enormous social upheavals of World War I and the 1917 Revolution, promoted a critical rejection of bourgeois culture. Like the aesthetes at the turn of the twentieth century, the avant-garde reacted to the increasing fragmentation of social life in industrialized society. But while aestheticism responded to the commercialization of art and its separation from life by substituting reflexive exploration of its own processes of creation for social relevance, the avant-garde attempted to reintegrate art into meaningful human activity by leading it back to social praxis (Burger 1984). As Raymond Williams has pointed out, there were innumerable variations on avant-garde complaints against the bourgeoisie – often articulating quite antithetical political positions – depending on the social and political structures of the countries in which these movements were active (1989, 54). Despite these variations, like queer theory and activism, avant-garde movements – among them Dada, Surrealism, Italian Futurism, the German Bauhaus, and Russian Constructionism – attacked the philosophical and political assumptions presupposed in the reigning bourgeois realist conceptions of representation and visibility. Like Queer Nation, Dada was a broad and disparate movement, crossing national boundaries as well as the ideological divisions between art, politics, and daily life. It, too, found expression in a variety of media: poetry, performance, painting, the cinema, and montage. Attacking the cultural, political and moral values on which the dominant social order relied, it set out to "shock the bourgeoisie" (Plant 1992, 40–41). The Surrealists, many of whom had participated in the Dadaist movement in France, rejected Dada's shock tactics and its purely negative approach and aimed instead to try to make use of Freud's theory of the unconscious in order to unleash the pleasures trapped in experience and unfulfilled by a social system dependent on rationality and the accumulation of capital (Plant 1992, 49). Convinced that the union of art and life, of the individual and the world, was "possible only with the end of capitalism and the dawn of a new ludic age," nonetheless, like other avant-garde movements, their experiments were pursued mainly in the cultural domain (Plant 1992, 52).

The Situationist International (SI) movement that surfaced in France in the late 1950s and lasted through 1972 is an interesting example of a political project that attempted to reclaim the revolutionary potential of the avant-garde and supersede the limitations of its cultural politics. The Situationists acknowledged the historical importance of their avant-garde antecedents' efforts as an effective means of struggle against the bourgeoisie, but were also critical of their failure to develop that spirit of revolt into a coherent critique. Consequently, they set out to transcend the distinction between revolutionary politics and cultural criticism once and for all, and in some respects went further than their predecessors in doing so (Plant 1992, 55–56).[11] Several of their strategies for disrupting the spectacular organization of everyday life in commodity culture share much in common with those of queer activism.

The tactic of *detournement*, for instance, is one – that is, the rearrangement of a preexisting text like an advertisement to form a new and critical ensemble. The SI's critique of consumer society, its political agitation in commodity culture, and efforts to form an international collective had both a revolutionary and a ludic dimension. Sorting out the contradictions in their vision and accounting for the failures in their attempt to revamp the avant-garde might be a useful project for queer intellectuals to pursue and learn from.

Historically, the dissolution of the more revolutionary aspirations and activities of the early avant-garde movements cannot be separated from political forces like Stalinism and Nazism that were responsible for the suppression of their potential oppositional force by the middle of the twentieth century. But their critical edge was also blunted by their own participation in the increasing commodification of social life by retreating to cultural experimentation as their principal political forum. That the term "avant-garde" now connotes primarily, even exclusively, artistic innovation is in this regard symptomatic. Seen from this vantage point, the distinction between the direction the avant-garde finally pursued and aestheticism seems less dramatic – as does the distinction in contemporary theory between poststructuralism's fixation on representation and more recent formulations of social postmodernism. Many of the aesthetic features of the avant-garde reverberate in this more worldly "social postmodernism": a tendency toward formalist modes of reading, a focus on performance and aesthetic experimentation, an idealist retreat to mythic/psychic spirituality, and the disparity between a professed agenda for broad social change and a practice focused exclusively on cultural politics. One way to begin to understand this gravitation toward cultural politics in the history of the avant-garde is to consider it in relation to the more general aestheticization of everyday life in consumer capitalism.

At the same time oppositional intellectuals struggle against the separation of art from daily life, capitalism's need for expanding markets has in its own way promoted the integration of art and life – but in accordance with the requirements of commodity exchange. The aestheticization of daily life is one consequence of this process. By "the aestheticization of daily life" I mean the intensified integration of cultural and commodity production under late capitalism by way of the rapid flow of images and signs that saturate myriad everyday activities, continuously working and reworking desires by inviting them to take the forms dictated by the commodity market. Advertising epitomizes this process and is its primary promoter. Along with computer technology, advertising permeates the fabric of daily life with an infinity of visual spectacles, codes, signs, and information bits. In so doing it has helped erase the boundary between the real and the image, an insertion of artifice into the heart of reality, an act for which Baudrillard has coined the term "simulation."

One effect of the aestheticization of daily life in industrial capitalism is that the social relations on which cultural production depends are even further mystified. The aestheticization of everyday life encourages the pursuit of new tastes and sensations as pleasures in themselves while concealing or backgrounding the labor that has gone into making them possible. In keeping with the aesthetic emphasis on cultural forms, "style" becomes an increasingly crucial marker of social value and identity. While the term has a more restricted sociological meaning in reference to specific status groups, "lifestyle" as a way of making sense of social relations crystallized in the 1980s in the United States as new forms of middle-class professionalism became the focal point for heightened involvement in consumption and the promotion of cosmopolitanism (Clarke 1991, 67–68).[12] The concept of identity as "lifestyle" serves to manipulate a system of equivalences that structures the connection between the economic functions of the new middle class and their cultural formation (Clarke 1991, 68). The economic remaking of the middle class depends on the rising significance of the sphere of circulation and consumption and the invisible though persistent extraction of surplus value through exploited human labor. Although their cultural formation is increasingly flexible, "middle-class identities" continue to be organized by gender and racial hierarchies as well as by a residual individualism. "Lifestyle" obscures these social hierarchies by promoting individuality and self-expression but also a more porous conception of the self as a "fashioned" identity. Advertising, especially, champions a highly coded self-consciousness of the stylized construction of almost every aspect of one's everyday life: one's body, clothes, speech, leisure activities, eating, drinking, and sexual preferences. All are regarded as indicators of individuality and style, and all can be acquired with a few purchases (Featherstone 1991, 83; Goldman

1992). Reconfiguring identities in terms of "lifestyles" serves in some ways, then, as a linchpin between the coherent individual and a more porous postmodern one. "Lifestyle" consumer culture promotes a way of thinking about identity as malleable because open to more and more consumer choices rather than shaped by moral codes or rules. In this way "lifestyle" identities can seem to endorse the breakup of old hierarchies in favor of the rights of individuals to enjoy new pleasures without moral censure. While the coherent individual has not been displaced, increasingly new urban lifestyles promise a de-centering of identity by way of consumer practices which announce that styles of life that can be purchased in clothes, leisure activities, household items, and bodily dispositions all dissolve fixed status groups. Concern with the stylization of life suggests that practices of consumption are not merely a matter of economic exchange but also affect the formation of sensibilities and tastes that in turn support more flexible subjectivities. At the same time, the capacity for hyperconsumption promoted by appeals to lifestyle as well as the constituent features of various "lifestyles" are class specific. For example, in the 1980s in the United States the class-boundedness of stylization became evident in the polarization of the mass market into "upscale" and "downscale," as middle-class consumers scrambled to shore up symbolic capital through stylized marks of distinction: shopping at Bloomingdale's or Neiman Marcus as opposed to K-Mart; buying imported or chic brand name foods (Beck's or Corona rather than Miller and Budweiser) or appliances (Kitchen Aid or Braun versus Sears' Kenmore) (Ehrenreich 1989, 228).

Aestheticization in consumer culture is supported by philosophies of the subject in postmodern theory that for all of their "social" dimensions nonetheless pose art – not social change – as the goal of a new ethics. In one of his last interviews, for instance, Michel Foucault protests,

But couldn't everyone's life become a work of art? Why should the lamp or the house be an object, but not our life? . . . From the idea that the self is not given to us, I think that there is only one practical consequence: we have to create ourselves as a work of art (1983, 236–37).

The aestheticized technology of the self here, and in Foucault's later writings generally, is taken straight from Nietzsche's exhortation to "give style to one's character – a great and rare art!" (1974, 290).[13] Queer theory and activism's conception of identities as performative significations anchored in individual psychic histories is not very far from this notion of identity as self-fashioning. For here, too, visibility is theatrical, a spectacle that shows up the always precarious stylization of identity. Foucault's equation of lamp, house, and life as "created" objects elides the different social relations that go into their making by securing them in individual creation. But the answer to why everyone's life couldn't become a work of art could take us somewhere else, to another story, one that makes visible the contradictory social relations the aestheticization of social life conceals. For even as the regime of simulation invites us to conflate style and life, some people's lives are not very artful or stylish, circumscribed as they are by limited access to social resources. How might the woman earning $50 a week for 60 hours of work operating a sewing machine in a sweatshop in the South Bronx or the exhausted migrant worker in the San Joaquin valley harvesting tomatoes for 12 hours a day at two dollars an hour make their lives an art? How artful was the life of Venus Xtravaganza, forced to support herself as a prostitute until she was murdered? Unless "art" is so re-understood as to be disconnected from individual creation or choice and linked to a strategy for changing the conditions that allow so many to suffer an exploited existence, making one's life an art is an intelligible possibility only for the leisured class and their new yuppie heirs. When queer theory reconfigures gender identity as a "style of the flesh" (Butler 1990a, 139), to use Judith Butler's phrasing, or as "the most stylish of the many attitudes on sale in the mall" (Berlant and Freeman 1992, 167), it is taking part in the postmodern aestheticization of daily life.

In the life(style): postmodern (homo)sexual subjects

It is not accidental that homosexuals have been most conspicuous in the primary domains of the spectacle: fashion and entertainment. In 1993 no fewer than five national straight news and fashion magazines carried positive cover stories on lesbians and gays. One of the most notable among them was the cover of *New York Magazine*'s May 1993 issue which featured a dashingly seductive close-up of k. d. lang dressed in drag next to the words "Lesbian chic: the bold, brave world of gay women." Every imaginable facet of gay and lesbian life – drag, transsexuality, gay teens, gay parents – has been featured on daytime talk shows. The *New York Times*'s recently inaugurated "Styles of the Times" section now includes along with the engagement and marriage announcements regular features on gay and lesbian issues, here explicitly figured as one of many life "styles." The drag queens Ru Paul and Lady Bunny have both been profiled in "Styles of the Times," and in 1993 the front page of the section carried full page stories on the Harlem balls and gay youth.

Gays and lesbians have been more visible than ever in arts and entertainment, despite the industry's still deeply entrenched investment in heteronormativity. Tony Kushner's "joyously, unapologetically, fabulously gay" *Angels in America* won the Pulitzer Prize in 1993 and was nominated for nine Tony Awards. The list of commercial film and video productions on gay subjects grows monthly and includes such notables as Neil Jordan's transvestite love story, *The Crying Game*; Sally Potter's film version of Virginia Woolf's transsexual, *Orlando*; Jonathan Demme's AIDS courtroom drama, *Philadelphia*; Barbara Streisand's film production of Larry Kramer's *The Normal Heart*; HBO's adaptation of Randy Shilts's AIDS exposé, *And the Band Played On*. While the movie industry still fears a subject it wouldn't touch five years ago, it goes where the money is, and so far in the 1990s "gay" is becoming a warmer if not a hot commodity.

Nowhere is gay more in vogue than in fashion, where homoerotic imagery is the epitome of postmodern chic. Magazines firmly situated in the middle-class mainstream like *Details*, *Esquire*, *GQ*, or *Mademoiselle* have all recently carried stories addressing some aspect of gay life and/as fashion, and it is here that gay and lesbian visibility blurs readily into a queer gender-bending aesthetic. The June 1993 issue of *Details*, for example, featured a story on couples that included one gay and one lesbian couple; another story offered a gay man's perspective on lifting the ban on gays in the military (including a graphic account of his one-night stand with a marine who is "not gay") and a favorable review by gay novelist David Leavitt of Michelangelo Signorile's *Queer in America* (1993). The first volume of *Esquire*'s new fashion magazine, *Esquire Gentleman*, carried a feature on "The Gay Factor in Fashion" that declared "Just about everyone dresses a little gay these days . . . It is now a marketing given that gay sensibility sells to both gay and straight" (Martin 1993, 140). *Esquire*'s regular June 1993 issue included a review of Potter's *Orlando* as well as a short story by Lynn Darling entitled "Single White Male Seeks Clue."

Darling's story is a symptomatic example of the incorporation of a queer aesthetic into the gender structure of postmodern patriarchy. "It's not easy to be the scion of a dying WASP culture," the cover blurb announces, "when women have more confidence, gay men have more style, and everyone seems to have the right to be angry with you." This is a tale of young urban professional manhood in crisis, a crisis managed through nostalgic detours into the "now vanished set of certainties" preserved in the world of boxing. As the story draws to a close, John Talbot, the single white male of the title, and his girlfriend look out of their hotel room and find in their view a gay couple "dry-humping" on a penthouse roof right below them. "Talbot was tempted to say something snide, but he checked himself. In fact, it was really sweet, he decided, and in his happiness he saw them suddenly as fellow travellers in the community of desire" (Darling 1993, 104). Talbot's inclusion of gays in the diverse community of "fellow travellers" offers an interesting rearticulation of Cold War moral and political discourses that once made all homosexuals out to be communists. Here gays are included in an elastic community of pleasure seekers and a tentatively more pliant heterosexual sex/gender system.

As Talbot's story suggests, the once-rigid links between sex, gender, and sexual desire that the invisible heterosexual matrix so firmly secured in bourgeois culture have become more flexible as the gendered divisions of labor among the middle class in industrialized countries have shifted. While these more accommodating gender codes are not pervasive, they have begun to take hold among the young urban middle class particularly. There are hints, for instance, that wearing a skirt, a fashion choice once absolutely taboo for men because it signified femaleness and femininity, is now more allowed because the gender system's heteronormative regime is loosening. The designers Betsy Johnson, Matsuda, Donna Karan, and Jean Paul Gaultier all have featured skirts on men in their spring and fall shows for the last few years. Some rock stars (among them Axl Rose of *Guns N Roses*) have worn skirts on stage. But skirts for men are also infiltrating more mundane culture. The fashion pages of my conservative local newspaper feature sarongs for men, and my fifteen-year-old daughter reports that at the two-week co-ed camp she attended in the summer of 1993 at least one of the male counselors wore a mid-calf khaki skirt almost every day.

As middle-class women have been drawn into the professional work force to occupy positions once reserved for men, many of them are now literally "wearing the pants" in the family, often as single heads of household, many of them lesbians and/or mothers. The "new man," like Talbot, has managed the crisis of "not having a clue" where he fits anymore by relinquishing many of the former markers of machismo: he expects women of his class to work outside the home and professes to support their professional ambitions, he "helps out" with the housework and the kids, boasts one or two gay friends, may occasionally wear pink, and perhaps even sports an earring. Men of Talbot's class might also read magazines like *GQ* or *Esquire* where the notion of the "gender fuck" that queer activists and theorists have presented as subversive cultural critique circulates as radical chic – in essays like David Kamp's piece on "The Straight Queer" (1993) detailing the appropriation of gay codes by hip heteros or in spoofs like "Viva Straight Camp" that parody ultra-straight gender codes by showing up their constructedness (Powers 1993).

Much like queer theory, the appropriation of gay cultural codes in the cosmopolitan revamping of gender displays the arbitrariness of bourgeois patriarchy's gender system and helps to reconfigure it in a more postmodern mode where the links between gender and sexuality are looser, where homosexuals are welcome, even constituting the vanguard, and where the appropriation of their parody of authentic sex and gender identities is quite compatible with the aestheticization of everyday life into postmodern lifestyles. In itself, of course, this limited assimilation of gays into mainstream middle-class culture does not disrupt postmodern patriarchy and its intersection with capitalism; indeed it is in some ways quite integral to it.

Because patriarchy has become a buzzword in some postmodern/-queer circles, I should explain what I mean by it here. I understand patriarchy to be a concept that explains the systematic gendered organization of all areas of social life – economic, political, and ideological – such that more social resources, power, and value accrue to men as a group at the expense of women as a group. In this sense, patriarchy is social, not merely cultural, and the privilege it accords some at the expense of others affects more than the making of meaning. Many poststructuralist critiques rightly target "the notion that the oppression of women has some singular form discernible in the universal or hegemonic structure of patriarchy or masculine domination" and remind us that any sort of monolithic theory of THE patriarchy fails to account for the workings of gender oppression in the concrete cultural contexts in which it exists (Butler 1990, 3). But often they also reduce patriarchy to contingent cultural forms or dismiss it as a viable concept altogether. Like capitalism, patriarchy is a politically urgent concept because it allows us to analyze and explain social hierarchies by which gender, sexuality, and their racial articulations are organized. Patriarchy is a variable and historical social totality in that its particular forms for organizing social relations like work, citizenship, reproduction, ownership, pleasure, or identity have had a persistent effect on heterogendered[14] structures in dominance at the same time these structures vary and are the sites of social struggle.

Some patriarchal formations entail kinship alliances ruled by fathers, although in industrialized countries this form of patriarchy has been unevenly and gradually displaced as the ruling paradigm by bourgeois patriarchy. In bourgeois patriarchy, kinship alliances are subordinate to a social organization split between public wage economy and unpaid domestic production, both regulated by the ideology of possessive individualism. In advanced capitalist countries, public or postmodern patriarchy has recently begun to emerge as the prevailing form. It is characterized by the hyperdevelopment of consumption and the joint wage-earner family, the relative transfer of power from husbands to professionals in the welfare state, the rise of single-mother-headed and other alternative households, and sexualized consumerism (Ferguson 1989, 110). While any one patriarchal formation may dominate, it often coexists with other contesting or residual forms. Policy debates like the current controversy over lifting the ban on gays in the US military as well as cultural narratives of various sorts (films like *A Few Good Men*, *Jungle Fever*, or *The Firm*, for instance) can be read as articulations of the struggle between bourgeois patriarchal formations and their accompanying moral ideologies and postmodern patriarchy's newer forms of family, gender, sexuality, and work.

Finally, patriarchy is differential. This means that while all women as a group are positioned the same (as subordinate or other) in relation to men, they are positioned differently in relation to each other and at times in relation to men in subaltern groups. Some women have access to resources – a professional job, an urban condo, a cleaning lady, a vacation home, a fancy car – that are only possible because of the work of other women and men who do not have these resources. Because patriarchy functions in concert with a racial system of white supremacy, disproportionate numbers of people of color, men and women alike, have historically occupied these exploited, under-resourced social positions. That more women than men fill the ranks of the impoverished speaks loudly to the ways class exploitation is reinforced by patriarchal structures. Similarly, some men have more patriarchal power than others, sometimes power over and at the expense of other men. This difference means that not all men benefit the same from patriarchy. Because the division of labor in general is racialized at the same time race is not necessarily congruent with class, the cultural capital people of color might gain on entry into any class can be canceled out or undermined by the operations of racism. Consequently, the white gay psychiatrist or lawyer is not in the same patriarchal position as his white straight colleagues nor is he in the same patriarchal position as a black gay man of the same class. Some women, lesbians among them, can claim patriarchal power over other women and men by virtue of their institutional privilege. For instance, women, lesbians included, in administrative or managerial positions can make use of their institutional positions to wield power over men and other women who work for them or are affected by the policies they draft. But even women who benefit from patriarchy in some areas of their lives are disadvantaged in a society that systematically accords men power over women. The pervasiveness of rape and wife-battering across classes and races and the general invisibility of lesbians in the culture demonstrate the systematic persistence of patriarchy despite the claims of a postmodern cosmopolitanism that gender hierarchies no longer operate or are readily subverted.

In positing male and female as distinct and opposite sexes that are naturally attracted to one another, heterosexuality is integral to patriarchy. Woman's position as subordinate other, as (sexual) property, and as exploited laborer depends on a heterosexual matrix in which woman is taken to be man's opposite; his control over social resources, his clear thinking, strength, and sexual prowess depend on her being less able, less rational, and never virile. As a pervasive institution within other institutions (state, education, church, media), heterosexuality helps guarantee patriarchal regulation of women's bodies, labor, and desires. Queer critiques of heterosexuality have often not acknowledged – in fact they often disavow – the relationship between heterosexuality and patriarchy. But the struggles of lesbians in groups like Queer Nation and other gay political organizations are testimony that gender hierarchies persist between men and women even when both are fighting against heterosexuality as a regime of power (Maggent 1991).

The gender flexibility of postmodern patriarchy is pernicious because it casts the illusion that patriarchy has disappeared. But behind this facade corporate interests are delighting in the discovery of new markets. Among the most promising are gays and lesbians in the new professional/managerial class. Among them are "lifestyle lesbians" like the Bay area vice president of a lesbian-owned business group who announced, "Here I am, this funny, warm person that you like and I happen to be a lesbian. I am bourgeois. I have a house in the suburbs. I drive a Saab" (Stewart 1991, 56). Given the increased "visibility" of this sort of gay consumer, "tolerance of gays makes sense" (Tobias 1992). Increasingly marketers of mainstream products from books to beer are aiming ads specifically at gay men and lesbians; *Fortune* magazine contends "it's a wonderful market niche, the only question is how to reach it" (Stewart 1991). Reaching it has so far involved manufacturing the image of a certain class-specific lesbian and gay consumer population. "Visibility is what it is all about," says David Ehrlich of Overlooked Opinions (Gluckman and Reed 1993, 16). These stereotypes of wealthy freespending gay consumers play well with advertisers and are useful to corporations because they make the gay market seem potentially lucrative; they cultivate a narrow but widely accepted definition of gay identity as a marketing tool and help to integrate gay people *as* gay people into a new marketing niche (Gluckman and Reed 1993, 17, 18). But if gay visibility is a good business prospect, as some companies argue, the question gay critics need to ask is "for whom?" Who profits from these new markets?

Out of sight, out of mind

Commodification structures much more than the exchange of goods on the market; it affects even as it depends on the knowledges that mediate what and how we see. The commodification of gay styles and identities in the corporate and academic marketplaces is integrally related to the formation of a postmodern gay/queer subjectivity, ambivalently gender coded and in some instances flagrantly repudiating traditional hetero and homo bourgeois culture. Nonetheless, as I have been arguing, to a great extent the construction of a new "homosexual/queer spectacle" perpetuates a class-specific perspective that keeps invisible the capitalist divisions of labor that organize sexuality and in particular lesbian, gay, queer lives. In so doing queer spectacles often participate in a long history of class-regulated visibility.[15] Beginning around the middle of the nineteenth century, the bourgeoisie mediated their experience of the working class through spatial as well as cultural/ideological arrangements. The erection of physical barriers – subway and rail construction and the siting of retail and residential districts – structured the physical arrangement of the city so as to foreclose the trauma of seeing the laboring classes (Kester 1993, 73). This physical regulation of class visibility was also compounded by the consolidation of a characteristically "bourgeois" mode of perception through an array of knowledges, the philosophic and aesthetic chief among them. The notion of an autonomous aesthetic perception, first developed by eighteenth-century philosophers (Kant, Hume, Shaftesbury), whereby perceived objects are abstracted from the social context of their creation, provided the foundation for a way of seeing that has dominated modern culture and aesthetics through the late twentieth century (Kester 1993, 74). This mode of perception reinforces and is indeed historically necessary to commodity exchange and comes to function as a "phenomenological matrix" through which the bourgeoisie confront an array of daily experiences through modes of seeing that erase the differently valued divisions of labor that organize visibility

(Kester 1993, 75). In late twentieth-century "postindustrial" societies like the United States, the (in)visibility of class divisions continues to be spatially regulated by urban planning, but it is also reinforced by changes in First World relations of production as industry has been increasingly consigned to sites in "developing countries" outside the United States. Capital has not been significantly dispersed or democratized in "First World" economies as a result, simply transferred to more profitable sectors, the so-called "tertiary" or service sectors: banking, finance, pension funds, etc. (Evans 1993, 43). The escalating domination of the ideological – the proliferation of information technologies, media images, codes – in postindustrial cultures has helped to reconfigure bourgeois modes of perception in First World populations, producing subjects who are more differentiated and less likely to experience capitalism collectively through production relations and more likely to experience it through relations of consumption. As a result, the neat subject/object split of Kantian aesthetics has been troubled and to some degree displaced, even as the invisibility of social relations of labor in corporate and intellectual commodity spectacles persists.

Gay-friendly corporations like Levi-Strauss, for example, reinforce the gender-flexible subjects their advertising campaigns promote through gay window-dressing strategies by way of public relations programs that boast of their progressive corporate policies for lesbians and gays. Levi-Strauss gives health insurance benefits to unmarried domestic partners of their employees, has created a supportive environment for employees who test HIV positive, and has a Lesbian and Gay Employees Association. Members of this association prepared a video for the company to use in its diversity training in which they, their parents, and their managers openly discuss their relationships (Stewart 1991, 50). But Levi-Strauss's workers in the sweatshops of Saipan who live in cramped and crowded barracks and earn as little as $2.15 an hour remain largely invisible. Although Levi-Strauss ended its contracts last year with the island's largest clothes maker after an investigation by the company found evidence of unsatisfactory treatment of workers in his factories, they still continue to make shirts at five plants there (Shenon 1993). Meanwhile, back in the United States, Levi-Strauss closed its San Antonio plant in 1990, laying off 1,150 workers, 92 percent of them Latino and 86 percent of them women, and moved its operations to the Caribbean where it can pay laborers $3.80 a day, roughly half the average hourly wage of the San Antonio workforce (Martinez 1993, 22). Displaying the gay-friendly policies of "progressive" US corporations often deflects attention from the exploitative international division of labor they depend on in the interests of the company's bottom line – profits.[16]

The formation of a gay/queer imaginary in both corporate and academic circles also rests on the suppression of class analysis. There have been all too few books that treat the ways gay history and culture has been stratified along class lines.[17] With several notable exceptions, studies of the relationship between homosexuality and capitalism are remarkably sparse, and extended analyses of lesbian and gay poverty are almost nonexistent.[18] To ask the more pointed question of how the achievement of lesbian and gay visibility by some rests on the invisible labor of others is to expose the unspeakable underside of queer critique.

The consolidation of the professional middle class during the 1980s brought with it an array of social contradictions. The recruitment of more and more women into the workforce bolstered the legitimation of both the professional "New Woman" and of academic feminism. The increasing, albeit uneven and complicated, investiture of lesbians and gays into new forms of sexual citizenship and the relative growth of academic gay studies accompanied and in some ways were enabled by these changes. But these were also decades when the chasm between the very rich and the very poor widened and poverty became more than ever feminized. As the 1990s began, a total of 33 million people in the United States – more than 13.5 percent of the population – were officially living in poverty. While estimates of the numbers of people who are homosexual are notoriously unreliable (ranging from the 1993 Batelle Human Research Center's 1.1 percent to the 1948 Kinsey Report's 10 percent), assuming that somewhere between 1 and 10 percent of the population are homosexual, it would be fair to say that there are between 1.65 and 3.3 million impoverished lesbians and gay men in the United States today.[19]

Most lesbians are leading less glamorous lives than their chic commodity images suggest, and poor lesbians of color are the most invisible and worst off. While the wage gap between women and men has supposedly narrowed in the 1980s – in 1990 women earned 72 percent of what men did – much of this change is due to a drop in men's earnings, while the incomes of women have stayed the same (US Bureau of the Census 1991). Furthermore, the bulk of necessary work at home, by some estimates 70 percent, is still left up to women. In other words, women as a group do more than half of all the work in this country and make less than half of what men do (Abelda, et al. 1988, 52). Of all poor people over 18, 63 percent are women, with 53 percent of poor families headed by women (Macionis 1993, 282). While there is no reliable data available on the numbers of poor who are lesbian or gay, the racialized and gendered division of labor suggests that there are more lesbians than gay men living in poverty and proportionately more of them are people of color.[20] Redressing gay invisibility by promoting images of a seamlessly middle-class gay consumer or by inviting us to see queer identities only in terms of style, textuality, or performative play helps produce imaginary gay/queer subjects that keep invisible the divisions of wealth and labor that these images and knowledges depend on. These commodified perspectives blot from view lesbians, gays, queers who are manual workers, sex workers, unemployed, and imprisoned. About a quarter to a half million homosexual and bisexual youths are thrown out of their homes and subjected to prostitution and violence in the streets (Galst 1992). Severing queer sexuality and homosexuality from the operations of class keeps these lives from view, forecloses consideration of the ways sexual identities are complicated by the priorities imposed by impoverishment, and keeps a queer political agenda from working collectively to address the needs of many whose historical situation is defined in terms of counterdominant sexual practices. That so little work has been done in the academy, even within lesbian and gay studies, to address these populations and the invisible social relations that maintain their marginality and exploitation speaks loudly to the ways a class-specific "bourgeois (homosexual/queer) imaginary" structures our knowledge of sexual identity, pleasure, and emancipation.

Critique-al visibility

Critique is a political practice and a mode of reading that establishes the intimate links between the visible and the historical by taking as its starting point a systemic understanding of the social. A radical critique of sexuality understands that the visibility of any particular construction of sexuality or sexual identity is historical in that it is shaped by an ensemble of social arrangements. As a way of seeing sexuality, critique insists on making connections between the emergence of a discourse or identity in industrialized social formations and the international division of labor, between sexy commodity images and labor, the spectacle and the sweatshop, style and class. This sort of critique-al intervention into heterosexuality, therefore, does not see sexuality as just the effect of cultural or discursive practice, merely the product of ideology or institutions, but as a regulatory apparatus that spans the organization of social life in the modern world and that works in concert with other social totalities – capitalism, patriarchy, colonialism.

As a political practice, critique acknowledges the importance of "reading" to political activism. Understood broadly as all those ways of making sense that enable one to be conscious, to be literate in the culture's codes, and so to be capable of acting meaningfully in the world, reading is an activity essential to social life. Although they often go unacknowledged, modes of reading are necessary to political activism. Paying attention to how we read and considering its implications and consequences are a key component of any oppositional political work. To ignore this crucial dimension of social struggle is to risk reproducing the very conditions we seek to change. The ways of making sense available in any historical time will tend to support the prevailing social order, but they are also contested. A critical politics joins in and foments this contest not just to reframe how we interpret the world but in order to change it. It is radical in the sense that it does not settle just for a change in the style or form of commodities but demands a change in the invisible social relations that make them possible.

I have tried to show that this way of reading is not just a matter of widening the scope of what we see, but of starting from a different place in how we see. Understanding social life to be "at once global and local" requires that we analyze what presents itself on first sight as obvious in order to show its connection to social structures that often exploit and oppress. While local situations (the commodification of pleasure in suburban malls, for instance) are necessary and important places to disrupt heteronormativity, they do not exist on their own, and we read them as such only at a cost. I am suggesting that a radical sexual politics that is going to be, in Judith Butler's words, "effectively disruptive, truly troubling," needs a way of explaining how the sexual identities we can see are systemically organized. We need a way of understanding visibility that acknowledges both the local situations in which sexuality is made intelligible as well as the ties that bind knowledge and power to commodity production, consumption, and exchange.

The critical way of reading I am proposing in this essay is indeed queer. If it is not very well received now in the academy or in activist circles – and it is not – that may be because in challenging the postmodern fetishizing of social life into discourse, culture, or local contexts, critique puts into crisis the investments of middle-class academics and professionals, queers among us, in the current social order. For this reason it is undoubtedly a risk. Perhaps it is also our best provisional answer to the question "what is to be done?"

Notes

For sharing her many resources and ideas and for her strong readings of various drafts of this essay, I want to thank Chrys Ingraham. I am also indebted to the students in graduate courses I taught in 1993 on the topics of Lesbian and Gay Theory and Critique of Commodity Culture at the University at Albany, SUNY. Their work inspired and challenged me and offered a critical forum for developing many of the arguments I present here.

1. For an astute analysis of the commodification of gay and lesbian culture see Gluckman and Reed 1993.
2. In *Bodies That Matter* (1993) Butler qualifies her earlier position by asserting that drag may not always be unproblematically subversive. Nonetheless, due to the theatrical gender trouble drag incites, it remains for her a commendable practice, perhaps the only viable form of political resistance to heterosexuality's regulatory power.
3. For a more detailed critique of Foucault's concept of discursive practice see Hennessy 1993, 37–46.
4. While the concept of the fetish has been taken up in some recent work in cultural theory (a few of the many recent examples include Adams 1989; Apter 1991; Findlay 1992; Mercer 1989), the relationship between Freud's theory of the fetish and Marx's theory of commodity fetishism has not been very rigorously addressed from a materialist perspective. Most analyses tend to draw upon one theoretical framework or the other, with the Freudian version receiving most attention. Zizek's work on ideology (1989), for example, makes use of Lacanian analysis and poststructuralist reconceptualizations of the social (vis à vis Laclau and Mouffe) to elaborate and extend the post-Marxist return to idealism in cultural theory; his endorsement of the Freudian concept of the fetish as "lack" ignores the possibility that the very notion of castration might be read as the effect of a positive network of (patriarchal) social relations.
5. For a much fuller elaboration of this distinction between the seeable and the visible and its bearing on the reception of film see Zavarzadeh 1991.
6. I have chosen this essay of de Lauretis's for its attention to issues of visibility but also because of its institutional impact which is indicated by its publishing history. Originally appearing in *Theatre Journal* (1988), it has since been reprinted in *Performing Feminisms* (Case 1990) and most recently in *The Lesbian and Gay Studies Reader* (Abelove, et al., 1993). The page numbers used here are from Abelove.
7. For summary-analyses of Queer Nation's history see Baker, et al. 1991; Berlant and Freeman 1992; Berube and Escoffier 1991; Bull 1992; Chee 1991; Duggan 1992; Signorile 1993, 88, 317–18; Smyth 1992. For more critical assessments see Fernandez 1991; Maggenti 1991; Mitchell and Olafimihan 1992; Smith 1993. Since 1992 Queer Nation, like ACT-UP, has been riven by internal strife over whether its focus and political actions

should also address issues of racism and sexism; as a result, several local chapters have been dissolved or fragmented.

8. For more extended lists of affinity groups see Berlant and Freeman 1992, 152 n. 3, and Berube and Escoffier 1991, 16.

9. For a more detailed analysis of the concept of nationhood in Queer Nation see Berlant and Freeman 1992.

10. Ann Cvetkovitch's chapter on *Capital* in her study of Victorian sensationalism (1992) offers an incisive reading of the relationship between visibility and the commodity.

11. On the SI see Knabb 1981; Marcus 1989; Plant 1992.

12. On the former connotations of lifestyle see Bourdieu 1984; Sobel 1982; Rojek 1985. On the latter see Ehrenreich 1989; Featherstone 1991.

13. See Callinicos 1989, 62–91 and 168–171, on the connection between poststructuralism and aestheticism, particularly in Foucault. See also Hennessy 1993, 55–59 on the relationship between the aesthetic and the ethical in Foucault.

14. For an elaboration of the concept of "heterogender" and its effects on the disciplining of knowledge see Ingraham 1994.

15. Grant Kester's fine essay (1993) on the imaginary space of postindustrial culture prompted my analysis of the class dimensions of visibility here; the phrase "out of sight, out of mind" is in part a reference to his title.

16. I am grateful to Catherine Sustana for pointing out to me the following detail: Levi-Strauss is owned by Robert Haas, the great-great-grandnephew of the company founder; when Haas staged a successful leveraged buyout to take the company private in 1985, profits rose by a staggering 31 percent (Sustana 1993).

17. Among the books that address the class dimension of lesbian and gay history and culture are: Bunch 1987; Faderman 1991; Kennedy and Davis 1993; Moraga 1983; Nestle 1987. Essays include D'Emilio 1983a; Franzen 1993; Weston and Rofel 1984.

18. On the relationship between (homo)sexuality and capitalism see Altman 1982; D'Emilio 1983a; Evans 1993. Most of the little work on gay poverty has, not accidentally, focused on lesbians and has circulated mostly in alternative/activist presses. Notable examples include Egerton 1990, Helmbold 1982, Levine 1992.

19. The accuracy of the federally funded Batelle Institute's findings has been questioned for a number of reasons: the study was aimed at addressing behavior related to AIDS, not homosexuality per se; the survey was based on self-reports from men; the interviewers were exclusively women who were not trained in sex research; and the questions about sex with men had a 30 percent non-response rate.

20. According to the US Bureau of the Census (1991) about 30 percent of the poor are black.

References

Abelda, Randy, Elaine McCrate, Edwin Melendez, June Lapidus, and the Center for Popular Economics. 1988. *Mink Coats Don't Trickle Down: The Economic Attack on Women and People of Color.* Boston: South End.

Abelove, Henry, Michele Aina Barale, and David Halperin, eds. 1993. *The Lesbian and Gay Studies Reader.* New York: Routledge.

Adams, Parveen. 1989. "Of Female Bondage." In *Between Feminism and Psychoanalysis*, ed. Teresa Brennan, 247–65. London: Routledge.

Altman, Dennis. 1982. *The Homosexualization of America.* Boston: Beacon Press.

Apter, Emily. 1991. *Feminizing the Fetish: Psychoanalysis and Narrative Obsession in Turn-of-the-Century France.* Ithaca, N. Y.: Cornell University Press.

Baker, James N., Anthony Duignan-Cabrera, Mark Miller, and Michael Mason. 1991. "What Is Queer Nation?" *Newsweek*, 12 Aug. 1991: 24.

Berlant, Lauren, and Elizabeth Freeman. 1992. "Queer Nationality." *boundary 2*, 19(1): 149–80.

Berube, Allan and Jeffrey Escoffier. 1991. "Queer Nation." *Out/Look*, 11: 12–14.

Bourdieu, Pierre. 1984. *Distinction: A Social Critique of the Judgement of Taste*, trans. R. Nice. London: Routledge and Kegan Paul.

Bull, Chris. 1992. "Queer Nation Goes on Hiatus in San Francisco." *Advocate*, 14 Jan. 1992: 24.

Bunch, Charlotte. 1987. *Passionate Politics.* New York: St. Martins.

Burger, Peter. 1984. *Theory of the Avant-Garde*, trans. Michael Shaw. Minneapolis: University of Minnesota Press.

Butler, Judith. 1990a. *Gender Trouble: Feminism and the Subversion of Identity.* New York: Routledge.

1990b. "Performative Acts and Gender Constitution: An Essay in Phenomenology and Feminist Theory." In *Performing Feminisms: Feminist Critical Theory and Theatre*, ed. Sue Ellen Case, 270–82. Baltimore: Johns Hopkins University Press.

1991. "Imitation and Gender Insubordination." In *Inside/Out: Lesbian Theories, Gay Theories*, ed. Diana Fuss. New York: Routledge.

1993. *Bodies That Matter: On the Discursive Limits of "Sex."* New York: Routledge.

Calinescue, Matei. 1987. *Five Faces of Modernity: Modernism, Avant-Garde, Decadence, Kitsch, Postmodernism.* Durham, N. C.: Duke University Press.

Callinicos, Alex. 1989. *Against Postmodernism: A Marxist Critique*. New York: St. Martins.

Case, Sue Ellen, ed. 1990. *Performing Feminisms: Feminist Critical Theory and Theatre*. Baltimore and London: Johns Hopkins University Press.

Chee, Alexander S. 1991. "Queer Nationalism." *Out/Look*, 11 (Winter): 15–19.

Clark, Danae. 1991. "Commodity Lesbianism." *Camera Obscura*, 25–26: 181–201.

Clarke, John. 1991. *Old Times, New Enemies: Essays on Cultural Studies and America*. London: Harper Collins.

Cvetkovich, Ann. 1992. *Mixed Feelings: Feminism, Mass Culture, and Victorian Sensationalism*. New Brunswick, N. J.: Rutgers University Press.

Darling, Lynn. 1993. "Single White Male Seeks Clue." *Esquire*, June 97–104.

De Lauretis, Teresa. 1991. "Film and the Visible." In *How Do I Look?*, ed. Bad Object Choices, 223–76. Seattle: Bay.

———. 1993. "Sexual Indifference and Lesbian Representation." In *The Lesbian and Gay Studies Reader*, ed. Henry Abelove, Michele Barale, and David Halperin, 141–58. New York: Routledge.

D'Emilio, John. 1983a. "Capitalism and Gay Identity." In *Powers of Desire: The Politics of Sexuality*, ed. Ann Snitow, Christine Stansell, and Sharon Thompson, 100–13. New York: Monthly Review.

———. 1983b. *Sexual Politics, Sexual Communities: The Making of a Homosexual Minority in the United States*. Chicago: University of Chicago Press.

Duggan, Lisa. 1992. "Making It Perfectly Queer." *Socialist Review*, 22 (1): 11–31.

Egerton, Jayne. 1990. "Out But Not Down: Lesbians' Experience of Housing." *Feminist Review*, 36 (Autumn): 75–88.

Ehrenreich, Barbara. 1989. *Fear of Falling: The Inner Life of the Middle Class*. New York: Harper.

Evans, David T. 1993. *Sexual Citizenship: The Material Construction of Sexualities*. London: Routledge.

Faderman, Lillian. 1991. *Odd Girls and Twilight Lovers: A History of Lesbian Life in Twentieth-Century America*. New York: Penguin.

Featherstone, Mike. 1991. *Consumer Culture and Postmodernism*. London: Sage.

Feinberg, Leslie. 1993. *Stone Butch Blues*. Ithaca, N. Y.: Firebrand.

Ferguson, Ann. 1989. *Blood at the Root: Motherhood, Sexuality, and Male Dominance*. London: Pandora.

Fernandez, Charles. 1991. "Undocumented Aliens in the Queer Nation." *Out/Look*, Spring: 20–23.

Findlay, Heather. 1992. "Freud's 'Fetishism' and the Lesbian Dildo Debates." *Feminist Studies*, 18.3: 563–79.

Foucault, Michel. 1983. "On the Genealogy of Ethics: An Overview of Work in Progress." In *Michel Foucault: Beyond Structuralism and Hermeneutics*, ed. Herbert Dreyfus and Paul Rabinow, 229–59. Chicago: University of Chicago Press.

———. 1990. *The History of Sexuality*, vol. 1, trans. Robert Hurley. New York: Vintage.

Franzen, Trisha. 1993. "Differences and Identities: Feminism and the Albuquerque Lesbian Community." *Signs*, 18.4 (Summer): 891–906.

Fuss, Diana. 1992. "Fashion and the Homospectatorial Look." *Critical Inquiry*, 18.4: 713–37.

Galst, Liz. 1992. "Throwaway Kids." *Advocate*, 29 December: 54.

Gluckman, Amy and Betsy Reed. 1993. "The Gay Marketing Moment." *Dollars and Sense*, Nov.–Dec.: 16–35.

Goldman, Robert. 1992. *Reading Ads Socially*. New York: Routledge.

Helmbold, Lois Rita. 1982. "Shopping Bag Lesbians." *Common Lives/Lesbian Lives*, 5 (Fall): 69–71.

Hennessy, Rosemary. 1993. *Materialist Feminism and the Politics of Discourse*. New York: Routledge.

Hooks, Bell. 1992. "Is Paris Burning?" In *Black Looks: Race and Representation*, 145–55. Boston: South End.

Ingraham, Chrys. 1994. "The Heterosexual Imaginary: Feminist Sociology and Theories of Gender." *Sociological Theory*, 12.2: 203–19.

Kamp, David. 1993. "The Straight Queer." *GQ*, July: 94–99.

Kennedy, Elizabeth Lapovsky, and Madeline D. Davis. 1993. *Boots of Leather, Slippers of Gold: The History of A Lesbian Community*. New York: Routledge.

Kester, Grant H. 1993. "Out of Sight Is Out of Mind: The Imaginary Spaces of Postindustrial Culture." *Social Text*, 35 (Summer): 72–92.

Knabb, Ken, ed. 1981. *Situationist International Anthology*. Berkeley: Bureau of Public Secrets.

Levine, Rebecca. 1992. "The Lesbian and Gay Prisoner Project: A Vital Connection." *Gay Community News*, 19.26: 5.

Maciones, John J. 1993 *Sociology*. Englewood Cliffs, N. J.: Prentice Hall.

Maggenti, Maria. 1991. "Women as Queer Nationals." *Out/Look*, 11: 20–23.

Marcus, Greil. 1989. *Lipstick Traces: A Secret History of the Twentieth Century*. Cambridge: Harvard University Press.

Martin, Richard. 1993. "The Gay Factor in Fashion." *Esquire Gentleman*, 13 July: 135.

Martinez, Elizabeth. 1993. "'Levi's, Button Your Fly – Your Greed Is Showing.'" *Z Magazine*, Jan.: 22–27.

Mercer, Kobena. 1989. "Skin Head Sex Thing." In *How Do I Look*, ed. Bad Object Choices, 169–222. Seattle: Bay.

Mitchell, Hugh, and Kayode Olafimihan. 1992. "Living." *Living Marxism*, Nov.: 38–39.

Moraga, Cherrie. 1983. *Loving in the War Years*. Boston: South End.

Nestle, Joan. 1987. *A Restricted Country*. Ithaca, N. Y.: Firebrand.

Nietzsche, Friedrich. 1974. *The Gay Science*. New York: Penguin.

Plant, Sadie. 1992. *The Most Radical Gesture: The Situationist International in a Postmodern Age*. London: Routledge.

Powers, Ann. 1993. "Queer in the Streets, Passing in the Sheets." *Village Voice*, 29 June: 24.

Rojek, Chris. 1985. *Capitalism and Leisure Theory*. London: Tavistock.

Shenon, Philip. 1993. "Saipan Sweatshops Are No American Dream." *New York Times*, 18 July: 1.

Signorile, Michelangelo. 1993. *Queer in America: Sex, the Media, and the Closets of Power*. New York: Random House.

Smith, Barbara. 1993. "Where's the Revolution?" *Nation*, 5 July: 12–16.

Smyth, Cherry. 1992. *Queer Notions*. London: Scarlet.

Sobel, E. 1982. *Lifestyle*. New York: Academic Press.

Stewart, Thomas. 1991. "Gay in Corporate America." *Fortune*, 16 Dec.: 42.

Sustana, Catherine. 1993. "The Production of the Corporate Subject." Conference on Literary/Critical Cultural Studies. University at Albany, SUNY, December.

Tobias, Andrew. 1992. "Three Dollar Bills." *Time*, 23 Mar.

Warner, Michael. 1993. "Introduction." *Fear of A Queer Planet*. Minneapolis, Minn.: University of Minnesota Press.

Weston, Kathleen and Lisa Rofel. 1984. "Sexuality, Class, and Conflict in a Lesbian Workplace." *Signs*, 9.4 (Summer): 623–46.

Williams, Raymond. 1989. *The Politics of Modernism*. London: Verso.

Zavarzadeh, Mas'ud. 1991. *Seeing Films Politically*. Albany, N.Y.: State University of New York Press.

Zizek, Slavoj. 1989. *The Sublime Object of Ideology*. London: Verso.

PART III

Postmodern approaches to the social

7

Gender as seriality: thinking about women as a social collective

Iris Marion Young

In the summer of 1989 I worked in Shirley Wright's campaign for a seat on the Worcester School Committee. Shirley is African-American in a city where about 5–7 percent of the population are African-American, and 7–10 percent are Hispanic. As in many other cities, however, more than 35 percent of the children in the public schools are black, Hispanic, or Asian, and the proportion of children of color is growing rapidly. For more than ten years all six of the school committee seats have been held by white people, and only one woman has served, for about two years. In her announcement speech Shirley Wright pledged to represent all the people of Worcester. But she noted the particular need to represent minorities, and she also emphasized the importance of representing a woman's voice on the committee.

A few weeks later a friend and I distributed Shirley Wright flyers outside a grocery store. The flyers displayed a photo of Shirley and some basics about her qualifications and issues. In the course of the morning at least two women, both white, exclaimed to me, "I'm so glad to see a woman running for school committee!" This African-American woman claimed to speak for women in Worcester, and some white women noticed and felt affinity with her as a woman.

This seemed to me at the time an unremarkable, easily understandable affinity. Recent discussions among feminists about the difficulties and dangers of talking about women as a single group, however, make such incidents appear at least puzzling. These discussions have cast doubt on the project of conceptualizing women as a group, arguing that the search for the common characteristics of women or of women's oppression leads to normalizations and exclusions. While I agree with such critiques, I also agree with those who argue that there are pragmatic political reasons for insisting on the possibility of thinking about women as some kind of group.

Clearly, these two positions pose a dilemma for feminist theory. On the one hand, without some sense in which "woman" is the name of a social collective, there is nothing specific to feminist politics. On the other hand, any effort to identify the attributes of that collective appears to undermine feminist politics by leaving out some women whom feminists ought to include. To solve this dilemma I argue for reconceptualizing social collectivity or the meaning of social groups as what Sartre describes as a phenomenon of serial collectivity in his *Critique of Dialectical Reason* (1976). Such a way of thinking about women, I will argue, allows us to see women as a collective without identifying common attributes that all women have or implying that all women have a common identity.

I

Doubts about the possibility of saying that women can be thought of as one social collective arose from challenges to a generalized conception of gender and women's oppression by women of color, in both the Northern and Southern hemispheres, and by lesbians. Black, Latina, Asian, and indigenous women demonstrated that white feminist theory and rhetoric tended to be ethnocentric in its analysis of gender experience and oppression. Lesbians, furthermore, persistently argued that much of this analysis relied on the experience of heterosexual women. The influence of philosophical deconstruction completed the suspension of the category of "women" begun by this process of political differentiation. Exciting theorizing has shown (not for the first time) the logical problems in efforts to define clear, essential categories of being. Let me review some of the most articulate recent statements of the claim that feminists should abandon or be very suspicious of a general category of woman or female gender.

Elizabeth Spelman (1988) shows definitively the mistake in any attempt to isolate gender from identities such as race, class, age, sexuality, and ethnicity to uncover the attributes, experiences, or oppressions that women have in common. To be sure, we have no trouble identifying ourselves as women, white, middle class, Jewish, American, and so on. But knowing the "right" labels to call ourselves and others does not imply the existence of any checklist of attributes that all those with the same label have in common. The absurdity of trying to isolate gender identity from race or class identity becomes apparent if you ask any individual woman whether she can distinguish the "woman part" of herself from the "white part" or the "Jewish part." Feminist theorists nevertheless have often assumed that the distinctive and specific attributes of gender can be identified by holding race and class constant or by examining the lives of women who suffer only sexist oppression and not also oppressions of race, class, age, or sexuality.

The categories according to which people are identified as the same or different, Spelman suggests, are social constructs that reflect no natures or essences. They carry and express relations of privilege and subordination, the power of some to determine for others how they will be named, what differences are important for what purposes. Because it has been assumed that women form a single group with common experiences, attributes, or oppressions, much feminist theorizing has exhibited privileged points of view by unwittingly taking the experience of white middle-class heterosexual women as representative for all women. Even when feminists attempt to take account of differences among women, moreover, they often manifest such biases because they fail to notice the race or class specificity of white middle-class women and how these also modify our gender. Much feminist talk about paying attention to differences among women, Spelman points out, tends to label only women of color or old women or disabled women as "different."

Chandra Talpade Mohanty believes that the "assumption of women as an already constituted, coherent group with identical interests and desires, regardless of class, ethnic or racial location, or contradictions, implies a notion of gender or sexual difference or even patriarchy which can be applied universally or even cross-culturally" (1991, 55). She believes that this category of "woman" as designating a single, coherent, already constituted group influences feminists to regard all women as equally powerless and oppressed victims. Rather than developing questions about how and whether women in a particular time and place suffer discrimination and limitation on their action and desires, questions that can then be empirically investigated, the assumption of universal gender categories bypasses such empirical investigation by finding oppression a priori. This tendency is especially damaging in the way European and American feminists think and write about women in the Southern and Eastern hemispheres. Assumptions about a homogeneous category of women helps create a homogeneous category of Third World women who stand as the other to Western feminists, who define Third World women as powerless victims of patriarchy.

Judith Butler draws more explicitly on postmodern theories to argue against the viability of the category of "woman" and of gender (1990).

In a Foucauldian mode, Butler argues that the idea of gender identity and the attempt to describe it has a normalizing power. The very act of defining a gender identity excludes or devalues some bodies, practices, and discourses at the same time that it obscures the constructed, and thus contestable, character of that gender identity.

Feminism has assumed that it can be neither theoretical nor political without a subject. Female gender identity and experience delineate that subject. Feminist politics, it is assumed, speaks for or in the name of someone, the group women, who are defined by this female gender identity.

The category of gender was promoted by feminism precisely to criticize and reject traditional efforts to define women's nature through "biological" sex. In its own way, however, according to Butler, gender discourse tends to reify the fluid and shifting social processes in which people relate, communicate, play, work, and struggle with one another over the means of production and interpretation. The insistence on a subject for feminism obscures the social and discursive production of identities.

In one of the most important arguments of her book, Butler shows that the feminist effort to distinguish sex and gender itself contributes to such obscuring by ignoring the centrality of enforced heterosexuality in the social construction of gender. However variable its content is understood to be, the form of gender differentiation is always a binary opposition between the masculine and the feminine. Inasmuch as sexual difference is classified only as man and woman, then, gender always mirrors sex. The binary complementarity of this sex/gender system is required and makes sense, however, only with the assumption of heterosexual complementarity. Gender identification thus turns out not to be a culturally variable overlay on a pregiven biological sex; rather, the categories of gender construct sexual difference itself. "Gender can delineate a *unity* of experience, of sex, gender and desire, only when sex can be understood in some sense to necessitate gender. The internal coherence or unity of either gender, man or woman, thereby requires both a stable and oppositional heterosexuality. Thus we see the political reasons for substantializing gender" (Butler 1990, 23).

This mutual reinforcement of (hetero)sex and gender as fixed categories suppresses any ambiguities and incoherences among heterosexual, homosexual, and bisexual practices. This unity of sex and gender organizes the variability of desiring practices along a single scale of normal and deviant behavior. Butler concludes that feminism's attempt to construct or speak for a subject, to forge the unity of coalition from the diversities of history and practice, will always lead to such ossifications. The primary task for feminist theory and politics is critical: to formulate genealogies that show how a given category of practice is socially constructed. Feminist discourse and practice should become and remain open, its totality permanently deferred, accepting and affirming the flows and shifts in the contingent relations of social practices and institutions.

These analyses are powerful and accurate. They identify ways that essentializing assumptions and the point of view of privileged women dominate much feminist discourse, even when it tries to avoid such hegemonic moves. They draw important lessons for any future feminist theorizing that wishes to avoid excluding some women from its theories or freezing contingent social relations into a false necessity. But I find the exclusively critical orientation of such arguments rather paralyzing. Do these arguments imply that it makes no sense and is morally wrong ever to talk about women as a group or, in fact, to talk about social groups at all? It is not clear that these writers claim this. If not, then what can it mean to use the term "*woman*"? More important, in the light of these critiques, what sort of positive claims can feminists make about the way social life is and ought to be? I find questions like these unaddressed by these critiques of feminist essentialism.

II

What is the genealogy of the essentializing discourse that established a normative feminist subject, woman, that excluded, devalued, or found deviant the lives and practices of many women? Like most discursive constructs, this one is overdetermined. But I suggest that one important source of the oppressive and paradoxical consequences of conceptualizing women as a group is the adoption of a *theoretical* stance. In large part feminist discourse about gender was motivated by the desire to establish a countertheory to Marxism, to develop a feminist theory that would conceive sex or gender as a category with as much theoretical weight as class. This desire employs a totalizing impulse. What *is* a woman? What *is* woman's social position such that it is not reducible to class? Are all societies structured by male domination, and of the same form or of variable forms? What are the origins and causes of this male domination?

These are all general and rather abstract theoretical questions. By "theory" I mean a kind of discourse that aims to be comprehensive, to give a systematic account and explanation of social relations as a whole. A theory tries to tell the way things are in some universal sense. From it one can derive particular instances or at least one can apply the theoretical propositions to particular facts that the theory's generalities are supposed to cover. A social theory is self-enclosed, in the sense that it offers no particular purpose other than to understand, to reveal the way things are.

Despite much work in the last twenty years to make such theories, feminists do not need and should not want theory in this sense. Instead, we should take a more pragmatic orientation to our intellectual discourse. By being pragmatic I mean categorizing, explaining, developing accounts and arguments that are tied to specific practical and political problems, where the purpose of this theoretical activity is clearly related to those problems (see, e.g., Bordo 1989). Pragmatic theorizing in this sense is not necessarily any less complex or sophisticated than totalizing theory, but rather it is driven by some problem that has ultimate practical importance and is not concerned to give an account of a whole. In this article I take the pragmatic problem to be a political dilemma generated by feminist critiques of the concept of "woman," and I aim to solve it by articulating some concepts without claiming to provide an entire social theory.

From this pragmatic point of view, I wish to ask, why does it matter whether we even consider conceptualizing women as a group? One reason to conceptualize women as a collective, I think, is to maintain a point of view outside of liberal individualism. The discourse of liberal individualism denies the reality of groups. According to liberal individualism, categorizing people in groups by race, gender, religion, and sexuality and acting as though these ascriptions say something significant about the person, his or her experience, capacities, and possibilities, is invidious and oppressive. The only liberatory approach is to think of and treat people as individuals, variable and unique. This individualist ideology, however, in fact obscures oppression. Without conceptualizing women as a group in some sense, it is not possible to conceptualize oppression as a systematic, structured, institutional process. If we obey the injunction to think of people only as individuals, then the disadvantages and exclusions we call oppressions reduce to individuals in one of two ways. Either we blame the victims and say that the disadvantaged person's choices and capacities render them less competitive, or we attribute their disadvantage to the attitudes of other individuals, who for whatever reason don't "like" the disadvantaged ones. In either case structural and political ways to address and rectify the disadvantage are written out of the discourse, leaving individuals to wrestle with their bootstraps. The importance of being able to talk about disadvantage and oppression in terms of groups exists just as much for those oppressed through race, class, sexuality, ethnicity, and the like as through gender (Young 1990, ch. 2).

The naming of women as a specific and distinct social collective, moreover, is a difficult achievement and one that gives feminism its specificity as a political movement. The possibility of conceptualizing ethnic, religious, cultural, or national groups, for example, rarely comes into question because their social existence itself usually involves some common traditions – language, or rituals, or songs and stories, or dwelling place. Women, however, are dispersed among all these groups. The operations of most marriage and kinship forms bring women under the identity of men in each and all of these groups, in the privacy of household and bed. The exclusions, oppressions, and disadvantages that women often suffer can hardly be thought of at all without a structural conception of women as a collective social position. The first step in feminist resistance to such oppressions is the affirmation of women as a group, so that women can cease to be divided and to believe that their sufferings are natural or merely personal. Denial of the reality of a social collective termed women reinforces the privilege of those who benefit from keeping women divided (Lange 1991).

Feminist politics evaporates, that is, without some conception of women as a social collective. Radical politics may remain as a commitment to social justice for all people, among them those called women. Yet the claim that feminism expresses a distinct politics allied with anti-imperialism, antiracism, and gay liberation but asking a unique set of enlightening questions about a distinct axis of social oppression cannot be sustained without some means of conceptualizing women and gender as social structures.

The logical and political difficulties inherent in the attempt to conceptualize women as a single group with a set of common attributes and shared identity appear to be insurmountable. Yet if we cannot conceptualize women as a group, feminist politics appears to lose any meaning. Is there a way out of this dilemma? Recent feminist discussions of this problem have presented two strategies for solving it: the attempt to theorize gender identity as multiple rather than binary and the argument that women constitute a group only in the politicized context of feminist struggle. I shall argue now that both of these strategies fail.

Spelman herself explores the strategy of multiple genders. She does not dispense with the category of gender but, instead, suggests that a woman's gender identity and gender attributes are different according to what race, class, religion, and the like she belongs to. Gender, she argues, is a relational concept, not the naming of an essence. One finds the specific characteristics and attributes of the gender identity of women by comparing their situation with that of men. But if one wishes to locate the gender-based oppression of women, it is wrong to compare all women with all men. For some women are definitely privileged when compared to some men. To find the gender-specific attributes of a woman's experience, Spelman suggests, one must restrict the comparison to men and women of the same race or class or nationality. Women of different races or classes, moreover, often have opposing gender attributes. In this reasoning, women as such cannot be said to be a group. Properly designated groups are "white women," "black women," "Jewish women," "working-class women," "Brazilian women," each with specific gender characteristics (Spelman 1988, 170–78).

In a recent paper Ann Ferguson proposes a similar solution to the contradictions and quandaries that arise when feminists assume that all women share a common identity and set of gendered attributes. "Instead of a concept of sisterhood based on a shared gender identity," she suggests, "it may be more helpful to posit different racial gender positions, and possibly different class gender positions. Processes of racialization in US history have created at least ten gender identities informed with racial difference if we consider the various subordinate races: black, Latino, Native American, and Asian, as well as the dominant white race" (Ferguson 1991, 114–15).

There is much to recommend this concept of multiple genders as a way of describing the differentiations and contradictions in the social experience of gender. The idea of multiple genders highlights the fact that not all men are equally privileged by gender. It also makes clear that some women are privileged in relation to some men, a privilege that derives partly from their gender. It allows the theorist to look for race or class in specific gender interactions and expectations without essentializing them. Multiple gender conceptualization may also address the problems of binarism and heterosexism that Butler finds in gender theory. According to a concept of multiple genders, the gender identity of lesbians, for example, can be conceptualized as different from that of straight women.

Despite its promising virtues, the strategy of multiplying gender also has some dangers. First, it is just not true, as Spelman suggests, that gender relations are structured primarily within a class, race, nationality, and so on. A working-class woman's gendered experience and oppression is not properly identified only by comparing her situation to working-class men. Much of her gendered experience is conditioned by her relation to middle-class or ruling-class men. If she experiences sexual harassment at work, for example, her harasser is at least as likely to be a middle-class professional man as a working-class assembler or delivery man. Examples of such cross-class or cross-race relations between men and women can be multiplied. In such relations it would be false to say that the class or race difference is not as important as the gender difference, but it would be equally false to say that the cross-class or cross-race relations between men and women are not gendered relations. But if we conceive of an African-American feminine gender, for example, as having one set of attributes in relation to African-American men and another in relation to white men, one of two things results: either we need to multiply genders further or we need to draw back and ask what makes both of these genders womanly.

Second, the idea of multiple genders presumes a stability and unity to the categories of race, religion, and ethnicity that divide women. To conceptualize "American Indian woman" as a single identity different from "white woman," we must implicitly assume "American Indian" or "white" as stable categories. As Bordo (1989) points out, feminist arguments against conceptualizing women as a single group often privilege categories of race or class, failing to challenge the appropriateness of these group categories. But the same arguments against considering these categories as unities can be used as the arguments against thinking about women as a unity. American Indians are divided by class, region, religion, sexuality, and ethnicity as well as by gender. Working-class people are divided by race, ethnicity, region, religion, and sexuality as well as by gender. The idea of multiple genders can solve the problems and paradoxes involved in conceptualizing women as a group only by presuming categorical unities to class and race.

This last point leads to the final objection to the idea of multiple genders. This strategy can generate an infinite regress that dissolves groups into individuals. Any category can be considered an arbitrary unity. Why claim that black women, for example, have a distinct and unified gender identity? Black women are American, Haitian, Jamaican, African, Northern, Southern, poor, working class, lesbian, or old. Each of these divisions may be important to a particular woman's gender identity. But then we are back to the question of what it means to call her a woman. The strategy of multiple genders, then, while useful in directing attention to the social specificities of gender differentiation and gender interaction, does not resolve the dilemma I have posed. Instead, it seems to swing back and forth between the two poles of that dilemma.

Some feminist theorists propose "identity politics" as a different answer to the criticism of essentializing gender while retaining a conception of women as a group. According to this view, an identity "*woman*" that unites subjects into a group is not a natural or social given but rather the fluid construct of a political movement, feminism. Thus Diana Fuss agrees that "*woman*" cannot name a set of attributes that a group of individuals has in common, that there is not a single female gender identity that defines the social experience of womanhood. Instead, she holds, feminist politics itself creates an identity "*woman*" out of a coalition of diverse female persons dispersed across the world. "Coalition politics precedes class and determines its limits and boundaries; we cannot identify a group of women until various social, historical, political conditions construct the conditions and possibilities for membership. Many anti-essentialists fear that positing a political coalition of *women* risks presuming that there must first be a natural class of women; but this belief only makes the fact that it is coalition politics which constructs the category of women (and men) in the first place" (Fuss 1989, 36).

Interpreting the theoretical writings of several black feminist writers, Nancie Caraway proposes a similar understanding of women as a group. She argues that unity and solidarity among women is a product of political discussion and struggle among people of diverse backgrounds, experiences, and interests who are differently situated in matrices of power and privilege. The process of discussion and disagreement among feminists forges a common commitment to a politics against oppression that produces the identity "woman" as a coalition. Thus, says Caraway, "Identity politics advances a space for political action, praxis, justified by the critical *positioning* of the marginalized subjects against hierarchies of power – the Enlightenment promise of transcendence . . . These emerging theories are codes about the fluid construction of identity. They are not racially specific; they speak to both white and Black feminists about the shared and differentiated faces of female oppression" (1989, 9).

The identity-politics position has some important virtues. It rightly recognizes that the perception of a common identity among persons must be the product of a social or political process that brings them together around a purpose. It retains a conception of women as a group that it believes feminist politics needs, at the same time clearly rejecting an essentialist or substantive conception of gender identity. There are, however, at least two problems with identity politics as a way to get out of the dilemma I have articulated.

Judith Butler points out the first. Even though identity politics' coalition politics and deconstructive discourse avoids the substantialization of gender, the dangers of normalization are not thereby also avoided. The feminist politics that produces a coalition of mutually identifying women nevertheless privileges some norms or experiences over others. Thus Butler suggests that feminist politics should be suspicious of settling into a unified coalition. The question of solidarity should never be settled, and identities should shift and be deconstructed in a play of possibilities that excludes no one.

My second objection to the idea that women are a group only as the construction of feminist politics is that it seems to make feminist politics arbitrary. Some women choose to come together in a political movement, to form themselves as a group of mutually identifying agents. But on the basis of what do they come together? What are the social conditions that have motivated the politics? Perhaps even more important, do feminist politics leave out women who do not identify as feminists? These questions all point to the need for some conception of women as a group prior to the formation of self-conscious feminist politics, as designating a certain set of relations or positions that motivate the particular politics of feminism.

III

Stories like Shirley Wright's race for school committee remind us that everyday language seems to be able to talk about women as a collective in some sense, even though women's experiences vary considerably by class, race, sexuality, age, or society. But Spelman, Mohanty, Butler, and others are right to criticize the exclusionary and normalizing implications of most attempts to theorize this everyday experience. We want and need to describe women as a group, yet it appears that we cannot do so without being normalizing and essentialist.

I propose a way out of this dilemma through a use of the concept of seriality that Sartre develops in his *Critique of Dialectical Reason*. I propose that we understand gender as referring to a social series, a specific kind of social collectivity that Sartre distinguishes from groups. Understanding gender as seriality, I suggest, has several virtues. It provides a way of thinking about women as a social collective without requiring that all women have common attributes or a common situation.

Gender as seriality, moreover, does not rely on identity or self-identity for understanding the social production and meaning of membership in collectives.

One might well question any project that appropriates Sartrian philosophy positively for feminist theory (see Murphy 1989). Much of Sartre's writing is hopelessly sexist and male-biased. This is certainly manifest in his theorization and functionalization of heterosexual relations. Perhaps more fundamentally, Sartre's early existentialist ontology presumes human relations as oppositional, egoistical, and basically violent. While his later philosophy on which I will draw is less individualistic than his early philosophy, the later thinking retains the assumption of human relations as latently violent. In it, boxing is a paradigm of the relation of self and other as mediated by a third.

Although Sartre's writing is sexist and his ontological assumptions about human relations tend to derive from masculine experience, I nevertheless have found the idea of seriality in particular, and its distinction from other kinds of social collective, of use in thinking about women as a collective. Linda Singer has talked about the feminist philosopher as a "Bandita," an intellectual outlaw who raids the texts of male philosophers and steals from them what she finds pretty or useful, leaving the rest behind (1992). I aim to approach Sartre's texts with the spirit of this Bandita, taking and rearticulating for my purposes the concepts I think will help resolve the dilemma I have posed. In doing so I need not drag all of Sartre with me, and I may be "disloyal" to him.

In the *Critique of Dialectical Reason*, Sartre distinguishes several levels of social collectivity by their order of internal complexity and reflexivity. For the purposes of addressing the problem of thinking about women as a social collective, the important distinction is between a group and a series. A group is a collection of persons who recognize themselves and one another as in a unified relation with one another. Members of the group mutually acknowledge that together they undertake a common project. Members of the group, that is, are united by action that they undertake together. In acknowledging oneself as a member of the group, an individual acknowledges oneself as oriented toward the same goals as the others; each individual thereby assumes the common project as a project for his or her individual action. What makes the project shared, however, is the mutual acknowledgement among the members of the group that they are engaged in the project together; this acknowledgement usually becomes explicit at some point in a pledge, contract, constitution, set of bylaws, or statement of purpose. The project of the group is a collective project, moreover, insofar as the members of the group mutually acknowledge that it can only be or is best undertaken by a group – storming the Bastille, staging an international women's conference, achieving women's suffrage, building an amphitheater (Sartre 1976, bk. 2, secs. 1, 2, and 3).[1]

So far in this article I have used the term "group" loosely, as does ordinary language, to designate any collection of people. Since my theorizing about women depends on Sartre's distinction between group and series, however, from now on in this article I shall reserve the term "group" for the self-consciously, mutually acknowledging collective with a self-conscious purpose. Much of an individual's life and action takes place in and is structured by a multitude of groups in this sense. Not all structured social action occurs in groups, however. As Sartre explains it, groups arise from and often fall back into a less organized and unself-conscious collective unity, which he calls a series.

Within Sartre's conception of human freedom, all social relations must be understood as the production of action. Unlike a group, which forms around actively shared objectives, a series is a social collective whose members are unified passively by the objects around which their actions are oriented or by the objectified results of the material effects of the actions of the others. In everyday life we often experience ourselves and others impersonally, as participating in amorphous collectives defined by routine practices and habits. The unity of the series derives from the way that individuals pursue their own individual ends with respect to the same objects conditioned by a continuous material environment, in response to structures that have been created by the unintended collective result of past actions.

Sartre describes people waiting for a bus as such a series. They are a collective insofar as they minimally relate to one another and follow the rules of bus waiting. As a collective they are brought together by their relation to a material object, the bus, and the social practices of public transportation. Their actions and goals may be different, and they have nothing necessarily in common in their histories, experiences, or identity. They are united only by their desire to ride on that route. Though they are in this way a social collective, they do not identify with one another, do not affirm themselves as engaged in a shared enterprise, or identify themselves with common experiences. The latent potential of this series to organize itself as a group will become manifest, however, if the bus fails to come; they will complain to one another about the lousy bus service, share horror stories of lateness and breakdowns, perhaps assign one of their number to go call the company, or discuss sharing a taxi.

Such serial collectivity, according to Sartre, is precisely the obverse of the mutual identification typical of the group. Each goes about his or her own business. But each is also aware of the serialized context of that activity in a social collective whose structure constitutes them within certain limits and constraints. In seriality, a person not only experiences others but also himself or herself as an Other, that is, as an anonymous someone: "Everyone is the same as the other insofar as he is Other than himself" (Sartre 1976, 260). Individuals in the series are interchangeable; while not identical, from the point of view of the social practices and objects that generate the series, the individuals could be in one another's place. It is contingent that I am third in line for the bus today. Thus in the series individuals are isolated but not alone. They understand themselves as constituted as a collective, as serialized, by the objects and practices through which they aim to accomplish their individual purposes. Often their actions take into account their expectations of the behavior of others in the series whom they nevertheless do not encounter. For example, I ask for a later schedule at work so that I will miss the crowd of bus riders at the rush hour.

Sartre uses the example of radio listening to illustrate some of the characteristics of seriality. The collective of radio listeners is constituted by their individual orientation toward objects, in this case radios and their material possibilities of sound transmission. As listeners they are isolated, but nevertheless they are aware of being part of a series of radio listeners, of others listening simultaneously linked to them indirectly through broadcasting. One's experience of radio listening is partly conditioned by the awareness of being linked to others from whom one is separated and of serving as other for them. Frequently the radio announcer explicitly refers to the serialized being of the listeners.

Sartre calls the series a practico-inert reality. The series is structured by actions linked to practico-inert objects. Social objects and their effects are the results of human action; they are practical. But as material they also constitute constraints on and resistances to action that make them experienced as inert. The built environment is a practico-inert reality. The products of human decision and action daily used by and dwelt in by people, the streets and buildings, are inert. Their material qualities enable and constrain many aspects of action.

Sartre calls the system of practico-inert objects and the material results of actions in relation to them that generate and are reproduced by serial collectives the milieu of action. The milieu is the already-there set of material things and collectivized habits against the background of which any particular action occurs. Thus for the series, commuters, for example, the milieu is the totality of the structured relations of the physical space of streets and rail lines, together with the predictable traffic patterns that emerge from the confluence of individual actions, together with the rules, habits, and cultural idiosyncracies of driving, riding, and walking.

Serialized action within the milieu results in *counterfinalities*: the confluence of individual intentional actions to produce a result that is counter to some purposes and that no one intended. Within a certain kind of milieu the series commuters will produce a gridlock; each individual driver pursues his or her own individual ends under material conditions that eventually makes a large cluster of them unable to move.

The collective otherness of serialized existence is thus often experienced as constraint, as felt necessities that often are experienced as given or natural. Members of the series experience themselves as powerless to alter this material milieu, and they understand that the others in the series are equally constrained. "A series reveals itself to everyone when they perceive in themselves and Others their common inability to eliminate their material differences" (Sartre 1976, 277). At the same time, the material milieu and objects are conditions of enablement for action. Objectives can be realized only through the mediation of already-there things, practices, and structures. A market is paradigmatic of such structured relations of alienation and anonymity that are felt as constraints on everyone. I take my corn to market in hopes of getting a good price, knowing that some people are trading on its price in a futures market and that other farmers bring their corn as well. We know that by bringing our large quantity of corn that we contribute to a fall in its price, and we might each play the futures market ourselves. But we are all equally as individuals unable to alter the collective results of these individual choices, choices that themselves have been made partly because of our expectations of what is happening to market prices.

Membership in serial collectives defines an individual's being, in a sense – one "is" a farmer, or a commuter, or a radio listener, and so on, together in series with others similarly positioned. But the definition is anonymous, and the unity of the series is amorphous, without determinate limits, attributes, or intentions. Sartre calls it a unity "in flight," a collective gathering that slips away at the edges, whose qualities and characteristics are impossible to pin down because they are an inert result of the confluence of actions. There is no concept of the series, no specific set of attributes that form the sufficient conditions for membership in it. Who belongs to the series of bus riders? Only those riding today? Those who regularly ride? Occasionally? Who may ride buses and know the social practices of bus riding? While serial membership delimits and constrains an individual's possible actions, it does not define the person's identity in the sense of forming his or her individual purposes, projects, and sense of self in relation to others.

Thus far the examples of seriality have been rather simple and one-dimensional. Sartre's theoretical purpose in developing the concept, however, is to describe the meaning of social class. Most of the time what it means to be a member of the working class or the capitalist class is to live in series with others in that class through a complex interlocking set of objects, structures, and practices in relation to work, exchange, and consumption.

Class-being does not define a person's identity, however, because one is a class member in a mode of otherness, otherness to oneself in one's subjectivity. If one says "I am a worker" in naming serialized class-being, this does not designate a felt and internalized identity but a social facticity about the material conditions of one's life. (To be sure, one can, and many do, say, "I am a worker," as a badge of pride and identity. But when this happens the class-being is not experienced in seriality; rather, one has formed a *group* with other workers with whom one has established self-conscious bonds of solidarity.) As serialized, class lies as a historical and materialized background to individual lives. A person is born into a class in the sense that a history of class relations precedes one, and the characteristics of the work that one will do or not do are already inscribed in machines, the physical structure of factories and offices, the geographic relations of city and suburb. An individual encounters other members of the class as alienated others, separated from one through the materiality of the things that define and delimit his or her class being – the factory with its machines, the physical movements and demands of the production process, the residential districts, buses, and highways that bring the workers into contact. As class members the individuals are relatively interchangeable, and nothing defines them as workers but the practico-inert constraints on their actions that they find themselves powerless to change. "If you want to eat, then you have to get a job," expresses the anonymous constraints on anyone who lacks independent means of support.

Let me now summarize the major elements in the concept of seriality. A series is a collective whose members are unified passively by the relation their actions have to material objects and practico-inert histories. The practico-inert milieu, within which and by means of whose structures individuals realize their aims, is experienced as constraints on the mode and limits of action. To be said to be part of the same series it is not necessary to identify a set of common attributes that every member has, because their membership is defined not by something they are but rather by the fact that in their diverse existences and actions they are oriented around the same objects or practico-inert structures. Membership in the series does not define one's identity. Each member of the series is isolated, other to the others, and as a member of the series other than themselves. Finally, there is no concept of the series within attributes that clearly demarcate what about individuals makes them belong. The series is a blurry, shifting unity, an amorphous collective.

Seriality designates a level of social life and action, the level of habit and the unreflective reproduction of ongoing historical social structures. Self-conscious groups arise from and on the basis of serialized existence, as a reaction to it and an active reversal of its anonymous and isolating conditions. Next I shall examine how gender is seriality and then explain the relationship between groups of women and the series, women.

IV

Applying the concept of seriality to gender, I suggest, makes theoretical sense out of saying that "women" is a reasonable social category expressing a certain kind of social unity. At the same time, conceptualizing gender as a serial collectivity avoids the problems that emerge from saying that women are a single group.

As I explained earlier, seriality designates a certain *level* of social existence and relations with others, the level of routine, habitual action, which is rule-bound and socially structured but serves as a prereflective background to action. Seriality is lived as medium or as milieu, where action is directed at particular ends that presuppose the series without taking them up self-consciously.

Thus, as a series "woman" is the name of a structural relation to material objects as they have been produced and organized by a prior history. But the series "women" is not as simple and one-dimensional as bus riders or radio listeners. Gender, like class, is a vast, multifaceted, layered, complex, and overlapping set of structures and objects. "Women" are the individuals who are positioned as feminine by the activities surrounding those structures and objects.

The loose unity of the series, I have said, derives from the fact that individuals' actions are oriented toward the same or similarly structured objects. What are the practico-inert realities that construct gender? Clearly female bodies have something to do with the constitution of the series "women" but it is not merely the physical facts of these female bodies themselves – attributes of breasts, vaginas, clitorises, and so on – that constructs female gender. Social objects are not merely physical but also inscribed by and the products of past practices. The female body as a practico-inert object toward which action is oriented is a rule-bound body, a body with understood meanings and possibilities. Menstruation, for example, is a regular biological event occurring in most female bodies within a certain age range. It is not this biological process alone, however, that locates individuals in the series of women. Rather, the social rules of menstruation, along with the material objects associated with menstrual practices, constitute the activity within which the women live as serialized. One can say the same about biological events like pregnancy, childbirth, and lactation.

The structure of the social body defining these bodily practices, however, is enforced heterosexuality. The meanings, rules, practices, and assumptions of institutionalized heterosexuality constitute the series, women, as in a relation of potential appropriation by men. Likewise the series "men" appears in the structures of enforced heterosexuality. The assumptions and practices of heterosexuality define the meaning of bodies – vaginas, clitorises, penises – not as mere physical objects but as practico-inert.

Even one so anti-essentialist as Gayatri Chakravorty Spivak locates heterosexuality as a set of material-ideological facts that constitute women cross-culturally. The material practices of enforced hetero-sexuality serialize women as objects of exchange and appropriation by men, with a consequent repression of autonomous active female desire. In Spivak's terms, "In legally defining woman as object of exchange, passage, or possession in terms of reproduction, it is not only the womb that is literally 'appropriated'; it is the clitoris and signifier of the sexed object that is effaced. All historical theoretical investigation into the definition of women as legal object – in or out of marriage; or as politico-economic passageway for property and legitimacy would fall within the investigation of the varieties of the effacement of the clitoris" (1987, 151).

Bodies, however, are only one of the practico-inert objects that position individuals in the gender series. A vast complex of other objects and materialized historical products condition women's lives as gendered. Pronouns locate individual people, along with animals and other objects, in a gender system. Verbal and visual representations more generally create and reproduce gender meanings that condition a person's action and her interpretation of the actions of others. A multitude of artifacts and social spaces in which people act are flooded with gender codes. Clothes are the primary example, but there are also cosmetics, tools, even in some cases furniture and spaces that materially inscribe the norms of gender. I may discover myself "as a woman" by being on the "wrong" dorm floor.

What usually structures the gendered relation of these practico-inert objects is a sexual division of labor. Though their content varies with each social system, a division of at least some tasks and activities by sex appears as a felt necessity. The division between caring for babies and bodies, and not doing so, is the most common sexual division of labor, over which many other labor divisions are layered in socially specific ways. Other sexual divisions of tasks and activities are more arbitrary but, in practice, also felt as natural. (Think, e.g., about the genderization of football and field hockey in most American colleges.) The context of the sexual division of labor varies enormously across history, culture, and institutions. Where the division appears, however, it usually produces a multitude of practico-inert objects that constitute the gendered series. The offices, workstations, locker rooms, uniforms, and instruments of a particular activity presuppose a certain sex. The language, gestures, and rituals of exclusion or inclusion of persons in activities reproduce the divisions by attracting people to or repelling people from those activities.

In short, then, bodies and objects constitute the gendered series "women" through structures like enforced heterosexuality and the sexual division of labor. As I have interpreted Sartre's concept, being positioned by these structures in the series women does not itself designate attributes that attach to the person in the series, nor does it define her identity. Individuals move and act in relation to practico-inert objects that position them as women. The practico-inert structures that generate the milieu of gendered serialized existence both enable and constrain action, but they do not determine or define it. The individuals pursue their own ends; they get a living for themselves in order to have some pleasures of eating and relaxation. The sexual division of labor both enables them to gain that living and constrains their manner of doing so by ruling out or making difficult some possibilities of action. The bathroom enables me to relieve myself, and its gender-marked door constrains the space in which I do it and next to whom.

The practico-inert structures of the gender series are abstract in relation to individuals and to groups of individuals. They are possibilities and orientations for concrete actions that give them content.[2] The gender structures are not defining attributes of individuals but are material social facts that each individual must relate to and deal with. The subjective experiential relation that each person has, and sometimes groups have, to the gender structure, are infinitely variable. In a heterosexist society, for example, everyone must deal with and act in relation to structures of enforced heterosexuality. But there are many attitudes a particular individual can take toward that necessity: she can internalize norms of feminine masochism, she can try to avoid sexual interaction, she can affirmatively take up her sexual role as a tool for her own ends, she can reject heterosexual requirements and love other women, to name just a few.

In seriality, I have said above, the individual experiences herself as anonymous, as other to herself and other to the others, contingently interchangeable with them. Sometimes when I become aware of myself "as a woman" I experience this serial anonymous facticity. The serialized experience of being gendered is precisely the obverse of mutual recognition and positive identification of oneself as in a group. "I am a woman" at this level is an anonymous fact that does not define me in my active individuality. It means that I check one box rather than another on my driver's license application, that I use maxipads, wear pumps, and sometimes find myself in situations in which I anticipate deprecation or humiliation from a man. As I utter the phrase, I experience a serial interchangeability between myself and others. In the newspaper I read about a woman who was raped, and I empathize with her because I recognize that in my serialized existence I am rapeable, the potential object of male appropriation. But this awareness depersonalizes me, constructs me as other to her and other to myself in a serial interchangeability rather than defining my sense of identity. I do not here mean to deny that many women have a sense of identity as women, an issue I will discuss in the next section. Here I only claim that the level of gender as series is a background to rather than constitutive of personal or group identity.

Sartre's main purpose in developing the concept of seriality is to describe unorganized class existence, the positioning of individuals in relations of production and consumption. Race or nationality can also be fruitfully conceptualized as seriality.[3] At the level of seriality racial position is constructed by a relation of persons to a materialized racist history that has constructed racially separated spaces, a racial division of labor, racist language and discourse, and so on. A person can and often does construct a positive racial identity along with others from out of these serialized positionings. But such racial identification is an active taking up of a serialized situation. Which, if any, of a person's serial memberships become salient or meaningful at any time is a variable matter.

Like gender structures, class or race structures do not primarily name attributes of individuals or aspects of their identity but practico-inert necessities that condition their lives and with which they must deal. Individuals may take up varying attitudes toward these structures, including forming a sense of class or racial identity and forming groups with others they identify with.

Thus the concept of seriality provides a useful way of thinking about the relationship of race, class, gender, and other collective structures, to the individual person. If these are each forms of seriality, then they do not necessarily define the identity of individuals and do not necessarily name attributes they share with others. They are material structures arising from people's historically congealed institutionalized actions and expectations that position and limit individuals in determinate ways that they must deal with. An individual's position in each of the series means that they have differing experiences and perceptions from those differently situated. But individuals can relate to these social positionings in different ways; the same person may relate to them in different ways in different social contexts or at different times in their lives.

A person can choose to make none of her serial memberships important for her sense of identity. Or she can find that her family, neighborhood, and church network makes the serial facts of race, for example, important for her identity and development of a group solidarity. Or she can develop a sense of herself and membership in group affiliations that makes different serial structures important to her in different respects or salient in different kinds of circumstances.

V

The purpose of saying that "women" names a series thus resolves the dilemma that has developed in feminist theory: that we must be able to describe women as a social collective yet apparently cannot do so without falling into a false essentialism. An essentialist approach to conceiving women as a social collective treats women as a substance, as a kind of entity in which some specific attributes inhere. One classifies a person as a woman according to whether that person has the essential attributes of womanness, characteristics all women share: something about their bodies, their behaviour or dispositions as persons, or their experience of oppression. The problem with this approach to conceptualizing women as a collective is that any effort to locate those essential attributes has one of two consequences. Either it empties the category "woman" of social meaning by reducing it to the attributes of biological female, or in the effort to locate essential social attributes it founders on the variability and diversity of women's actual lives. Thus, the effort to locate particular social attributes that all women share is likely to leave out some persons called women or to distort their lives to fit the categories.

Conceptualizing gender as seriality avoids this problem because it does not claim to identify specific attributes that all women have. There is a unity to the series of women, but it is a passive unity, one that does not arise from the individuals called women but rather positions them through the material organization of social relations as enabled and constrained by the structural relations of enforced heterosexuality and the sexual division of labor. The content of these structures varies enormously from one social context to the next. Saying that a person is a woman may predict something about the general constraints and expectations she must deal with. But it predicts nothing in particular about who she is, what she does, how she takes up her social positioning.

Thinking of gender as seriality also avoids the problem of identity. At least since Nancy Chodorow developed her theory of the psychodynamics of mother–infant relations (1978), gender has been understood as a mode of personal identity. By identity, I mean one of two conceptions, which sometimes appear together. First, identity designates something about who persons are in a deep psychological sense. This is the primary meaning of identity in Chodorow's theory of gender identity. She argues that feminine gender identity gives women more permeable ego boundaries than men, thus making relations with other persons important for their self-conception. Many recent moral and epistemological theories have been influenced by this notion of gender identity and suggest that theories, modes of reasoning, and ways of acting tend to be structured by those feminine and masculine identities.

Second, identity can mean self-ascription as belonging to a group with others who similarly identify themselves, who affirm or are committed together to a set of values, practices, and meanings. This is the sense of identity expressed by theorists of identity politics. Identity here means a self-consciously shared set of meanings interpreting conditions and commitments of being a woman.

Criticisms of gender as identity in either of these senses are similar to criticisms of gender essentialism. This approach either leaves out or distorts the experience of some individuals who call themselves or are called women. Many women regard their womanness as an accidental or contingent aspect of their lives and conceive other social group relations – ethnic or national relations, for example – as more important in defining their identity. Many women resist efforts to theorize shared values and experiences specific to a feminine gender identity – in a caring orientation to relationships, for example – claiming that such theories privilege the identities of particular classes of women in particular social contexts. Even among women who do take their womanhood as an important aspect of their identity, the meaning of that identity will vary a great deal (Ferguson 1991).

Thinking about gender as seriality disconnects gender from identity. On the one hand, as Elizabeth Spelman argues, at the level of individual personal identity there is no way to distinguish the "gender part" of the person from her "race part" or "class part." It may be appropriate, as Butler argues, to think of subjects or personal identities as constituted rather than as some transcendental origin of consciousness or action. It nevertheless would be misleading to think of individual persons as mixtures of gender, race, class, and national attributes. Each person's identity is unique, the history and meaning she makes and develops from her dealings with other people, her communicative interactions through media, and her manner of taking up the particular serialized structures whose prior history position her. No individual woman's identity, then, will escape the markings of gender, but how gender marks her life is her own.

Conceptions of gender as an identity, however, more often seek to name women as a group – that is, a self-conscious social collective with common experiences, perspectives, or values – than to describe individual identity. Conceiving gender as seriality becomes especially important for addressing this mistake. In Sartre's conceptualization, a group is a collection of persons who do mutually identify, who recognize one another as belonging to the group with a common project that defines their collective action. A series, on the other hand, is not a mutually acknowledging identity with any common project or shared experience. Women need have nothing in common in their individual lives to be serialized as women.

A relationship between series and groups does exist, however. As self-conscious collectives of persons with a common objective that they pursue together, groups arise on the basis of and in response to a serialized condition. The group in fusion is a spontaneous group formation out of seriality. When those who have waited for the bus too long begin complaining to each other and discussing possible courses of action, they are a group in fusion. Once groups form and take action, they either institutionalize themselves by establishing meetings, leaders, decision-making structures, methods of acquiring and expending resources, and so on, or they disperse back into seriality. Social life consists of constant ebbs and flows of groupings out of series; some groups remain and grow into institutions that produce new serialities, others disperse soon after they are born.

At its most unreflective and universal level, being a woman is a serial fact. But women often do form groups, that is, self-conscious collectives that mutually acknowledge one another as having common purposes or shared experiences. Let me give an example of a movement from women as a serial collective to a group of women. In her novel, *Rivington Street* (1982), Meredith Tax vividly portrays the lives of Russian Jewish immigrant women in the Lower East Side of Manhattan at the turn of the century.

In one episode of the novel, some women in the neighborhood discover that a local merchant has manipulated the chicken market in order to make more profits. They talk with one another with anger and then go about their business. One of them, however, thinks a bit more in her anger and decides to act. She calls her three or four women friends together and tells them that they should boycott the butcher. The women organize a boycott by going from apartment to apartment talking to women. Gradually these neighborhood women, formerly serialized only as shoppers, come to understand themselves as a group, with some shared experiences and the power of collective action. When the boycott succeeds, they hold a street celebration and honor their leader, but then they quickly disperse back into the passive unity of the series.

The gendered being of women's groups arises from the serial being of women, as taking up actively and reconstituting the gendered structures that have passively unified them. The chicken boycott arises from the serialized condition of these women defined by the sexual division of labor as purchasers and preparers of food. While the gendered series "*women*" refers to the structured social relations positioning all biologically sexed females, groups of women are always partial in relation to the series – they bring together only some women for some purposes involving their gender serialized experience. Groups of women are usually more socially, historically, and culturally specified than simply women – they are from the same neighborhood or university, they have the same religion or occupation. Groups of women, that is, will likely, though not necessarily, emerge from the serialities of race and class as well as gender. The chicken boycotters live in the same neighborhood, speak the same Russian-Yiddish, and are passively united in a marginal working-class series in the class structure of Manhattan. All of these serialized facts are relevant to their story and partially explain their grouping.

The chicken boycott example shows a case of women grouping self-consciously as women and on the basis of their gendered condition, but the boycott is not feminist. There can be many groupings of women as women that are not feminist, and indeed some are explicitly antifeminist. Feminism is a particularly reflexive impulse of women grouping, women grouping as women in order to change or eliminate the structures that serialize them as women.

In order to clarify and elaborate the relation of series and group in understanding women as a collective, let me return to my story of Shirley Wright. In her announcement of her candidacy for school committee, when Shirley Wright says that she intends to represent women, she is referring to a gender series defined primarily by the sexual division of labor. *"Women"* names a position in the division of labor that tends to be specifically related to schools, the primary parent to deal with schools, at the same time that it names a position outside authority structures. In that speech Wright is not claiming a group solidarity among the women of Worcester, either around her candidacy or in any other respect, but is referring to, gesturing toward, a serial structure that conditions her own position and that she aims to politicize. To the degree that Shirley Wright aims to politicize gender structures in her campaign and on the school committee, she invites or invokes the positive grouping of women out of the gender series, but her candidacy speech neither names a group nor generates it. Her claiming to represent "minorities" is also a reference to a serial structure of race and racism that she claims conditions her position and that she aims to politicize.

The women who responded to my handing them a flyer with satisfaction at seeing a woman running are also serialized, as women, as voters. Their identification with Shirley Wright as a woman, however, makes for a proto-group. If some women are motivated to come together to form a "Women for Shirley Wright" committee, they have constituted an active grouping. In relation to the series, women, or even to the series, the women of Worcester, the group is necessarily partial – it will probably attract only certain kinds of women, with only some kinds of experiences, and it will focus only on some issues.

In summary, then, I propose that using the concept of seriality and its distinction from the concept of a group can help solve the conundrums about talking about women as a group in which feminist theory has recently found itself. "Woman" is a serial collective defined neither by any common identity nor by a common set of attributes that all the individuals in the series share, but, rather, it names a set of structural constraints and relations to practico-inert objects that condition action and its meaning. I am inclined to say that the series includes all female human beings in the world, and others of the past, but how and where we draw the historical lines is an open question. We can also claim that there are also social and historical subseries. Since the series is not a concept but a more practical-material mode of the social construction of individuals, one need not think of it in terms of genus and species, but as vectors of action and meaning.

Unlike most groups of women, feminist groups take something about women's condition as the explicit aim of their action, and thus feminist groups at least implicitly refer to the series, women, which lies beyond the group. Feminist politics and theory refers to or gestures toward this serial reality. Feminist reflection and explicit theorizing draw on the experience of serialized gender, which has multiple layers and aspects. Feminism itself is not a grouping of women; rather, there are many feminisms, many groupings of women whose purpose is to politicize gender and change the power relations between women and men in some respect. When women group, their womanliness will not be the only thing that brings them together; there are other concrete details of their lives that give them affinity, such as their class or race position, their nationality, their neighborhood, their religious affiliation, or their role as teachers of philosophy. For this reason groupings of women will always be partial in relation to the series. Women's groups will be partial in relation to the series also because a group will have particular objectives or purposes that cannot encompass or even refer to the totality of the condition of women as a series. This is why feminist politics must be coalition politics. Feminist organizing and theorizing always refers beyond itself to conditions and experiences that have not been reflected on, and to women whose lives are conditioned by enforced heterosexuality and a sexual division of labor who are not feminist and are not part of feminist groups. We should maintain our humility by recognizing that partiality and remaining open to enquiring about the facts of the series beyond us.

Notes

I am grateful to Linda Alcoff, David Alexander, Sandra Bartky, Sonia Kruks, Lynda Lange, Bill McBride, Uma Narayan, Linda Nicholson, Vicki Spelman, and anonymous reviewers for *Signs* for comments on earlier versions of this article.

1. Sartre in fact distinguished several levels of group: the group in fusion, the statutory group, the organization, and the institution. Each is less spontaneous, more organized and rule-bound, and more materialized than the last. All come under the more general definition I am offering here, which is all that is necessary to develop my argument. Although my summaries of Sartre throughout this article leave out a great deal of detail, I believe they are nevertheless adequate to the text and sufficient for developing my argument.

2. In terms of Sartre's early work, I am here interpreting seriality as a condition of facticity that helps constitute a situation but in no way determines action. Action, the having of projects and goals, the realizing of ends, I am saying here, is what constitutes the identities and experiences of persons. Action is situated against a background of serialized existence, which means that it is constrained but neither general nor determined.

3. While Sartre does not thematize race as such, I think he provides grounds for understanding race positioning as seriality. He describes being Jewish as initially belonging to a series. As a social fact or social label, being Jewish in a society that marks or devalues Jews does not name some concept, a set of specific attributes a person must be identified as having in order to be classed as Jewish. In the social relation of being Jewish, there is no separate substance that Jews have in common that makes them Jews. The group label is never real, specific limited, here; it always names an alien otherness coming from elsewhere, from the facticity of "them," the anonymous others who say things about the Jews, who "know" what the Jews are:

> In fact, the being-Jewish of every Jew in a hostile society, which persecutes and insults them, and opens itself to them only to reject them again, cannot be the only relation between the individual Jew and the anti-semitic, racist society which surrounds him; it is this relation insofar as it is lived by every Jew in his direct or indirect relations with all the other Jews, and insofar as it constitutes him, through them all, an Other and threatens him in and through the Others. To the extent that, for the conscious, lived Jews, being-Jewish (which is his status to *non-Jews*) is interiorized as his responsibility in relation to all other Jews and his being-in-danger, out there, owing to some possible carelessness caused by Others who mean nothing to him, over whom he has no power and every one of whom is himself like Others (in so far as he makes them exist as such in spite of himself,) the *Jew*, far from being *the type* common to each separate instance, represents *on the contrary* the perpetual being *outside-themselves-in-the-other* of members of this practico-inert grouping.   (Sartre 1976, 268)

Sartre also discusses colonialism as a serial social relation, mediated by an anonymous public opinion that constitutes racist discourse. He says that the most important thing about racist ideas and utterances is that they are not *thoughts*. Racism as operative in everyday life and as a medium of works and beliefs for reproducing practically congealed social relations of oppression and privilege is not a *system* of beliefs, thought through and deliberated. On the contrary, the racist language is unconsidered, uttered as the obvious, and spoken and heard always as the words of an other. Everyday repeated stereotypes such as that blacks are lazy or more prone to be aggressive, or that they prefer to stay with their own kind,

> have never been anything more than this system itself producing itself as a determination of the language of the colonists in the milieu of alterity. And for this point of view, they must be seen as material exigencies of language (the *verbal milieu* of all practico-inert apparatuses) addressed to colonialists both in their eyes and in those of others, in the unity of a gathering . . . The sentence which is uttered, as a reference to the common interest, is not presented as the determination of language by the individual himself, but as his *other* opinion, that is to say, the claims to get it from and give it to others, insofar as their unity is based purely on alterity.
>
> (Sartre 1976, 301)

References

Allen, Jeffner, and Iris Marion Young, eds. 1989. *The Thinking Muse: Feminism and Modern French Philosophy.* Bloomington, Ind.: Indiana University Press.

Bordo, Susan. 1989. "Feminism, Postmodernism, and Gender-Scepticism." In *Feminism/Postmodernism*, ed. Linda Nicholson. New York: Routledge.

Butler, Judith. 1990. *Gender Trouble: Feminism and the Subversion of Identity.* New York: Routledge.

Caraway, Nancie. 1989. "Identity Politics and Shifting Selves: Black Feminist Coalition Theory." Paper presented at American Political Science Association.

Chodorow, Nancy. 1978. *Reproduction of Mothering: Psychoanalysis and the Sociology of Gender.* Berkeley: University of California Press.

Ferguson, Ann. 1991. *Sexual Democracy: Women, Oppression, and Revolution.* Boulder, Colo.: Westview.

Fuss, Diana. 1989. *Essentially Speaking.* New York: Routledge.

Lange, Lynda. 1991. "Arguing for Democratic Feminism: Postmodern Doubts and Political Amnesia." Paper presented to the meeting of the American Philosophical Association, midwest division, Chicago.

Mohanty, Chandra Talpade. 1991. "Under Western Eyes: Feminist Scholarship and Colonial Discourses." In *Third World Women and the Politics of Feminism*, ed. Chandra Talpade Mohanty, Ann Russo, and Lourdes Torres. Bloomington, Ind.: Indiana University Press.

Murphy, Julien. 1989. "The Look in Sartre and Rich." In Allen and Young 1989.

Sartre, Jean-Paul. 1976. *Critique of Dialectical Reason*, trans. Alan Sheridan Smith, ed. Jonathan Ree. London: New Left Books.

Singer, Linda. 1992. *Erotic Welfare*. New York: Routledge.

Spelman, Elizabeth. 1988. *Inessential Woman*. Boston: Beacon Press.

Spivak, Gayatri Chakravorty. 1987. "French Feminism in an International Frame." In *In Other Worlds: Essays in Cultural Politics*. New York: Methuen.

Tax, Meredith. 1982. *Rivington Street*. New York: Morrow.

Young, Iris Marion. 1990. *Justice and the Politics of Difference*. Princeton, N.J.: Princeton University Press.

8

Refiguring social space

Cindy Patton

> . . . the principles consistently advocated by the civil rights movement
> for two centuries following the American Revolution – individual rights
> and equality under law – . . . which were abandoned in the mid-1960s
> by the modern civil rights establishment, translate neatly into a viable,
> forward-looking civil rights program that can at once counter the left's
> agenda while it confronts the civil rights issues that exist today.
>
> Clint Bolick, "A Conservative Civil Rights Agenda,"
> *Human Events*, February 20, 1988

It may seem farfetched to imagine the American new right as the appropriate inheritors of the civil rights tradition. But from their rise as a far-right fringe in the late 1970s to the diffusion of their politics in the PC debates beginning in the late 1980s, the new right systematically poached progressive political discourse. By the end of the 1980s, the relationships among a cluster of concepts and their easy association with political positions (for example, family=right; culture or identity=left) had broken down. This labor on discursive terrain was not simply a series of rhetorical appropriations between two easily defined sides but marked a careful gambit in which the new right challenged the meaning and practical effects of civil rights by refiguring the idea which had once secured them.

The partially secularized new right of the 1980s entered politics through adoption of an identity, modeled, ironically enough, on the last entrant into civil rights claims: the most articulately voiced identity of the 1980s – "gay" identity. But combating the proliferating ethnic, sexual, and other identities required more from these rightists than simply adopting their own name. The minoritizing discourse progressive factions used to gain access to civil rights presumed that social space could accommodate everyone, if only by carving out imaginary and separate domains for any claimants to minority status. The new right could not eliminate the offending identities if it was merely another among many identities. In order to combat identity with identity, the right needed to defeat the partitioning which liberal pluralist notions of minority tried to secure as "civil rights." The new right would attempt to neutralize identity by taking up identity against identity, instead of taking it up in order to gain civil rights, breaking the calculus that linked identity claims with access to civil rights. Unlike the other identities, the new right sought not visibility but revenge.

In the 1970s, the far right had opposed civil rights, understood as an extension of integration through special hiring "quotas" for African-Americans. By the mid-1980s, however, the new right understood the linkage of civil rights and minority as an ethical balkanization which resulted in the loss of a unifying sensibility for "Americans." By the end of the 1980s, a mainstreamed new right (now "cultural conservatives") finally embraced civil rights by arguing that the pluralization of space which had underwritten the notion of civil rights as expressed in the 1960s had decreased "true" civil rights. This reinterpretation of the spaces of minorities was accomplished through asserting the primacy of "culture" (by definition, Western and just barely crypto-Christian) *regardless* of race.

In order to make this revision, the new right set black claims to civil rights *in opposition to* rather than *in coalition with* other groups' similar claims: the 1960s was rewritten not as a high point for the civil rights movement but as a drift away from the "original" (post-American Revolution) civil rights.[1] Renarrating the Post-World War II expansion of civil rights as a deviation from a longer process of limiting government interference in equality and liberty deracialized the inaugurating moment of civil rights activism as most white liberals and progressives know it and explicitly rejected the logic of minority status on which Post-World War II civil rights claims rest. In this fatal gambit, the new right quietly sought to destroy the grounds for making remedies to those who faced systematic oppression. "Civil rights" ceased to mean the inclusion of groups excluded by an evolving hegemony and became instead the erasure of the marks of difference through which those exclusions had been publicized.

I Identity and the politics of disidentification

By 1981, with the publication of Richard Viguerie's *The New Right: We're Ready to Lead*, the emerging political movement acknowledged its need to recruit African-American and Latino support if it was to break the perceived hegemony of "minorities" which came to be known as the Rainbow Coalition and which the new right later dubbed "PC." The new right used two strategies to attract African-Americans: first, the new right created a non-racialized identity with which to distance itself from the overtly white-supremacist identity which had preceded it. But second, if the black cultural discourse which celebrated Africanness proved too strong to undergo the deracialization required to enter the new assimilationism, the new right promoted disidentification[2] with a common other.

Recognizing religious commitment as the strongest ground for coalition with conservative African-American leaders, the new right hammered at the crack between the progressive, liberation-theology-inspired black leadership and the more conservative black Christian leadership. In particular, the new right pressed hard on the machismo obvious in the 1960s liberation movements (also viewed as "communist"). The new right courted black conservatives by promoting shared disdain ("disidentification") for the image of the black revolutionary to which the (white) right contrasted a bootstrap-style of black masculinity.

Jesse Jackson and his 1984 and 1988 presidential campaigns became the icon against which the new right would promote their disidentificatory coalition. The new right capitalized on dissent among black leaders by questioning the strength of political consensus within the black community, supporting the tiny number of black conservatives, and pretending that these conservatives actually directly supported the organizations of the new right.[3] The new right's claim that the black conservatives who shared their dislike of liberationist black leaders actually *identified with* the new right's racial politics was so practiced by 1992 that it operated as a political presumption. Clarence Thomas had difficulty maintaining himself as the bootstrap version of "respectable" black masculinity while challenging the overt racism of the white senators interrogating him. Because she was, in this agon of heterosexuality, *opposed* to Thomas, Anita Hill, herself another version of black conservative, was insistently constructed as a black progressive, even a black feminist.

The new right media of the 1980s was full of articles attacking Jesse Jackson. But in order to capitalize on the disidentificatory possibilities of hating Jackson, when possible, the new right put the critique of progressive blacks in the mouth of conservative blacks. A particularly striking example of this complex strategy was *Conservative Digest*'s posthumous publication of an article by Clarence M. Pendleton, Jr. (1988), who was Reagan's Chairman of the US Commission on Civil

Rights until his death, "on June 5, 1988, . . . two days after putting the final touches on the article above. America will miss him," as the *Digest's* editor avowed. Pendleton attacks the connotative meaning of minority as "all but created [by Democrats] so that they could have somebody to protect . . . against the tyranny of their white brothers" (Pendleton 1988, 15).

Playing out the rich analogy set up in the article's title – "Guess Who's Coming to Dinner with the White Folks?" – Pendleton argues that "the Democrats no more want a black on their national ticket than Tracy wanted Poitier to marry his daughter" (1988,15). Jackson is figured simultaneously as the frightening black buck who threatens white womanhood and the shucking dupe who does what massa wants, but never gets his reward. But Jackson is also the *cause* of black adherence to the Democratic Party, resulting in a fellatious gang rape of "individual" Americans:

He convinced 90 percent or more of black voters that it is unmitigated heresy for us to be anything but liberal Democrats. He has provided the glue for the black–white liberal Democratic and Republican coalition led by the civil-rights groups . . . This coalition has built a political juggernaut that has ramrodded special-interest group privileges and protections down the throats of freedom-loving and law-abiding individual Americans . . . Those champions of equality . . . used the issues of equality, privacy, and sensitivity to politically castrate Judge Robert Bork.   (Pendleton 1988, 16–17)

But Pendleton doesn't stop at the complex and contradictory racial troping ("signifyin'," in the sense suggested by Gates 1988) on Jackson's manhood: rejected as a "mate," dismembered to become a phallic-coalition, even while it is Bork, not Jackson who is "castrated." Midway through the article, Pendleton shifts address from the (presumably) largely white readers of the periodical, to whom he has been describing Jackson's activities in third person, and begins to speak *to* Jackson ("Jesse") in second person.[4] This shift eerily recreates a paranoid plantation fantasy: white readers can imagine that they are overhearing a private strategic discussion *between* black leaders. But the second-person address also incorporates Jackson as a reader of the digest, pressing the white reader to identify with the textual embodiment of one of these warring forms of black masculinity. In order to avert their most immediate readerly identification as/with the object of a second-person address, the white reader must labor to become instead the "I" who has authored the castigating words; Pendleton's words are placed in the white reader's mouth. This logofellatio (more performative than the one crudely implied in the text) is dangerous since it equalizes the white reader and the black author's "right" to occupy the coveted universal pronoun: "I." If recognized, this pronoun-shifting miscegenation (already invoked in the terrifyingly unstable "who" in the title of the popular film punned in the article's headline) enables the white readers to sustain their presumption that they are non-racist, repressing the final solution of the plantation fantasy in which slave revolts are suppressed by the Ku Klux Klan, who have their own conspiratorial intentions.

Even for those white readers who would shudder at the recognition of their own cross-race identification, the morphology of *dis*identification represses the implication of converging, raced, first-person pronouns to allow the readers to differentiate between a second-person address aimed at "Jesse" and one to "them." This is the most basic, grammatical production of disidentification – reversal, double reversal, convergence of self-claims, splitting of object[5] – and it accomplishes the new right's purpose of reinforcing any points of ideological convergence, if only palpable as shared hatred of a common object. The object-splitting which holds off a cross-racial identification between the white readers and the black patriarch is finally secured through Pendleton's plays on the white cultural ambivalence toward black adulthood/masculinity: scolding "Jesse" diminishes "Jackson's" masculine status, making him doubly "boy" – the younger and less dignified of the two black men and the boy-man object of racist insult.

But even worse than Jackson's persona was the fact that he had managed to unite identity-politics factions with more traditionally conceived groups from the left. Inclusion of "lavender" in the Rainbow Coalition for the first time legitimized lesbians' and gay men's social organizations, so heroically displayed in the personal and community response to the AIDS epidemic. Though incredibly important for gays and lesbians, this incorporation provided an additional line of attack on Jackson. Another new right author, obviously an avid reader of leftist periodicals (the verb "revealed" is a slip, a displacement of the author's conspiracy-theory belief that it is *he*, and not the *commie* writer who has uncovered the nefarious plot), tells readers of *Conservative Digest* that:

> *The Progressive* magazine has revealed that at the 1986 founding convention of [Jackson's] political arm, the Rainbow Coalition, militant homosexuals and lesbians wanted a piece of his action, and although blacks objected that this violated their Christian beliefs (with all the opposition reportedly black while all the proponents were white), Jackson insisted that the perverts be included. Jesse Jackson once again embraced these creatures at a Washington demonstration this fall . . . Jesse backed their demands to allow child custody to homosexuals and passage of a federal pervert-rights bill. (Hoar 1988)

Adding homosexuals to the fellating ramrod, Jackson not only "embraces" the "perverts," but also gives up "a piece of his action."

Hoar neatly repeats the stereotype which displaces homophobia and shores up racism. Describing the "opposition" as "black" and the "proponents" as "white" he effects the same maneuver as Pendleton, only squared. Hoar enlists the biracial conservative dissent toward Jackson, allowing readers to unite in their disdain of "these creatures" and their white liberal supporters without actually endorsing their implicit allegiance with "black Christians." The racial disloyalty of opposing other whites while aligning with blacks is glossed over in the central and increasingly useful disdain of queers. Hoar also skates on the thin ice of miscegenating logofellatio when he deploys the racist stereotype of the black con man in order to lay claim to the blandest version of civil rights activism for the disidentifying white reader. In order to experience outrage at having the famous words stolen, Hoar all but puts Martin Luther King's words in the white reader's mouth: he lampoons Jackson, implying that Jackson (reversing King) has actually said, "I have a Scheme" (Hoar 1988, 35).

Though more elegantly than Hoar, Pendleton doesn't stop at associating Jackson with a queer invasion of the Democratic Party. Using some of the most labile metaphors of the 1980s and invoking the sexual tropes which have so constrained black masculinity, Pendleton instructs "Jesse" that "they suckered you." He ups the ante from mere logofellatio to coalitional anal intercourse, raising the spectre of HIV transmission and hinting that even when you "know your partners," as mainstream safe-sex advice admonishes, they might still lie about their "status":

In the more than thirty years that you've been a leader you didn't know that white liberal Democrats are seropositive for discrimination. Well, now you know. With your candidacy the fear of the liberal Democrats who control your party has become FULL-BLOWN RACISM!   (Pendleton 1988, 18)

Again, a double-reversal, only here, fear of one kind of blood and its meaning is turned into fear of another kind of blood and its medical result: the racial misrecognition – passing as white – which might ensue after generations of "miscegenation" is replaced by the spectre of undisclosed HIV status of one's sexual partner. Two registers of fear (held by white racists and by uninformed heterosexuals) are made one: *recognizing* race is transformed into ra*cism*, a central maneuver in the new right's growing attempts to form coalition with conservative blacks.[6]

Jackson, politically infected and infectious (he transmitted Democratic Party allegiance to black voters), is effectively neutralized as – and because he is – a *black* leader.

This tactic of reversing the accusation of racism became the centerpiece of the new right strategy to attract black conservatives; extended in the PC debates it transformed mainstream white perceptions about the meaning and cause of continuing racial strife and inequity. Charging welfare liberals with racism solidified points of convergence between conservatives across race, an ideological assimilation staged in collective disregard for the racial dimensions of the current recession. Enter free-market economics, promising equal opportunity for bootstrap tuggers of all colors.

The economic proposals which went along with the strategy of reversing the charge of racism were first publicly articulated by George Gilder (1981), popular free-market theorist and Reagan's close advisor on "supply-side" economic policy. But the new right of the late 1980s would recycle these ideas as their own in a manifesto called *Cultural Conservatism: Toward a National Agenda* (Lind and Marshner 1987), published by the new right Free Congress Research and Educational Foundation, under the auspices of its Institute for Cultural Conservatism. Paul M. Weyrich, then president of the Foundation, defended cultural conservatism against its detractors among the more traditional ultra-right wing[7] in an interview in *Conservative Digest*, another part of his direct-mail and magazine empire and for which he has sometimes served as editor. Weyrich is more strident than either Gilder or the manifesto when he exposes the racial agenda underlying the supposedly race-blind free-market economics. The material assurances of the welfare state will be exchanged for a cultural glass floor:

We've said we'll make a pact with the minority community that, if they'll inculcate traditional values in their people, and help us discourage welfarism, then we'll make sure there is a safety net in the Western tradition.

(Weyrich 1988, 64)

But Weyrich doesn't stop at offensive, stinging pronouns ("*their* people") or near-red-baiting ("welfar*ism*") which belie the promise of a non-racialized American dream. If the "minority community" can't "inculcate traditional values" on "their" own, he is more than happy to interfere in the political processes internal to those communities:

the present political leadership of the minority community won't accept this challenge . . . it's in their vested interest to keep people on welfare because that keeps these leaders powerful. If the present leaders are unwilling to enter into this pact, we should encourage creation of an alternative leadership for the minority community. Such leaders would be traditionally oriented and dedicated to leading people from dependency to the freedom of self-reliance.

(Weyrich 1988, 64)

Alluding to the previous month's article trashing Jackson, Hoar's "I Have a Scheme," Weyrich claims as his allies and henchmen an "alternative leadership" which Reaganism brought to Washington. Richard Viguerie had already identified some of these "freedom fighters" in his 1981 inaugural new right manifesto: Clarence Thomas, among others.

Civil rights as social space

The new right's success in altering the terms and conditions of political debate makes their rhetorical intervention deeply troubling. But more problematic is the reality that the new right has achieved its goals without ever garnering the "body count" produced by the various progressive factions (evidenced, for example, in a variety of kinds of massive marches on Washington): apparently, "movements" can now exist largely as simulacra. Powerful ideological coalitions with legible political identities can now be formed through means other than those held near and dear by liberationist-movement architects of the post-World War II era: consciousness-raising, criticism/self-criticism, and democratic, grass-roots organizing are no longer necessary ingredients for oppositional political subjectivities. But I want to argue that discursive agonistics do *more* than affect the terms of debate: insofar as some terms undergird the production of the spaces occupied by bodies, discursive intervention is itself material.

Of course, we have not "just discovered" that there are linkages between discursive and extra-discursive elements; Althusser pointedly argued that ideology is material in that it exists in and as state apparatuses. Foucault went further, arguing that as the body or "subjectivities" are the stage of intersecting discursive and institutional practices, neither is prior to or contingent on the other. I want to go further here: securing body-space and community-space through civil rights, as in the post-World War II era, has produced a new form of political subjectivity which is partially autonomous of "the state" as conceived by Althusser and generative *of*, not hailed *by*, an "apparatus." The present situation in the United States is yet different from the modern mode of governmentality described by Foucault: securing social space through identity (the crossing of ontonominative speech acts[8] and objectivist social scientific measurement), albeit in relation to already established modes of knowledge, engenders a new means of administering bodies and goods which commodifies "rights" at the same time that it blurs the distinction between governance of the politico-economic body and the participation in "the state" by the ethical body.

However this critical shift may be described and evaluated (the continuation of the Enlightenment project, the rupture into postmodernity), it seems to be linked in the United States with the specific engagements between the black, feminist, and gay social movements and the new right. The first part of this essay described a particular kind of discursive maneuver used by the new right. I now want to discuss the undergirding concept of space as it evolves from its first articulation in evidently reactionary activism and stopping just as the new right laundered its theory in the academy as anti-"PC."[9] I will chart this development through two shifts in new right activism: the new right's implosion of liberal pluralism's "social" into the new right's late 1970s notion of "the family," and the transformation of this collection of relations into a space called "culture" in the late 1980s. These two moves defaced both liberal pluralism's tripartite social-political-cultural and neo-Marxism's economic-social-cultural, inserting in their place a mono-spatial structure encompassing the new right's crypto-theocratic idea of the United States.

The most frightening effect of this reconceptualization was the deconstruction (still partial) of the spatial concept underlying civil rights: the new right theorists sought to shift the idea and use of civil rights away from a system of remedy for those who could mark themselves as a minority situated outside the social, political, or economic mainstream and instead proposed that civil rights are always and already proper[10] to the defensive space of the uncleaved "true" America. In fact, argued these new rightists, the proliferation of spaces under liberal pluralism and "the left" had been the cause of economic and political inviability of those who call themselves minorities. The metaphysics of the new right reversed a secular division largely accepted by Americans from a wide variety of political positions, the division between "real" material and economic factors and "concepts" like culture, society, and civil space which organize "basic needs" or arise from "relations of production." For the new right, theocratic space, and not the material used to display election within it, is "the real."

In the moves I will describe, the right dislinked the social from the political and economic, denying the validity of measures of oppression which had been used to make the claim to minority status *and* to specify the forms remedies might take, scientific data which rationalized "demands" – for equal opportunity programs based in statistical representation of salaries, for the end of racial covenants based on detailed analysis of housing patterns, for the establishment of police training and for decrease in violent prejudicial attitudes based on reporting and tabulation of hate crimes. Attempting to eliminate the performative dimension[11] of claims to minority status by ruling out use of "objective"[12] markers of status difference, the new right argued for a minimal and passive notion of civil rights for those who assimilate to the mainstream, an idea which excluded claims for remedy by deeming them requests for "special privileges." This repudiation threatened to replace a more expansive and active notion of civil rights that *incorporated* indexable minorities into the majority presumed to possess such rights already. The new right shifted debate away from the issues and practices of minority recognition and compensation and toward the nature and obligation of rights. For the new right, "special privileges" are an illegitimate attempt to secure as inalienable rights which are to be bestowed only on those who perform duties to God and culture.

I want to detail some of the theoretical apparatus which has proved helpful to me in rethinking new right political discourse as a battle for space. I will then describe the emergence of the new right as an identity movement under the sign of family and the shift of an accelerating movement to the rubric of "culture." When I conclude by contemplating the end of civil rights as we know them, I hope to have made clear that these shifts, and my concerns about their significance, are directly contingent on propositions about space.

II Rethinking the social: inessential identity

Foucault proposed that a shift from sovereignty over bodies and space to management of the relations between them signaled a rupture into a modern "governmentality." This modern system of distributing bodies and their relations proliferated, refining a once general space of sovereignty into specialized spaces of relation: political, social, economic, and cultural. Foucault effects a disavowal of the Marxist metanarrative ("economic determinism in the last instance"), deconstructing and seeking to improve upon models of state–body relations, obliquely, perhaps, models like that of Althusser, his teacher. However, Foucault's governmentalized bodies still appear to be more subject to disciplining than they appear capable of maneuvering through the regimes that practice it. His much-complained-about failure to give a detailed account of "resistance" is perhaps most evident in the gap between the description of governmentality or his later critique of American gay politics (1989) and the reconstruction of the state performed through the US gay movement's attempts to claim civil rights. But the rise of desiring bodies to their official status as identitarian subjects is symptomatic of a partial dissolution of modern governmentality, at least in the United States. Making sense of the effects of "gay identity" on US politics requires adding a chapter to Foucault's account (1980) of the emergence of modern concepts of sexual identity. In fact, the role of the "gay movement" and its "identity" in altering civil rights might square two parts of Foucault's work which have troubled commentators: the relation to self and the "resistance" engendered by power. How has the introjection of the "secret" of sexuality into a legitimated political subject of civil rights altered the multiple relational spaces which arose as the means through which modern governance would be effected?

While the "economic" and "political" spaces continue to look like what Foucault was describing, the "social" – the space of "lifestyle" governmentalized through expansion of civil rights and establishment of the "right to privacy" – and the "cultural" – governmentalized through censorship of "art" – no longer integrate bodies' relationships under government, but are *spaces of territorial competition which threaten government's capacity*. I want to argue that these alterations occurred through discursive and spatial engagements *among* political factions despite and in opposition to the apparently cohesive discourse and practices of the governmental state: *the bodies transformed authorized discourse and practices of subject formation to invent themselves as a new kind of political actor*.

The analysis of the new right which forms the third section of this essay builds on my earlier work (1993) describing the emergence of the new right as an identity movement. That argument rested on the claim that identity is deontologically constructed through rhetoric rather than ontologically grounded in self-discovery or escape from ideology.[13] The new right's emergence as an identity movement was not simply an appropriation of the mantle white-heterosexual-mainstream, but a refiguration. The once "silent/moral majority" was rearticulated as a minority in relation to the new right's construction as the new hegemony of the minorities who had earlier articulated themselves against the "white heterosexual mainstream."

The minority movement's legibility had occurred through a reverse discourse (Foucault 1980); the move made by the right could be characterized as a double-reversal, a reverse discourse that is related to, but does not merely reoccupy the space indicated by, a reverse discourse. This discursive procedure is characterized by refiguration of, rather than rejection of or dialectical engagement with, existing terms of debate. The double-reversal placed the coalition of minorities (however truly fractious) in the awkward position of having to deny their unity if they were to sustain their claim to marginality: if the new right was successful at evacuating the phantasmatic center, part of the logic of minority identity was lost. I want to continue that argument here, suggesting that the notion of social space underwriting the pluralization of minorities was also subjected to a double-reversal by the new right, with disastrous consequences not just for identity *movements*, but also for bodies' individual and collective ability to mark themselves as appropriate subjects of civil rights discourse and its governmental apparatus.

This project is a rejoinder on behalf of identity politics, not in order to salvage identity but to suggest that the stage for the identities which critics of identity politics have rightly viewed as performative is itself radically under assault. My reading of new right rhetoric suggests that while *we* are deconstructing identity, the new right is deconstructing the social space that *our* identity predicates. Defending social space (if this is, indeed, desirable) while avoiding the problems of identitarian politics requires a broader critique than has so far been offered by critics of essentialized identity: if, as many argue, identity is performative or a performance, then identity is necessarily always in context or in practice. In order to be useful and not merely nihilistic (not that I object in principle to regular doses of nihilism), the deconstruction of this identity must be accompanied by an analysis of the spaces posited by or through identity.

Recovering a "progressive" project requires understanding the limitations of performative personae as well as evaluating the role of the field which they posit and struggle on behalf of themselves. One of the crucial analytic issues, then, is considering how to think about the space in which performative identities are in play, how to interrogate identity as it is situated in fields of power. Power must not be treated monolithically or viewed as isomorphic or continuous across the various forms of space ("culture," "political," "social") which identities inhabit, however performatively. The role of institutions and the significance of "the state" must be reevaluated, and new ways of understanding the successes (and not just the tawdry "essentialist failures") of the gay movement must be imagined,[14] not by reintroducing once (and properly) discarded ideas about the subject or the state, but by queering social theory.

My argument here uses Bourdieu's (1972; 1980; 1984; 1985; 1986; Bourdieu and Wacquant 1992) notion of fields, which usefully distinguishes among different performances by defining a field as constituted through and constitutive of a value – "capital" – which organizes benefits and the struggles for them. Capital is possessed by actors within a field, but is distinguishable as and sustained as a value through the rules of ongoing struggle in a field. Together, possession of capital and control over the rules of its valuation constitute power: power does not transcend fields but is a function of the value and rules of struggle within them. Capitalization of a value is quasi-material: consolidating capital conveys specific, material power. Thus, there are several forms of power. The visibility of power is contingent on apprehending the field(s) in which it is operative; the force of power is sustained through its institution as the possession/ rules within a field. Power is always at risk of dispossession if the rules for distinguishing capital change.

For Bourdieu, there are a limited number of forms of capital which an individual might possess, but these may be used in any field in which such capital is or can be made effective. Of the forms of capital which Bourdieu's various studies have identified – symbolic, educational, cultural, social, and political – the last would seem to come closest to explaining the rise of gay politics. But political capital (Bourdieu 1991) applies to the power achieved by elites in asserting themselves as the proper representatives of the people and in securing the value of their skills as uniquely necessary, a different view of the same condition which Foucault described as governmentality. The prerequisites for attaining political capital are leisure time and cultural capital (knowledge obtained through education). For example, Reagan secured "communication" as uniquely necessary, a skill which Bush lacked. Bush, however, secured his class and military background, while Clinton, as "Bubba," transformed his lack of class status and military service into "authenticity" through a perpetual and guileless surprise at his own presidentialness. But this does not capture the possession which seems to be at stake in the evolving use of civil rights. The identities of contemporary US minorities are inscribed precisely through their *lack* of prestige, *lack* of leisure, and *lack* of specialized skills: minority identity secures its legitimacy through representation of the people, but the people dispossessed.[15]

Bourdieu's notion of social capital and its transformation is critical to reconceptualizing civil rights under pressure from lesbian and gay politics:

Social capital is the sum of resources, actual or virtual, that accrue to an individual and group by virtue of possessing a durable network of more or less institutionalized relations of mutual acquaintance and recognition.

(Bourdieu and Wacquant 1992, 119)

Minority identity, partly encouraged by the political capital that extended civil status as a "right," but partly through its local struggles to increase the value of its networks of recognition, imposed itself on the political field and partially changed the rules of subject formation. Civil rights, as a system of rules for subject formation, institutes a means to convert social capital into political capital. Linked through value equivalency, both the political field and the social field from which minorities extracted their initial capital are altered. "Essential identities" are *predicated on*, not *a precondition for*, the successful transformation of social into political capital.

Capital and field provide a limited concept of agency by providing a description of the situated struggle or play that bodies may be observed to undertake. If we understand identity as a sign of capital in relation to one or more fields, then the "essentialism" supposedly characterizing naive activists appears to be more like a resistance to ceding a material benefit, a stubborn unwillingness to hand over a hard-won stash of capital. Possessing a form of capital which is signed "identity" is not itself performative: *our* identity's much-vaunted performativity arose when queerly desiring bodies entered the field in which political subjects are formed and succeeded in bending the rules of game until "lesbians and gay men" were legible as subject-bodies of civil rights.

Put bluntly, this description is a partial account of what happened when lesbians and gay men began to claim an identity and demand civil rights on the model which appeared to have been successful for African-Americans during the 1950s and 1960s. Lesbians and gay men generalized the mark of race to allow for additional claims of discrimination to be quantified through new kinds of evidence, especially kinds having to do with affection and domestic relations and their legitimation through housing, employment benefits, etc. Sexuality-based claimants may have produced anxiety for race-based claimants, but, in the case of "hate crimes," also created the new indicators of "oppression" which produced the conditions for making a previously impossible claim. Once it was possible to obtain power in this way, identity elites tried to control the exact means of articulating "gay and lesbian identity" so as to maintain the maximum distinction for their specific type of identity capital. It might seem that less-specific rules would enable more bodies to be counted as "gay and lesbian." On the contrary, it is the distinctiveness of the capital which makes it possible for those who possess it to assert its value. Blurring definitions diminished the ability to take up space in the political field.

In addition to the tendency internal to the "gay and lesbian minority" to narrow the means of capitalizing identity, the differences between various minorities' modes of mutual recognition and aid meant that transferring social capital accumulated as racial community versus social capital accumulated as sexual community was not exactly the same. Differences in degree of transferability of capital created the appearance of a hierarchy of legitimacy in claims to civil rights. This disjuncture is the soft point in the logic of civil rights extensions at which the new right continues to hammer away.

The success of the gay movement might then be understood as a series of strategies of individual and group capital formation parlayed into a stronger form of capital which has had a significant role in altering contemporary modes of political subject formation. The bodies that gained publicity as a "community" in the post-gay liberation era may have initially accumulated social capital – codes of recognition and commitments to mutual aid – designed to offset the difficulties of accumulating cultural (and perhaps gender?[16]) capital in the existing heteroperformative social field. But that social capital was moved into another field: that of political subject formation, previously occupied principally by race-based (and almost exclusively African-American) claimants to civil rights. This move, though logically feasible under liberal–pluralist governance – which views the space of the social as infinitely partitionable and thus, infinitely expandable – in fact, ruptured the boundary between social and civil. Civil rights was no longer a compensatory, temporary conduit designed to incorporate a class of bodies viewed as historically always present but excluded as subjects, but an open door that permitted more bodies to make different claims to subject status.

III The new right

Until the mid-1970s, the conservative political factions which would in 1980 name themselves the new right, consciously avoided uniting their activisms. Concerned that top-down national organizing and coalition building would result in too much conflict to move issues forward, key strategists avoided large gatherings like the marches and assemblies of the post-war progressive, environmental, and civil rights groups and were reluctant to articulate a clear national agenda (Viguerie

1980; Crawford 1980). Other than unsystematic attempts to shape the platforms of the two major political parties, leaders generally argued that whatever there was to be done was already written in the Bible or the Constitution or was self-evident in the general ideas of "Western civilization" and the "American Dream."

But in the mid-1970s, two elements changed: first, Richard Viguerie's direct-mail empire transformed the worship-at-home sensibility of radio and television evangelism into a separatist, check book activism (Quebedeaux 1981). Initially used to raise funds and create a sense of common cause among individuals who held right-wing positions on any of a number of issues, Viguerie's computer database experienced financial success that suggested a new means for organizing an electoral base. Second, the idea of defending "family" emerged as a means of uniting the diverse conservative social issues under a rubric. Together, these created the organizational means and the ideological frame for rapidly assembling a rightist social movement similar in structure, style, and ambitions to the progressive social movements which emerged in the post-World War II era.

"Family" as social movement

Unlike contemporaneous attempts to forge a single national movement from the range of so-called new social movements, the new right did not emerge from local organizers combining their efforts and forming larger democratic organizations. The new right coalesced through the heavily mediated intersection of ultra-conservative elected officials and a variety of single-issue activist groups. The attempts to call constitutional conventions and demonstrations for the Family Protection Act in the 1970s were some of the few occasions when a rightist mass would stage its physical presence as a national movement.[17] If uniting resistant bodies against material conditions or state tyranny is a condition for social movements, then the new right was a simulacrum which simulated its object of revulsion, too. There need not be a homosexual next door. Like gay liberation's own gloss, "we are everywhere," the new right deconstructed the idea of separated social spaces by dispersing the objectional bodies: *anywhere* was too close. And yet, the new right was obsessed with the mass staging of the gay movement. For several years, Jerry Falwell (or his son) would "secretly" attend the gay and lesbian pride march in San Francisco, using photographs "dangerously" obtained there as fundraising fodder.

There were two other peculiarly new right stagings of mass national presence, which themselves suggest a shift in form of claims-making. The STOP ERA campaign of Phyllis Schlafly's Eagle Forum added direct-mail fundraising to counterfeminism, but faded from the political scene once the decade window for passing state ERAs closed. The Moral Majority also used direct mail and its own newspaper to form an imagined community (Anderson 1987) considerably more like the new social movements than like previous moral purity campaigns. Though STOP ERA involved activist engagement of the state and of another social movement (the women's movement), the Moral Majority was primarily the discursive site through which a negative link to the newly consolidated notion of "minority" was initially made.

From the 1970s to the mid-1980s, when the Moral Majority and Eagle Forum, respectively, folded or withdrew from public prominence, the new right produced itself as a movement through allegiance to a broad and polysemous cultural ideal to be promoted through individual single-issue campaigns. The first major coalition effort came under the rubric of "pro-family" or "family protection," which encompassed the range of issues and actions of the variety of conservative groups. A proposed constitutional amendment, the Family Protection Act, did not pass, but, like the ERA, much of what it encompassed was passed piecemeal at the state and local level during the 1980s. This narrowing differs markedly from the liberationist movements, which, during the same period, sought to close gaps between grassroots groups by expanding the political brief of each to include the issues of the others. The liberationist, cross-identificatory effort culminated in the formation and electoral ambitions of the Rainbow Coalition; the disidentificatory efforts of the new right continue to spawn campaigns of hatred.

From hearth and home to the representative house

By the late 1970s, a few right-wing politicians took up the rhetoric of the new right: the new right, now a collection of criss-crossed direct-mail lists, began to have legislative and party ambitions. As a first step, they sought influence in state elections by targeting liberals through personal or political smear campaigns or by backing ultra-conservatives with little chance of winning. Both types of campaign focused attention on single issues in the respective candidates' campaigns: usually abortion, busing, or gay rights, but also longstanding right-wing issues like law and order, evident, for example, in efforts to get rid of Miranda and search and seizure restrictions, introduce or maintain the death penalty, decrease state regulation of gun ownership, and "keep" the Panama Canal. Although winning ultra-right candidates had often not come from the ranks of the new right itself and while the liberals who were unseated were generally replaced by moderates, the new right considered itself successful at the ballot box.

Although there continued to be significant local activism, the ideologic leadership and nominative power now came from the top: but the handful of strategists proposed and managed an ideological center more than they attempted to organize or direct the activities of individual groups. The direction and membership of the diffuse new right was constituted through the central rhetoric and its logical elaboration. Discursive coherence maintained at the highest level did not interfere with the needs and focus of local projects.

Richard Viguerie's 1981 *New Right: We're Ready to Lead*, a book widely distributed through his direct-mail empire and the supporting college[18] and popular news media, increasingly identified with the emerging brand of conservatism. Viguerie's book together with Falwell's editorial persona in his monthly *Moral Majority Report* inaugurated a new self-conception for this growing political conservatism. No longer an uneasy alliance of single-issue conservatives, the new right saw itself as a unified movement with a coherent set of beliefs, a majority united through opposition to the extension of "special privileges" to those whom they viewed as having disavowed the Christian, family lifestyle which was the condition for deserving the benefits of the social contract. Widely interpreted as a simple backlash, this new right movement did not register on a political scale now used to dealing in minorities. Thus, by the early 1980s, the "moral majority" reunderstood itself as a numerical minority comprised of true, universal Americans. The "white-heterosexual-male-as-minority" logic quickly proliferated, enabling stronger specific claims to "reverse discrimination" and making it more difficult to make the case for introducing courses addressing racism, sexism, and homophobia in college curricula.

The move into identity politics placed the new right and several progressive forces in contention within the same space. If initially the new right seemed content to occupy another of liberal pluralism's expanding social spaces, it quickly recognized the means of deconstructing social space while capitalizing its own identity as the *central* – and, they hoped, the only – form of subject-constitution within the ultimately imploded field of unmarked (anti-minoritarian) bodies. This bid for territorial dominance did not go unrecognized by progressive factions; a series of skirmishes over "family" and "minority" partially created the conditions for the new right's final move to reintegrate the fields mapped as separate under secular, liberal-plural discourse.

Coming to grips with the social

The discursive convergence of left and right, or at least, their arrival on the same turf, was the result of disjunct but related capitulations by each: the ceding of family by the left and the acquiescence to "minority" by the right. Critically, the space in which these asymmetrical shifts occurred was the "social," which suffered a double reshaping. The left expanded the social to include the cultural, bringing "cultural workers" and their projects under the sign of social movement. But at the same time, the right imploded the social into the family:

> the marketplace *can't* solve all our problems . . . [I]n fact, the community must take responsibility for dealing with many social problems. And the community begins, of course, with the family. It extends to the church and to other mediating structures of the community. Government should get involved only as the last resort.   (Weyrich 1988, 66)

This competing expansion and implosion of the social created an accidental alliance *between* the new left and new right through opposition to a third force. While the new left and new right were positioning themselves through the use of "family," feminist, gay, and nationalistically oriented ethnic and racial activisms staked their tents in the space of minority. For the left, what came to be called identity politics emerged as a significant and viable alternative to socialist and issue-oriented modes of coalition.

During Jesse Jackson's two campaigns, Rainbow Coalition progressives attempted to unite the identity-based movements with more recognizable forms of oppositional political movement. Because the identity movements were struggling primarily for self-determination and cultural status – struggles which eroded once-clear lines between social and political – their demands always seemed less specific than those of the labor, ecology, or antidiscrimination groups. Identity-based issues were usually incorporated through more classically stated demands on the government. The movement's critiques of gender and heterosexism were transformed into demands for employment and housing nondiscrimination or more government funding for AIDS. While most progressives were able to support the nondiscrimination demands, many were uncomfortable with the larger social critique.

While the left generally moved to incorporate racially signifying cultural workers, some leftists, in the effort to claim a broader notion of "family" *for* the left, refused to accept similar claims to minority and cultural autonomy made by parts of the feminist and gay movements. For writers like *In These Times* editorialist John Judis, a progressive recapturing of family rhetoric excluded gay people's place in any alternative family; gay rights could be endorsed, but only insofar as such demands were made by single individuals. For both the new left and new right – though from different directions – family and social were linked but civil rights were something else. The right explicitly staged its political efforts to save the family as a response to the rise of the gay and feminist movements. The equivocal response to "family" by the remnants of the new left made it possible for the new right to drive a wedge between gender or sexuality-related identities and those associated with race. The new right capitalized on the left's equivocal acceptance of the identity-based movements by asserting that black community is grounded in the black family and that feminists, gays, and "trait-loyal" blacks opposed that family. The new right also defeated the left's attempts to subsume "cultural work" in its concept of social by substituting a different notion of Culture as the final foundation of *family*.

Through several decades of cultural drift, the values, standards, and principles that Americans could count on other Americans to share have been dwindling in number and content . . . The depleted stock of our common ethos must be replenished . . . Culture . . . shapes all of us in our daily lives, in our families, communities, places of work.   (Lind and Marshner 1987)

Dampening strong notions of *temporal* progression ("decades" of "drift"), by fusing *spaces* (daily lives, families, communities, places of work), the new right's double-reversal of Culture laid the groundwork not for a return, but for a respatialization which would be called anti-PC. Despite the invocation of lost values, it is not a past but a future to which cultural conservatism's secular millennialism points. History will begin once the spatial fragmentation of the present has ended, when space is reduced to one.

From family to culture

The subordination of the social to the family might have been a sufficient distance into politics for the new right. But, paradoxically, the more it squeezed on family, the more perversion seemed to "come out." The ultimate incorporation of lesbians and gays into the Rainbow Coalition solidified an image of progressives for the new right: at first, the presumed coalition of feminist, gay, and black nationalists appeared as the new political force threatening the family, irrespective of the family's race.[19] But this move required actually recruiting black conservatives to the new right's position. The easiest solution was to sever civil rights from its leftist heritage, tacitly refiguring civil rights as part of the foundation of the United States, as all but Biblical. The typical form of this rhetorical maneuver was to invoke the queer–feminist–nationalist triumvirate as the image of civil rights gone awry and as the rallying point to attract the newly desirable black conservative:

Most individuals who were not involved in the civil rights movement against racism tend to lump the traditional civil rights movement with the later feminist and gay liberation campaigns. This hijacking of the freedom train by middle-class careerists and sexual adolescents has virtually destroyed the real civil rights movement.   (Pence 1987)

But this was a complicated rhetorical maneuver because the civil rights of the post-World War II era and the "tradition" of civil rights which the new right wanted to imagine itself inheriting had conflicting conceptions of space: although forced to operate under a Constitutional separation of church and state, and, in the post-World War II era, a legislated and litigated racial integration, neither fundamentalist Christian theology nor white supremacist ideology accepted the divisions of social, political, and cultural which play such a significant role in liberal pluralism and in progressive coalition politics. Not only did they reject the tripartite distinction which had enabled liberal pluralism to manage a range of political differences by allocating them to an infinitely expandable and non-competing set of social spaces, but they proposed their own theory of space based in religious separatist and segregationist conceptions of only two, mutually hostile spaces: Christian or white space and the secular or race-mixing world, which would be eradicated by God at the millennium.

Up to this complex attempt to refigure social space, Christian separatists and segregationists simply tried to protect their space, in the first case, by largely withdrawing from the secular world, both "political" and "social" (Marty and Appleby, 1992; Ammerman 1991), into a space which to the outside read as cultural, or in the second case, through local terrorism designed to keep blacks and race-mixers out of white territory. The first implied an imaginary space of mutual recognition, the second had a quite literal one.

By the end of the 1980s, the new right would take the basic division of pious and evil worlds and siphon off the "cultural," until then a stronghold of progressive conceptions of political space, and introduce a new idea of "culture" as the *principal* foundation for the holy, but now very politically active, world.

The *Cultural Conservatism* report (Lind and Marshner 1987) described the situation of the mid-1980s mainstream politics as a battle between economic plans in which liberals had become obsessed with the welfare state while conservatives had become obsessed with economic freedom and growth:

both parties have had to reach out to activist movements built around values, life-styles, and other non-economic issues. Although they are often castigated as "one-issue" interest groups, these movements are in fact the vanguards of a profound political change. The politics that carry us into the twenty-first century will be based not on economics but on culture. (1)

This renarration of political history situated new left/identitarian progressives and the new right contending forces in a power and leadership vacuum in which progressives, via their influence on a bankrupt Democratic Party, are ascendent. The family, though still critical to the solution, and attacks on it, though still symptomatic, were no longer the primary site of contestation. "Culture" eclipsed "family," even though the latter emerged (but as virtual pastiche) in the presidential rhetoric and counterrhetoric (Bush: "family values"; Clinton: "value families") in the 1992 Presidential election.

Culture war

Progressives had treated culture somewhat aesthetically, invoking an ahistorical tradition outside the historical high culture of Western tradition. The attempt to redraw the boundary to include cultural workers in the "social" movement was trumped by "cultural conservatism," a broad ideological position which had many adherents but virtually no mass constituency. The culture asserted by the new right was also ahistorical, but here, it was the time of secularism which was rejected. Instead of remaining a hazy space to be protected through pluralistic extension, the new right refigured culture as the material basis of the economy and the territory of the nation.

What is culture? . . . It is a nation's collective mind, its sense of right and wrong, the way it perceives reality, and its definition of self . . . Culture is the foundation for everything else. On it depends the economy, civic order, the well-being of families and communities, and, simply, whether things work: whether a nation's products are thoughtfully designed and well made, whether its services function as they should, whether its industry can compete . . . whether its standard of living and its standing in the world are rising or falling.

(Lind and Marshner 1987, 4–5)

With culture as the generative bedrock, the new right shifts the battle away from the familiar pendulum swinging left and right and instead examines the best means of cultural reproduction: "a liberationist left . . . offering nothing less than a unified agenda of cultural radicalism" and "the alternative, which has slowly been building in the hearts of a majority of Americans, many of them Democrats, and many of them not notably religious" (Lind and Marshner 1987, 5) – to wit, cultural conservatism.

The cultural conservative position is explicitly constructed in opposition to a disastrous cultural radicalism which threatens to:

refashion the culture of our society to make it conform to certain newly perceived moral imperatives or to certain allegedly scientific (especially psychological or ecological) requirements. Strident demands to eliminate "sexism" and "homophobia" are examples of such moral imperatives. Alleged scientific requirements include the elimination of male aggressiveness as the source of war, the achievement of zero population growth, and the elimination of dogmatic religion as a form of "maladjustment" (Lind and Marshner 1987, 6)

and which "rejects what might be called 'the reality standard,' which is a realistic sense of what is achieved or achievable in history" (6). The new right (now cultural conservatives) no longer constructs its opponents as a fragmented lunatic fringe ("the customary menagerie of feminist, gays, black militants and chowder-headed clerics": Buchanan 1989, 15) but now argues that various groups, individuals, and media are multiple sites of the enactment of the cultural radical ideology.

We encounter cultural radicalism in many settings. On a typical university campus, one need not wander over to the Womens' Studies Department; one can find it as well in the treatment of literature ("deconstruction") or in classes at the law school ("Critical Legal Studies"). Off campus, we can find it in prurient arrogance of a television show host, in the patronizing tone of a "committed" clergyman or social worker, in the disruptive wake of a court order, and (in a different sense) in many a rock video. Major institutions, such as our schools and colleges, have been weakened – and personal morals have been altered – because of ideas popularized and the "revolutions" proclaimed by cultural radicals in the 1960s.   (Lind and Marshner 1987, 7–8)

It may seem bizarre to hear neoconservatives speak of the cultural dimensions of radicalism; the forms of "culture" developed and promoted in the ever-vilified 1960s – the recovery of Africanicity, of women's modes of art and craft, of "peace" – are more often figured by the right as "me-isms" that are opposed to Culture. But the discursive unbounding of the *spaces* of these cultural forms, and their supposed role in undermining institutions makes it possible to lump anyone who is not part of the cultural conservative consensus into the radical camp by default. The new right constitutes a disidentification in relation to a shared enemy, this time, an improbable combination of ideas and institutions otherwise considered to occupy totally separate domains. The bimorphic structure of space – a defiant "us" in a bounded "here" all but engulfed by "them" in a mutating, proliferating "everywhere else" – is similar to the paranoid divisions of Christian separatists and white supremacists initially secularized and racially demarked by the new right of the late 1970s. But where the new right had to tread carefully between the two constituted parties, and dance around the problems of combining millennial theology and the pragmatics of secular politics, the cultural conservative could be "Democrats[,] . . . not notably religious," and even black or Hispanic. Through double-reversal of "culture," the now-despatialized anti-culture of cultural radicalism (it is "everywhere") is now contained by broadening the possibility for disidentifying with it: disdain any of its parts – the multicultural academy, left and identity-based politics, Donahue (the figure of wimpy liberalism in many new right articles), or MTV – etches a border around the whole which defends cultural conservatism "here."

The end of civil rights as we know them

The implosion of civil rights threatens the performative – and extremely powerful, if now deeply contested – gesture which united the descriptions of objectivist sociology with the ontonominative voice of disempowered bodies to produce the class of claimants now largely accepted as the referent subjects of post-World War II civil rights discourse and practice. It marks the end of the procedure liberalism had allowed as "difference" and which in part formed the rhetorical structure with which minorities understood and expressed their "experience of exclusion."

While the strategy of linking identity, minority, and civil rights was enormously successful in creating a political mass and in achieving more favorable status for at least some of the bodies in resistance, the ability to name and deploy identity did not stay within the control of progressive identity movements. The new right finally acknowledged the identity claims of gays and feminists, but in order to oppose their inclusion in the very civil rights discourse such identities intended to access. The new right's acceptance of feminists and gays as militant political actors at first seemed like right-wing capitulation to civil rights discourse. But where the single-issue right-wing campaigns of the 1970s used the spectre of desexed (but too sexual) women and of decadent homosexual men largely to mobilize conservative feelings of revulsion, the new right of the 1980s would use the feminist and gay movements to drive a wedge between the conservative and progressive black approaches to antiracism.

As identity increasingly became the currency of post-1960s political participation, the new right chose to reconstitute itself not as the "moral majority" but as the gnomon space of an eroded national and cultural consensus. The new right placed itself as the minority which could absorb all "true Americans," the always-already space of rights set against the fleeting fashions of "special privileges" of groups making false claims on civil and social life. Thus, while much of the surface content of the New Right's concerns was not new – moral purity, anticommunism, free-market economics – the discursive modus operandi and the *place* created for the "average American" was quite different than both earlier and contemporaneous conservatisms. The right had long valorized the authoritarian and implicitly heterosexual male and the subordinate, moral, feminine, and hetero(de)sexual female: these characters attained positive status and attracted identifying bodies through the new right's identity discourse and its proliferation in popular culture through the media coverage of the academy's PC debates.[20] This phenomenon was not mimicry of the 1970s liberation movements whose social agenda the new right wished to contest but a significant move into a different form of political engagement. While articulated in *terms* of civil rights, new right identity effectively destroys the administrative apparatus of civil rights by altering the modes of staging minority.

However ideologically effective the new right's careful assault on civil rights, minority, and liberalism, the new right also knew that their best ammunition against the Rainbow Coalition was visible black support that did not assert itself in minority discourse. From at least 1980, the new right actively courted black conservatives, proffering a view of civil rights that argued for the capacity of a theocratized United States to address the plight of black people in the post-civil rights era. The new right expanded *through* and over space, rather than marking off the space*s* of difference we now think of as minorities. New right identity eliminates the comparative claims which made the invocation of class oppression possible; any failure to feel at home in the United States is individual, noniterable, in fact *caused* by the pluralization of values created through liberalism. The new right severed the claim to identity from the claim to rights by denying the relation of each to the crucial term which had come to link them – minority. By breaking the logic that enabled historically oppressed groups to mark themselves as political subjects – and under the very sign, culture, that had once generated community and radical opposition – the new right destroyed part of the basis for civil rights as we know them.

The difficulty with "identity politics" is not so much that we mistakenly "believed" in our self-namings but that we believed in the promise of inalienable rights, rights which would accrue once our status as political subjects was secured. I hope I have shown that this promise was substantially contingent on a concept and practice of space which has now been substantially challenged from the new right. Whether we keep or reject our ontonominative voice may be less relevant than the question of how to maintain our *space*, the tiny bivouac we have carved out, without the substantial, but now importantly less accessible, apparatus of civil rights.

Notes

Thanks for comments to: Harry Denny, Toril Moi, Mandy Merck, and Eve Sedgwick and her graduate seminar at Duke University, especially Jose Munoz, Katy Kent, Greta Nu, Mandy Berry, and Jonathan Flatley. Thanks to the National Humanities Center, Australian National University, Canberra, for offering me a splendid work environment during my fellowship there in 1993.

1. The battle over the meaning of the American Revolution is as long as US history, standing both as a closure and as a promise. Abolitionists and their foes struggled over the meaning of the revolution. Orators from Grimkes and Frederick Douglass to the Black Panthers and Chuck D have invoked the language of the Declaration of Independence and attempted to reshape the cultural memory of that "revolution" as the sign of a promise yet to be fulfilled.

2. I have argued elsewhere that identification and disidentification are formally separable modes of group formation. In practice, they often occur in tandem, as in a disidentification with homosexuality which also claims to be heterosexuality, or alternatively, a claim to black nationalist identity which is also a claim against white pluralist identity. But they may occur separately: a claim to black cultural identity which does not oppose itself to other forms of

racialized identity, or a disavowal of homosexuality which does not require claiming a particular form of heterosexuality. In the 1993 debates about gays in the military, the black conservative church seemed to disavow the white, middle-class homosexuality of the most visible gay civil rights movement while not stating itself as heterosexual, in principle leaving open a space of non-heterosexual, black identity. This disidentification easily aligned with white disavowal of homosexuality, even if black identity did not lay claim to the particular form of white heterosexuality (monogamous, bourgeois) quite overtly claimed by conservative whites.

3. The traditionally anticommunist, crypto-white-supremacist Washington watchdog newspaper *Human Events* began writing about the activities of black conservatives on Capitol Hill in the early 1980s, offering columns to those who appeared to support Reagan or his policies, such as, for example, economic theorist Thomas Sowell.

4. If we read the first part of Pendleton's article as "signify-in'" rather than discrediting Jackson's political achievements by describing them through white racist tropes of black masculinity, then *this* section has a sermonic element: the sinner is talked *about* and then singled out and talked *to*. If one were inclined to read Pendleton's posthumously published article as hijacked, or as a subversive writing operating only superficially in support of white crypto-racism, then this second section might also be read as a "call and response" in which it is supportive of conservative black readers whose *active participation* is sought and not disidentifying white readers whose *passive alignment* is sought. Whatever the "intention" of the article, its public appearance from the heart of the new right media enterprise suggests the ease with which the new right accommodated itself to particular black rhetorical forms.

5. Reversal: Jackson forms the Rainbow Coalition as a collection of interests framed as the "others" of white, crypto-racist mainstream society.
   Double-reversal: new right describes this collection as a minority trying to "cram its politics down the throat" of the majority.
   Convergence of "I": those who individually oppose the various "others" are now placed in the same place, producing intolerable bedfellows, resolved through:
   Splitting of objects: by suppressing the prepositional aspect of oppositional political speech and highlighting the objects. An unstable alliance is formed through shared disdain which does not require *association*.

Again, it is critical to note that within contemporary US politics, with its expectations regarding party membership and social movement allegiance, an alignment formed through disidentification is probably less predictable and cohesive than politics effected through identification. If the Rainbow Coalition experienced internal strife it was because differences were addressed head on, and only to a lesser extent is the monolith of middle America still used as a disidentificatory rallying point. I am suggesting that this was possible because participants believed that there would ultimately be enough "social space" to accommodate everyone.

For the new right, there is always a recognition that different interests are co-occupying the same space, the *only* space. Hence, the "final solution" is to convert all differences into the index "I," the unraced, god-fearing, heterosexual, family-oriented gender-appropriate male or female.

It may seem unwarranted to suggest that the new right is genocidal or supremacist, given my detailed discussion of their attempts to unmark race. And their activism and rhetoric from the 1970s to 1990 was principally concerned with family. However, in the early 1990s, the new right began to militate about immigration law, using the stance concerning civil rights and race I am describing here as their defence against charges of racism.

6. Clarence Thomas would be caught in the duplicity of this strategy – arguing during the regular portions of the confirmation hearings that his race was irrelevant to his nomination and to his judicial beliefs, but then casting himself as a victim of racism – "high-tech lynching" – during the special hearings concerning charges of sexual harassment. He split himself: the raceless potential judge and the brutalized black body.

7. It is difficult to assess how much of the debate concerning cultural conservatism actually occurred among far right theorists. A series of articles and interviews attacked and defended the book, which was treated as a policy document produced by a think tank. The chief point of contention seemed to be the role of government: the cultural conservative position enlisted the government in quasi-theocratic intervention against what was perceived to have been amoral social engineering by secular humanists. There was very little debate about the book itself in other neoconservative media. The manufacture of controversy may have served needs internal to the new right: *Conservative Digest* may have been attempting to position the new label ("cultural conservative") as distinct from the older, anti-big-government ultra-right. The need to construct a battle with old-line secular ultra-conservatives may stem from the need to rationalize alliance with the government for once-separatist Christian members of the rapidly politicizing new right. Despite the persistence of official crypto-Christianity (how many of the last two decades' liberal politicians have felt compelled to assure the country of their Christian devotion?), there remains a deep suspicion of overt governmental ties to the administrative institutions of Christianity (ties to any other religion would seem simply preposterous). The slow erasure of Christian terminology from cultural conservatism's official positions does not diminish its reliance on a fundamentally millennial world view. Cultural conservatism performs the same compromise that Jerry Falwell had made earlier when he proclaimed that if the moral majority didn't intervene *now* there wouldn't be a world to transform into the Kingdom of God (Ammerman 1991).

8. This neologism indicated the gap between a claim to a "truth" of one's identity and the *belief* in that identity. In highlighting the dual aspect of current claims to identity, it presumes that the claimant is an agent in, rather than a dupe of, the gesture of naming. Identity is double: at present, and as it has developed in conjunction with the notion of civil rights, identity gestures toward objectivist social scientific data (usually surveys) and toward a sign taken as a name for the truth of the body's meaning. Together, these are what I am calling ontonominative. Either alone may be legible – social science produces all manner of "classes on paper," as Bourdieu (1985) describes them, which are not taken up by those indicated, and there are all kinds of group and individual self-namings which do not seek or cannot lay claim to "official" descriptions. It is their combination in differing ratios which seems common to virtually all of the identity/cultural movements in the United States which now attempt to secure space through civil rights claims. It has been crucial in the development of social policy and allocation of resources to specify numbers of bodies and degrees of disenfranchisement. Social scientific data is the accepted means of closing the gap between bodies in resistance and official acts of redress. In short, identity, as we now critique it, is an act of self-naming that occurs in a context in which social scientific data is accepted as verification of the presence of those bodies. Self-naming outside that domain, for which data is unavailable or withheld, or for reasons other than claims on the body politic, is something different.

9. There are, of course, subsequent chapters to this story. As the PC debates became institutionalized and contained in the early 1990s, the new right moved its concept of culture in a new direction. Some new rightists began to argue that however bad the demise of the family was, it was not due as much to homosexuals and feminists as it was to the influx of non-Westerners in the wake of 1966 changes in immigration law. On one hand, this is obviously a new style of racist argumentation. However, in action, it pits Asians against African-Americans, creating a shared disidentification between African-Americans and white neoconservatives.

10. Several French poststructural writers pun this word – propriety, proper to, property – usefully materializing the notion of ownership/tropic association of concepts. See Derrida's *Positions* (1981), de Certeau's *The Practice of Everyday Life II* (1988), Cixious's "The Laugh of Medusa" (1981), Irigary's "When the Goods Get Together" (1981), or Wittig's "The Straight Mind" (1980).

11. There is still an ethical dimension to claims to civil rights, even if a group cannot adequately demonstrate a history of systematic ill-treatment. Though linked to civil rights discourse, claims made through detailing cases of "hate speech" lack the same force of social scientific validation (because its intensity is difficult to quantify, its meaning too receiver-dependent), but are still partially accepted because fair play, dignity, and civility are

values held independently of the more materialized policies of equality of opportunity, antidiscrimination, and compensation.

12. Obviously, I do not believe that measures which count as "objective," in particular research and policy discourses, have any special relationship to anything, much less to a "real" phenomenon. Nevertheless, specific politico-scientific regimes accept particular kinds of "data" as expressions of the "phenomenon" they administer, that is, they are the scientific branch of modern governmentality. If a regime is concerned to articulate subjects with identities, something must count as evidence of such identities; identity claims in the context of civil rights politics (and the issues of "visibility" they produce) join "objective social facts" with ontonominative voice – self-naming speech thought to originate in the essential traits of the person.

    Both the marks of oppression and the identities formed in relation to them are legible because rules of political discourse – including rules of subject formation – make them so. Identity and the social scientific data which it depends on in part are both constructions, and both in relation to less clearly articulated political regimes. The relative lack of clarity about the best mode of constructing subject status in the current political climate has been at issue in the evolving strategy of gay activists in Colorado: whether to align the claims to identity with the legitimated claims to scientific knowledge. By the same token, the new right sometimes tries to argue against the existence of a minority (Buchanan 1989), but more consistently tries to disallow the basic argument that the claim to a "minority identity" is equivalent to a claim to civil rights.

13. I argued that identity is less a positive statement of who one *is* than a statement of what "a person like me does," in which the "sense of duty" – which is really an apprehension of place, of the intersection of relational lines constitutive of the "position" of a body in fields of power – precedes the articulation of "self." Identity is always agonistic, not simply performatively inventing itself, but *placing* itself in relation to a set of alliances and obligations, or rather, deducing "who it is" from its interpretation of "where it is" in an active field of power.

    While this position shares in common with Althusser a notion of interpellation, it centers the construction of the subject closer to the body-actant than to the "apparatus": that is, the fields in which accumulations of power are observable do not hail bodies as subjects, but rather, bodies observe themselves at play in the field and consider the market of names offered for those positions. In arguing that a "new" form of "governmentality" or, to stay closer to Bourdieu's way of speaking, a "new" set of rules for capital formation in the field of political representation has emerged, I am suggesting that a rare event has occurred. The Althusserian frame, finally deterministic as it is, has difficulty accounting for this innovation in the first instance of subject formation. By contrast, Bourdieu argues that structural imposition and subject activation are only homologous, and not causally related, there remains the possibility for a fracture in the "apparatus" or "structuring structure" (however unlikely it is for this gap to produce revolution or even express a significant "change"), such as emergence and reversal of "identity politics" that I am taking pains to describe in this particular way.

As a mode of describing the recent predicament concerning "identity politics" and its utility, this position holds two additional advantages over the Althusserian position. First, it suggests that subjectivities arise only in part in relation to "institutions," since the calculation of "self" may take into account any elements which mark its position, not only the ones extending from an ideological state apparatus. Elements of "culture" and popular memory that survive underneath the line of vision of the state are also fair game in identity construction.

Second, it affords a weak form of agency to the body, which now does not merely wait around to be hailed, but is already actively engaged in struggle for position, "deducing" itself from the fluctuations and maneuvers within always materially and spatially structured fields of power.

14. Examples include, in particular, the essays in Warner 1993, but also Lisa Duggan's "Queering the State" (1994), and Henry Abelove's "From Thoreau to Queer Politics" (1993).

15. Toril Moi suggested to me that in order to be consistent with Bourdieu's terminology, the proper name for the capital formed in the field of subject formation should be subject capital, or the capital called identity ought to be positioned in a field of identity. Admittedly, the slide between the identity in the social field and the identity of the political field creates a terminological confusion. However, rather than alter one term, I have chosen to retain this confusion for now, in hopes that readers will recognize, as I did, that the "identity" we critique operates in multiple ways, sometimes affording power through presumptions of social interdependence with others who share our identity (social capital) and sometimes through political interdependence with people of other identities, but ones formed through similar subject-creating rules (governmental capital). This recognition renders incoherent the now de rigueur claims about the "essential essentialness" of the ego-development concept of identity that supposedly created identity politics: which identity is meant?

Identity is the sign of capital, a sign of power in a specific field – it marks different degrees and forms of power in the field of subject formation than in the social field where networks of mutual aid are formed. The identity of so-called identity politics is neither a sign of ego-development ("essentialist") nor performative (inventing itself only in context) but both, depending on what kind of capital it stands for, what field it is observed operating within, and whether we focus more on classes of bodies as they activate the range of assets at their disposal across and between fields or whether we describe a single field.

16. Bourdieu does not specify gender capital, although he considers gender conformity to be an aspect of cultural capital. I am uncertain whether gender does constitute a field, or whether it is an aspect of capital formation in several fields.

17. Because of the active involvement of Catholic liberals and some new left radicals, anti-abortion activism must be treated separately. A case could be made that by the late 1980s, it too constituted a movement; indeed, anti-abortion protest increasingly became the most visible scene of new right activist presence, in part because of media attention linking the two. What I mean to suggest here is that with the exception of the 1970s profamily period, the new right rarely staged national actions as evidence of its status as a fractional group, but instead produced issue-specific activism. This presentation is consonant with the new right's general perception of itself as already present, already the ground zero of America.

18. The Dartmouth Review, one of the many college new right periodicals, was a significant example of this convergence of media and political interests: Dinesh D'Souza would later parlay his experience there into the opening assault of the PC debates.

19. Clearly, the still-lively debate about the supposed pathology of the black family, stimulated by the mid-1960s publication of the Moynihan report, fueled the new right's analysis of the importance for everyone of the family. The Thomas–Hill confrontation played the same cards, demonstrating the final undecidability of the value to conservatives of the long-asserted ideas about the black family. Hill was the product of the conservative's favorite kind of family and Thomas the refuge from the kind thought responsible for the black community's failure.

20. AIDS discourse, and the new right's pressure on it, also promoted positive self-identification as heterosexual. For discussion of the new right and AIDS discourse, see Patton 1993.

References

Abelove, Henry. 1993. "From Thoreau to Queer Politics." *Yale Journal of Criticism*, 6 (2).

Ammerman, Nancy. 1991. "North American Protestant Fundamentalism." In *Fundamentalisms Observed*, ed. Martin Marty and R. Scott Appleby. Chicago: University of Chicago Press.

Anderson, Benedict. 1983. *Imagined Communities: Reflections on the Origins and Spread of Nationalism*. London: Verso.

Bourdieu, Pierre. 1972. *Outline for a Theory of Practice*. Cambridge: Cambridge University Press.

1980. "The Production of Belief: Contribution to an Economy of Symbolic Goods." *Media, Culture and Society*, 2: 261–93.

1984. *Distinction: A Social Critique of the Judgement of Taste.* Cambridge: Harvard University Press.

1985. "The Social Space and the Genesis of Groups." *Social Science Information*, 24 (2): 195–220.

1986. "From Rules to Strategies." *Cultural Anthropology*, February: 110–20.

1991. *Language and Symbolic Power.* Cambridge: Harvard University Press.

Bourdieu, Pierre, and Loic J. D. Wacquant. 1992. *An Invitation to Reflexive Sociology.* Chicago: University of Chicago Press.

Buchanan, Patrick J. 1989. "The Great Hoax of Dr. Kinsey." *New Dimensions*, n.d.

Butler, Judith. 1990. *Gender Trouble: Feminism and the Subversion of Identity.* New York: Routledge.

Cixious, Helene. 1981. "The Laugh of Medusa." In *New French Feminisms*, ed. Elaine Marks and Isabelle de Courtivron. New York: Schocken Books.

Crawford, Alan. 1980. *Thunder on the Right: The "New Right" and the Politics of Resentment.* New York: Pantheon.

De Certeau, Michel. 1988. *The Practice of Everyday Life.* Berkeley: University of California Press.

Derrida, Jacques. 1981. *Positions.* Chicago: University of Chicago Press.

Duggan, Lisa. 1992a. "Making It Perfectly Queer." *Socialist Review*, 22 (1): 11–31.

1992b. "Theory and Practice." *Village Voice Literary Supplement.* June.

1994. "Queering the State." *Social Text*, 39 (Summer): 1–14.

Foucault, Michel. 1979. "On Governmentality." *I & C*, 6: 5–22.

1980. *The History of Sexuality: Vol. 1, An Introduction.* New York: Vintage.

1989. "Friendship as a Way of Life." In *Foucault Live*, Foreign Agent Series. New York: Semiotext(e).

Gates, Henry Jr. 1988. *The Signifying Monkey.* Oxford: Oxford University Press.

Gilder, George. 1981. *Wealth and Poverty.* New York: Bantam.

Hoar, William P. 1988. "Have the Democrats All Gone Crazy?" *Conservative Digest*, May/June.

Irigary, Luce. 1981. "When the Goods Get Together." In *New French Feminisms*, ed. Elaine Marks and Isabelle de Courtivron. New York: Schocken Books.

Lind, William, and William Marshner. 1987. *Cultural Conservatism:*

Toward a New National Agenda. Free Congress Research and Educational Foundation. Lanham, Md.: UPA Inc.

Marty, Martin, and R. Scott Appleby. 1992. *The Glory and the Power.* Boston: Beacon Press.

Patton, Cindy. 1993. "Tremble Heteroswine." In *Fear of a Queer Planet,* ed. Michael Warner, 143–77. Minneapolis, Minn.: University of Minnesota Press.

Pence, David. 1988. "Address to Physicians, Grand Rapids, Michigan, November 4, 1987." In *Vital Speeches,* December.

Pendleton, Clarence M. Jr. 1988. "Guess Who's Coming to Dinner with the White Folks?" *Conservative Digest,* June.

Quebedeaux, Richard. 1981. *By What Authority?* San Francisco: Harper and Row.

Viguerie, Richard. 1981. *The New Right: We're Ready to Lead.* Falls Church, Va.: Viguerie Co.

Warner, Michael, ed. 1993. *Fear of a Queer Planet.* Minneapolis, Minn.: University of Minnesota Press.

Weyrich, Paul. 1988. "Why Cultural Conservatism Is Drawing Heavy Fire." *Conservative Digest,* May/June.

Wittig, Monique. 1980. "The Straight Mind." *Feminist Issues,* 1: 103–10.

9

Just framing: ethnicities and racisms in a "postmodern" framework

Ali Rattansi

Introduction

What I propose to do in this essay is to posit a "postmodern" frame, in order to provide a particular "take" on issues around racism and ethnicity. By placing the term "postmodern" consistently in quotation marks, I am registering reservations about its distinctiveness and indicating a provisionality about its usage and usefulness which are discussed at length elsewhere (Rattansi 1994).

The "postmodern" frame

My construction of the "postmodern" frame draws eclectically upon a wide range of authors – Foucault (1977, 1979, 1980), Derrida (1977, 1978, 1981), Bauman (1989, 1991), Laclau (1990), Giddens (1990a, 1990b), Butler (1990), Hekman (1990), Said (1978, 1993), Hall (1992a, 1992b, 1992c, 1992d), and Bhabha (1983, 1986), among others (see Rattansi 1994).

The following features of a "postmodern" frame as an analytic device are highlighted, and their implications explored, in the understanding of questions of racism and ethnicity:

1 The "postmodern" condition as primarily an *intellectual* condition characterized by reflection on the nature and limits of Western modernity.

2 "Modernity" as a theoretical category: the form of conceptualization adopted here focuses especially on the dualities of modernity; for example, between the formation of democratic institutions and disciplinary complexes of bureaucracy and power/knowledge; between

250

the excitement of rapid change and the simultaneous anxiety of societies seemingly out of control; and the constant destabilization of identities and continuous reinvention of "traditions."

3 The role of Western modernity's Others, both internal and external, *the Other* real and imagined, especially in the context of various imperialisms and colonialisms, as potent forces in the formation and continuous reconstruction of Western identities, in particular by processes of the marginalization of Others as binary opposites of supposedly Western characteristics. Derridean "deconstructive" strategies are brought into play to display the artifice involved in the construction of binarities in Western discourses and cultural identities, and to destabilize the way in which oppositions such as male/female, active/passive, culture/nature, rational/emotional, civilized/savage, white/black, and so forth have become superimposed on each other to hold together, precariously, a phallocentric "Occidentalism" against feminized "Orients" and barbaric "Africans" to take just two examples (Rattansi 1994).

4 An exploration of the profound impact of new phases of globaliz- *globalization* ation, theorized as uneven processes, but as corrosive of old national boundaries and playing a creative role in the formation of new, hybrid, syncretic transnational identities.

5 The project of "de-centering" and de-essentializing both "subjects" *de-centering* and the "social": the individual is no longer conceptualized as *the subject* a fully coherent, "rational," self-knowledgeable agent capable of direct access to reality and truth, and is theorized as living within the tension of a variety of potential and actual subject positions; social formations are no longer regarded as tightly knit complexes of institutions with necessary, predetermined forms of connection or logics of development – there are no final determining instances or levels such as the economy, and no laws of motion as posited in most versions of Marxism.

6 Analyses of temporality and spatiality as constitutive features of the *temporality* social, of subjectivities, and of processes of identification. Neither *spatiality* time nor space are privileged over the other (Soja 1989; Urry 1991; Adam 1990; Lash and Urry 1994); moreover, both are seen as being in a constant state of flux, in contrast to a widespread tendency to view time as dynamic and space as static – a form of conceptualization which, among other things, has allowed time to be associated with "progress," activity, and the masculine while space has been construed as passive and "feminine" (Massey 1993). Moreover, in conditions of "late modernity" and its associated intensified globalization,

there is an emphasis on what Harvey (1989) has called "time–space compression," that is, the diminution of space by technologies of mass communication and travel and the increasing simultaneity of experience across the globe. There are specific "postmodernist" aesthetic strategies and cultural movements associated with these transformations which are crucial to a sense of the "postmodern" as a cultural and political formation (Boyne and Rattansi 1990).

7   A reconsideration of the relation between the "psychic" and the "social" which takes seriously a specifically psychoanalytic de-centering of the subject, positing it as constitutively split between a conscious self and the disruptions of unconscious desire, emotional attachments and hostilities, the operations of ambivalence, splitting, fantasy, paranoia, projection, and introjection (Rattansi 1994).

8   An engagement with questions of sexuality and sexual difference, both as theorized within poststructuralist and "postmodern" feminisms, which destabilize and de-essentialize the categories of "woman" and "women" and question the simple binarities of sex/gender and public/private (Butler 1990; Hekman 1990; Flax 1990 and 1993), and as analyzed in attempts to understand the sexualization of "race" (Fanon 1986; Gilman 1992: Stepan 1990; Nandy 1983 and 1990; Kabbani 1986; Frosh 1989; Rattansi 1994).

Having set in place, albeit in outline form, the elements of a particular "postmodern" framework I turn now to exhibiting some of its uses in tackling questions of racism and ethnicity.

Defining ethnicities and racisms

A "postmodern" frame's intrinsic suspicion of doctrines of "pure" origins makes it inherently corrosive of discourses that invoke notions of historically formed cultural essences. Its de-essentializing and de-centering tendencies inevitably provoke conflict with political projects which rely on strong classificatory systems, whether based on conceptions of "ethnicity," "nation," or "race." Moreover, conventional ideas of ethnicity and racism as elaborated in the truth-regimes of the human sciences find themselves equally vulnerable to the deconstructive power of "postmodern" analysis.

The social sciences have had predictably little success in furnishing uncontentious definitions of ethnicity and racism. There is little agreement except around the points that the term "ethnicity" derives from the

Greek *ethnos*, meaning a people, a collectivity sharing certain common attributes; and that ethnicity ought essentially to be regarded as a cultural marker or, indeed, container in which some conception of shared origin and characteristics is crucial (Rex 1986, 26–29, 79–98). But what precisely is meant here by "culture"? Is any particular shared "cultural" attribute more important than any other – for instance, language, territoriality, or religion? Do not notions of "shared origin" smuggle in ideas of shared *biology* (Nash 1989, 5)? How is "ethnicity" to be consistently and usefully distinguished from "race," and "ethnocentrism" from "racism," and both of these from "xenophobia" and "nationalism"? How distinctive is the current notion and practice of "ethnic cleansing" from the Nazi project of "racial cleansing"?

The inherent conceptual difficulties of strong classificatory programs in the human sciences have, around these questions, been hopelessly exacerbated by becoming intertwined and having to come to terms with the astonishingly complex manner in which populations appear to draw and redraw, and maintain and breach, and narrow and widen the boundaries around themselves and others.

De-centering and de-essentializing ethnicity, "race," and racism

In this context the first "postmodern" move must be to decenter and de-essentialize, by postulating what is often glimpsed but rarely acknowledged and accepted with any degree of comfort: there are no unambiguous, water-tight definitions to be had of ethnicity, racism, and the myriad terms in between (Omi and Winant 1986, 68–69). Indeed, all these terms are permanently in between, caught in the impossibility of fixity and essentialization. There is a "family resemblance" between them, a merging and overlapping of one form of boundary formation with another, coupled with strong contextual determinations. One programmatic conclusion would be for "postmodern" frame analyses to eschew tight definitions, and instead engage in Foucauldian genealogical and archeological projects, exploring the accretion of meanings, political affiliations, subject positions, forms of address, regimes of truth, and disciplinary practices involved in the construction of particular myths of origin, narratives of evolution, and forms of boundary marking and policing engaged in by different "communities" in particular historical contexts. "Ethnicity," "race," "the nation," and so on, carry infinitely rich connotations and continue to be harnessed to a wide variety of political and cultural projects; such genealogies and archeologies can and have explored the continuities and discontinuities in the discursive practices involved.

The debate about whether there is now a "new racism" provides an illustration of the necessity for de-centering and de-essentializing concepts of "race," "ethnicity," and "nation."

Racisms "old" and "new": undoing a binary opposition

The political projects and the disciplinary matrices involved in the formation of "race" as a marker in Western modernity have, of course, been extensively studied, especially in forms of "scientific racism" of the nineteenth and early twentieth centuries which were intertwined with conceptions of non-European others, sexual difference, anti-Semitism, and the culturally assimilationary thrust of the nation-state. "Scientific racisms" have had two enduring characteristics: a biological definition of "race," therefore "racializing" the body and conceiving of a population as having a commonality of "stock" and phenotypical features, such as coloration, hair type, shape of nose, and skull, and even type of foot in the case of representations of Jewishness, as Gilman (1991, 38–59) has pointed out; and, secondly, attempts to create a *hierarchy* of races which, despite representing some "white" races as racially inferior to others have consistently consigned "non-white" populations to the lowest rungs of the racial ladder (Banton and Harwood 1975).

But the difficulty of extrapolating from "scientific racism" to contemporary forms of inferiorization, discrimination, and exclusion to define racism is evident in the controversy over the "new racism" as well as in attempts to provide legislative and judicial protection to populations subjected to discriminatory practices. The term "new racism" is already burdened by having two different referents. Martin Barker (1981), who appears to have first used the label, mainly targeted the recent appropriation of the doctrines of sociobiology by the British new right, who have deployed sociobiological conceptions in postulating a supposedly "natural" equivalence between cultural, especially *national* difference, and cultural and political antagonisms against those deemed to be "obviously different," that is, foreign and alien. They have attempted thereby to legitimize policies for the repatriation of British Asian and British African-Caribbean populations, and to underwrite de facto segregation in schooling, especially in areas with a large concentration of British Asian, particularly Muslim, populations. Balibar (1991), also keen to highlight the relatively novel phenomenon in which overt doctrines of biological inferiority have been abandoned in Europe (although legitimation for domination, discrimination, repatriation, and forms of segregation or separation continue to be found there), speaks of the new racism as primarily a form of "cultural racism"; a "differentialist racism," in which cultural difference replaces the earlier and now scientifically discredited biological theorizations. Support for culturalist interpretations of new forms of racism has come from a number of other influential commentators (e.g., Gilroy 1987, 43–51).

But how "new" is the "new racism"? Its credentials for novelty have been questioned by Miles (1987), whose argument that the "scientific racism" of the nineteenth and twentieth centuries, although rooted in biological features, always revolved around a conception of cultural/national character and uniqueness and that there has always been a powerful connection between racist and nationalist discourses, challenges the claims of Barker, Balibar, and the rest.

My purpose in referring to this discussion is not to adjudicate between these particular disputants – I return to some of these questions later as part of a wider commentary on forms of racism in conditions of a possible "crisis" of modernity – but to suggest that inside a "postmodern" frame it seems clear, on the one hand, that without a very detailed archeological and genealogical exercise it would be impossible to grasp the continuities and discontinuities between the two, but also that a simple old/new binary homogenizes each discourse and delimits its field of application, effectiveness, and articulation in a singularly unhelpful manner. Both "scientific racism" and "differentialist racism" are complex enough formations to merit being referred to in the plural, and any effective comparative exercise requires an understanding of their articulation with discourses and disciplinary practices not merely around the "nation" as has hitherto been the case, *but also around sexual difference, and the cultural codes of social class difference.* My argument acquires particular relevance at a period in European history that has seen the resurgence of racisms which combine older fascist, anti-Semitic ideologies with a differentialist rhetoric mobilized against migrant com-munities with "Third World" origins. Some of these movements are not afraid to speak openly of a commitment to racism, while still maintaining a rhetoric of differentialism. Thus Derek Beackon, elected as councillor for the British National Party in the Millwall Ward in London's East End in September 1993, is reported to have said, "I am happy to describe myself as a racist. I just want to live amongst my own people" (*Sun*, 18 September 1993, 7). Elsewhere his rhetoric appeals to a nationalism of Britishness and a territorialization which invites racist mobilization to return Britain to the British and cleanse the streets of "rubbish" –

256   Ali Rattansi

that is, the Asian communities (see the report in the *Daily Mirror*, 18 September 1993, 2).

The discourses of "race," nation and ethnicity: no necessary political belonging

Note, too, the ways in which racializing, exclusionary discourses can take antiracist campaigning principles based on multiculturalism and equal respect for all cultures, and egalitarian appeals based on rights of citizenship, and turn them around so that multiculturalism becomes transmuted into a defense of the rights of white cultures to retain their "purity," and the rhetoric of citizenship is mobilized to underwrite demands for forms of segregation in schooling and housing. This can then be conjoined with claims that the real problem is that whites have become "second-class citizens" in their own countries, all ploys which are evident in the discourse of the Ku Klux Klan, or in the appeals of the British extreme right as well as in British popular culture (on the latter, see Cohen 1993 and the British National Party statements, for example, in the wake of their victory in the local council election in London's East End (*Daily Mirror*, 18 September 1993)).

Moreover, while the British extreme right has generally espoused a traditional stance on the role of women and "family values," there has in fact been an internal struggle over attempts by some members to articulate their racism with feminism, and attract more women members, by arguing for more egalitarian approaches (Durham 1991, 274).

The only way to make sense of these complex and ever-changing reconfigurations of what one might call color, culture, and political discourse is to de-center and de-essentialize concepts of "race," ethnicity, and nation as recommended here *and to acknowledge that they have no necessary political belonging*. Although it is arguable that historically concepts of "race" have contained a strong biological element, the degree of centrality accorded to biology is obviously subject to enormous variation, as is its articulation with conceptions of nationality, sexual difference, class, and democratic rights. There are, moreover, shifts of discourse and policy depending upon targeted populations – "black," "Asian," "Oriental," "Celtic," and so on. In other words, there are racism*s*, not a singular racism.

Nor can it be assumed that the concept of "race" and nation will only function in a manner that underwrites projects of domination and inferiorization. Their capacity for mobilization as resources for resistance is evident in conceptions of Afrocentrism and in other projects which rely on a notion of an African "race" and nation, particularly in the populations of the African diaspora in the United States and Britain. And it certainly cannot be ruled out that some of the discourses and practices of those committed to doctrines of racial and cultural purity amongst the ethnic minorities might be regarded in some respects and contexts as "racist." Hence, in part, the futility of merely proclaiming the scientific falsity of the concept of "race." From "postmodern" perspectives, as from others, such attributions of fixed origin appear reprehensible in their attempts at closure around mythic collectivities, but there is no denying their potential for cultural and political mobilization.

Thus, as with "race," the various elements that go to make up the notion of ethnicity – language, religion, notions of common origin, codes of kinship, marriage, and dress, forms of cuisine, and so forth – *have no necessary political belonging* (see Laclau 1977, 160–72 and 1990, 28–29 for a discussion of the relative motility of various discursive figures in the "trench war" of political struggles) and can be mobilized for apparently incongruous alliances, for example, between the "cultural racists" of the British new right and British Muslim communities demanding the right to separate schooling, between the black nationalism of the African-American Louis Farrakhan and elements of the white American extreme right – anti-Semitism being one of the uniting political strands – (and in South Africa, not so long ago, between sections of the Zulu population and white right-wing groups, each demanding separate "homelands"), thus demonstrating the complex articulations that become possible around projects of nationalism, racism, and ethnicity, white and black. The language of cultural difference, as part of ethnicity, "race," and nation has no necessary political belonging.

Ethnicity, representation, and racialization

A "postmodern" framing conceptualizes *ethnicity* as part of a *cultural politics of representation*, involving processes of "self-identification" as well as formation by disciplinary agencies such as the state, and including the involvement of the social sciences, given their incorporation in the categorization and redistributive activities of the state and campaigning organizations.

"Representation" in this conceptualization is being used in a double sense. On the one hand it refers to issues of authority and accountability in the articulation of communal views and "interests." It poses questions about who is authorized to speak for whom, and immediately opens up the issue of conflicts within designated ethnic communities. It also encourages analyses of projects of hegemony within and between ethnic communities (Cohen 1988, 26–27; Winant 1994). Moreover, by foregrounding institutional politics, it reveals what is so often at stake in the conflicts within and between collectivities: a voice in the allocation and redistribution of resources, often from local and national state agencies.

But the emphasis on "representation" is also important, for it focuses attention on the significance of the construction and constant recreation of ethnic identities through the production of images and narratives in visual and written texts of "popular" and "high" culture: newspapers, novels, television documentaries and drama, cinema, the theatre, music, painting, and photography. Ethnic identity is a "social imaginary," to adapt a term from Castoriadis (1987), or to borrow Anderson's, an "imagined community" (1983), that is, amongst other things, a collectivity bonded together by forms of literary and visual narration which locate in time and space, in history, memory, and territory.

The formation of ethnic identities may be regarded as part of a process of *racialization* when categories of "race" are explicitly invoked or when popular or specialized biological and quasi-biological discourses are drawn upon to legitimate projects of subject-formation, inclusion and exclusion, discrimination, inferiorization, exploitation, verbal abuse, and physical harassment and violence. However, individual acts and collective projects of boundary formation, discrimination, exploitation, and violence may or may not involve explicit inferiorization and may or may not contain references to biological notions of "stock," "blood," genetic differences, and bodily attributes such as color and capacities such as "intelligence." Note, too, that appeals to ethnicity and cultural difference, by invoking ideas of shared origin, "kith and kin," and "nation" may in fact smuggle in quasi-biological conceptions. Moreover, as Cohen (1988) in particular has emphasized, rhetorics of social class have often contained appeals to biology, enshrined in ideas of "codes of breeding."

The de-centering and de-essentialization of "race" and "ethnicity" that is being recommended here makes for a much more fruitful analytical engagement with these processes of flux, contextual transformation and dislocation, and the complex overlapping and cross-cutting of boundaries that characterizes the formation of ethnic and racialized identities. This is not to argue that definitions of racism are not necessary, both for purposes of legal protection and redress, and the specification of objects of social, political, and economic analysis, but that strict definitions are always liable to find themselves confounded by the complex intertwining of the very wide range of cultural repertoires being drawn upon by individuals and collectivities.

The difficulties of drawing neat boundaries around concepts such as ethnicity, ethnocentrism, race, racism, and so forth, are now becoming more widely acknowledged, as are the difficulties of finding unambiguous and acceptable ethnic labels in practices of regulation and policy, as for example, in census questions. Some have even doubted the value of the notion of ethnicity (Omi and Winant 1986). Others (Anthias 1992) appear to regard ethnicity as the primary concept, with "race" as a subset, although this then leads to another set of classificatory conundrums around definitions of racism (see Mason's critique (1992) of Anthias).

The significance of a "postmodern" framing of these difficulties lies in elaborating a framework that makes these problems intelligible in a specific manner, and in proposing avenues for research. The "postmodern" point is not merely one of highlighting a perennial excess of "things" over "words," that is, that definitions and analyses are always partial, but one of exhibiting particular forms of interpenetration between "words" and "things" in which discourses of "race" and ethnicity are *productive* of objects of analysis in forms that prevent simple "empirical" adjudication between competing discourses. This involves an undermining of the cultural/material distinction, and is overlaid by the potential destabilizing effects of *différance* as a property of language and discourse, both in everyday life and specialized disciplines, and deconstruction as an analytical strategy that allows the unraveling and displacement of binaries, for example, that of "old/new" racism.

These general aspects of a "postmodern" framing raise a number of questions and open up several avenues for elaboration. Given the constraints of space, four issues only are now briefly highlighted to exhibit further the particular emphases of "postmodern" framing. The discussion that follows will thus be confined to (a) the effects of a "postmodern" de-centering, de-essentialization, and "detotalization" or "undoing" of the social; (b) a de-centering of the racist subject; (c) issues of sexual difference, ambivalence, and pleasure in racializing processes, in the context of time/space relations and new forms of global/local configurations; and (d) the phenomenon of the so-called "new ethnicities."

Racism and the de-centering of the social

De-centering and detotalizing the social has the consequence, amongst the other things referred to, of treating the "social" within a "post-modern" frame as always relatively open, in the process of becoming "closed," but always subject to the play of contingency, dislocation, opposition, and dis-integration, which prevents closure around discursive practices within and between contextual, institutional sites. Framed in this mode, the variety and contradictions of ethnic and racialized discourses, as constitutive of the social, are particularly highlighted, pointing up the complexity and relative contingency and openness of the processes by which identities are constructed in "routine" everyday practices, as well as in more explicit political projects of ethnic and racialized hegemony.

Take the case of "stereotypes" of British Asians and British African-Caribbeans, as part of the cultural repertoire of inferiorization, exclusion, abuse, and discrimination in contemporary Britain. A "post-modern" framing is alert to significant *dislocations* in a process often portrayed as all-encompassing and monolithic, smoothly reproducing racialized stereotypes and practices of discrimination in institutional sites, for example, schools. To put it differently, a "postmodern" framing requires that we break with "reproductive" models in which, say, the academic performance, suspension rates, and so forth, of British Asian and British African-Caribbean pupils are portrayed as an outcome of "stereotypes" of these pupils held by teachers which lead to acts of discrimination against them, for example, placing them in less academic streams and sets. This picture oversimplifies (Rattansi 1992). Racialization processes in schools are coming to be seen as uneven and contradictory in their operation. Not all teachers hold stereotypes; the stereotypes are often contradictory in their attributions of characteristics such as "lazy," "unacademic," "stupid," "bright," as between different British Asian and British African-Caribbean pupils; other forms of discrimination may or may not follow from the expression of stereotyping abuse in the classroom; the "reproduction" of racialized stereotypes and discourses more generally is negotiated and resisted by pupils through a varied repertoire of strategies. Some of these appear to be gendered, with some British African-Caribbean female pupils "settling" for a truce in which resistance to racialized and gendered schooling practices is strategically controlled to prevent an open confrontation which could lead to serious disciplinary measures. Codes of black masculinity drawn upon in disciplinary contexts may well prevent some black male pupils adopting the relatively conciliatory pose of young black females (see Rattansi 1992 for a more detailed discussion of relevant research).

While British research monographs in the social sciences (Jenkins 1986, 1992; Genders and Player 1989) have noticed the occurrence of contradictory stereotypes, neither their general significance, nor the import of their gendered mode, has been sufficiently noticed; nor, as we shall see, the role of "modernity" as a constitutive category, and the significance of time and space in the operation of these dislocations and contradictions.

In understanding these problems, a shift of conceptual vocabulary from conventional social science to a more poststructuralist one is useful. One translation to make here is again a Foucauldian one: studies of recruitment of ethnic minorities to employment (example Jenkins 1986, 1992), of discriminatory treatment in schools (Rattansi 1992) and allocation procedures for public housing (Henderson and Karn 1984, 1987), for example, may be said to point up the extent to which stereotyping discourses, working as legitimation for exclusion from jobs, higher streams and sets in schools, and better public housing are based on *normalizing, disciplinary* judgements – thus part of what Foucault has called "bio-politics" – enshrined in managerial and allocatory practices which regard good time-keeping, lack of "trouble-making," and possible attributes of cleanliness, hygiene, bodily deportment and technique, and so forth as the relevant criteria which determine access and the allocation of resources. These considerations override conceptions of skill, academic ability, and need, and neglect the possibility of greater acceptance of cultural relativism in matters of "taste" and lifestyle. Moreover, these judgements are gendered and class-specific as well as racialized: to elaborate upon just one of the instances mentioned above, it is clear that judgements which have worked against certain families being allocated public housing on the basis of size of family, type of "taste" in decoration, lifestyle, and so forth, are the product of a form of professional and managerial disciplinary, bio-political gaze and practice, routinized in the procedures of modern public bureaucracies, which have disadvantaged both ethnic minorities *and* particular sections of the white working class. This is how Henderson and Karn's research (1987) may be read within a "postmodern" frame.

Institutional racism

The concept of "institutionalized racism," of course, has been deployed to point up processes of this kind, but a "postmodern" frame sees this not as a smooth, reproductive machine but as an internally contradictory set of processes, bound up with the specificity of *modern* disciplinary institutions, which amongst other things embody particular "standards" of deportment and hygiene, involving not merely racialized, but gendered and class-specific discursive practices of judgement and discrimination involving bodily attributes, everyday aesthetics, capacities for self-control (drinking, time-keeping, lack of disruptive behavior), and ordering the immediate environment (tidiness, cleanliness, etc.). Moreover, the assumption of "uniform" judgements, consistently "applied," cannot necessarily be made, although the consistently discriminatory outcomes of allocatory processes may provide particular clues to the forms of "normalizing" discrimination involved.

Undoing the social in this manner has, of course, general implications for the way in which the operation of racialized power relations is theorized. That is, it cannot be conceptualized as working and reproducing through a small number of tightly knit sites such as those of state and capital, aided and abetted by a capitalist media supposedly only interested in dividing black and white workers, as set out in some influential British Marxist works (for cruder versions of this thesis see, for example, Sivanandan 1974; for a more sophisticated but nevertheless class-reductionist rendering of this type of argument, see Sarup 1986, 40, 95–98). Instead, racialized power relations may be seen more usefully in neo-Foucauldian terms which do not deny the importance of the state and capital but see these as far more fragmented and internally divided, together with a multiplication of sites for the operation of racisms – playgrounds, streets, classrooms, doctors' surgeries, mental hospitals, offices, etc. – with an important constitutive role assigned to specialized configurations of power/knowledge such as psychiatry or educational psychology, and professional ideologies, for example, among British teachers, the popular liberal notion of treating individual students in supposedly "color-blind" terms, which has the effect of ignoring the effects of racism and racialized economic disadvantage on students (a form of "professionalism" criticized in the State-commissioned Rampton Report (Department of Education and Science 1981)).

Moreover, attempts to understand struggles to improve the treatment of ethnic minorities, for instance, in the workplace, have to give much greater importance to the question of discursive contestations. Jewson and Mason's analysis (1992) of the rhetorical ploys and countermoves in struggles over the meaning of "equal opportunities" in particular workplaces furnishes an especially well-researched illustration of a widespread strategy of resistance by those opposed to such policies.

*Sexuality, time/space, the body, pleasure, ambivalence, and the
spectacular in racialization*

The question of the gendering of racialized discursive practices has
already featured in my discussion above. Several other dimensions
can be highlighted. For instance, the ways in which the black and
Asian presence in British inner cities, in other words "the inner city"
as a *racialized* "place," is also *sexualized* by reference to the "threat"
posed to white women by black men in a variety of discourses, including
those of the popular press, politicians, and the police (Ware 1992).
The British extreme right has certainly been adept at exploiting this
particular form of appeal to its male and female members in texts
likely to generate fear in the women and masculine protectiveness in
the men. Thus, the National Front youth paper *Bulldog* has covered its
front page with a story headlined "Black Pimps Force White Girls into
Prostitution," while *National Front News* consistently carried reports of
alleged sexual offences perpetrated by black men against white women.
The front page was used to caption a photograph of a white family
with the appeal: "White Man! You Have a Duty to Protect Your
Race, Homeland and Family!," and *Bulldog* advised its readers to
"think of the safety of your White womenfolk . . . think of your
mother, your sister, your girlfriend" (Durham 1991, 272). Amongst
other things, these examples also manage to convey the significance
of the articulations betwen "family" and "home" as symbols of race and
space (Cohen 1993). They also repeat, at a temporal and spatial distance,
the colonial discourse whereby the idea of the empire as a dangerous
place where women needed protection and were to stay at "home"
allowed the construction of aggressive and protective masculinities,
with a privileged placing in the "public" arena, confining women to
the "domestic" sphere.

Of course, the racializing of space, especially in the city, takes a
variety of forms, from the relative segregation of communities by
housing policies and the phenomenon of "white flight" (Cohen 1993),
as well as black expulsion – ethnic minority families forced out by
vicious harassment – to the connotative "fixing" of drug and crime
issues to the black presence. And the sexualization of the inner city
also has an autonomous logic involving prostitution and the activities
of pornographers, and "panics" around the gay and lesbian presence,
although here again the racialization and the sexualization can be
articulated to each other via the supposed power of black pimps, a
representation circulated by various forms of media including film –

take the case of the highly popular *Mona Lisa*, whose racializing and sexual dynamics, involving a world of black pimps and black and white prostitutes, are acutely explored by Pajaczkowska and Young (1992) – and panics about black homophobia (Burston 1993). The gendering and sexualization of the nation is another important element in the dynamics of the sexualization of "race." Women, as Yuval-Davis and Anthias (1989, 8–10) have pointed out, and as is evident from the discussion of the discourse of the extreme right above, play a pivotal role in the construction of ethnicity and nationality: as biological reproducers; as boundary markers – hence the attempts to police their sexual relations with "others"; as transmitters of the culture; as crucial symbols, for example, in notions of the motherland; and of course as actual participants in national struggles.

Hence, surely, the significance of the metaphor of "rape" in discussions of the impact of immigration on British culture (see for example the speech by John Stokes, MP, reproduced, although not with this point in mind, by Barker 1981, 18), and the actuality of rape in so many projects of what have come now to be called "ethnic cleansing." If "woman" is a key signifier of both culture and territory, then the sexual violation of her body is an assertion of masculinist ethnicity, or nationality, or "race," which emasculates the other (although thereby enmeshing the rapist in the contradictions of defilement by such biological intercourse and the probable birth of a "miscegenated" population). But masculinization may function in an oppositional mode, for example, in struggles for nationhood, while simultaneously being part of the discursive practices which subordinate women in that community. An instance may be found in Yuval-Davis and Anthias's recounting of a popular, presumably male, Palestinian saying of the 1980s which referred to the higher birthrates among the Palestinian population: "The Israelis beat us at the borders but we beat them in the bedrooms" (1989, 8).

Space, then, is not only feminized but masculinized. This sexualization too feeds into the racialization of locales. In British cities this often happens through the staking out of territorial claims, and their continued policing by young working-class males to keep an area "clean" of "wogs," "Pakis," and "niggers." Amongst other things, the discursive practices involved attempt to humiliate these others by physical assaults and verbal abuse which "prove" the masculinity of the attackers and "reduce" the victims to "sissies": a form of emasculation and effeminization (Willis 1978). And the significance of masculinist cultures was emphasized by the Macdonald Enquiry into the murder of an Asian pupil at Burnage High School in Manchester, England, by a white schoolmate: a strong masculinist culture of violence in the all-boys school was, the report argued, an important constitutive feature of the racism in the school (Macdonald, et al. 1989).

But it is important to remember that there may be complex variations in the racializing dynamics involved, with alliances between white and African-Caribbean males against Asians or, as in some areas, the skirmishes being confined to whites and Asians, coexisting with the presence of African-Caribbeans in local colleges of further and higher education (Cohen 1993). And as we shall see in the next section, the Macdonald Enquiry also had some interesting remarks on the complexity of racialized networks of alliance and cooperation.

There is precious little research on the connections between classed masculinities, the territorialization of social relations, and racism in Britain to draw upon (Cohen's work being a notable exception). I would suggest that amongst the elements that such research would need to consider are the *pleasures* of male bonding and violence in various urban contexts where there is a perennial search for excitement thwarted by a chronic lack of material and cultural resources and opportunities. The possibilities for gaining fame and notoriety through media coverage gives added pleasure and affirmation, and provides motivation for a continuation of the violence despite the threat and actuality of prison and other sanctions. (What applies to racist activities can surely also be true of the pleasures of antiracist involvements. For discussions of "pleasure" in cultural politics, see the pioneering attempt in Bennett, et al. 1983.)

Some of this becomes evident in recent accounts of those involved in soccer violence and in the activities of Britain's far right organizations. Here, for example, are extracts from an interview with a soccer "hooligan":

He talks of his days with the Subway Army (so named because of the way they ambushed opposition fans in Wolverhampton's subway network) . . . with an unmistakable air of nostalgia. They were heady days of male bonding. You looked after your mates, and they looked after you . . . The fighting would go on for as long as the police would let it. Tony freely admits he wasn't much interested in the football. What attracted him was the thrill of the violence. "It's just a buzz. A feeling of power. Knowing you are with a bunch of geezers who can do another firm."   (Weale 1993; see also Williams, et al. 1987)

The same report explores the attractions of participating in violence abroad and the pleasures of national and international notoriety in a world of international media coverage:

The up-and-coming soccer yobs have . . . been looking abroad for action, where they can be sure of a bigger stage which will attract widespread media attention and where they can make their names. Some, like Paul Scarrot from Nottingham, who earned the title of super-yob after being expelled from the 1990 World Cup in Italy go on to achieve international notoriety.

(Weale 1993)

And a contemporaneous account of a neo-Nazi group not only recounted the pleasures of violence and listening to racist rock bands, but contained the following remarks on the significance to the group of media coverage:

This is a fan club whose cult is itself and its own doings. No group was ever more besotted by its reflection in the media, whether it is in its own *Blood and Honour* fanzine or in the furiously hostile publicity granted to the skinhead racist scene by the mainstream press and television. When they are in jail, which is fairly frequently, members devour the anti-racist magazine *Searchlight*, which is devoted to exposing the neo-Fascist right. They find their own names and doings and are happy. (Ascherson 1993)

A globalized, media-saturated world is in some senses constitutive of this group: its name, Blood and Honour, is in fact borrowed from the South African neo-Nazi party, the AWB, while part of the pleasures of media coverage are bound up with a sense of connection with an international network of neofascist organizations, but are also perhaps a compensation for the drab anonymity of an ordinary existence in a soulless new English town, Milton Keynes.

 The body and its insertion into an economy of the cultural politics of pleasure and spectacle thus emerges as an important site for exploration that future research into racializing processes must address. Think for example of the ways in which so many younger members of the extreme right fashion distinctive bodily adornments from tattoos to skinhead and "mohican" haircuts, "badges" of membership, identification, and affirmation directly imprinted on the body, but allied to particular conceptions of bodily hygiene and a lifestyle which allows them to construct their identities in often imaginary differentiation from both blacks and "Pakis" and groups like "new-age travelers" (see, again, Ascherson 1993 on the Blood and Honour Group). Musical preferences for raucous rock and modes of dance – often accompanied by violence – set their bodies in motion, to borrow a phrase from Mort (1983).

These accounts give added weight to Silverman's recent suggestion that an understanding of contemporary forms of racism, and racist violence in particular, requires an acknowledgement of Bauman's emphasis on the symbolic nature of the "struggle for survival" today and its desire to imprint itself on "the public imagination" (Silverman 1993). A shift to a relatively novel racism in which the symbolic has a more privileged role, whether in the form of the desecration of Jewish graves or attacks on Muslim and other places of worship, takes place as part of a change of emphasis in racialized discourses to the language of "difference," which I have discussed earlier.

Silverman usefully yokes his argument to recent discussions of economic and political transformations in Western Europe, whether theorized in terms of "postmodernization" or, as Wieviorka has done in his *L'Espace du Racisme* (1991) and in Wieviorka (1994), under the rubric of "postindustrialism," an analysis which points to the marginalization of older labor movements and the numerical decline and fragmentation of the communities built around the male manual working class due to a fundamental restructuring of the industrial and urban infrastructure, combined with crises of national identity and state institutions. This is the "space" in which there is a relatively new politics of cultural difference organized around "new" social movements, including racist and antiracist movements well aware of symbolic gestures and the staging of events, operating in a political environment in which governments, too, are enmeshed in a strategy of the symbolic management of racialized discrimination and conflict.

One consequence of the new industrial, urban, and cultural transformations is a disembedding of traditions and a collapse of employment and other infrastructures, and feelings of rootlessness, generating anxieties which become exploited and mobilized around endless searches for "roots" and projects of racialized nationalisms. There is a sense in which this gives rise to particular racisms which are novel, and enable the thesis of a "new racism" to be reformulated in a more convincing fashion.

But as I have argued above, such analyses will have to accomplish far more than documentation of some of these sorts of processes of "postmodernization" or the crisis of "modernity." We need to theorize them rigorously by a more direct rethinking of the formation of identities, subjectivities, and the social and in which issues of sexuality, pleasure, temporality, and spatiality have a role entirely neglected not only in the work of Wieviorka but also Silverman. It is important to note, too, that the form of analysis I am recommending is different in quite fundamental ways from discussions of urban racism based either on albeit sophisticated versions of the "false consciousness" thesis as posited by Phizacklea and Miles (1980; for an appreciative but critical discussion see Rattansi 1992, 31–33) or a resource-conflict model of the type proposed by Wellman (1977) in which white racism is seen primarily as a legitimating ideology for white privilege.

The differences involved are further underscored once the question of *ambivalence* and its great significance is appreciated. Racialized discourses, and those involving degrees of sexualization in particular, are not merely differentiating, inferiorizing, and legitimating, but involve forms of ambivalence which interrupt their subordinating charge.

I have remarked elsewhere on the ambivalence around the figure of the British Asian woman, at once the guardian and pillar of the "tightly knit" Asian family – much admired, especially by the right for its "family values" and discipline; but also a symbol of the "backwardness" of Asians, for she is both seen as subject to extraordinary subordination and, by her adherence to Asian conventions, regarded as an obstacle to the assimilation of Asians into British culture or "the English way of life"; and sexually alluring, the dusky heiress to the Kama Sutra and the Oriental harem (Rattansi 1992).

The ambivalence surrounding the British Asian family, especially on the right, is nicely captured by a recent headline in the conservative *Daily Mail*: "Britain's Traditional Family is Now Asian' (29th January 1993). The accompanying text continues: "Asians have taken over from whites as the traditional British family, a new report reveals. Seventy per cent of Pakistani and Bangladeshi households here consist of husband, wife and children – the accepted norm for generations – compared with only 25 per cent of whites." The discourse combines a nostalgia for a golden age, and an implicit admiration for the "family values" of Asians, with the anxiety of being "taken over" as well as overtaken by a population not granted the status of really belonging – they are still described as Pakistani and Bangladeshi households who happen to be "here."

But in this instance and others around the discussion of "the Asian woman" discussed earlier, we can also see how the category of "modernity," conceptions of time and space, and the sexualization of discourses around cultural "others" can combine in distinctive ways. That is, discourses around British Asians, their families, "their women," their supposed business success, and so forth can be understood by analogy with Bauman's analysis (1989; 1991) of the Jew as eternal "stranger," falling foul of modernity's drive for classificatory order and its abhorrence of the disruptive, unassimilable figure. It is arguable, that is, that British Asians generate a series of contradictory responses in discourses in modern British culture, partly because of their transgression of a series of culturally produced boundaries which attempt to hold British modernity in place: *British Asians are, in effect, too premodern, too modern, and too postmodern.* The "premodernity," *the lack of coevality in time* of British Asians, is symbolized by the supposedly all-effective subjugation of "their women," as well as by patterns of dress, religious "fundamentalism," "uncivilized" and "backward" practices of ritualized animal slaughter, and so forth; their *modernity-in-excess* is symbolized, as with the Jews, by their supposedly disproportionate involvement in commerce, their eagerness to accumulate, and by their shops replacing the "traditional" English cornershop, symbol of the cosy British working-class community-neighborhood – the "kith and kin" element is important here – but they are also too "postmodern," too mobile, a diasporic, "deterritorialized" community with links in India, Pakistan, Canada, the United States, Singapore, Hong Kong, and elsewhere, disturbing the settledness of Britain's "island race" culture, bringing in brides and husbands from India, while setting up transnational businesses and refusing to support the British cricket team in its (currently disastrous) encounters with India, Pakistan, and the West Indies. And yet, this is a form of cultural disruption always overlaid with the ambivalence of unconscious desire and the more explicit pulls of admiration and envy.

So there is not just the often-noted *double bind* of racist discourses which traps the racialized subject into inferiorization and transgression – as Fanon put it, "When people like me, they tell me it is in spite of my colour. When they dislike me, they point out it is not because of my colour. Either way, I am locked into the infernal circle" (1986, 116) – but also a *triple bind* which is revealed when temporality and spatiality are more explicitly built into the analysis of racializing processes.

De-centering the racist subject

If the proliferation of contradictory and ambivalent discourses is indicative of dislocations internal to and constitutive of the social and its relative openness, it is also to be seen as part of the structuration which makes available a series of different "subject positions." In effect, part of the process by which, in this instance, racist identities are de-centered is by being invited to occupy a variety of enunciative modes and engage in a range of practices. A "postmodern" frame posits racist identities, like other identities, including that of the "antiracist," as de-centered, fragmented by contradictory discourses and by the pull of other identities. Therefore, as not necessarily consistent in their operation across different contexts and sites, and not available in the form of transparent self-knowledge to the subjects.

British researchers like Billig (1978 and 1984), more aware of the complexities of racialized identity formation, have furnished a range of examples of relevant subjects and contexts. For instance, the trade union official, a member of the explicitly racist National Front, who appeared to have been elected to his union position by both blacks and whites because of his record of fighting equally for both sets of members, and his personal relations of friendliness to black colleagues; the white girl interviewed at school, who expressed strong racist views, but was then seen leaving school arm in arm with an Asian girl; and so forth (see also Jones 1988, 177–227). Even the Macdonald Enquiry into the murder of a British Pakistani pupil at Burnage High School in Manchester was forced to conclude that the racism of his killer, a white fellow pupil, was not of a "simple" kind: he had earlier established alliances and friendships with other black and Asian pupils (see Rattansi 1992 for a more detailed discussion). Moreover, as I pointed out earlier, the Enquiry also in effect argued that what has to be understood is not only the complexity of his racism, but the effect of his masculinity as embedded in the aggressive and violent culture of his all-boys school.

The form of de-centeredness of racist and racializing subjectivities and identities cannot however be understood simply in Foucauldian terms as the structured effects of different discourses and the subject positions thus made available, for example around both "race" and masculinity.

For example, disavowal statements of the kind "I'm not a racist, but . . . (there are too many of them)," or "Some of my best friends are black, but . . . (it's the rest)," etc., need to be seen as part of complex rhetorical strategies by subjects as reflexive *agents*, attempting to articulate different subject positions within a framework of perceived interests and drawing upon a variety of what Weatherall and Potter (1993) have called interpretive repertoires. Discourses of liberalism and even egalitarianism may be rhetorically mobilized not merely against racialized forms of discrimination and exclusion but to legitimate them.

Weatherall and Potter's discourse analysis frame for the exploration of the highly complex rhetoric involved in the "working out" of white New Zealanders' construction of Maoris as racial problems and their legitimation of exclusionary and exploitative practices against Maoris may be regarded as a particularly fruitful illustration of a type of "postmodern" analysis of racism. Eschewing reductive accounts of racism as simply "false consciousness," and the "racist" as a unified subject, they explore how social categories and arguments are deployed by white New Zealanders around specific instances and fields such as education, crime, land claims, and so forth, but, for Weatherall and Potter, always with a view to understanding these rhetorical moves in a historical context of relations of power, domination, and advantage, while drawing out the tension of contradictory pulls of "racist" and "antiracist" positions.

Amongst other things, Weatherall and Potter's *Mapping the Language of Racism* accomplishes a critique of the common conception of racism as "prejudice," with its psychologically reductive, individualistic, and pathologizing tendency. It reveals at the same time the Enlightenment residue of the "rational/prejudiced" binary which underlies much of this type of analysis (see also Rattansi 1992 for a critique of "prejudice" as used in the discourse of "multicultural education"). And it establishes the productiveness of the strategy recommended in this essay, of avoiding supposedly water-tight definitions of racism in favor of actually examining how racial logics and categories work in relation to specific events and social fields.

However, amongst a number of my reservations with regard to Weatherall and Potter's project, three interrelated ones are particularly relevant here. First, while justifiably skeptical of attempts within social psychology to construct typologies of subjects along a spectrum of adherence to racist views (Weatherall and Potter 1993, 194), by default they end up not merely de-centering but almost completely denuding subjects of identities altogether: "Conflict, ambivalence, inconsistency and contradiction seem to be endemic. They do not, that is, seem to be associated with just one group of individuals or one type of person. Everybody is a dilemmatician – anti-racist to the same extent as racist" (1993, 198). But this evades the issue of the different "investments" that individuals may have in particular identities and identifications in a wide range of contexts. To take rather extreme cases to illustrate the point, while both the long-standing National Front activist and the "liberal" or other kind of antiracist activist may both draw on conflicting logics and face discursive dilemmas in justifying their (subject) positions, to homogenize them as "dilemmaticians" – Weatherall and Potter's term – is to ignore vital differences in how each may engage in social practices towards racialized groups at work and in other fields, and the degree to which each is likely to initiate and respond to various projects of racialized or racializing mobilization. Unwittingly no doubt, Weatherall and Potter appear to be aligned to the crasser forms of "postmodernist" conceptions of "multiple identities," mainly as a consequence of wanting to avoid equally problematic theorizations of "identity" in social psychology (1993, 43–49).

At this point a second difficulty becomes apparent: the neglect of psychoanalytic accounts. Weatherall and Potter distance themselves, not without good reason, from the "authoritarian personality" studies (1993, 49–57), but apart from a passing nod of approval to the possibilities of mobilizing Horney's "neo-Freudian" work for reading racist discourse (1993, 54), they fail to engage with the psychoanalytic possibilities that might prove fruitful. Not surprisingly, while borrowing from aspects of Bhabha's work (Weatherall and Potter 1993, 142–43), his use of psychoanalytic theory, and the related emphasis on "ambivalence" go unnoticed, and it is tempting to attribute Weatherall and Potter's complete neglect of the gendering and sexualization of racial discourse, and this is my third reservation, in part to the absence of psychoanalytic theory in their construction of discourse analysis.

Psychoanalysis and the de-centered racist subject

Psychoanalytic theorizations, as an earlier part of this essay has suggested, must be regarded as important to a "postmodern" de-centering of the subject and in principle could yield interesting accounts of de-centered, "racialized" subjects – here to include those with investments in racist *and* antiracist positions, and also those who are the objects of racism. Franz Fanon's *Black Skins, White Masks* (1986) is a key reference point for understanding some of the psychic costs of racism to its victims – I use the latter term without imputing passivity to them. However, it is not at all clear that, to date, the psychoanalytic literature has produced work of serious power and scope in understanding the psychic economy of racism, although Fanon himself offers some interesting observations, and the work of Kovel (1988), Rustin (1991, 57–84), Kristeva (1991), and others (see Gordon 1992 and Young 1993 for brief surveys), may be regarded as having made a start. Amongst those I have already discussed, Bhabha, Gilman, and Cohen, from different theoretical stances, have deployed psychoanalytic concepts productively.

The *ambivalence* of racism, although deriving from a variety of sources that I have remarked upon, is particularly open to psychoanalytic interpretation, for it is in psychoanalysis that the notion has its strongest roots. Curiously, the Klein-influenced commentators, Gordon, Young, and Rustin, appear not to grasp its significance; indeed, they neglect it altogether, one consequence being their noticeable pessimism (this being slightly less true of Rustin), the effect of reducing racism to an uncontradictory pathology.

"Postmodern" framing obviously requires a form of psychoanalytic theorization which, in addition to being aware of the racist involvements of psychoanalytic theory and politics, does not reduce all racisms merely to supposedly eternal and universal psychic mechanisms, but also reflects on the specificity of modernity and its constitutive role in the formation of racism. Psychoanalytic attempts to grapple with colonialism and the Holocaust have been forced to confront racism in a more historically specific register, with the Frankfurt School's "Authoritarian Personality" studies perhaps being the most explicit in their efforts to delineate some of the interconnections between modernity and racism.

One of the more interesting recent attempts is that by Stephen Frosh (1989; also 1987 and 1991), who sketches out the links between racism and modernity, sexuality, and masculinity, while mindful of the significance of ambivalence, although his account is written with little engagement with "colonial discourse analysis." Frosh analyzes racism as one response of the threatened ego, an ego that is generically fragile, split, and fragmented in both Kleinian and Lacanian senses, but under further pressure from the multiplicitous, disintegrating, constantly changing, fast-moving forces of social life under conditions of modernity. Sexuality is crucially important in his account: in the Fanonian sense, with the white man seeing the black man as biological other – a vehicle for the projection of unwanted feelings about the body – as well as a sexual threat (Fanon 1986, 163–78). Repressed homosexual desire creates an ambivalence that connects up with other forms of ambivalence that permeate feeling toward others, whether Jews, blacks, or Asians. Modernity is one of the other sources of ambivalence. It is experienced as threatening, but in part exciting. Other forms of ambivalence see the objects as not only disgusting and hateful, but powerful, fascinating, and erotic and possessors of qualities admired by racist subjects. Hence the plausibility of conspiracy theories in which the enemy is seen as having conquered what terrifies the racist – chaos, change, disorder, fragmentation, disintegration.

This is not an appropriate place to enter into a lengthy consideration of the merits of psychoanalytic approaches to issues of racism. Here I only wish to register the general point that in my view neither the general de-centeredness of the (racist) subject nor the sexualization and ambivalences of racism can be fully grasped without some hypothesization of the self as constitutively divided between the conscious and the unconscious, without understanding the centrality of sexuality, and without some consideration of splitting, fantasy, pleasure, introjection, projection, and so on, as possible mechanisms by which identifications and subjectivities operate and change. Clearly, complex issues arise for practices of antiracism, too, if psychoanalytic insights are granted credibility.

Ethnicities, "new" and "old"

The "de-centering" and "de-essentializing" moves of the "postmodern" frame have played a key role in this essay: in mobilizing a general conception of identities, in pointing to its effects on the dissolution of "woman" as a figure in feminism, in suggesting its possible ramifications for understanding the nature of "race," the formation of racist identities, subjectivities, and discourses, and in emphasizing that ethnicities, nationalisms, and other forms of collective identity are products of a process to be conceptualized as a cultural politics of representation, one in which narratives, images, musical forms, and popular culture more generally, have a significant role.

Contemporary forms of globalization, the formation of diasporas and diasporic identities, and the creation of new hybrid and synthetic cultural forms, I have earlier argued, are also of key interest within a "postmodern" frame, as is Hall's conception of the "new ethnicities" (1992a), for similar reasons, in what he now refers to as a "notorious" piece (1992d). Written in the context of a debate on the place of "black film" in British cinema, Hall's "New Ethnicities" (1992a) reflects on the particularities of an apparently curious conjunction between poststructuralism, a series of iconoclastic "black" cinematic projects – Hanif Kureishi's *My Beautiful Launderette* and Sankofa's *Passion of Remembrance* being two outstanding examples – and the formation of a new configuration in ethnic minority politics in Britain where the saliency of "black" as a unifying signifier has been gradually losing its potency. This is in effect a double interwoven transition. A shift, first, from an earlier period characterized by *a struggle over relations of representation* – taking the form of demands for access to the apparatuses and technologies of representation and the contestation of gross stereotypes and their replacement with "positive" images – to *a politics of representation* where the demands of the "positive" image are now regarded as suffocating the possibilities for exploring the huge variety of ethnic, subcultural, and sexual identities pulsating in the minority communities. Moreover, there is an experimentation with modernist and "postmodernist" forms which break from an equally stifling aesthetic of "realism" imposed by the demands of the "positive image" (usually privileging middle-class heterosexuality). And relatedly, we see the beginnings of a new phase which Hall describes as the demise of "the essential black subject" in which the oppositional political unity forged by ethnic minorities of African-Caribbean and South Asian descent under the sign of blackness – influenced by the Black Power movement in the United States – is giving way to new types of political "subjects" involving new forms of identity-formation and a new phase in the politics of cultural difference.

Poststructuralism doubles here as both a *form of analysis*, which reads this as a de-essentializing moment, and a *constitutive element* in the formation of the new ethnicities insofar as some of the cultural workers and activists involved have themselves been influenced by poststructuralist currents (not least by the writings of Hall himself). By the same token, the "postmodern" frame as defined here is also doubly valorized (although I hasten to add that the essential black subject is being undermined by rather more than the adoption of versions of poststructuralism by artists and film-makers).

Questions of sexuality have been crucial to the projects comprising the new ethnicities, for many of the de-essentializing cultural and political projects have been produced by black feminists and gay and lesbian activists intent upon challenging the codes of black masculinity that had hitherto marginalized other sexual identities in the minority communities.

Issues of globalization and diaspora are also central, given the impetus provided by decolonization processes in general, the influence of "Third World" cinema, and the creation of new "hybrid" cultural forms by borrowing from Western, Asian, African, African-American, and other cultural practices.

Commenting on these new cultural politics, and indeed deploying the term "new ethnicities" is, for Hall, also a way of rescuing the concept of ethnicity from its connotative links with nation and "race." Here we encounter another doubling, for at the same time that Hall himself contributes to a de-essentialization of the black subject by pointing to the cultural and political possibilities opened up by the new cultural politics, he also wants to emphasize that there can be no form of representation, no sort of political enunciation, no kind of positioning which does not have to operate with historically given languages and cultural codes; in other words, with ethnicities.

The "new ethnicities," then, is Hall's way of conceptually inserting the minority communities into the more generally commented upon politics of cultural difference of late modernity or "postmodernity," a politics that has also seen the demise and fracturing of other previously essentialized subjects: social classes and women.

The precise meaning of "ethnicity" still remains elusive, but in my view Hall's general project is nevertheless indispensable, for it attempts to chart and indeed to recommend new, more open, non-absolutist forms of cultural politics within and between the minority communities and their articulation with the politics of the "center" – a project to which Paul Gilroy has also made powerful contributions (see 1992 and 1993b) while not falling into the trap of assuming a utopian emancipation from all forms of cultural essentialization, an escape from the positionings of time and space, narrative, memory, and territorialization which make cultural production and politics possible. It is here that the "strategic essentialism" recommended by Spivak (1990) and others finds its place in an oppositional politics of coalition and cooperation rather than an endless multiplication of identities and fragments incapable of effective collective mobilization. In all these senses Hall's account of the "new ethnicities" can be mined for its suggestiveness for what in very general terms may be regarded as the political implications of the "postmodern" frame, especially as they relate to questions of "race" and ethnicity.

But this is a politics that has to contend with a variety of different political projects of cultural difference in the minority diasporic communities of Britain and the United States, and the "blacklash" they have had to endure. For one thing, versions of the "old" ethnicities are very much alive, a point hardly to be labored in the wake of the Rushdie affair in which revamped Islamic "fundamentalisms" were met in turn with a retreat into virulent assimilationism by some white liberals. Fay Weldon's *Sacred Cows* (1989) provides an instructive illustration of the arguments of Mendus (1989) and Parekh (1994) about the strong limits to "liberal" toleration. At the same time, many new black cultural forms and projects, from rap to the films of Spike Lee, have attempted to reconstruct traditional masculinities, have colluded with or actively promoted misogynistic and homophobic currents, and have supported black nationalisms which run quite counter to the optimistic openness tracked in Hall's "new ethnicities" (on Spike Lee, see, for instance, the critiques by Michelle Wallace 1992 and Paul Gilroy 1993b).

Rap is clearly a contradictory cultural form. There is on the one hand the misogyny of Ice-T and others, with some black cultural critics making a particularly strong stand against 2 Live Crew (Baker 1992 and 1993). Stephens (1991), on the other hand, regards rap as a "clearly postmodern artform," characterized by "indeterminacy, decanonisation, hybridisation, performance and participation, and immanence," although his oxymoronic construction of rap as a form of Afrocentric "postmodernism" fails to convince. A more likely candidate for the label "postmodernist" rap in the sense used in this essay is the music and performance of the British South Asian rapper Apache Indian, who not only mocks the misnaming of native Americans – although this may be an unwitting consequence of borrowing the name from an Indo-Caribbean musical hero (see Back 1993a) – and borrows a musical form produced by members of the African diaspora, but in songs like "Arranged Marriage," "Sharabi" (alcoholic), and "Caste System" he also challenges cultural practices amongst the British South Asian communities which subordinate women, valorize hard-drinking displays of masculinity, and reinforce boundaries of caste, class, and ethnicity (Back 1993a, 1993b). More recently, the rapper has become involved in the antiracist campaigns provoked by the victory of the British National Party and the serious escalation in racist violence in London's East End and has released a single, "Moving On" (Back 1993b), with part of the proceeds going to a variety of grass-roots East End Bengali campaigning organizations (Back 1993b).

This is not to argue that only "progressive" forms of rap can qualify as "postmodernist" but that the essentialism of a strongly committed form of Afrocentrism surely disqualifies. Stephens (1992), however, does usefully place rap as a "postmodern" musical form and reflects on the mixed audiences for it, and now the "interracial" performers of the music.

By way of conclusion: racialization and the politics of identities

A distinctive thrust of this essay has been the recommendation of a strategy of "postmodern," especially poststructuralist, "deconstruction" which de-centers racist and antiracist subjects and de-essentializes and detotalizes racialized social structures. Attention has been focused on the mobility and variability of "race" as a signifier in political processes, and an attempt has been made to treat the "racist" subject as the site of contradictory identities which result from the contextual juggling of the variety of subject positions that "Western" capitalist liberal democracies make potentially available: citizen, democrat, worker, employer (note the significance of *class* here), man/woman, or masculine and feminine. These articulate with many others, but especially with various ethnic and racialized positions – white, black, African, Asian, and all the myriad others forged in long struggles for recognition, entitlements, and freedoms. Very often the tensions between positions have been explicitly acknowledged, especially by subordinated minorities – one only has to think of "African-American" or "black British" – in an attempt to work within syncretic spaces and desynchronized temporalities. That is, to work with fragments, from the margins, attempting to get some place in the structures, narratives, and imaginations of the centers.

But these emphases are often taken to imply that the institutionaliz-ation, the sheer "materiality" of power, and the necessity and possibility of broadly based struggles for transformation are dissolved and denied in this type of "postmodern" politics. Fragmented, "local" struggles are all we are supposedly left with in the debris left after the demolition of centered subjects and brute, enduring socioeconomic oppressions. If individual subjects are fragmented, what hope can there be for the formation of collective subjects and movements? If the "social" is de-essentialized such that no necessary links between power structures are posited, how can strategic programs of broad reform be formu-lated which might allow alliances between "antiracists," "feminists," workplace struggles, and so forth?

Although such political and strategic implications *may* be inferred from a "deconstructive" approach, they are by no means the only points of destination. Other routes are equally plausible, for there has been another set of thematics consistently present in the analysis presented here. The interpretive strategy advocated here has emphasized, for one thing, the *institutional* forms of bio-power and the material effects of discursive regimes of power which inscribe the bodies and subjectivities of individual subjects. Forms of racialized discrimination in education, employment, public housing allocation, and so forth have been shown to operate within *patterned structures of power and domination* – that is, public and private bureaucracies. Although these are no longer posited as monolithic, reproductive machines, there is no denial of the embeddedness of power relations in these institutions, sedimented over long periods. The operations of power within these fields can be analyzed in their historical and contemporary actualities, and the strategies, rules, and procedures, activated by dominant and subordinate reflective agents through the use of institutional resources, can be excavated by various forms of struggle and research. The detailed workings of discriminatory practices can be scrutinized, central nodal points of subject-formation and power networks identified, and weak points hypothetically specified where strategic pressure may make parts of institutions susceptible to reform in the direction of nondiscriminatory and redistributive practices. In this essay a number of studies of racist discrimination in schools, private enterprises, and public bureaucracies have been cited which can form the basis of strategies to challenge, dismantle, and restructure the regimes of power and "truth."

Moreover, an emphasis on historical and cultural specificities in the workings of power relations does not necessarily condemn struggles to the desert of infinite difference and permanent fragmentation. Analyses of discriminatory practices in Britain discussed in this essay have shown the ways in which the procedures and practices which disadvantage one group, for example, black and Asian pupils, black and Asian workers seeking employment, or black, Asian, and Irish families applying for public housing, may also work against white English working-class individuals and families. The white professional and managerial, often male bio-political, gaze which attempts to identify and exclude the "abnormals" – the subversive or recalcitrant pupil, the "undisciplined" worker, or the unhygienic family – creates both classed and racialized collectivities of the disadvantaged. In specific historical and political circumstances this may create the possibility of broader "race"–class alliances, for example, in the inner city. The gendered and sexualized forms of "racial" and ethnic conflicts and discriminations create the potential for local and national alliances which target hypermasculinities (themselves classed and territorialized in form). The "locales" or sites of struggle may even extend beyond the whole national polity, given the regulatory reach of corporations and state agencies, on the one hand, and the existence of diasporas on the other – the "black Atlantic" (Gilroy 1993a) and the Indian, Irish, and Jewish diasporas (as well as movements of indigenous peoples) immediately spring to mind as collectivities that have been able to mobilize transnationally.

Moreover, the operation of de-centered subjectivities and identities can work both ways. Potentially they can fragment as well as *unite*. If racist subject positions in liberal democratic polities are also open to the pull of others, such as "liberal," "good citizen," "unprejudiced," and thus other political discourses too – "fairness," equal opportunities," "justice" – then the potential always exists for the mobilization of otherwise disparately located subjects by movements struggling for antidiscriminatory and redistributive reform. Note too the possibly progressive effects of various forms of ambivalence highlighted in this essay.

However, my conceptualization does not regard identities as completely "free-floating," nor does it assume that each subject position has equal saliency for any particular individual. There is no collapse into what I have earlier called a "vulgar postmodernism" of multiple selves. Individual subjects have different degrees of "investment" in particular identities which have effectiveness over a number of contexts. Thus reformist alliances cannot be guaranteed. Perhaps one of the most important lessons of the present era is that there are no guarantees, period. But the point is that these are all grounds for *optimism* as well as pessimism. The "postmodern," especially Foucauldian, emphasis on

[handwritten margin notes: "but are they more likely to fragment?"]

[handwritten margin notes: "ambivalence is progressive?"]

the ubiquity of relations of power, domination, and resistance opens up the whole terrain of the "social," however its boundaries are drawn in specific circumstances, to political practice. And the emphasis on the significance of new hybrid and syncretic identities shows the potential for crossover identities which destabilize old ethnic absolutisms; this was part of the point of my discussion of rap and new youth identities in Britain.

The contemporary politics of "race" and ethnicity in all the liberal democracies of Europe and in the United States are witnessing a struggle between forms of "ethnic absolutism" on the one hand – white supremacist movements, neofascisms of various types, forms of black nationalism – and on the other hand, attempts to build broader, "rainbow" coalitions to contest racialized disadvantage, subordination, and violence. While there are transnational patterns, they take local, historically specific forms (Miles 1994; Wieviorka 1994; Lloyd 1994). No universal programs of reform can be prescribed. And no particular types of struggle and strategy can be universally proscribed, although it is worth pointing out that one implication of the type of analysis recommended in this essay is the need to recognize the limitations of overly "rationalist" (Enlightenment) strategies which neglect the strength of emotions, fantasy, and pleasure in sustaining racisms (see Rattansi 1992 for a discussion of the significance of this in projects of antiracist education). But what forms of reform are likely to be effective and what discourses will be capable of progressive mobilization – "citizenship," "equal rights," "democracy," "justice," "fairness" – can only be contextually decided. Strategies can only be forged in active politics and have to be endlessly revisable in the light of struggles and results.

References

Adam, B. 1990. *Time and Social Theory*. Cambridge, England: Polity Press.

Anderson, B. 1983. *Imagined Communities: Reflections on the Origins and Spread of Nationalism*. London: Verso.

Anthias, F. 1992. "Connecting 'Race' and Ethnic Phenomena." *Sociology*, 26 (3): 421–38.

Anthias, F., and N. Yuval-Davis. 1993. *Racialised Boundaries*. London: Routledge.

Ascherson, N. 1993. "Scenes from Domestic Life." *Independent on Sunday*, 17 Oct.

Back, L. 1993a. "X Amount of Sat Siri Akall: Apache Indian, Reggae Music, and Intermezzo Culture." Mimeo.

1993b. "The Unity Beat." *Guardian*, 13 Oct.

Baker, H. Jr. 1992. "You Caint' Trus' It': Experts Witnessing the Case of Rap." In *Black Popular Culture*, ed. M. Wallace and G. Dent. Seattle: Bay Press.

1993. *Black Studies, Rap, and the Academy*. Chicago: University of Chicago Press.

Balibar, E. 1991. "Is There a Neo-racism?" In *Race, Nation, and Class*, ed. E. Balibar and L. Wallerstein. London: Verso.

Banton, M., and J. Harwood. 1975. *The Race Concept*. Newton Abbot: David and Charles.

Barker, M. 1981. *The New Racism*. London: Junction Books.

Bauman, Z. 1989. *Modernity and the Holocaust*. Cambridge, England: Polity Press.

1991. *Modernity and Ambivalence*. Cambridge, England: Polity Press.

Bennett, T., V. Burgin, and J. Donald, eds. 1983. *Formations of Pleasure*. London: Routledge.

Bhabha, H. 1983. "The Other Question . . ." *Screen*, 24 (6): 18–36.

1986. "Of Mimicry and Man: The Ambivalence of Colonial Discourse." In *Politics and Ideology*, ed. J. Donald and S. Hall. Milton Keynes: Open University Press.

Billig, M. 1978. *Fascists: A Social Psychological View of the National Front*. London: Harcourt, Brace, Jovanovich.

1984. "I'm Not National Front, But . . ." *New Society*, 68 (21): 255–58.

Boyne, R. and A. Rattansi, eds. 1990. *Postmodernism and Society*. London: Macmillan.

Burston, P. 1993. "Batties Bite Back: Gays, Homophobia, and Racism." *Guardian Weekend*, 20 Nov.

Butler, J. 1990. *Gender Trouble: Feminism and the Subversion of Identity*. London: Routledge.

Castoriadis, C. 1987. "The Imaginary." In *The Real Me: Postmodernism and the Question of Identity*, ed. L. Appignanesi. London: Institute of Contemporary Arts.

Cohen, P. 1988. "The Perversions of Inheritance: Studies in the Making of Multiracist Britain." In *Multiracist Britain*, ed. P. Cohen and H. Baines. London: Macmillan.

1993. *Home Rules: Some Reflections on Racism and Nationalism in Everyday Life*. London: New Ethnicities Unit, University of East London.

282   Ali Rattansi

Department of Education and Science. 1981. *West Indian Children in Our Schools* (The Rampton Report). London: Department of Education and Science.

Derrida, J. 1977. *Of Grammatology*. Baltimore, Md.: Johns Hopkins University Press.

1978. *Writing and Difference*. London: Routledge.

1981. *Positions*. Chicago: University of Chicago Press.

Durham, M. 1991. "Women and the National Front." In *Neo-Fascism in Europe*, ed. L. Cheles, R. Ferguson, and M. Vaughan. London: Longman.

Fanon, F. 1986. *Black Skins, White Masks*. London: Pluto Press.

Flax, J. 1990. *Thinking Fragments: Psychoanalysis, Feminism, and Postmodernism in the Contemporary West*. Berkeley: University of California Press.

1993. *Disputed Subjects: Essays on Psychoanalysis, Politics, and Philosophy*. New York: Routledge.

Foucault, M. 1977. *Discipline and Punish*. London: Allen Lane.

1979. *The History of Sexuality: Vol. I, An Introduction*. London: Allen Lane.

1980. *Power/Knowledge: Selected Interviews, 1972–77*, ed. C. Gordon. Brighton: Harvester Press.

Frosh, S. 1987. *The Politics of Psychoanalysis*. London: Macmillan.

1989. "Psychoanalysis and Racism." In *Crises of the Self*, ed. B. Richards. London: Free Association Books.

1991. *Identity Crisis: Modernity, Psychoanalysis, and the Self*. London: Macmillan.

Genders, E., and E. Player. 1989. *Race Relations in Prisons*. Oxford: Clarendon Press.

Giddens, A. 1990a. *The Consequences of Modernity*. Cambridge, England: Polity Press.

1990b. "Modernity and Utopia." *New Statesman and Society*, 3 (125): 20–22.

Gilman, S. 1991. *The Jew's Body*. London: Routledge.

1992. "Black Bodies, White Bodies: Toward an Iconography of Female Sexuality in Late Nineteenth-Century Art, Medicine, and Literature." In *"Race," Culture, and Difference*, ed. J. Donald and A. Rattansi. London: Sage.

Gilroy, P. 1987. *There Ain't No Black in the Union Jack*. London: Hutchinson.

1992. "Cultural Studies and Ethnic Absolutism." In *Cultural Studies*, ed. L. Grossberg, C. Nelson, and P. Treicher. London: Routledge.

1993a. *The Black Atlantic: Modernity and Double Consciousness.* London: Verso.

1993b. *Small Acts: Thoughts on the Politics of Black Cultures.* London: Serpent's Trail.

Gordon, P. 1992. "Souls in Armour: Towards a Psychoanalytic Understanding of Racism." Mimeo.

Hall, S. 1992a. "The New Ethnicities." In *"Race," Culture, and Difference,* ed. J. Donald and A. Rattansi. London: Sage.

1992b. "The Question of Cultural Identity." In *Modernity and Its Futures,* ed. S. Hall and A. McGrew. Cambridge, England: Polity Press.

1992c. "The West and the Rest: Discourse and Power." In *Formations of Modernity,* ed. S. Hall and B. Giegen. Cambridge, England: Polity Press.

1992d. "What Is This 'Black' in Black Popular Culture?" In *Black Popular Culture,* ed. M. Wallace and G. Dent. Seattle: Bay Press.

Harvey, D. 1989. *The Condition of Postmodernity.* Oxford: Blackwell.

Hekman, S. 1990. *Gender and Knowledge: Elements of a Postmodern Feminism.* Cambridge, England: Polity Press.

Henderson, J., and V. Karn. 1984. "Race, Class, and the Allocation of Public Housing in Britain." *Urban Studies,* 21: 115–28.

1987. *Race, Class, and State Housing.* Aldershot: Gower.

Jenkins, R. 1986. *Racism and Recruitment.* Cambridge: Cambridge University Press.

1992. "Black Workers in the Labour Market: The Price of Recession." In *Racism and Antiracism: Inequalities, Opportunities, and Policies,* ed. P. Braham, A. Rattansi, and R. Skellington. London: Sage.

Jewson, N., and D. Mason. 1992. "The Theory and Practice of Equal Opportunities Policies: Liberal and Radical Approaches." In *Racism and Antiracism: Inequalities, Opportunities, and Policies,* ed. P. Braham, A. Rattansi, and R. Skellington. London: Sage.

Jones, S. 1988. *Black Culture, White Youth.* London: Macmillan.

Jordan, W. 1974. *The White Man's Burden.* Oxford: Oxford University Press.

Kabbani, R. 1986. *Europe's Myths of Orient.* London: Macmillan.

Kovel, J. 1988. *White Racism: A Psychohistory.* London: Free Association Books.

Kristeva, J. 1991. *Strangers to Ourselves.* New York: Columbia University Press.

Laclau, E. 1977. *Politics and Ideology in Marxist Theory: Capitalism, Fascism, Populism.* London: NLB.

1990. *New Reflections on the Revolution of Our Time*. London: Verso.

Lash, S., and J. Urry. 1994. *Economies of Sign and Space*. London: Sage.

Lloyd, C. 1994. "Universalism and Difference: The Crisis of Antiracism in France and the UK." In *Racism, Modernity, and Identity*, ed. A. Rattansi and S. Westwood. Cambridge, England: Polity Press.

Macdonald, I., R. Bhavnani, L. Khan, and G. John. 1989. *Murder in the Playground*. London: Longsight Press.

Mason, D. 1992. *Some Problems with the Concept of Racism*. Leicester: Leicester University Discussion Papers in Sociology.

Massey, D. 1993. "Politics and Spaced Time." In *Place and the Politics of Identity*, ed. M. Keith and S. Pile. London: Routledge.

Mendus, S. 1989. *Liberalism and the Limits of Tolerance*. Cambridge: Cambridge University Press.

Miles, R. 1987. "Recent Marxist Theories of Nationalism and Racism." *British Journal of Sociology*, 38 (1): 24–43.

1994. "Explaining Racism in Europe." In *Racism, Modernity, and Identity*, ed. A. Rattansi and S. Westwood. Cambridge, England: Polity Press.

Mort, F. 1983. "Sex, Signification, and Pleasure." In *Formations of Pleasure*, ed. T. Bennett, et al. London: Routledge.

Nandy, A. 1983. *The Intimate Enemy: Loss and Recovery of Self Under Colonialism*. Delhi: Oxford University Press.

1990. *The Tao of Cricket: On Games of Destiny and the Destiny of Games*. New York: Viking.

Nash, M. 1989. *The Cauldron of Ethnicity in the Modern World*. Chicago: University of Chicago Press.

Omi, M., and H. Winant. 1986. *Racial Formation in the United States: From the 1960s to the 1980s*. New York: Routledge.

Pajaczkowska, C., and L. Young. 1992. "Racism, Representation and Psychoanalysis." In *"Race," Culture, and Difference*, ed. J. Donald and A. Rattansi. London: Sage.

Parekh, B. 1994. "Decolonising Liberalism." In *Decolonising the Imagination*, ed. J. N. Piterse and B. Parekh. London: Zed Books.

Phizacklea, A., and R. Miles. 1980. *Labour and Racism*. London: Routledge.

Rattansi, A. 1992. "Changing the Subject? Racism, Culture, and Education." In *"Race," Culture, and Difference*, ed. J. Donald and A. Rattansi. London: Sage.

1994. "'Western' Racisms, Ethnicities, and Identities in a 'Postmodern' Frame." In *Racism, Modernity, and Identity*, ed. A. Rattansi and S. Westwood. Cambridge, England: Polity Press.

Rex, J. 1986. *Race and Ethnicity*. Milton Keynes: Open University Press.

Rustin, M. 1991. *The Good Society and the Inner World*. London: Verso.

Said, E. 1978. *Orientalism*. London: Routledge.

1993. *Culture and Imperialism*. London: Chatto and Windus.

Sarup, M. 1986. *The Politics of Multiracial Education*. London: Routledge.

Silverman, M. 1993. "Symbolic Violence and the New Communities." Paper presented to Antiracist Strategies and Movements in Europe workshop, University of Greenwich, London.

Sivanandan, A. 1974. *Race, Class, and the State*. London: Institute of Race Relations.

Soja, E. 1989. "Spatializations: A Critique of the Giddensian Version." In *Postmodern Geographies*, ed. E. Soja. London: Verso.

Spivak, G. 1990. *The Post-Colonial Critic: Interviews, Strategies, Dialogues*. London: Routledge.

Stepan, N. L. 1990. "Race and Gender: The Role of Analogy in Science." In *Anatomy of Racism*, ed. D. Goldberg. Minneapolis, Minn.: University of Minnesota Press.

Stephens, G. 1991. "Rap Music's Double-Voiced Discourse: A Crossroads for Interracial Communication." *Journal of Communication Inquiry*, 15 (2): 70–91.

1992. "Interracial Dialogue in Rap Music." *New Formations*, 16.

Urry, J. 1991. "Time and Space in Giddens' Social Theory." In *Giddens' Theory of Structuration*, ed. C. Bryant and D. Jary. London: Routledge.

Wallace, M. 1992. "'Boyz n the Hood' and 'Jungle Fever.'" In *Black Popular Culture*, ed. M. Wallace and G. Dent. Seattle: Bay Press.

Ware, V. 1992. *Beyond the Pale: White Women, Racism, and History*. London: Verso.

Weale, S. 1993. "Foreign Fields of Violent Dreams." *Guardian*, 16 Oct.

Weatherall, M., and J. Potter. 1993. *Mapping the Language of Racism*. Hemel Hempstead: Harvester Wheatsheaf.

Weldon, F. 1989. *Sacred Cows: A Portrait of Britain, Post-Rushdie, Pre-Utopia*. London: Chatto and Windus.

Wellman, D. 1977. *Portraits of White Racism*. Cambridge: Cambridge University Press.

Wieviorka, M. 1991. *L'Espace du racisme*. Paris: Seuil.

1994. "Racism in Europe: Unity and Diversity." In *Racism, Modernity, and Identity*, ed. A. Rattansi and S. Westwood. Cambridge, England: Polity Press.

Williams, J., E. Dunning, and P. Murphy. 1987. *Hooligans Abroad*. London: Routledge.

Willis, P. 1978. *Learning to Labour*. Farnborough: Saxon House.

Winant, H. 1994. "Racial Formation and Hegemony." In *Racism, Modernity, and Identity*, ed. A. Rattansi and S. Westwood. Cambridge, England: Polity Press.

Young, R. M. 1993. "Psychoanalysis and Racism: A Loud Silence." Mimeo.

Yuval-Davis, N., and F. Anthias, eds. 1989. *Woman–Nation–State*. London: Macmillan.

10

Politics, culture, and the public sphere: toward a postmodern conception

Nancy Fraser

Recent years have seen a burgeoning of interest in the United States of the concept of the public sphere. This concept finds its most sophisticated theoretical elaboration in Jürgen Habermas's 1962 book, *The Structural Transformation of the Public Sphere*. In fact, it was the belated publication of an English translation of this book in 1989 that sparked the current revival of interest in this topic (Habermas 1989).[1]

This revival is in my view quite salutary. The idea of the public sphere is a valuable conceptual resource for contemporary critical theory. It designates a theatre in modern societies in which political participation is enacted through the medium of talk. It is the space in which citizens deliberate about their common affairs, hence, an institutionalized arena of discursive interaction. This arena is conceptually distinct from the state; it a site for the production and circulation of discourses that can in principle be critical of the state. The public sphere in this sense is also conceptually distinct from the official economy; it is not an arena of market relations but rather one of discursive relations, a theatre for debating and deliberating rather than for buying and selling. Thus, this concept of the public sphere permits us to keep in view distinctions between state apparatuses, economic markets, and democratic associations. Such distinctions are essential to democratic theory. They are especially important today, when "democracy" has once again become a keyword of political life, invoked to justify various postcommunist scenarios, even as its meaning is hotly contested.

If the idea of the public sphere is an indispensable resource for the political theory of contemporary democracy, it is no less important for contemporary cultural critique. The public sphere is a site where social meanings are generated, circulated, contested, and reconstructed. It is a primary arena for the making of hegemony and of cultural common sense. The concept thus allows us to study the discursive construction of social problems and social identities. But unlike some other approaches, it situates discursive processes in their social-institutional context. The idea of the public sphere enables us to study the ways in which culture is embedded in social structure and affected by social relations of domination. It thus provides an alternative to the sort of free-floating, decontextualized discourse analysis that dissociates cultural studies from critical social theory.

In this essay, I want to explore both uses of the concept of the public sphere. I shall look first at its uses in democratic theory and then at its uses in cultural studies. In both cases, however, I shall argue that the standard *modern liberal conception of the public sphere* is not wholly satisfactory for contemporary critique. I shall suggest that it needs to be supplanted by a new *postmodern, postliberal conception of the public sphere*.

I. Beyond the modern public sphere: a political-theoretical critique

The modern liberal conception of the public sphere depends on three constitutive assumptions, each of which is problematic.[2] The three are:

1. the assumption that it is possible for interlocutors in a public sphere to bracket status differentials and to deliberate "as if" they were social equals; the assumption, therefore, that social equality is not a necessary condition for political democracy;

2. the assumption that the proliferation of a multiplicity of competing publics is necessarily a step away from, rather than toward, greater democracy, and that a single, comprehensive public sphere is always preferable to a nexus of multiple publics;

3. the assumption that discourse in public spheres should be restricted to deliberation about the common good, and that the appearance of "private interests" and "private issues" is always undesirable (Fraser 1991).

None of these assumptions can withstand critical scrutiny, however. Let us briefly consider each of them in turn.

Open access, participatory parity, and social equality

A central meaning of the modern notion of publicity is open access. Thus, defenders of the modern liberal public sphere have proclaimed it to be open and accessible to all. Historically, of course, this was not so. Women of all classes and ethnicities were long excluded from official political participation on the basis of their gender, while plebeian men were formally excluded by property qualifications. And in many cases, women and men of racialized ethnicities of all classes were excluded on racial grounds. In time, of course, such formal exclusions were eliminated. Is open access therefore finally a reality?

The modern liberal conception of the public sphere implies yes. It assumes that open access is achieved when no formal barriers to participation remain so that all can deliberate as peers. Social inequalities may persist, to be sure, but these need not vitiate participatory parity. In the liberal conception of the public sphere, interlocutors are supposed to set aside differences in birth and fortune and speak to one another as if they were social and economic peers. The operative phrase here is "as if." The social inequalities among the interlocutors are not in fact eliminated, but only *bracketed*, held in suspence and supposedly rendered inoperative.

Can such bracketing really guarantee equal access and parity of participation? The historical record to date is not encouraging. Historians such as Joan Landes (1988), Geoff Eley (1991), Mary Ryan (1990, 1991), and Evelyn Brooks-Higginbotham (1993) have shown that discursive interaction within official bourgeois public spheres has consistently been governed by protocols of style and decorum that were also markers of status inequality. These protocols functioned *informally* to marginalize women, plebeians, and members of subordinate racialized groups, preventing them from participating as peers *even after their formal incorporation*.

Informal impediments to participatory parity can persist even after everyone is formally and legally licensed to participate. When this happens, deliberation can mask domination. As Jane Mansbridge (1990, 127) puts it, "the transformation of 'I' into 'we' brought about through political deliberation can easily mask subtle forms of control. Even the language people use as they reason together usually favours one way of seeing things and discourages others. Subordinate groups sometimes cannot find the right voice or words to express their thoughts, and when they do, they discover they are not heard. [They] are silenced, encouraged to keep their wants inchoate, and heard to say 'yes' when what they have said is 'no'" (1990, 127). Thus, social inequalities tend to infect deliberation, even in the absence of formal exclusions.

Here we encounter a very serious difficulty with the modern liberal conception of the public sphere. Insofar as the bracketing of social inequalities in deliberation means proceeding as if they don't exist when they do, this does not foster participatory parity. It usually works instead to the advantage of dominant groups in society and to the disadvantage of subordinates. In most cases, it would be more appropriate to *unbracket* inequalities in the sense of explicitly thematizing them.

The modern liberal conception of the public sphere also contains another flaw. This conception assumes that a public sphere is or can be a space of zero degree culture, so utterly bereft of any specific ethos as to accommodate with perfect neutrality and equal ease interventions expressive of any and every cultural ethos. But this assumption is counterfactual, and not for reasons that are merely accidental. In stratified societies, unequally empowered social groups tend to develop unequally valued cultural styles. The result is to marginalize the contributions of members of subordinated groups both in everyday life contexts and in official public spheres.[3]

These considerations cast doubt on any conception of the public sphere that purports to bracket, rather than to eliminate, social inequalities. It will not be possible for interlocutors to deliberate *as if* they were peers in specially designated discursive arenas, when these arenas are situated in a larger context that is pervaded by structural relations of dominance and subordination. In order to have a public sphere in which interlocutors can deliberate as peers, it is not sufficient merely to bracket social inequality. Instead, it is a necessary condition for participatory parity that systemic social inequalities be eliminated. This does not mean that everyone must have exactly the same income, but it does require the sort of rough equality that is inconsistent with systemically generated relations of dominance and subordination. Pace modern liberalism, then, political democracy requires substantive social equality.[4]

Equality, diversity, and multiple publics

A second constitutive assumption of the modern liberal conception is that there should be one and only one public sphere. It is assumed that the institutional confinement of public life to a single, overarching public sphere is a positive and desirable state of affairs, whereas the proliferation of a multiplicity of publics represents a departure from, rather than an advance toward, democracy. But this assumption, too, is implausible.

We have already seen that in stratified societies full parity of participation in public debate and deliberation is not possible. But there can nevertheless be better and worse institutional arrangements. What arrangements would minimize the parity-of-participation gap between dominant and subordinate groups?

I contend that in stratified societies arrangements that promote contestation among a plurality of competing publics better promote the ideal of participatory parity than does a single, comprehensive, overarching public. This follows from the previous argument. As we saw, where societal inequality persists, deliberative processes in public spheres will tend to operate to the advantage of dominant groups and to the disadvantage of subordinates. These effects will be exacerbated, however, where there is only a single, comprehensive public sphere. In that case, members of subordinated groups would have no arenas for deliberation among themselves about their needs, objectives, and strategies. They would have no venues in which to undertake communicative processes that were not, as it were, under the supervision of dominant groups. In this situation, they could have difficulty "find[ing] the right voice or words to express their thoughts" and could tend rather "to keep their wants inchoate." They would thus be hindered from articulating and defending their interests in the comprehensive public sphere and from exposing modes of deliberation that mask domination by "absorbing the less powerful into a false 'we' that reflects the more powerful" (Mansbridge 1990).

Historically, therefore, members of subordinated social groups – women, workers, peoples of color, and gays and lesbians – have repeatedly found it advantageous to constitute alternative publics. I have called these "subaltern counterpublics" in order to signal that they are parallel discursive arenas where members of subordinated social groups invent and circulate counterdiscourses. Subaltern counter publics permit them to formulate oppositional interpretations of their identities, interests, and needs.[5] In the contemporary US feminist subaltern counterpublic, for example, feminist women have invented new terms for describing social reality, including "sexism," "the double shift," "sexual harassment," and "marital, date, and acquaintance rape." Armed with such language, we have recast our needs and identities, thereby reducing, although not eliminating, the extent of our disadvantage in official public spheres.[6]

Because such counterpublics emerge in response to exclusions within dominant publics, they help expand discursive space. In principle, assumptions that were previously exempt from contestation will now have to be publicly argued out. In general, then, the proliferation of subaltern counterpublics means a widening of discursive contestation. In stratified societies, this expansion represents a movement toward greater democracy.

It remains the case, of course, that participatory parity is not fully realizable where systematic inequalities persist. Nevertheless, the ideal is more closely approximated by arrangements that encourage contestation among a plurality of competing publics than by a single, comprehensive public sphere. Once we acknowledge this, however, we must modify the modern liberal view that treats deliberation as the privileged mode of public-sphere interaction. Relations among differentially empowered publics in stratified societies are more likely to be *contestatory* than deliberative.

Public spheres, common concerns, and private interests

One important object of such contestation is the appropriate boundaries of the public sphere. Here the central questions are: what counts as a public matter and what, in contrast, is private? This brings me to the third problematic assumption underlying the modern liberal conception of the public sphere, concerning where the line between the public and private should be drawn.

The modern liberal public sphere was supposed to be a discursive arena in which "private persons" deliberated about "public matters." There are several different senses of privacy and publicity in play here. "Publicity," for example, can denote (1) state-related; (2) accessible to everyone; (3) of concern to everyone; and (4) pertaining to a common good or shared interest. Each of these corresponds to a contrasting sense of "privacy." In addition, there are two other senses of "privacy" hovering just below the surface here: (5) pertaining to private property in a market economy; and (6) pertaining to intimate domestic or personal life, including sexual life.

I have already discussed the sense of "publicity" as open or accessible to all. Let us now examine some of the other senses, beginning with (3), of concern to everyone. This is ambiguous between what objectively affects or has an impact on everyone, as seen from an outsider's perspective, on the one hand, and what is recognized as a matter of common concern by participants, on the other hand. Now, the idea of a public sphere as an arena of collective self-determination does not sit well with approaches that would appeal to an outsider perspective in order to delimit its proper boundaries. Thus, it is the second – participant's – perspective that is relevant here. Only participants themselves can decide what is and what is not of common concern to them. However, there is no guarantee that all of them will agree. Until quite recently, for example, feminists were in the minority in thinking that the behavior they named "sexual harassment" was a matter of common concern and thus a legitimate topic for public deliberation. The great majority of people considered such behavior to be innocent flirting, hence a private matter. Then, feminists formed a subaltern counterpublic from which we disseminated a view of sexual harassment as an abuse of power and an instrument of domination, hence a widespread systemic feature of male-dominated societies. Eventually, after sustained discursive contestation – culminating in the dramatic confrontation between Clarence Thomas and Anita Hill – we succeeded in *making* it a common concern.

Contrary to the modern liberal view, there are no natural or a priori boundaries here. What will count as public in the sense of being a matter of common concern will be decided precisely through discursive contestation. It follows that no topics should be ruled off-limits in advance of such contestation. On the contrary, democratic publicity requires positive guarantees of opportunities for minorities to convince others that what in the past was not public in the sense of being a matter of common concern should now become so.

What, then, of the sense of publicity as pertaining to a common good or shared interest? This sense is in play in the modern liberal conception when the public sphere is held to be an arena in which the topic of discussion is restricted to the common good and in which discussion of private interests is ruled out. This conception, once again, is problematic. It conflates the ideas of deliberation and the common good by assuming that deliberation must be deliberation *about* the common good. It limits deliberation to talk framed from the standpoint of a single, all-encompassing "we," thereby ruling claims of self-interest and group interest out of order. Yet this works against one of the principal aims of deliberation, namely, helping participants clarify their interests, even when those interests turn out to conflict. Mansbridge (1990, 131), once again, puts the point well: "Ruling self-interest [and group interest] out of order makes it harder for any participant to sort out what is going on. In particular, the less powerful may not find ways to discover that the prevailing sense of 'we' does not adequately include them."

In general, there is no way to know in advance whether the outcome of a deliberative process will be the discovery of a common good in which conflicts of interest evaporate as merely apparent or, rather, the discovery that conflicts of interests are real and the common good is chimerical. But if the existence of a common good cannot be presumed in advance, then there is no warrant for putting any strictures on what sorts of topics, interests, and views are admissible in deliberation.[7] This point is especially important in stratified societies. When social arrangements operate to the systemic profit of some groups of people and to the systemic detriment of others, there are prima facie reasons for thinking that the postulation of a common good shared by exploiters and exploited may well be a mystification. Any consensus that purports to represent the common good in this social context should be regarded with suspicion, since this consensus will have been reached through deliberative processes tainted by the effects of dominance and subordination.

It follows, then, that we need to take a harder, more critical look at the terms "private" and "public." These terms are not simply straightforward designations of preexisting societal spheres; rather, they are cultural classifications and rhetorical labels. In political discourse, they are frequently deployed to delegitimate some interests, views, and topics and to valorize others.

This brings me to two of our other senses of privacy, which often function ideologically to delimit the boundaries of the public sphere in ways that disadvantage subordinate social groups. These are sense (5), pertaining to private property in a market economy; and sense (6), pertaining to intimate domestic or personal life, including sexual life. Each of these senses is at the center of a rhetoric of privacy that has historically been used to restrict the universe of legitimate public contestation.

The rhetoric of domestic privacy seeks to exclude some issues and interests from public debate by personalizing and/or familializing them; it casts these as private-domestic or personal-familial matters in contradistinction to public, political matters. The rhetoric of economic privacy, in contrast, seeks to exclude some issues and interests from public debate by economizing them; the issues in question here are cast as impersonal market imperatives or as "private" ownership prerogatives or as technical problems for managers and planners, all in contradistinction to public, political matters. In both cases, the result is to enclave certain matters in specialized discursive arenas and thereby to shield them from broad-based debate and contestation.

This curtaining off usually works, of course, to the advantage of dominant groups and individuals and to the disadvantage of their subordinates.[8] Labeling sexual harassment a "personal" matter, for example, serves to reproduce gender dominance and subordination. Similarly, if questions of workplace democracy are labeled "economic" or "managerial" problems and if discourse about these questions is shunted into specialized institutions associated with, say, "industrial relations" sociology, labor law, and "management science," it serves to perpetuate class (and usually also gender and race) dominance and subordination.

Once again, the lifting of formal restrictions on public-sphere participation does not suffice to ensure inclusion in practice. On the contrary, even after women and workers have been formally licensed to participate, their participation may be hindered by conceptions of economic privacy and domestic privacy that delimit the scope of debate. These notions, therefore, are vehicles through which gender and class disadvantages may continue to operate subtextually and informally, even after explicit, formal restrictions have been rescinded.

Toward a postmodern conception of the public sphere

What conclusions can we draw from this critique of the modern liberal conception of the public sphere? We have seen that this conception is seriously flawed, but the upshot is not simply negative. The discussion provides some clues as to how we might begin to devise a better conception of the public sphere – a *postmodern, postliberal* conception.

Three counterassumptions should inform a postmodern conception of the public sphere:

(1) a postmodern conception of the public sphere must acknowledge that participatory parity requires not merely the bracketing, but rather the elimination, of systemic social inequalities;
(2) where such inequality persists, however, a postmodern multiplicity of mutually contestatory publics is preferable to a single modern public sphere oriented solely to deliberation; and
(3) a postmodern conception of the public sphere must countenance not the exclusion, but the inclusion, of interests and issues that bourgeois masculinist ideology labels "private" and treats as inadmissible.

II. The postmodern public sphere and cultural critique: rereading the Clarence Thomas/Anita Hill struggle

A postmodern conception of the public sphere can be a powerful instrument of cultural criticism. For one thing, it can render visible the ways in which social inequality taints deliberation within existing publics in late capitalist societies. For another, it can show how inequality affects relations among different publics in such societies, how various publics are differentially empowered or segmented, and how some are involuntarily enclaved and subordinated. Finally, a postmodern conception of the public sphere can expose ways in which the labeling of some issues and interests as "private" limits the range of problems, and of approaches to problems, that can be widely contested in contemporary societies. Unlike the modern liberal conception, then, it can be genuinely critical of contemporary politics and culture.

These advantages become clear when we reconsider the 1991 struggle over the confirmation of Associate Supreme Court Justice Clarence Thomas. That struggle raised in a dramatic and pointed way many of the issues we have already examined concerning the political theory of the public sphere.[9]

If we were to accept the modern liberal conception of the public sphere, we would tell the story essentially like this: the Senate Judiciary Committee hearings on Hill's claim that Thomas sexually harassed her constituted an exercise in democratic publicity. The hearings opened to public scrutiny an aspect of government functioning, namely the nomination and confirmation of a Supreme Court Justice. They thus subjected a decision of state officials to the force of public opinion. Through the hearings, in fact, public opinion was constituted and brought to bear directly on the decision itself, affecting both the decision-making process and its outcome. As a result, state officials were held accountable to the public by means of a discursive process of opinion and will formation.

Most of us know, however, that this modern liberal narrative does not tell the whole story of these events. If we examine the struggle over the Thomas confirmation more closely, we see that part of what was at stake was the very meaning and boundaries of the concept of publicity. The way the struggle unfolded, moreover, depended at every point on who had the power to define successfully and authoritatively where the line between the public and the private would be drawn. It depended as well on who had the power to police and defend that boundary.

Let us return to the events of October 1991.

Gender struggle

The first phase of the struggle was played out as a gender struggle, and it laid bare important gender asymmetries concerning privacy and publicity. These asymmetries were not the familiar orthodoxies of an earlier stage of feminist theory, which protested women's alleged confinement to the private sphere and lack of public-sphere participation. Rather, the asymmetries here concerned women's lesser power in drawing and enforcing the boundary between public and private, their greater vulnerability to unwanted, intrusive publicity, and their lesser ability to define and defend their privacy.

These issues first emerged at the very outset of the struggle. At Anita Hill's first public news conference, held soon after the story of her accusations against Thomas broke, she was already having to defend herself against two apparently contradictory charges: first, that she had failed to make public her allegations in a timely fashion, as any bona-fide victim of sexual harassment supposedly would have; but second, that in making these charges she was seeking publicity and self-aggrandizement. Hill sought to explain her actions, first, by insisting that "control" over these disclosures "never rested with me," and second, by acknowledging her difficulty in balancing her need for privacy against her duty to disclose information in response to the committee's enquiry (Hill 1991). As it turned out, she never succeeded in fully dispelling many people's doubts on these points.

Meanwhile, the breaking of the story revealed that "control" over Hill's story had to that point "rested with" the Senate Judiciary Committee. It became known that they had earlier chosen not to publicize her charges against Thomas, electing thereby to delimit the scope of the public hearings and to contain public debate about the nomination. Once Hill's charges were made public, however, the committee lost control of the process. Instead, its members became embroiled in a public struggle with feminists who objected to the privatization of an important gender issue and accused the senators of "sexism" and "insensitivity."

This gender struggle was widely reported in the media in counterpoint with a counterdiscourse of outrage over "the leak." These two rival schemata – "sexism in the Senate" (Dowd 1991a) and "the leak" – vied for interpretative preeminence, as a struggle unfolded over whether to delay the Senate vote on the nomination and to hold an extraordinary second round of hearings. The vote *was* delayed, the hearings *were* reopened, and momentarily at least the feminists had won. We succeeded in broadening the space of the official national political public sphere to encompass, for the first time, the subject of sexual harassment.

To get an issue on the public-sphere agenda, however, is not necessarily to control its discussion. While public debate focused on the question of the Senate's "insensitivity," White House strategists worked behind the scenes to shape the focus of the hearings and the interpretation of events.

As it turned out, the administration plan to shape public debate and limit the scope of the hearings had three crucial features. First, the White House sought to prevent or marginalize any new allegations of sexual harassment by other victims in order to shape the hearings as a "he said, she said" affair. Second, they sought to rule off-limits any interrogation of what was defined as Thomas's "private life," including what the *New York Times* called his "well-documented taste for watching and discussing pornographic movies while he was at Yale Law School" (Dowd 1991b).[10] Third, they sought to exclude expert testimony about the nature of sexual harassment and the characteristic responses of victims, so that, in the words of one administration spin doctor, they could "prevent this from turning into a referendum on two thousand years of male dominance and sexual harassment" ("Bush Emphasizes" 1991).

Together these three moves cast Clarence Thomas and Anita Hill in very different relations to privacy and publicity. Thomas was enabled to declare key areas of his private life off-limits. Hill, in contrast, was cast as someone whose motives and character would be subject to intense scrutiny and intrusive speculation, since her "credibility" was to be evaluated in a conceptual vacuum. When the Senate Judiciary Committee adopted these ground rules for the hearings, they sealed in place a structural differential in relation to publicity and privacy that worked overwhelmingly to Thomas's advantage and to Hill's disadvantage. Thus, Senator Alan K. Simpson (1991, 14546) could predict on the Senate floor that "Anita Hill will be sucked right into the very thing she wanted to avoid most. She will be injured and destroyed and belittled and hounded and harassed, real harassment, different from the sexual kind."

Meanwhile, Clarence Thomas was attempting to define and defend his privacy. His opening statement to the committee clearly announced this aim: "I am not here to put my private life on display for prurient interests or other reasons. I will not allow this committee or anyone else to probe my private life . . . I will not provide the rope for my own lynching or for further humiliation. I am not going to engage in discussions, nor will I submit to roving questions, of what goes on in the most intimate parts of my private life, or the sanctity of my bedroom. These are the most intimate parts of my privacy, and they will remain just that: private" (Thomas 1991a). Throughout the hearings, he refused to entertain questions that breached his "privacy" as he defined it.

Members of the Senate Judiciary Committee generally accepted Thomas's definition of his "privacy," and they did not trespass on that space as he had demarcated it. They didn't enquire into his sexual history or his fantasy life, and he was not in fact questioned about his practice of viewing and discussing pornographic films. (The one time when this subject was broached, by Senator Leahy at the session of October 12, Thomas successfully repulsed the enquiry, and the question was not pursued.) Later, after the Senate confirmed the nomination, Democratic members of the Judiciary Committee defended their failure to cross-examine Thomas vigorously by saying that he had put up a "wall" and refused to answer questions about his private life (Dowd 1991b, A14).

Soon the country was awash in speculation concerning the character, motives, and psychology of Anita Hill. Yet there was no comparable speculation about Thomas. No one wondered, it seemed, what sort of anxieties and hurts could lead a powerful and successful self-made black man who had grown up in rural poverty to sexually harass a black female subordinate from a similar background.

Anita Hill also sought to define and defend her privacy, but she was far less successful than Thomas. Despite her efforts to keep the focus on her complaint and on the evidence that corroborated it, the principal focus soon became her character. During the course of the struggle, it was variously suggested that she was a lesbian, a heterosexual erotomaniac, a delusional schizophrenic, a fantasist, a vengeful spurned woman, a perjurer, and a malleable tool of liberal interest groups. Yet the Democratic committee members made no effort to limit the scope of enquiry into her "privacy."

Hill's lesser success in drawing the line between public and private testifies to the implication of these categories in gender hierarchy. It also by contrast sheds light on some of the deeper issues at stake in Thomas's insistence on avoiding the "humiliation" of a "public probe" into his "privacy." This insistence can be understood in part as a defense of his masculinity; to be subject to having one's privacy publicly probed is to risk being feminized.

Women's difficulty in defining and defending their privacy was also attested by an extremely important absence from the hearings: the nonappearance of Angela Wright, a second black woman who claimed to have been sexually harassed by Thomas and whose testimony to that effect was to have been corroborated by another witness. Given that disbelief of Hill was often rationalized by the claim that there were no other complainants, the nonappearance of Wright was significant. Had she testified and proved a credible witness, the momentum of the struggle might have shifted decisively. Why then did Angela Wright not appear? Both sides had reasons to privatize her story. Thomas's supporters feared a second accusation would be extremely damaging and threatened to discredit her by introducing information concerning her personal history. Hill's legal team apparently feared that a woman described in the press as presenting "a more complex picture than Professor Hill" (Applebone 1991, A11) would lack credibility and undermine Hill's as well. Thus, the silencing of a complainant who lacked Hill's "respectability" was a crucial and possibly even decisive factor in the dynamics and outcome of the struggle.

The struggle over "race"

During the first, gender-dominated, phase of the struggle, the issue of race was barely discussed. That silence was soon shattered, however, when Thomas himself broached the issue by famously claiming that the hearings were a "high-tech lynching" designed to stop an "uppity Black who deigned to think for himself." He spoke about his vulnerability to changes that played into racial stereotypes of black men as having large penises and unusual sexual prowess (Thomas 1991b, A1).

By combining references to lynching with references to stereotypes about black men's sexual prowess, Thomas artfully conflated two distinct racial stereotypes. The first is the stereotype of the black man as sexual stud, capable of providing women great sexual pleasure. This was the figure that emerged from Hill's testimony, according to which Thomas's harassment of her involved bragging about his [hetero] sexual virtuosity. The second stereotype is that of the black man as rapist, a lust-driven animal, whose sexuality is criminal and out of control. There was no hint of that stereotype in Hill's testimony.

Both these stereotypes have been embraced by white racists, to be sure, but they nevertheless differ significantly. The first, but not the second, has also been embraced by some black men.[11] By conflating these two stereotypes, Thomas was able to suggest that Hill's reports of his behaviour as a would-be stud were equivalent to southern white racist fabrications of criminal sexuality and rape.

This turned out to be a rhetorical master stroke. The Democrats on the committee were too cowed by the charge of racism to question the nominee's logic. Many leading African-American liberals seemed too caught off-guard to respond effectively; most simply denied that race had any relevance in the case at all.

One of the most important features of the entire struggle was the absence from the hearings and from the mainstream public sphere debate of a black feminist analysis. No one who was in a position to be heard in the hearings or in the mainstream mass media spoke about the historic vulnerability of black women to sexual harassment in the United States and about the use of racist-misogynist stereotypes to justify such abuse and to malign black women who protest.[12] There was no widely disseminated perspective that persuasively integrated a critique of sexual harassment with a critique of racism. At this stage, then, the struggle was cast as *either* a gender struggle *or* a race struggle. It could not, apparently, be both at once.

The result was that it became difficult to see Anita Hill as a black woman. She became, in effect, functionally white. Certainly, Thomas's references to lynching had the effect of calling into question her blackness. The lynching story requires a white woman as "victim" and pretext. To my knowledge, no black man has ever been lynched for the sexual exploitation of a black woman. Thomas's charge thus implied that Hill might not really be black. Perhaps because she was a "tool of white interest groups." Or perhaps because she had internalized the uptight, puritanical sexual morality of elite white feminists and mistaken Thomas's lower-class African-American courting style for abuse, a view propounded by Orlando Patterson (1991). Or perhaps most ingeniously of all because, like Adela Quested, the white female protagonist of E. M. Forster's *A Passage to India*, Hill was an erotomaniacal spinster who fantasized abuse at the hands of a dark-skinned man out of the depths of her experiences of rejection and sexual frustration.

Whichever of these scenarios one chose to believe, the net effect was the same: Anita Hill became functionally white. The result was to cast black women who seek to defend themselves against abuse at the hands of black men as traitors or enemies of the race. Consequently, when the struggle was cast exclusively as a racial struggle, the sole black protagonist became the black man. The black woman was erased from view.

This erasure prompted the founding of a group called African-American Women in Defense of Ourselves, whose inaugural statement is worth quoting at some length:

Many have erroneously portrayed the allegations against Clarence Thomas as an issue of either gender or race. As women of African descent, we understand sexual harassment as both. We further understand that Clarence Thomas outrageously manipulated the legacy of lynching in order to shelter himself from Anita Hill's allegations. To deflect attention away from the reality of sexual abuse in African American women's lives, he trivialized and misrepresented this painful part of African American people's history. This country, which has a long legacy of racism and sexism, has never taken the sexual abuse of Black women seriously. Throughout US history, Black women have been sexually stereotyped as immoral, insatiable, perverse; the initiators in all sexual contact – abusive or otherwise. The common assumption in legal proceedings as well as in the larger society has been that Black women cannot be raped or otherwise sexually abused. As Anita Hill's experience demonstrates, Black women who speak of these matters are not likely to be believed.

(AAWIDO 1991, A19)

What is so important about this statement is its rejection of the view, widely held by many supporters of Anita Hill, that race was simply irrelevant to this struggle, apart from Thomas's manipulation of it. Instead, the statement implies that the categories of privacy and publicity are not simply gendered categories; they are racialized categories as well. Historically African-Americans have been denied privacy in the sense of domesticity. As a result, black women have been highly vulnerable to sexual harassment at the hands of masters, overseers, bosses, and supervisors. At the same time, they have lacked the public standing to claim state protection against abuse, whether suffered at work or at home. Black men, meanwhile, have lacked the rights and prerogatives enjoyed by white men, including the right to exclude white men from "their" women and the right to exclude the state from their "private" sphere.

Perhaps, then, it is worth exploring the hypothesis that in making his case before the white tribunal, Clarence Thomas was trying to claim the same rights and immunities of masculinity that white men have historically enjoyed, especially the right to maintain open season on black women. Or perhaps he wasn't claiming exactly the same rights and immunities as white men. Perhaps he wasn't seeking these privileges vis à vis all women. After all, no white woman claimed to have been sexually harassed by him. Is that because in fact he never sexually harassed a white woman, although he married one? And if so, is that because he felt less of a sense of entitlement in his interactions with his white female subordinates at work? If so, then perhaps his references to lynching were not merely a smokescreen, as many people assumed. Perhaps they were also traces of the racialization of his masculinity. In any event, we need more work that theorizes the racial subtext of the categories of privacy and publicity and its intersection with the gender subtext.[13]

Class struggle?

Sexual harassment is not only a matter of gender and racial domination but one of status and class domination as well. The scene of harassment is the workplace or educational institution; the protagonists are superordinate bosses, supervisors, or teachers, on the one hand, and subordinate employees or students, on the other; the effect of the practice is to maintain the control of the former over the latter.[14] Sexual harassment, therefore, implicates the classic issues of workers' power in the workplace and student power in the school. It should be high on the agenda of every trade union, labor organization, and student association.

Yet these dimensions of the struggle over Thomas's confrontation were not aired in any straightforward way in the public-sphere debates. No trade unionist or workers' or students' representative testified in the hearings. Nor did any publish an op-ed piece in the mainstream press. In general, no one in a position to be widely heard articulated support for Anita Hill grounded in class solidarity. No one foregrounded the accents of class to rally workers and students to her side.

The absence of a straightforward discourse of class conflict in the United States is no surprise. What is more surprising perhaps was the deployment in the final phase of the struggle of a counterdiscourse of class resentment to mobilize support for Thomas.

On the day before the Senate confirmation vote, the *New York Times* printed an op-ed piece by former Reagan speechwriter Peggy Noonan (1991, A15). Noonan predicted victory for Thomas based on a "class division" between the "chattering classes" supporting Hill and the "normal humans," who believed Thomas. She also glossed this as a division between the "clever people who talk loudly in restaurants and those who seat them":

> You could see it in the witnesses. For Anita Hill: the professional, movement-y, and intellectualish Susan Hoerchner, who spoke with a sincere, unmakedupped face of inherent power imbalances in the workplace. For Clarence Thomas, the straight-shooting Maybellined J. C. Alvarez, who once broke up a mugging because she hates bullies and who paid $900 she doesn't have to get there because she still hates 'em . . . Ms. Alvarez was the voice of the real, as opposed to the abstract America: she was like a person who if a boss ever sexually abused her would kick him in the gajoobies and haul him straight to court.   (Noonan 1991, A15)

Here Noonan appealed in familiar terms to the "real American" workers (tough and macho, even if wearing eyeliner) to resist the effeminate (albeit make-up-free) intellectuals who impersonate them and feign concern for their interests, but whose Americanness is suspect (shades of communism). The scenario thus appeared to oppose "the real worker," J. C. Alvarez, to "the intellectual," Susan Hoerchner. Yet Alvarez here actually represented Thomas, the boss, while the actual aggrieved subordinate, Anita Hill, disappeared once again. By painting "the worker" as a Maybellined tough guy, moreover, Noonan simultaneously updated and perpetuated masculinist stereotypes. The result was that it became hard to see most women, who do not repay sexual harassment with a kick to the groin, as "workers."

Noonan's rhetoric mobilized class resentment in support of Thomas by disappearing Anita Hill as a worker. A similar tack was taken by Orlando Patterson (1991, E15), whose own *New York Times* op-ed piece appeared the following week in the guise of a more analytical postmortem. Patterson treated Hill exclusively as a tool not simply of whites or of feminists, but of elite, upper-class white feminists bent on using the law to impose a class-specific sexual morality on poor and working-class populations with different, less repressive norms. Workers were in effect called to defend their class culture – by siding with the boss against his assistant.

Both Noonan and Patterson in effect bourgeoisified Anita Hill, just as Thomas had earlier whitened her. Her actual social origins in rural poverty, which she had stressed in her opening statement to the committee, had by the end of the affair become so clouded by the rhetoric of class resentment that to many she was just another yuppie. The "class struggle" in this affair, then, was largely a matter of manipulating the signifiers of class to mobilize resentment in the interests of management.

Yet class may nevertheless have affected the way these events were viewed. Some news reports following closely upon Thomas's confirmation portrayed white working-class women and women of color of all classes as unsympathetic to Hill. The *New York Times* (Barringer 1991, A1) reported that blue-collar women were put off by her softspokenness and what they construed as her inability to take care of herself. The *Times* contrasted this "working-class" view with the views of female lawyers, human service professionals, and politicians, who strongly sympathized with and believed Hill. But the *Times* did not consider the possibility that these putative class differences could be rooted in different class work structures. It could be the case, for example, that working-class people who felt that Hill should simply have told Thomas off and quit and found another job were not attuned to professional "career" structures, which require cultivation of one's reputation in the profession via networking and long-term maintenance of relationships.

Polls taken soon after Thomas's confirmation showed that party affiliation was the most statistically significant factor distinguishing his supporters from Hill's (Kolbert 1991). Part of what was at stake, then, was the continuation – or not – of the Reagan–Bush agenda, broadly conceived. For a moment, the question of sexual harassment became the condensation point for a host of anxieties, resentments, and hopes about who gets what and who deserves what in the United States. In our current political culture, those anxieties, resentments, and hopes are usually articulated in terms of gender and race, but they are also necessarily about status and class. Noonan and Patterson notwithstanding, class remains the great unarticulated American secret. As such, it remains highly susceptible to manipulation and abuse.

III. Conclusion

The Thomas/Hill struggle proves beyond any doubt the continuing importance of the public sphere in relation to state power. However, it also demonstrates the need to revise the standard modern liberal view of the public sphere. If this struggle shows nothing else, it proves that the categories of publicity and privacy are multivalent and contested. And not all understandings of these categories promote democracy.

Clearly, male-supremacist constructions of publicity enshrine gender hierarchy by privatizing practices of domination like sexual harassment. They enforce men's privacy rights to harass women with impunity in part by smearing in public any woman who protests. As a result, women are in effect asked to choose between quiet abuse in private and noisy discursive abuse in public.

However, the gendered character of the categories "publicity" and "privacy" cannot today be understood in terms of the Victorian separate-spheres ideology, as some feminists have assumed. It is not the case now, and never was, that women are simply excluded from public life; nor that men are public and women are private; nor that the private sphere is women's sphere and the public sphere is men's; nor that the feminist project is to collapse the boundaries between public and private. Rather, feminist analysis shows the political, ideological nature of these categories. And the feminist project aims in part to overcome the gender hierarchy that gives men more power than women to draw the line between public and private.

Yet the categories of public and private also have a racial-ethnic dimension. The legacy of US slavery and racism has denied black women even the minimal protections from abuse that white women have occasionally managed to claim, even as their disadvantaged economic position has rendered them more vulnerable to sexual harassment. Black men have lacked white men's privacy rights and have sometimes tried to claim them in ways that endanger black women. Hence the need to develop an antiracist project that does not come at black women's expense, one that simultaneously attacks the racial and gender hierarchy embedded in hegemonic understandings of privacy and publicity.

Recognizing the gendered and raced dimensions of these categories points up several further inadequacies of the modern liberal conception of the public sphere. Contrary to that conception, privacy and publicity are not properly viewed in relation to state power exclusively. Rather, discursive privatization supports the "private" power of bosses over workers, husbands over wives, and whites over blacks. Publicity is not therefore only a weapon against state tyranny, as its bourgeois originators and current Eastern European devotees assume. It is also potentially a weapon against the extra-state power of capital, employers, supervisors, husbands, and fathers, among others. There was no more dramatic proof of the emancipatory potential of publicity in relation to private power than the way in which the Thomas/Hill events momentarily empowered many women to speak openly for the first time of heretofore privately suffered humiliations of sexual harassment.

Nevertheless, publicity is not always simply and unambiguously an instrument of empowerment and emancipation. For members of subordinate groups, it will always be a matter of balancing the potential political uses of publicity against the dangers of loss of privacy.

It also follows that publicity as a political weapon cannot be understood simply in terms of making public what was previously private. On the contrary, merely publicizing some action or practice is not always sufficient to discredit it; that is only the case where the view that the practice is wrong is already widely held and uncontroversial. Where, in contrast, the practice is widely approved or contested, publicity means staging a discursive struggle over its interpretation. Certainly, a key feature of the Thomas/Hill confrontation was the wider struggle it sparked over the meaning and moral status of sexual harassment.

The way that struggle played out, moreover, reflected the current state of US political culture. The drama unfolded at a point at which a feminist vocabulary for naming and interpreting the behavior ascribed to Thomas had already been created in the feminist counterpublic sphere and disseminated to a broader public. Not only was that vocabulary thus available and ready to hand, but it was also even encoded in law. However, the feminist interpretation of sexual harassment was neither deeply rooted nor widely accepted. Consequently, it was contested and resisted throughout these events, despite its official legal standing. This disjuncture between its official legal acceptance, on the one hand, and the widespread popular resistance it met, on the other, helped determine the shape of the struggle. Much of the disbelief of Anita Hill may well have been a disguised rejection of the feminist view of sexual harassment as a wrong, a rejection that could not easily be openly expressed and that was displaced onto doubts about Hill. Moreover, because the feminist understanding had legal legitimacy before it had widespread popular legitimacy, it could become a target for the expression of class, ethnic, and racial resentments. While it is not the case, in other words, that the feminist perspective is elitist, white, upper-class, etc., it was vulnerable to being coded as such. Consequently, people with any number of a range of class, ethnic, or racial resentments, as well as those with gender resentments, could express them by disbelieving Hill.[15]

Yet an undeniable result of these events has been a sharpening and broadening of the battle of interpretation. On the one hand, consciousness-raising processes were initiated that have promoted feminist understandings. As noted before, many women were empowered by these events to rename and confront harms long ago suffered in silence. A poll taken one year after Thomas's confirmation, moreover, showed a decisive shift in opinion; whereas one year earlier the majority had claimed to believe Thomas, now the majority professed to believe Hill. It should not be forgotten, finally, that all future Supreme Court or cabinet nominees will be vetted in background checks for sexual harassment.

Nevertheless, the antifeminist side of the struggle has further developed its discursive weapons for the continuing battle over interpretation. It has refined a rhetoric of opposition that paints harassment complainants as enforcers of "political correctness," authoritarian prudes interfering with men's rights of free speech. Thus, the struggle over interpretation in the public sphere is continuing apace.

If one result of the Thomas/Hill struggle was increased contention over sexual harassment, another was the fracturing of the myth of homogeneous "communities." The "black community," for example, is now fractured into black feminists versus black conservatives versus black liberals versus various other strands of opinion that are less easy to fix with ideological labels. The same thing holds for the "women's community." This struggle showed that women don't necessarily side with women just because they are women. Rather, for what they're worth (and it may not be much), the polls showed that a plurality of women in every age, income, and education group said they believed Clarence Thomas more than Anita Hill. Perhaps these events should lead us to consider replacing the homogenizing, ideological category of "community" with the potentially more critical category of "public" in the sense of a discursive arena for staging conflicts.

This last point suggests that if these events expose some weaknesses in the modern liberal conception of the public sphere, they also point in the direction of a better, postmodern conception. Such a conception takes as its starting point the multivalent, contested character of the categories of privacy and publicity with their gendered and racialized subtexts. It acknowledges that in highly stratified late capitalist societies, not everyone stands in the same relation to privacy and publicity; some have more power than others to draw and defend the line. Further, a postmodern conception of the public sphere theorizes both the multiplicity of public spheres in contemporary late capitalist societies and also the relations among them. It distinguishes, for example, official governmental public spheres, mass-mediated mainstream public spheres, counterpublic spheres, and informal public spheres in everyday life; and it shows how some of these publics marginalize others. Such a conception certainly helps us better understand discursive struggles like the Thomas/Hill confrontation. Perhaps it could also help inspire us to imagine, and to fight for, a more egalitarian and democratic society.

Notes

This essay combines material from two previously published essays (Fraser 1991 and 1992). I am grateful for helpful comments from Craig Calhoun, Joshua Cohen, Laura Edwards, Jim Grossman, Moishe Postone, Susan Reverby, David Schweikart, and Eli Zaretsky.

1. For Habermas's later use of the category of the public sphere, see Jürgen Habermas 1987. For a critical secondary discussion of Habermas's later use of the concept, see Fraser 1989a.
2. What follows is a drastically abbreviated summary of an argument I have elaborated in Fraser 1991.
3. In *Distinction* (1979), Pierre Bourdieu has theorized these processes in an illuminating way in terms of the concepts of "cultural capital" and "class habitus."
4. My argument here draws on Karl Marx's still unsurpassed critique of liberalism in Part I of "On the Jewish Question."
5. I have coined this expression by combining two terms that other theorists have recently used with very good effects for purposes that are consonant with my own. I take the term "subaltern" from Gayatri Spivak 1980. I take the term "counterpublic" from Rita Felski 1989.
6. For an analysis of the political import of oppositional feminist discourses about needs, see Fraser 1989b.

7. This point, incidentally, is in the spirit of a strand of Habermas's recent normative thought, which stresses the procedural, as opposed to the substantive, definition of a democratic public sphere; here, the public sphere is defined as an arena for a certain type of discursive interaction, not as an arena for dealing with certain types of topics and problems. There are no restrictions, therefore, on what may become a topic of deliberation. See Seyla Benhabib's account (1991) of this radical proceduralist strand of Habermas's thought and her defense of it as the strand that renders his view of the public sphere superior to alternative views.

8. Usually, but not always. As Josh Cohen (1990) has argued, exceptions are the uses of privacy in *Roe v. Wade*, the US Supreme Court decision legalizing abortion, and in Justice Blackmun's dissent in *Hardwick v. Bowers*, the decision upholding state anti-sodomy laws. These examples show that the privacy rhetoric is multivalent rather than univocally and necessarily harmful. On the other hand, there is no question but that the weightier tradition of privacy argument has buttressed inequality by restricting debate. Moreover, many feminists have argued that even the "good" privacy uses have some serious negative consequences in the current context and that gender domination is better challenged in this context on other grounds.

9. The following analysis abridges the account in Fraser 1992.

10. The mainstream press frequently referred to Thomas's alleged porn habit. See Michael Wines (1991) for an account by one of his fellow Yale Law School students.

11. In a roundtable discussion on a local Chicago television talk show, three black male journalists, Salim Muwakkil (*In These Times*), Ty Wansley (WVON radio), and Don Wycliff (*Chicago Tribune*), agreed with the suggestion of black political satirist Aaron Freeman (author of the play *Do the White Thing*), that many black men embrace the stereotype of the sexual stud.

12. The one exception was Ellen Wells, a witness who corroborated Hill's version of events by testifying that Hill had told her that Thomas was harassing her at the time. In the course of her testimony, Wells explained why Hill might have nonetheless maintained contact with Thomas:

> My mother told me, and I'm sure Anita's mother told her. When you leave, make sure you leave friends behind, because you don't know who you may need later on. And so you do at least want to be cordial. I know I get Christmas cards from people that I . . . quite frankly do not wish to [see]. And I also return their cards and will return their calls. And these are people who have insulted me and done things which have degraded me at times. But these are things you have to put up with. And being a black woman you know you have to put up with a lot. And so you grit your teeth and you do it.
>
> (Wells 1991, A13)

13. A good beginning has been made in two important articles that appeared shortly after the end of the struggle: Nell Irvin Painter 1991 and Rosemary L. Bray 1991. See also the essays in Morrison 1992.
14. There is in addition another variety of sexual harassment, in which male workers harass female co-workers who are not formally under their supervisory authority. This sort of harassment is frequent when very small numbers of women enter heavily male-dominated and masculinized occupations such as construction, firefighting, and military service. Women in these fields are often subject to harassment from co-workers who are technically their peers in the occupational hierarchy – in the form, for example, of the display of pornography in the workplace, sexual taunts, noncooperation or sabotage, and even having male co-workers urinate in front of them. This sort of "horizontal" harassment differs significantly from the "vertical" variety discussed in the present essay, which involves harassment of an occupational subordinate by a superordinate. "Horizontal" harassment merits a different sort of analysis.
15. Perhaps this helps explain the otherwise surprising fact, disclosed in polls, that large numbers of people who claimed to believe Hill nonetheless supported Thomas's confirmation, either minimizing the seriousness of her accusations, or judging her to be too prudish, or insisting that she should have handled the situation herself by simply telling him where to get off (Kolbert 1991).

References

AAWIDO. 1991. "African American Women in Defense of Ourselves." Advertisement. *New York Times* (17 November), A19.

Applebone, Peter. 1991. "Common Threads between the Two Accusing Thomas of Sexual Improprieties." *New York Times* (10 October), A11.

Barringer, Felicity. 1991. "Women See Hearing from a Perspective of Their Own Jobs." *New York Times*, midwest ed., (18 October), A1.

Benhabib, Seyla. 1991. "Models of Public Space: Hannah Arendt, the Liberal Tradition, and Juergen Habermas." In *Habermas and the Public Sphere*, ed. Craig Calhoun, 73–98. Cambridge: MIT Press.

Bourdieu, Pierre. 1979. *Distinction: A Social Critique of the Judgment of Pure Taste*. Cambridge: Harvard University Press.

Bray, Rosemary L. 1991. "Taking Sides Against Ourselves." *New York Times Magazine*. (17 November), 56, 94–95, 101.

Brooks-Higginbotham, Evelyn. 1993. *Righteous Discontent: The Women's Movement in the Black Baptist Church, 1880–1920*. Cambridge: Harvard University Press.

"Bush Emphasizes He Backs Thomas in Spite of Uproar." 1991. *New York Times* (10 October), A10.

Cohen, Joshua. 1990. "Comments on Nancy Fraser's 'Rethinking the Public Sphere.'" Unpublished manuscript presented at meetings of the American Philosophical Association, Central Division, New Orleans.

Dowd, Maureen 1991a. "The Senate and Sexism." *New York Times* (8 October), A1.

1991b. "Image More Than Reality Became Issue, Losers Say." *New York Times* (16 October), A14.

Eley, Geoff. 1991. In *Habermas and the Public Sphere*, ed. Craig Calhoun, 289–339. Cambridge: MIT Press.

Felski, Rita. 1989. *Beyond Feminist Aesthetics*. Cambridge, Mass.: Harvard University Press.

Fraser, Nancy. 1989a. "What's Critical about Critical Theory? The Case of Habermas and Gender." In *Unruly Practices: Power, Discourse and Gender in Contemporary Social Theory*, ed. Nancy Fraser, 113–43. Minneapolis, Minn.: University of Minnesota Press.

ed. 1989b. "Struggle over Needs: Outline of a Socialist-Feminist Critical Theory of Late-Capitalist Political Culture." In *Unruly Practices: Power, Discourse and Gender in Contemporary Social Theory*, ed. Nancy Fraser, 161–87. Minneapolis, Minn.: University of Minnesota Press.

1991. "Rethinking the Public Sphere: A Contribution to the Critique of Actually Existing Democracy." In *Habermas and the Public Sphere*, ed. Craig Calhoun, 109–42. Cambridge: MIT Press.

1992. "Sex, Lies, and the Public Sphere: Some Reflections on the Confirmation of Clarence Thomas." *Critical Inquiry* 18 (Spring): 595–612.

Habermas, Jürgen. 1987. *The Theory of Communicative Action, Vol. 2: Lifeworld and System: A Critique of Functionalist Reason*. Trans. Thomas McCarthy. Boston: Beacon Press.

1989. *The Structural Transformation of the Public Sphere: An Inquiry into a Category of Bourgeois Society*, Trans. Thomas Burger with Frederick Lawrence. Cambridge: MIT Press.

Hill, Anita. 1991. "Excerpts of News Conference on Harassment Accusations against Thomas." *New York Times*, 8 Oct., A20.

Kolbert, Elizabeth. 1991. "Most in National Survey Say Judge is More Believable." *New York Times*, 15 Oct., A1, A20.

Landes, Joan B. 1988. *Women and the Public Sphere in the Age of the French Revolution*. Ithaca, N.Y.: Cornell University Press.

Mansbridge, Jane. 1990. "Feminism and Democracy." *American Prospect*, 1 (Spring) 127.

Morrison, Toni, ed. 1992. *Race-ing Justice, En-gendering Power: Essays on Anita Hill*. New York: Pantheon.

Noonan, Peggy. 1991. "A Bum Ride." *New York Times*, 15 Oct., A15.

Painter, Nell Irvin. 1991. "Who Was Lynched?" *Nation*, 11 Nov., 577.

Patterson, Orlando. 1991. "Race, Gender, and Liberal Fallacies." *New York Times*, 20 Oct. E15.

Ryan, Mary P. 1990. *Women in Public: Between Banners and Ballots, 1825–1880*. Baltimore: Johns Hopkins University Press.

1991. "Gender and Public Access: Women's Politics in Nineteenth-Century America." In *Habermas and the Public Sphere*, ed. Craig Calhoun, 259–88. Cambridge: MIT Press.

Simpson, Alan K. 1991. *Congressional Record*. 102nd Cong. 1st sess., 137, pt. 143: 14546.

Spivak, Gayatri Chakravorty. 1980. "Can the Subaltern Speak?" In *Marxism and the Interpretation of Culture*, ed. Cary Nelson and Larry Grossberg, 271–313. Chicago: University of Illinois Press.

Thomas, Clarence. 1991a. "Hearing of the Senate Judiciary Committee." (11 Oct., morning sess.) In Nexis Library. FEDNWS file, Federal News Service.

1991b. "Thomas Rebuts Accuser: 'I Deny Each and Every Allegation.'" *New York Times*, 12 Oct., A1.

Wells, Ellen. 1991. "Questions to Those who Corroborated Hill Account." *New York Times*, 14 Oct., A13–14.

Wines, Michael. 1991. "Stark Conflict Marks Accounts Given by Thomas and Professor." *New York Times*, 10 Oct., A18.

PART IV

Postmodern approaches to the political

11

Feminism, citizenship, and radical democratic politics

Chantal Mouffe

Two topics have recently been the subject of much discussion among
Anglo-American feminists: postmodernism and essentialism. Obviously
they are related since the so-called "postmoderns" are also presented as
the main critics of essentialism, but it is better to distinguish them since
some feminists who are sympathetic to postmodernism have lately come
to the defense of essentialism.[1] I consider that, in order to clarify the
issues that are at stake in that debate, it is necessary to recognize that
there is not such a thing as "postmodernism" understood as a coherent theoretical approach and that the frequent assimilation between
poststructuralism and postmodernism can only lead to confusion. Which
is not to say that we have not been witnessing through the twentieth
century a progressive questioning of the dominant form of rationality
and of the premises of the modes of thought characteristic of the Enlightenment. But this critique of universalism, humanism, and rationalism has
come from many different quarters and it is far from being limited to
the authors called "poststructuralists" or "postmodernists." From that
point of view, all the innovative currents of this century – Heidegger
and the post-Heideggerian philosophical hermeneutics of Gadamer, the
later Wittgenstein and the philosophy of language inspired by his work,
psychoanalysis and the reading of Freud proposed by Lacan, American
pragmatism – all have from diverse standpoints criticized the idea of
a universal human nature, of a universal canon of rationality through
which human nature could be known as well as the traditional conception
of truth. Therefore, if the term "postmodern" indicates such a critique of
Enlightenment's universalism and rationalism, it must be acknowledged
that it refers to the main currents of twentieth-century philosophy and
there is no reason to single out poststructuralism as a special target. On
the other side, if by "postmodernism" one wants to designate only the

315

very specific form that such a critique takes in authors such as Lyotard and Baudrillard, there is absolutely no justification for putting in that category people like Derrida, Lacan, or Foucault, as has generally been the case. Too often a critique of a specific thesis of Lyotard or Baudrillard leads to sweeping conclusions about "the postmoderns" who by then include all the authors loosely connected with poststructuralism. This type of amalgamation is completely unhelpful when not clearly disingenuous.

Once the conflation between postmodernism and poststructuralism has been debunked, the question of essentialism appears in a very different light. Indeed, it is with regard to the critique of essentialism that a convergence can be established among many different currents of thought and similarities found in the work of authors as different as Derrida, Wittgenstein, Heidegger, Dewey, Gadamer, Lacan, Foucault, Freud, and others. This is very important because it means that such a critique takes many different forms and that if we want to scrutinize its relevance for feminist politics we must engage with all its modalities and implications and not quickly dismiss it on the basis of some of its versions.

My aim in this article will be to show the crucial insights that an anti-essentialist approach can bring to the elaboration of a feminist politics which is also informed by a radical democratic project. I certainly do not believe that essentialism necessarily entails conservative politics and I am ready to accept that it can be formulated in a progressive way. What I want to argue is that it presents some inescapable shortcomings for the construction of a democratic alternative whose objective is the articulation of the struggles linked to different forms of oppression. I consider that it leads to a view of identity that is at odds with a conception of radical and plural democracy and that it does not allow us to construe the new vision of citizenship that is required by such a politics.

The question of identity and feminism

One common tenet of critics of essentialism has been the abandoning of the category of the subject as a rational transparent entity that could convey a homogeneous meaning on the total field of her conduct by being the source of her action. For instance, psychoanalysis has shown that far from being organized around the transparency of an ego, personality is structured in a number of levels which lie outside of the consciousness and the rationality of the agents. It has therefore undermined the idea of the unified character of the subject. Freud's central claim is that the human mind is necessarily subject to division between two systems of which one is not and cannot be conscious. Expanding the Freudian vision, Lacan has shown the plurality of registers – the Symbolic, the Real, and the Imaginary – which penetrate any identity, and the place of the subject as the place of the lack which – though represented within the structure – is the empty place which at the same time subverts and is the condition of constitution of any identity. The history of the subject is the history of his/her identifications and there is no concealed identity to be rescued beyond the latter. There is thus a double movement. On the one hand, a movement of de-centering which prevents the fixation of a set of positions around a preconstituted point. On the other hand, and as a result of this *essential* nonfixity, the opposite movement: the institution of nodal points, partial fixations which limit the flux of the signified under the signifier. But this dialectics at nonfixity/fixation is possible only because fixity is not given beforehand, because no center of subjectivity precedes the subject's identifications.

In the philosophy of language of the later Wittgenstein, we also find a critique of the rationalist conception of the subject that indicates that the latter cannot be the source of linguistic meanings since it is through participation in different language games that the world is disclosed to us. We encounter the same idea in Gadamer's philosophical hermeneutics in the thesis that there is a fundamental unity between thought, language, and the world and that it is within language that the horizon of our present is constituted. A similar critique of the centrality of the subject in modern metaphysics and of its unitary character can be found under several forms in the other authors mentioned earlier. However, my purpose here is not to examine those theories in detail but simply to indicate some basic convergences. I am not overlooking the fact that there are important differences among all those very diverse thinkers. But from the point of view of the argument that I want to make, it is important to grasp the consequences of their common critique of the traditional status of the subject and of its implications for feminism.

It is often said that the deconstruction of essential identities, which is the result of acknowledging the contingency and ambiguity of every identity, renders feminist political action impossible. Many feminists believe that, without seeing women as a coherent identity, we cannot ground the possibility of a feminist political movement in which women could unite as women in order to formulate and pursue specific feminist aims. Contrary to that view, I will argue that, for those feminists who are committed to a radical democratic politics, the deconstruction of essential identities should be seen as the necessary condition for an adequate understanding of the variety of social relations where the principles of liberty and equality should apply. It is only when we discard the view of the subject as an agent both rational and transparent to itself, and discard as well the supposed unity and homogeneity of the ensemble of its positions, that we are in the position to theorize the multiplicity of relations of subordination. A single individual can be the bearer of this multiplicity and be dominant in one relation while subordinated in another. We can then conceive the social agent as constituted by an ensemble of "subject positions" that can never be totally fixed in a closed system of differences, constructed by a diversity of discourses among which there is no necessary relation, but a constant movement of overdetermination and displacement. The "identity" of such a multiple and contradictory subject is therefore always contingent and precarious, temporarily fixed at the intersection of those subject positions and dependent on specific forms of identification. It is therefore impossible to speak of the social agent as if we were dealing with a unified, homogeneous entity. We have rather to approach it as a plurality, dependent on the various subject positions through which it is constituted within various discursive formations. And to recognize that there is no a priori, necessary relation between the discourses that construct its different subject positions. But, for the reasons pointed out earlier, this plurality does not involve the *coexistence*, one by one, of a plurality of subject positions but rather the constant subversion and overdetermination of one by the others, which make possible the generation of "totalizing effects" within a field characterized by open and indeterminate frontiers.

Such an approach is extremely important to understand feminist as well as other contemporary struggles. Their central characteristic is that an ensemble of subject positions linked through inscription in social relations, hitherto considered as apolitical, have become loci of conflict and antagonism and have led to political mobilization. The proliferation of these new forms of struggle can only be tackled theoretically when one starts with the dialectics and de-centering recentering described earlier.

In *Hegemony and Socialist Strategy* (1985), Ernesto Laclau and I have attempted to draw the consequences of such a theoretical approach for a project of radical and plural democracy. We argued for the need to establish a chain of equivalence among the different democratic struggles so as to create an equivalent articulation between the demands of women, blacks, workers, gays, and others. On this point our perspective differs from other nonessentialist views where the aspect of detotalization and de-centering prevails and where the dispersion of subject positions is transformed into an effective separation, as is the case with Lyotard and to some extent with Foucault. For us, the aspect of articulation is crucial. To deny the existence of an a priori, necessary link between subject positions does not mean that there are not constant efforts to establish between them historical, contingent, and variable links. This type of link, which establishes between various positions a contingent, unpredetermined relation is what we designated as "articulation." Even though there is no necessary link between different subject positions, in the field of politics there are always discourses that try to provide an articulation from different standpoints. For that reason every subject position is constituted within an essentially unstable discursive structure since it is submitted to a variety of articulatory practices that constantly subvert and transform it. This is why there is no subject position whose links with others is definitively assured and, therefore, no social identity that would be fully and permanently acquired. This does not mean, however, that we cannot retain notions like "working class," "men," "women," "blacks," or other signifiers referring to collective subjects. However, once the existence of a common essence has been discarded, their status must be conceived in terms of what Wittgenstein designates as "family resemblances" and their unity must be seen as the result of the partial fixation of identities through the creation of nodal points.

For feminists to accept such an approach has very important consequences for the way we formulate our political struggles. If the category "woman" does not correspond to any unified and unifying essence, the question can no longer be to try to unearth it. The central issues become: how is "woman" constructed as a category within different discourses? How is sexual difference made a pertinent distinction in social relations? And how are relations of subordination constructed through such a distinction? The whole false dilemma of equality versus difference is exploded since we no longer have a homogeneous entity "woman" facing another homogeneous entity "man," but a multiplicity of social relations in which sexual difference is always constructed in very diverse ways and where the struggle against subordination has to be visualized in specific and differential forms. To ask if women should become identical to men in order to be recognized as equal, or if they should assert their difference at the cost of equality, appears meaningless once essential identities are put into question.[2]

Citizenship and feminist politics

In consequence, the very question of what a feminist politics should be has to be posed in completely different terms. So far, most feminists concerned with the contribution that feminism could make to democratic politics have been looking either for the specific demands that could express women's interests or for the specific feminine values that should become the model for democratic politics. Liberal feminists have been fighting for a wide range of new rights for women to make them equal citizens, but without challenging the dominant liberal model of citizenship and politics. Their view has been criticized by other feminists who argue that the present conception of the political is a male one and that women's concerns cannot be accommodated within such a framework. Following Carol Gilligan, they oppose a feminist "ethics of care" to the male and liberal "ethics of justice." Against liberal individualist values, they defend a set of values based on the experience of women *as* women, that is, their experience of motherhood and care exercised in the private realm of the family. They denounce liberalism for having constructed modern citizenship as the realm of the public, identified with men, and for having excluded women by relegating them to the private realm. According to this view, feminists should strive for a type of politics that is guided by the specific values of love, care, the recognition of needs, and friendship. One of the clearest attempts to offer an alternative to liberal politics grounded in feminine values is to be found in "maternal thinking" and "social feminism" principally represented by Sara Ruddick (1989) and Jean Bethke Elshtain (1981). Feminist politics, they argue, should privilege the identity of "women as mothers" and the private realm of the family. The family is seen as having moral superiority over the public domain of politics because it constitutes our common humanity. For Elshtain "the family remains the locus of the deepest and most resonant human ties, the most enduring hopes, the most intractable conflicts" (1983, 138). She considers that it is in the family that we should look for a new political morality to replace liberal individualism. In women's experience in the private realm as mothers, she says, a new model for the activity of citizenship is to be found. The maternalists want us to abandon the male liberal politics of the public informed by the abstract point of view of justice and the "generalized other" and adopt instead a feminist politics of the private, informed by the virtues of love, intimacy, and concern for the "concrete other" specific to the family.

An excellent critique of such an approach has been provided by Mary Dietz (1985) who shows that Elshtain fails to provide a theoretical argument which links maternal thinking and the social practice of mothering to democratic values and democratic politics. Dietz argues that maternal virtues cannot be political because they are connected with and emerge from an activity that is special and distinctive. They are the expression of an unequal relation between mother and child which is also an intimate, exclusive, and particular activity. Democratic citizenship, on the contrary, should be collective, inclusive, and generalized. Since democracy is a condition in which individuals aim at being equals, the mother/child relationship cannot provide an adequate model of citizenship.

Yet a different feminist critique of liberal citizenship is provided by Carole Pateman.[3] It is more sophisticated, but shares some common features with "maternal thinking." Pateman's tone bears the traces of radical feminism, for the accent is put, not on the mother/child relation, but on the man/woman antagonism.

Citizenship is, according to Pateman, a patriarchal category: who a "citizen" is, what a citizen does and the arena within which he acts have been constructed in the masculine image. Although women in liberal democracies are now citizens, formal citizenship has been won within a structure of patriarchal power in which women's qualities and tasks are still devalued. Moreover, the call for women's distinctive capacities to be integrated fully into the public world of citizenship faces what she calls the "Wollstonecraft dilemma": to demand equality is to accept the patriarchal conception of citizenship which implies that women must become like men while to insist that women's distinctive attributes, capacities, and activities be given expression and valued as contributing to citizenship is to demand the impossible because such difference is precisely what patriarchal citizenship excludes.

Pateman sees the solution to this dilemma in the elaboration of a "sexually differentiated" conception of citizenship that would recognize women *as* women, with their bodies and all that they symbolize. For Pateman this entails giving political significance to the capacity that men lack: to create life, which is to say, *motherhood*. She declares that this capacity should be treated with equal political relevance for defining citizenship as what is usually considered the ultimate test of citizenship: a man's willingness to fight and to die for his country. She considers that the traditional patriarchal way of posing an alternative, where either the separation or the sameness of the sexes is valorized, needs to be overcome by a new way of posing the question of women. This change can be effected through a conception of citizenship that recognizes both the specificity of womanhood and the common humanity of men and women. Such a view "that gives due weight to sexual difference in a context of civil equality, requires the rejection of a unitary (i.e., masculine) conception of the individual, abstracted from our embodied existence and from the patriarchal division between the private and the public" (Pateman 1986, 24). What feminists should aim for is the elaboration of a sexually differentiated conception of individuality and citizenship that would include "women *as* women in a context of civil equality and active citizenship" (Pateman 1986, 26).

Pateman provides many very interesting insights into the patriarchal bias of the social-contract theorists and the way in which the liberal individual has been constructed according to the male image. I consider that her own solution, however, is unsatisfactory. Despite all her provisos about the historically constructed aspects of sexual difference, her view still postulates the existence of some kind of essence corresponding to women *as* women. Indeed, her proposal for a differentiated citizenship that recognizes the specificity of womanhood rests on the identification of women *as* women with motherhood. There are for her two basic types of individuality that should be expressed in two different forms of citizenship: men *as* men and women *as* women. The problem according to her is that the category of the "individual," while based on the male model, is presented as the universal form of individuality. Feminists must uncover that false universality by asserting the existence of two sexually differentiated forms of universality; this is the only way to resolve the "Wollstonecraft dilemma" and to break free from the patriarchal alternatives of "othering" and "saming."

I agree with Pateman that the modern category of the individual has been constructed in a manner that postulates a universalist, homogeneous "public" that relegates all particularity and difference to the "private" and that this has very negative consequences for women. I do not believe, however, that the remedy is to replace it by a sexually differentiated, "bigendered" conception of the individual and to bring women's so-called specific tasks into the very definition of citizenship. It seems to me that such a solution remains trapped in the very problematic that Pateman wants to challenge. She affirms that the separation between public and private is the founding moment of modern patriarchalism because

the separation of private and public is the separation of the world of natural subjection, i.e. women, from the world of conventional relations and individuals, i.e. men. The feminine, private world of nature, particularity, differentiation, inequality, emotion, love and ties of blood is set apart from the public, universal – and masculine – realm of convention, civil equality and freedom, reason, consent and contract.   (Pateman 1986, 7–8)

It is for that reason that childbirth and motherhood have been presented as the antithesis of citizenship and that they have become the symbol of everything natural that cannot be part of the "public" but must remain in a separate sphere. By asserting the political value of motherhood, Pateman intends to overcome that distinction and contribute to the deconstruction of the patriarchal conception of citizenship and private and public life. As a result of her essentialism, however, she never deconstructs the very opposition of men/women. She therefore ends up, like the maternalists, proposing an inadequate conception of what should be a democratic politics informed by feminism. This is why she can assert that "the most profound and complex problem for political theory and practice is how the two bodies of humankind and feminine and masculine individuality can be fully incorporated into political life" (Pateman 1989, 53).

My own view is completely different. I want to argue that the limitations of the modern conception of citizenship should be remedied, not by making sexual difference politically relevant to its definition, but by constructing a new conception of citizenship where sexual difference should become effectively nonpertinent. This, of course, requires a conception of the social agent in the way that I have defended earlier, as the articulation of an ensemble of subject positions, corresponding to the multiplicity of social relations in which it is inscribed. This multiplicity is constructed within specific discourses which have no necessary relation but only contingent and precarious forms of articulation. There is no reason why sexual difference should be pertinent in all social relations. To be sure, today many different practices, discourses, and institutions do construct men and women (differentially), and the masculine/feminine distinction exists as a pertinent one in many fields. But this does not imply that it should remain the case, and we can perfectly imagine sexual difference becoming irrelevant in many social relations where it is currently found. This is indeed the objective of many feminist struggles.

I am not arguing in favor of a total disappearance of sexual difference as a pertinent distinction; I am not saying either that equality between men and women requires gender-neutral social relations, and it is clear that, in many cases, to treat men and women equally implies treating them differentially. My thesis is that, in the domain of politics, and as far as citizenship is concerned, sexual difference should not be a pertinent distinction. I am at one with Pateman in criticizing the liberal, male conception of modern citizenship but I believe that what a project of radical and plural democracy needs is not a sexually differentiated model of citizenship in which the specific tasks of both men and women would be valued equally, but a truly different conception of what it is to be a citizen and to act as a member of a democratic political community.

A radical democratic conception of citizenship

The problems with the liberal conception of citizenship are not limited to those concerning women, and feminists committed to a project of radical and plural democracy should engage with all of them. Liberalism has contributed to the formulation of the notion of universal citizenship, based on the assertion that all individuals are born free and equal, but it has also reduced citizenship to a merely legal status, indicating the rights that the individual holds against the state. The way those rights are exercised is irrelevant as long as their holders do not break the law or interfere with the rights of others. Notions of public-spiritedness, civic activity, and political participation in a community of equals are alien to most liberal thinkers. Besides, the public realm of modern citizenship was constructed in a universalistic and rationalistic manner that precluded the recognition of division and antagonism and that relegated to the private all particularity and difference. The distinction public/-private, central as it was for the assertion of individual liberty, acted therefore as a powerful principle of exclusion. Through the identification between the private and the domestic, it played indeed an important role in the subordination of women. Recently, several feminists and other critics of liberalism have been looking to the civic republican tradition for a different, more active conception of citizenship that emphasizes the value of political participation and the notion of a common good, prior to and independent of individual desires and interests.

Nevertheless, feminists should be aware of the limitations of such an approach and of the potential dangers that a communitarian type of politics presents for the struggle of many oppressed groups. The communitarian insistence on a substantive notion of the common good and shared moral values is incompatible with the pluralism that is constitutive of modern democracy and that I consider to be necessary to deepen the democratic revolution and accommodate the multiplicity of present democratic demands. The problems with the liberal construction of the public/private distinction would not be solved by discarding it, but only by reformulating it in a more adequate way. Moreover, the centrality of the notion of rights for a modern conception of the citizen should be acknowledged, even though these must be complemented by a more active sense of political participation and of belonging to a political community.[4]

The view of radical and plural democracy that I want to put forward sees citizenship as a form of political identity that consists in the identification with the political principles of modern pluralist democracy, namely, the assertion of liberty and equality for all. It would be a common political identity of persons who might be engaged in many different purposive enterprises and with differing conceptions of the good, but who are bound by their common identification with a given interpretation of a set of ethico-political values. Citizenship is not just one identity among others, as it is in liberalism, nor is it the dominant identity that overrides all others, as it is in civic republicanism. Instead, it is an articulating principle that affects the different subject positions of the social agent while allowing for a plurality of specific allegiances and for the respect of individual liberty. In this view, the public/private distinction is not abandoned, but constructed in a different way. The distinction does not correspond to discrete, separate spheres; every situation is an encounter between "private" and "public" because every enterprise is private while never immune from the public conditions prescribed by the principles of citizenship. Wants, choices, and decisions are private because they are the responsibility of each individual, but performances are public because they have to subscribe to the conditions specified by a specific understanding of the ethico-political principles of the regime which provide the "grammar" of the citizen's conduct.[5]

It is important to stress here that if we affirm that the exercise of citizenship consists in identifying with the ethico-political principles of modern democracy, we must also recognize that there can be as many forms of citizenship as there are interpretations of those principles and that a radical democratic interpretation is one among others. A radical democratic interpretation will emphasize the numerous social relations in which situations of domination exist that must be challenged if the principles of liberty and equality are to apply. It indicates the common recognition by the different groups struggling for an extension and radicalization of democracy that they have a common concern. This should lead to the articulation of the democratic demands found in a variety of movements: women, workers, blacks, gays, and ecological, as well as other "new social movements." The aim is to construct a "we" as radical democratic citizens, a collective political identity articulated through the principle of democratic *equivalence*. It must be stressed that such a relation of *equivalence* does not eliminate *difference* – that would be simple identity. It is only insofar as democratic differences are opposed to forces or discourses which negate all of them that these differences are substitutable for each other.

The view that I am proposing here is clearly different from the liberal as well as the civic republican one. It is not a gendered conception of citizenship, but neither is it a neutral one. It recognizes that every definition of a "we" implies the delimitation of a "frontier" and the designation of a "them." That definition of a "we" always takes place, then, in a context of diversity and conflict. Contrary of liberalism, which evacuates the idea of the common good, and civic republicanism, which reifies it, a radical democratic approach views the common good as a "vanishing point," something to which we must constantly refer when we are acting as citizens, but that can never be reached. The common good functions, on the one hand, as a "social imaginary": that is, as that for which the very impossibility of achieving full representation gives to it the role of an horizon which is the condition of possibility of any representation within the space that it delimits. On the other hand, it specifies what I have designated, following Wittgenstein, as a "grammar of conduct" that coincides with the allegiance to the constitutive ethico-political principles of modern democracy: liberty and equality for all. Yet, since those principles are open to many competing interpretations, one has to acknowledge that a fully inclusive political community can never be realized. There will always be a "constitutive outside," an exterior to the community that is the very condition of its existence. Once it is accepted that there cannot be a "we" without a "them" and that all forms of consensus are by necessity based on acts of exclusion, the question cannot be any more the creation of a fully inclusive community where antagonism, division, and conflict will have disappeared. Hence, we have to come to terms with the very impossibility of a full realization of democracy.

Such a radical democratic citizenship is obviously at odds with the "sexually differentiated" view of citizenship of Carole Pateman, but also with another feminist attempt to offer an alternative to the liberal view of the citizen: the "group differentiated" conception put forward by Iris Marion Young (1987 and 1989). Like Pateman, Young argues that modern citizenship has been constructed on a separation between "public" and "private" that presented the public as the realm of homogeneity and universality and relegated difference to the private. But she insists that this exclusion affects not only women but many other groups based on differences of ethnicity, race, age, disabilities, and so forth. For Young, the crucial problem is that the public realm of citizenship was presented as expressing a general will, a point of view that citizens held in common and that transcended their differences. Young argues in favor of a repoliticization of public life that would not require the creation of a public realm in which citizens leave behind their particular group affiliation and needs in order to discuss a presumed general interest or common good. In its place she proposes the creation of a "heterogeneous public" that provides mechanisms for the effective representation and recognition of the distinct voices and perspectives of those constituent groups that are oppressed or disadvantaged. In order to make such a project possible, she looks for a conception of normative reason that does not pretend to be impartial and universal and that does not oppose reason to affectivity and desire. She considers that, despite its limitations, Habermas's communicative ethics can contribute a good deal to its formulation.

Whereas I sympathize with Young's attempt to take account of other forms of oppression than the ones suffered by women, I nevertheless find her solution of "group-differentiated citizenship" highly problematic. To begin with, the notion of a group that she identifies with comprehensive identities and ways of life might make sense for groups like Native Americans, but is completely inadequate as a description for many other groups whose demands she wants to take into account like women, the elderly, the differently abled, and others. She has an ultimately essentialist notion of "group," which accounts for why, in spite of all her disclaimers, her view is not so different from the interest-group pluralism that she criticizes: there are groups with their interests and identities already given, and politics is not about the construction of new identities, but about finding ways to satisfy the demands of the various parts in a way acceptable to all. In fact, one could say that hers is a kind of "Habermasian version of interest-group pluralism," according to which groups are not viewed as fighting for egoistic private interests but for justice, and where the emphasis is put on the need for argumentation and publicity. So politics in her work is still conceived as a process of dealing with already-constituted interests and identities while, in the approach that I am defending, the aim of a radical democratic citizenship should be the construction of a common political identity that would create the conditions for the establishment of a new hegemony articulated through new egalitarian social relations, practices, and institutions. This cannot be achieved without the transformation of existing subject positions; this is the reason why the model of the rainbow coalition favored by Young can be seen only as a first stage toward the implementation of a radical democratic politics. It might indeed provide many opportunities for a dialogue among different oppressed groups, but for their demands to be construed around the principle of democratic equivalence, new identities need to be created: in their present state many of these demands are antithetical to each other, and their convergence can only result from a political process of hegemonic articulation, and not simply of free and undistorted communication.

Feminist politics and radical democracy

As I indicated at the outset, there has been a great deal of concern among feminists about the possibility of grounding a feminist politics once the existence of women *as* women is put into question. It has been argued that to abandon the idea of a feminine subject with a specific identity and definable interests was to pull the rug from under feminism as politics. According to Kate Soper,

feminism, like any other politics, has always implied a banding together, a movement based on the solidarity and sisterhood of women, who are linked by perhaps very little else than their *sameness* and "common cause" as women. If this sameness itself is challenged on the ground that there is no "presence" of womanhood, nothing that the term "woman" immediately expresses, and nothing instantiated concretely except particular women in particular situations, then the idea of a political community built around women – the central aspiration of the early feminist movement – collapses.   (1990, 11–17)

I consider that Soper here construes an illegitimate opposition between two extreme alternatives: either there is an already given unity of "womanhood" on the basis of some a priori belonging or, if this is denied, no forms of unity and feminist politics can exist. The absence of a female essential identity and of a pregiven unity, however, does not preclude the construction of multiple forms of unity and common action. As the result of the construction of nodal points, partial fixations can take place and precarious forms of identification can be established around the category "women" that provide the basis for a feminist identity and a feminist struggle. We find in Soper a type of misunderstanding of the anti-essentialist position that is frequent in feminist writings and that consists in believing that the critique of an essential identity must necessarily lead to the rejection of any concept of identity whatsoever.[6]

In *Gender Trouble*, Judith Butler asks, "What new shape of politics emerges when identity as a common ground no longer constrains the discourse of feminist politics?" (1990, xi). My answer is that to visualize feminist politics in that way opens much greater opportunity for a democratic politics that aims at the articulation of the various different struggles against oppression. What emerges is the possibility of a project of radical and plural democracy.

To be adequately formulated, such a project requires discarding the essentialist idea of an identity of women *as* women as well as the attempt to ground a specific and strictly feminist politics. Feminist politics should be understood not as a separate form of politics designed to pursue the interests of women *as* women, but rather as the pursuit of feminist goals and aims within the context of a wider articulation of demands. Those goals and aims should consist in the transformation of all the discourses, practices, and social relations where the category "woman" is constructed in a way that implies subordination. Feminism, for me, is the struggle for the equality of women. But this should not be understood as a struggle for realizing the equality of a definable empirical group with a common essence and identity, women, but rather as a struggle against the multiple forms in which the category "woman" is constructed in subordination. However, we must be aware of the fact that those feminist goals can be constructed in many different ways, according to the multiplicity of discourses in which they can be framed: Marxist, liberal, conservative, radical-separatist, radical-democratic, and so on. There are, therefore, by necessity many feminisms and any attempt to find the "true" form of feminist politics should be abandoned. I believe that feminists can contribute to politics a reflection on the conditions for creating an effective equality of women. Such a reflection is bound to be influenced by the existing political and theoretical discourses. Instead of trying to prove that a given form of feminist discourse is the one that corresponds to the "real" essence of womanhood, one should intend to show how it opens better possibilities for an understanding of women's multiple forms of subordination.

My main argument here has been that, for feminists who are committed to a political project whose aim is to struggle against the forms of subordination which exist in many social relations, and not only in those linked to gender, an approach that permits us to understand how the subject is constructed through different discourses and subject positions is certainly more adequate than one that reduces our identity to one single position – be it class, race, or gender. This type of democratic project is also better served by a perspective that allows us to grasp the diversity of ways in which relations of power are constructed and helps us to reveal the forms of exclusion present in all pretensions to universalism and in claims to have found the true essence of rationality. This is why the critique of essentialism and all its different forms – humanism, rationalism, universalism – far from being an obstacle to the formulation of a feminist democratic project, is indeed the very condition of its possibility.

Notes

This chapter was originally published in *Feminists Theorize The Political*, ed. Judith Butler and Joan Scott (New York: Routledge, 1992).

1. See the issue of the journal *differences*, 1 (September 1989), entitled "The Essential Difference: Another Look at Essentialism" as well as the recent book by Diana Fuss, *Essentially Speaking* (1989).
2. For an interesting critique of the dilemma of equality versus difference which is inspired by a similar *problematique* from the one I am defending here, see Scott 1988, part IV. Among feminists the critique of essentialism was first developed by the journal *m/f* which during its eight years of existence (1978–86) made an invaluable contribution to feminist theory. I consider that it has not yet been superseded and that the editorials as well as the articles by Parveen Adams still represent the most forceful exposition of the antiessentialist stance. A selection of the best articles from the 12 issues of *m/f* are reprinted in *The Woman in Question* (Adams and Cowie 1990).
3. See Pateman 1988 and 1989, as well as numerous unpublished papers on which I will also be drawing, especially the following: "Removing the Obstacles to Democracy: The Case of Patriarchy"; "Feminism and Participatory Democracy: Some Reflections on Sexual Difference and Citizenship"; "Women's Citizenship: Equality, Difference, Subordination."
4. I analyze more in detail the debate between liberals and communitarians in Mouffe 1988.
5. The conception of citizenship that I am presenting here is developed more fully in Mouffe 1991.
6. We find a similar confusion in Diana Fuss, who, as Anna Marie Smith indicates in her review of *Essentially Speaking* (Smith 1991), does not realize that the repetition of a sign can take place without an essentialist grounding. It is for that reason that she can affirm that constructionism is essentialist as far as it entails the repetition of the same signifiers across different contexts.

References

Adams, Parveen, and Elisabeth Cowie, eds. 1990. *The Woman in Question*. Cambridge: MIT Press and London: Verso.

Butler, Judith. 1990. *Gender Trouble: Feminism and the Subversion of Identity*. New York: Routledge.

Dietz, Mary G. 1985. "Citizenship with a Feminist Face: The Problem with Maternal Thinking." *Political Theory*, 13 (1).

Elshtain, Jean Bethke. 1981. *Public Man, Private Woman*. Princeton, N. J.: Princeton University Press.

1983. "On 'The Family Crisis.'" *Democracy*, 3 (1): 138.

Fuss, Diana. 1989. *Essentially Speaking*. New York: Routledge.

Laclau, Ernesto, and Chantal Mouffe. 1985. *Hegemony and Socialist Strategy: Towards a Radical Democratic Politics*. London: Verso.

Mouffe, Chantal. 1988. "American Liberalism and Its Critics: Rawls, Taylor, Sandel, and Walzer." *Praxis International*, 8 (2): 70–82.

1991. "Democratic Citizenship and the Political Community." In *Community at Loose Ends*, ed. Miami Theory Collective. Minneapolis: University of Minnesota Press.

Pateman, Carole. 1986. "Feminism and Participatory Democracy." Unpublished paper presented at Meeting of the American Philosophical Association, St. Louis, Mo. (May).

1988. *The Sexual Contract*. Stanford, Calif.: Stanford University Press.

1989. *The Disorder of Women*. Cambridge, England: Polity Press.

Ruddick, Sara. 1989. *Maternal Thinking*. Boston: Beacon.

Scott, Joan W. 1988. *Gender and the Politics of History*. New York: Columbia University Press.

Smith, Anna Marie. "Review of Diana Fuss's *Essentially Speaking*." *Feminist Review*, 38.

Soper, Kate. 1990. "Feminism, Humanism and Postmodernism." *Radical Philosophy*, 55: 11–17.

Young, Iris Marion. 1987. "Impartiality and the Civic Public." In *Feminism as Critique*, ed. Seyla Benhabib and Drucilla Cornell. Minneapolis: University of Minnesota Press.

1989. "Polity and Group Difference: A Critique of the Ideal of Universal Citizenship." *Ethics*, 99.

12

The space of justice: lesbians and democratic politics

Shane Phelan

The task of formulating visions of prolesbian society and of its means of achievement has been blocked by the seemingly incompatible aims and perspectives of the two major discourses on lesbianism – lesbian-feminism in its 1970s version and poststructuralist challenges to lesbian identity – that currently vie for the allegiance of white lesbians. While lesbian-feminism provided a powerful analysis and vision of the future, it was too often perceived and used as a "party line" from which individuals strayed only at the cost of a loss of membership in lesbian community. Deconstructive treatments of lesbian identity, on the other hand, have been leery of positive formulations. Thinkers such as Judith Butler and Diana Fuss have called for coalition politics, but even the most subtle and original thinkers have failed to flesh out what this coalition politics would mean.

Fuss has noted that politics is the "aporia in much of our current political theorizing," and she has linked the popularity of the "politics of x" formula, such as "the politics of theory" or "textual politics" to this ambiguity; "politics" denotes struggle and activism, but so vaguely that it can satisfy a myriad of needs by its invocation (Fuss 1989, 105). As someone whose training is in political theory, I would go even further. The term "politics of x" has thrown political theory into a crisis, as we try to untangle the implications of new social movements that do not operate simply on a logic of self-interest or a fight for material goods. Nevertheless, the idea of a wider "politics" has also served those who resist large-scale institutional politics but who want to discuss power. While this has been an important avenue for new insights, the "politics of x" idea has sometimes led to the refusal to discuss institutional or movement politics, leaving us with the narrowest, popularly US American, vision of "politics" as the terrain of power, but never of common

vision or justice or citizenship. Simply pointing out and condemning
oppression or inequality becomes political activism. That one can do
this as an isolated academic as well as in concert with others means
that this version of politics serves to neglect the force of atomization
and isolation in modern US society.

In order to begin to theorize postmodern lesbian politics we need
to move beyond calls for "subversion" to a more concrete and specific
agenda.

First, we need to critically discuss our goals. We presently remain
locked within dichotomies of "assimilation vs. transformation," "reform
vs. revolution," and the like that can limit our conceptions. It is time for
lesbians to confront whether we can and should envision a future, and
what that future should be. Following that, we need to examine how to
achieve these goals. Specifically, we need to think in more detail about
what postmodern alliances and coalitions might look like, and how to
maintain them. That will be my purpose in this chapter.

Outlaws and solid citizens

The most striking thing about lesbians is not our difference(s) from
heterosexuals, or something distinctive about lesbian cultures and communities, but our diversity. There are politically conservative lesbians,
antifeminist lesbians, separatist lesbians (both feminist and nonfeminist),
Marxist lesbians, radical feminist lesbians, liberal lesbians, apolitical
lesbians, and others. This mosaic was a problem for traditional identity
politics because such politics posited an intimate connection between
one's sexuality[1] and one's political sympathies or "true interest." This
was best conceived along the lines of standpoint theory. A given lesbian
might not presently adopt a "lesbian" standpoint, seeing things from a
"prolesbian" perspective, but the elements of that standpoint are implicit
in her life, waiting for consciousness to catch up.

While many lesbians may believe that the daily texture of lesbians'
lives in the United States provides the ground for a common vision,
the experience of the last twenty-five years indicates that a broad or
comprehensive vision is not in fact shared at this point. While white
lesbians are notably and consistently more liberal in their voting patterns
than are either heterosexual women or men of any sort, they are far from
monolithic.[2] Even among feminist lesbians, there are many disputed
questions. For example, should lesbians fight for the right to be legally
married, with the tax preferences, property understandings, and other
legal powers that currently accompany marriage in the United States,

or should we critique an institution that is inherently patriarchal? Would legal marriage present an improvement for lesbians, or would it signal their assimilation into a heterosexual paradigm? Similar questions arise concerning issues of lesbian motherhood. An even more painful case is that of lesbians in the military. Should we fight for the chance to serve in the military, or be grateful and even proud that we are unwelcome in a destructive and oppressive institution?

Ruthann Robson refers to the two sides in these arguments as "separatist" and "assimilationist." The debate in general, as she puts it, is this:

> Are we sexual outlaws, and perhaps political outlaws as well, who recognize that the law is founded upon the rule of men, upon enforced heterosexuality, and upon violence? Or are we legitimate citizens who have been wrongly excluded from legal recognitions and protections because our private lives are slightly different from some mythical norm?[3]

This is a hard choice. It is also a mistaken one. First, the exclusive choice between being law-abiding and being a criminal, between being within (and under, subject to) the law and being an "outlaw," is not logically given, but is socially structured by the current regime of power/knowledge. In this regime, breaking the law "makes" one into something – a "criminal," an "outlaw" – that then, for many, becomes a badge of pride. For others, the encompassing nature of the identity becomes a deterrence to certain sorts of activity – while I wouldn't mind stealing, someone might say, I wouldn't want to "be a thief." We already see this in the many men and women who have regular sexual relations with other men and women but refuse the identities of "gay" or "lesbian" because they are stigmatized, "outlaw" identities. Full assimilationists are those who accept the label but refuse stigmatization; they say, "yes, I am a lesbian, but I'm not a criminal; I'm a law-abiding normal citizen."

This dynamic relies on the assumption that "everyone else" is in fact law-abiding and "normal." It is the hegemonic assumption, the assumption that exempts (white, middle-class) heterosexuals from problematization. This assumption assigns difference to the under-privileged side of what is actually a relation of difference. Instead of noting that both sides of an opposition are "different" from one another, the hegemony works to render the relation invisible and to describe difference as something inherent in one side.

In this (hetero) sexist social ontology, there are two distinct groups: "Americans" and "gays and lesbians." This ontology is shared among

Americans of all political stripes. As an example, remember Ross Perot's statement in the 1992 Presidential campaign that he would not have "homosexuals and adulterers" in his cabinet because they would be "controversial" with "the American people." It had evidently not occurred to him that heterosexual adultery is the norm among men, or that homosexuals are also among the American people. The strength of feminist and separatist positions has been the ability to question this hegemonic presentation, to challenge the "normality" of the normal citizen/subject. These analyses have exposed the assumed maleness and heterosexuality of the citizen. Problems reemerge when we accept the idea that lesbians should not or cannot become citizens. This repudiation serves to erase all the (usually, but not always, closeted) lesbians who live "normal" or "exemplary" lives.

The second mistake implicit in Robson's choice is the belief that "legitimate citizens" must not be subject to (or aware of?) social dominance. The guiding assumption of assimilationists is that heterosexuals are not daily coerced and shaped into fit subjects. Because of this assumption, they can see inclusion as enough; if only "outsiders" are coerced and subjected, then becoming "insiders" will suffice for freedom. But they are mistaken in this belief. "Other" populations can be effectively targeted only when the "core" population is safely domesticated.

In fact, Robson argues, assimilationists and separatists are not necessarily opposed: they are instead the result of legal thought that occludes recognition of differences as other than dichotomous and enduring. "The law's pronouncement that a person is either law-abiding or a criminal may be a dichotomy that serves the law's interests and does not serve lesbian interests" (Robson 1992, 19). This statement presumes in its very structure that lesbians are distinct from "the society" in which they live. Such positions work for those who experience themselves as true insiders mistakenly disenfranchised, but it does nothing to problematize the inside. And without that problematization of the "inside," the hegemonic core of social structures, we will continually return to unsatisfying choices.

One of the most important insights of poststructuralist work has been the strong deconstruction of "society." While Marx recognized that societies were processes as well as structures, and that the conceptual separation of the individual from society was deceptive, liberal political theory has never made this leap. In Marxism, the problem of society has been that of viewing these systems of processes as a monolithic structure, ruled by "the economic system." This formulation still assumes a unity of system in the economy, instead of a plurality of processes and events and positions. Increasingly, these systems, and thus "society," are giving way to "the social" as the theoretical space of negotiation of identity and difference. And with this, the liberal vision of the individual and his/her society finally breaks down. We are "society," we shifting, incomplete beings. We do indeed live within social formations that possess a certain fixity and provide channels and links and productions of power and meaning, but these formations are not, strictly speaking, separable from us. We are, we speak, those formations.

This insight has been paralleled by the work of writers, especially historians, who have insisted that it is a mistake to distinguish "gays and lesbians" from "society." The question is not, do we "fit into" "society" or not, but where and how do we find out places in social formations, and where do we want to be? This is not a question that admits of a singular answer such as "lesbians fit x" or "lesbians are y" or even "lesbians should do/be z." We cannot simply piggyback onto metanarratives about the progress of freedom and enlightenment that were partial and flawed in their formation without being carried along by their defective assumptions. Lesbian political theory requires a different, more fluid consciousness to move through these dilemmas, exploring our interests and how to further them.

Lesbian interests

Having said the above, the question of what is to be done is not obvious. Robson urges us to center "lesbian interests," but it is far from clear what that means. For her it seems to mean the ability of lesbians to choose their circumstances of life. While seemingly concrete in its refusal to privilege certain choices or desires as more lesbian than others, this formulation quickly reveals its inadequacy. In her desire to "put lesbians at the center," to construct a "lesbian legal theory," Robson argues that such a theory must center lesbians over any others. She gives as an example child custody rules. She reminds us that not all lesbians will want custody of their children. If the lesbian does not want custody, then "lesbian legal theory" should support that decision regardless of the desires of the child or other parents. If a lesbian desires custody, such a theory must "privilege her position to choose custody" (Robson 1992, 134). For Robson, then, lesbian legal theory privileges any given lesbian over any nonlesbian. While this may sound inviting to those of us (most of us!) who have been told in our lives to subordinate our desires and needs to those of others, her alternative is not an improvement.

First, this rule presumes that we know who lesbians are, a presumption belied both by current theory and by political controversies. Are women who occasionally sleep with men lesbians? How often is too often? If a lesbian were to become heterosexual, would Robson recommend that her ex-lover be given child custody? The instability of lesbian identity makes this a much more difficult proposition than it first appears.

Second, Robson's recommendation rests on an impoverished conception of the social landscape. Lesbians become the privileged, whose desires are the command of the law. If I can certify my lesbianism, and I want to abandon my child, then Robson's theory would support that decision. While Robson is not intending a world of all-powerful lesbian choosers, her theory does not sufficiently address the networks of relationships that lesbians emerge in and live within.

Robson's proposal in fact has no content beyond particular interests at particular times. It is not a standard that is appropriate to any real humans in all social relations, much less a full public life. It only speaks to lesbians as consumers of rights, characterized as social or political goods, in a world in which choice is the greatest good. Such a conception of a desired end is unable to articulate with other struggles in any terms other than "choice," which will not do. At some point, individuals' choices will conflict. If we do not have some sense of how to adjudicate these conflicts beyond the a priori privilege given to one party over another, we will be unable to sustain a common world. Such a "lesbian legal theory" as Robson proposes guarantees that lesbians will be isolated from others, both in the rigidity of our identities and in the privilege accorded us as consumers of the law.

Behind Robson's recommendation lies a conception of interest that is inimical to building democratic alliances. This conception assumes, first, that identities are easily demarcated, and, second, that interests are attached to identities. A more specific analysis calls into question the simple delineation of identities. If our basis for theory is social practice and structure, rather than rational/logical categorization, it becomes immediately clear that no one fits within any identity; we are all "citizens of the lack," as it were, all members of an incompletely filled or unstable social space. This lack is what makes politics possible. We all live within multiple valid descriptions of ourselves, choosing from situation to situation which description – which identity – shall come to the fore.

The full political implications of this point only emerge when we look at the second assumption. Its message is that each "identity" carries with it an identifiable "interest." Both interest-group liberalism and Marxism share these two assumptions. They differ in their conception of the goal of politics. For interest-group liberalism the goal of politics is the adjudication through compromise of competing interests. For Marxism, "politics" is largely secondary, if not distracting; while democratic socialists allow for parliamentary, democratic forms of change, Leninists and many others disavow it. For both orthodox Marxists and liberals, politics is the work of advancing essentially pre- or nonpolitical "interests."

Theodore Lowi describes the "model" of "interest-group liberalism" as follows:

(1) Organized interests are homogeneous and easy to define. Any duly elected representative of any interest is taken as an accurate representation of each and every member. (2) Organized interests emerge in every sector of our lives and adequately represent most of those sectors, so that one organized group can be found effectively answering and checking some other organized group as it seeks to prosecute its claims against society. And (3) the role of government is one of insuring access to the most effectively organized, and of ratifying the agreements and adjustments worked out among the competing leaders.

(Lowi 1979, 51)

Thus, interest-group liberalism gives us a description of politics in which the business at hand is that of effecting compromises between, e.g., farmers and consumers. To the extent that it surfaces at all, justice is a matter of optimal distribution of goods. Within this model, the purpose of coalitions is to lend support to another's interest in return for their support of yours.

This model works best for interests that are economically defined. The rise of interest-thinking coincides with and reinforces the modern capitalist state, with its primary business of negotiating between competing classes. James Madison underscores this point when he argues that "the most common and durable source of factions has been the verious [sic] and unequal distribution of property. Those who hold and those who are without property have ever formed distinct interests in society. . . . The regulation of these various and interfering interests forms the principal task of modern legislation . . ." (Madison 1961, 79). The modern category of the "consumer" has problematized even these identities and interests. A farmer is also a consumer. If interests are attached to identities, as interest-group pluralism suggests, then most of us will find ourselves in positions of internal conflict. When we move beyond economic "identities" to sociocultural ones, things get even more confusing.

Interest talk may make sense if all the members of a group share every "relevant" social characteristic or submerge difference(s) among themselves, but this eventuality is increasingly unlikely. In modern societies, where overlapping social movements and identities are increasingly present, interest becomes as unstable as identity. It is at least in part this instability of overlapping identities that has given rise to the attacks on identity politics from across the political spectrum. Seeing interest as concretely and stably linked to particular social identities, such commentators have seen in the proliferation of identities a fragmentation of the social world and the impossibility of common action.

Interest and the space of citizenship

If this is all there is to interest, then the poststructuralist critique of identity and the identity politics of new social movements seem to demolish the possibility of interests as the basis of politics. A shift of focus, however, enables us to see these proliferations as the opening to a new citizenship and public life, to a new interest. Without the presumption of stability and predictability of political subjects, the position of "interest" is opened for reexamination.

Anna Jonasdottir has begun this reexamination. She reminds us that in its root "interest" does not simply refer to the content of people's desires, needs, or demands, but to the space of politics itself. Its initial construction, from the Latin *inter* ("among, between") and *esse* ("to be") suggests that interest is also the claim to *publicity* of certain needs or wants; that is, the concept of interest marks those things that are of legitimate public concern, in contrast to those desires and needs that are "private," my business alone. Thus, claiming something as an interest is both a substantive claim to a good and a formal claim to participation and public recognition.[4] Jonasdottir argues that the formal claim of interest is more "relevant" than the substantive (content) claim. The formal claim of an interest – say as a lesbian – does not yet commit a lesbian to a particular desire or need. It establishes lesbianism as a relevant political identity from which to proceed. This provides the space to articulate a "lesbian good" without predetermining what that good will be. It also opens the category of "lesbian" to negotiation – claiming lesbianism as a relevant identity cannot simply avoid "common sense" notions of what such an identity is, but it need not rest with those notions either. The identity itself becomes open to politics.

This flexibility is not something unique to lesbianism, or to sexual categories in general. Consider the case of the farmer again. Claiming an interest as a farmer will lead many to conclusions about what that person – the "farmer" – will want and support. It is not given from the establishment of that interest/identity exactly who will be defined as a farmer, however, nor is it given that the farmer *must* support subsidies or oppose decent wages for migrant workers, or in general think only in the narrowest terms of individual economic advantage. The farmer is also (at least potentially) a *citizen* – not as "another" identity, but as the basis of the claim of interest. The farmer may conclude that the nation cannot afford subsidies, or that decent wages and living conditions are a requirement of justice, without abandoning her "interest" as a farmer.[5]

In the same way, claiming an interest as a lesbian in this view is a civic act. It embeds the lesbian in her political community(ies), implicating her in responsibilities as well as rights and demands. This point is often missed, both in mainstream political science treatments of interest and in discussions of lesbian politics. Claims made on a community are inseparable from recognition of that community. When lesbians seek to further our interests in US society and law, we are at the same time involving ourselves in the larger affairs of that society. And this involvement is crucial if we are actually to have the option to live "lesbian-centered" lives. As Michael Walzer points out, within a political community "the denial of membership is always the first of a long train of abuses" (1983, 62), and thus anyone interested in eliminating persecution and oppression must work immediately for recognition of the membership of lesbian citizens. If lesbians are to claim any interest at all, the first interest must be recognition as members of the political community.

If we transform our identity politics from one that assumes an automatic correlation between identity and politics to one based on the spaces of citizenship itself we might, ironically, find more to share both with other lesbians and with nonlesbians. Such a politics will recognize relevant differences in the specific situations of our lives while leaving the political meaning of those differences open to negotiation. This situation need not be contradictory, though it may sound paradoxical.

We can get at this problem by considering what counts as a lesbian issue. While some might argue that lesbian issues should be only those that concern all lesbians or affect lesbians *qua* lesbians, these issues break down quickly. Lesbian motherhood is not an issue for all lesbians; many cannot have children, and others are not interested. While lesbophobic violence against lesbians may seem a clear "lesbian issue," it is irrelevant in less violent cultures or locations in the United States. More basically, any such requirements for lesbian issues presume a stability to lesbian identities that is belied by recent theory as well as many women's experiences. What is it to act "as a lesbian," or to have a concern "in one's capacity as a lesbian?" These essentialisms and reifications have broken down, and with them falls the question of a lesbian issue construed as unique.

Consider the goal of decent housing for all. Surely this is a concern for many lesbians, and is therefore a "lesbian" issue. It is also a concern for many others, however, and for them it is not configured as "lesbian." The difficulty that poor lesbians face in finding decent housing, especially if they try to live openly as lesbians, is lesbian-specific *and* reaches beyond lesbians to the problem of decent housing at affordable cost for all. Here we can distinguish the difficulties faced by women marked as lesbians, stigmatized in a heterosexist identitarian society, without attributing to them any essential features or qualities. We can thus establish a limited political agenda without essentializing or overgeneralizing.

We could approach this problem in several ways, but I will focus on two here. In this first, lesbian-centered approach, lesbians will work with other lesbians to provide decent housing for lesbians. This will include construction, oversight of landlords and municipalities for maintenance and rate fairness, and efforts to ensure that lesbians are not discriminated against on the basis of their sexuality. Nonlesbians will be ignored, except insofar as they either control housing or provide something desirable. This is the separatist solution, and there is much to be said for it as an occasional tactic. Working with and for other lesbians is exhilarating and empowering. It cannot be our only position, however.

In the second approach, lesbians will work with everyone concerned to provide decent housing to all citizens. This approach will look like the first in many ways, but there are some differences. First, the nonlesbians will need continual prodding to understand and work on issues of discrimination. Secondly, the lesbians will have to commit to working with and for people who are not lesbians. In so doing, they will not be able to focus solely on lesbians, but will have to work for and talk about the problems faced by the other members and potential members of the group. This widened focus does not make decent housing no longer a lesbian issue, however; it simply removes the divide between lesbians and everyone else. Making decent housing a lesbian issue does not remove it from the public agenda, nor from that of any other identifiable group. The lesbian concerns may be specific to lesbians, but that does not mean that those concerns cannot be shared and fought for by all.

In this second scenario, the specific problems and desires of lesbians are relevant to the whole group, insofar as it wants to include lesbians as equal members of a democratic organization or polity. This does not mean that the specifics of being lesbian are irrelevant to membership in the group; each is welcome and has an equal voice without regard to sexuality. The equality of membership in the group requires that the group treat all equally, and that means paying attention to the situations and needs of all. It does not mean allowing only those in a given situation to participate in decision making, however; that violates equality.[6]

Such a politics allows both for the presentation of something like a "lesbian interest" and for the recognition that many (if not most) lesbians will not share that interest. In the model described by Lowi, an interest was only a "real" interest if it was shared by every member of the homogeneously defined group. Thus, if not all lesbians agree on a policy, it must not be a "lesbian interest." If we abandon presumptions of homogeneity and identity, however, if we get specific, we can say that nondiscrimination in housing is a lesbian interest without thereby excluding others from having that interest or requiring that all lesbians share it.

It becomes a lesbian interest both in that it does affect some lesbians and in its *potential* to directly affect all lesbians *qua* lesbians. While wealthy lesbians may find themselves able to evade the strictures of rents or mortgages, the strictures exist nonetheless. There is a distinct difference between knowing that you can afford a decent place to live because you can finance that dwelling without any help and knowing that you can afford it because while you need a loan or need to pay rent, the rules of your society prohibit landlords and lenders from refusing to rent or lend to you. In the first case privilege enables some to escape the general social consequences of lesbianism; in the second lesbianism is socially recognized as a potential and invalid source of discrimination. There is thus an overt social commitment to the membership of lesbians, without any prescription as to the particulars of lesbians' lives. It is this recognition of membership that forms the basis for a lesbian interest, as well as the particulars of the policy.

On the other hand, nondiscrimination is not a uniquely lesbian interest. Within systems of discrimination, heterosexuals are forced to prove their membership as well. Suspicion of lesbianism can deny to single heterosexual women the rights supposedly held by women, as the history of discrimination against women in the military shows. The policing of nonlesbian identities concomitant with lesbian oppression provides the possibility of a common interest, and shifts the focus of activism from lesbians and their "similarity" with or "difference" from heterosexuals to the network of power that binds everyone in differential relation.

If this treatment of interest leaves us with a less monolithic agenda, the focus on the public nature of lesbian interest invites us into a realm of shared concern extending beyond lesbian communities or groups. Feminist lesbians may be forced to admit that not all lesbians share any version of a feminist agenda, but on the other hand we have a greater opening to work with feminist nonlesbians as well as others with whom we may share a great deal. If interest as inter-esse challenges the grand claims of shared lesbian interests and identities, it raises the claims on the larger polity to the demand that lesbians be acknowledged as equal citizens, with equal participation and recognition not "in spite" of our lesbianism, but with and through it. Our membership is not qualified or limited by our lesbianism, and thus our concerns, even our concerns as lesbians, are legitimately public ones. Our presence as lesbians is prior to any particular claims we make, and does not require proof of our sameness with heterosexuals. Membership acknowledges our existence, our presence, and it is this which interest group politics contains in an abstract claim for certain rights or benefits. The primary right properly claimed by advocates of identity politics is the right of membership. This right is more subversive than any number of laws or protections based on the desire to ignore our differences and allow us to be just like the mythical (monogamous, religious, hardworking) heterosexual.

Thus, rethinking interest moves us from identity, with the assumptions of homogeneity and privatized consumerist concerns and agendas, to politics as an activity that is valuable in itself. This shift is not the subsumption or transcendence of "identity politics," but a recognition of the fullness of politics that cannot be encapsulated by identity. It is the return of identity politics to its formulation by the Combahee River Collective. They did not say that their only political concerns would arise from their self-interest, which was to be unquestioned and unchallenged; they said that they would no longer accept other people's agendas and models for their politics, that they would look to the specific circumstances of their own lives for their politics. This linkage between the personal and the larger public that shapes and limits individual lives invites us to examine the relations between us rather than isolating us in our "private" concerns or "special" interests. "Identity politics" is not fragmenting or divisive; it is the failure to acknowledge and respond to the inequalities and injustices that mark some identities that is divisive. The later problems of identity politics have followed the corruption of this vision into interest-group liberalism. The homogeneity presumed by interest-group liberalism provided an essentialist vision of masses of women, of lesbians, etc., with a unified interest. The recognition of the diversity of these groups gave rise to descriptions of "difference," but for many white (and probably many nonwhite) people this looked like the end of politics, the death of a shared world, because "differences" appeared as discrete entities, singular atoms on a blank social space, rather than as nodes in social constellations. The refiguration of differences as specificities, as crystallizations of differential relations between equally "different" people, enables us to return to the strength of identity politics without leading to abandonment of those who do not obviously share our identities.

Getting specific introduces the possibility of thinking of lesbians not as outlaws, nor as solid citizens, but as lesbian citizens. These lesbian citizens are "queer" in existing models of citizenship, but this queerness is not itself a virtue. The revolutionary potential of lesbian citizens lies not in separatism, nor in continual elaboration of the law to privilege "lesbian interests," but in forcing the political and legal systems to stretch and re-form to do justice to our lives. It does indeed demand that legislators and judges consider lesbian interests, but not as a list of criteria based upon known characteristics. It requires that they learn to frame legislation and adjudication from the standpoint of a lesbian in a given case, to ask what she needs as well as what nonlesbians need. It is not a privileging of lesbians above others; it is, in Martha Minow's words, a process of "making all the difference," moving to see fields of relations rather than discrete persons labeled as "different." The shift from thinking of people as single condensed entities to envisioning identities as social processes then calls into question the position and interest of "not marked by difference" in dominant discourses. If "difference" is no longer the property of one group, but is the mark of a relation of (dis)similarity, then it is not enough to fit "others" into a previously existing frame, nor can we simply modify the frame to include them. There is no avoiding it; what is needed is not a specific result, but a process – that of public deliberation among a group all of whose members are treated as equal participants. While certain particulars, such as civil rights, are a prerequisite for this process, they are not the sum of the goal. The other part is our need for choice if we are truly to reshape institutions and practices. Lesbian citizens will thus be part of the larger project of radical democracy that aims at making all the difference, at eliminating the privilege of hegemonic identity.

Opening the space of citizenship addresses the needs of US lesbians for recognition and self-determination, inclusion, and safety. It also provides a means of linking lesbian struggles to other demands for these same things without assuming a priority among those struggles or suggesting a hierarchy of oppressions. It enables lesbians and others to be specific about their own circumstances, to make connections between their circumstances and those of others, and to formulate a common agenda for concrete changes that does not play into zero-sum games of power. The demand for the broadest range of civil rights is not a "special interest" demand, sought at the expense of the civic good or that of another "group," but a demand for equal membership in a democratic polity.

In the end, our goal should be to articulate a lesbian agenda as part of a radical democratic creed shared across sexualities and other differences. In such a future, the interest of lesbians in their lives will be shared by others, and will not need to include reminders that we should not be raped, killed, intimidated, "cured," or ignored. We will thus be ready for specific citizenships, entry into the multiplicity of public realms that await postmodern citizens.

Interest in the house of difference

Postmodern politics means that as we enter public discourse we do so, not as "Lesbians" with a fixed, eternal identity, but as lesbians, people occupying provisional subject positions in heterosexual society. As such, we might acknowledge that speaking and being heard does not mean simply drawing on our "experience" in an unmediated way, but means articulating our lives, interpreting and reinterpreting them in ways that link us to others. Coalitions of the future will require us to maintain the subject position of lesbians and our belief in our voices with the growing awareness that our own subjectivity is part of the terrain of possible change. To paraphrase Foucault, "we have to work on *becoming* [lesbian] and not be obstinate in defining what we are" (Foucault 1989, 204). Thus, the problem for coalition politics is not, what do we share? but rather, what *might* we share as we develop our identities through the process of coalition? Coalition cannot be simply the strategic alignment of diverse groups over a single issue, nor can coalition mean finding the real unity behind our apparently diverse struggles. Our politics must be informed by affinity rather than identity, not simply because we are not all alike, but because we each embody multiple, often conflicting, identities and locations (Haraway 1990, 197).

As an example of the construction of interest and identity as monolithic and natural, we can use the best-selling book on gay politics, *After The Ball* (Kirk and Madsen 1989). This book was written by two white male Harvard graduates currently working at high-prestige, high-income jobs. They propose a "marketing strategy" to overcome homophobia in the United States. This strategy includes advertisements that plant the idea that gays and lesbians are "just like everyone else." This proposition is not just strategic; they believe that

When treated with respect and friendship, we're as happy and psychologically well adjusted as they . . . we look, feel, and act just as they do; we're hardworking, conscientious Americans with love lives exactly like their own.

(Kirk and Madsen 1989, 379)

This statement is fascinating because it follows 100 pages of castigation of gay male sexual, political, and personal behavior. They continually contrast the pathology of gay life to the nice, normal picture of heterosexuality. They manage this dissonance by separating the "bad gays" from the "good gays," and claiming that "good gays" are just like heterosexuals. They experience themselves as just like their straight friends, and so they are embarrassed by the "deviants."

There is much to take exception with in this book, and much to think about. Here I just want to focus on a few points. The first is the ease with which these two men subsume lesbians into the category of "gay." While they occasionally acknowledge that lesbians do not have the proclivity for casual sex that gay men do (a difference of which they approve) and that we face some problems as women, the bulk of the book makes no distinction between gays and lesbians. This erasure is not simply sexist, but reflects their ability to see gayness as a singular distinguishing mark in their lives. Were it not for their "sexual orientation," they would be just like their (white?) heterosexual friends and fellow Harvard graduates. Thus, "gayness" appears to them as a discrete identifier, and the "gay" they are discussing emerges as male, white, and middle- (or upper-) class. They seek simply to end antigay prejudice, to secure equal rights (e.g., formal marriages) with heterosexuals, and eventually, just to fit in with every other white affluent citizen. They have no problem with any other structures of oppression in the United States, and so they urge "gays" not to distract themselves from the fight for gays by "admixture with superfluous issues that might further upset or distract ordinary Americans" (Kirk and Madsen 1989, 180). Included in the list of "superfluous" or "utterly extraneous" causes are racial justice, feminism, environmentalism, and others. They disdain the Rainbow Coalition concept as a distraction.

What is a lesbian to make of this? What is a Chicana (or black, or Asian, or Native American, or poor, or . . .) lesbian to think? Kirk and Madsen are telling us that feminism is not simply not equivalent to lesbianism, but that it is dangerous to the cause of gay rights. Discussions of race or class are divisive.

Imagine the response of Audre Lorde. In *Zami: A New Spelling of My Name*, Lorde describes her position as a black lesbian among lesbians in Greenwich Village:

> Being women together was not enough. We were different. Being gay-girls together was not enough. We were different. Being Black together was not enough. We were different. Being Black women together was not enough. We were different. Being Black dykes together was not enough. We were different . . . It was a while before we came to realize that our place was the very house of difference rather than any one particular difference.   (Lorde 1982, 226)

Within the "house of difference," Kirk and Madsen's advice is inadequate. And not only black lesbians dwell in that house; the differences were differences among that progressively more narrowly defined group, inseparable from the individuality of its members. From this perspective, Kirk and Madsen's prescription is both politically naive and theoretically incoherent. It rests on the idea of gayness as a discrete identifier, in the manner of interest-group liberalism, and reduces that identifier, to who we have sex with. It then colonizes all those who have or would like to have sex with members of the same sex (or gender? who knows?) as "gays," and tells them to address that in isolation from the rest of their lives. While their aim is to "keep the message focused," the effect is to isolate white bourgeois gay men from any potential allies other than straight white men. Just as the phrase "as a woman" has been discredited in feminism as "the Trojan horse of feminist ethnocentrism" (Spelman 1988, 13), we cannot rest with "as a gay" or "as a lesbian"; we need to produce public spaces to discuss what these words can mean, and we need to recognize their insufficiency in fully capturing the nature of our sexualities.

Kirk and Madsen provide us with an example of how a simple white identity politics can fail. While they have many good suggestions for media campaigns to convince heterosexuals that we are "just like them," they fail to provide any reason for the majority of lesbians or queers of color to work with them. Theirs is a pre-Stonewall, prefeminism politics. (While they state that "the gay revolution has failed," that post-Stonewall gay activism has been a "disaster," the legal and social advances of lesbians and gays in the last two decades, when compared to the advances under homophile organizations, are staggering.)

The narrowness of this prescription rests on the assumption of a clear "gay interest." As we saw earlier, this notion is problematic. Even if we could/can posit a discrete "gay interest," however, there is no entailment between such an interest and the rejection of coalition. One could assume such an interest and still advocate coalition politics. The motivation of such a politics would be a quid pro quo understanding: I'll protect you from "them" if you protect me. I'll support racial or class advances if you support feminism and lesbian rights.

Such models collapse in the face of specific thinking about our lives. "Overlapping" memberships in various social groups may cause some people to hold "several agendas" for change at once: black lesbians will have an agenda on the basis of race, on gender, and on sexuality. Thus for some, coalitions will be the only way to do justice to their concerns, their "interests." Even so, this argument still remains in the realm of essentialist thinking about social groups. It conceives of "blacks" and "lesbians" as distinct and uniform groups; the anomaly of black lesbians is precisely that they do not fit the modal version of either group. From an essentialist viewpoint, black lesbians become "bridges" between groups that are otherwise coherent. But none of these groupings is "natural." *All* are the result of particular historical discourses about race, sexuality, and gender. The coherence and unity of the category of "blacks," "whites," "lesbians," etc., is a politico-historical event, not a logical or a natural one.[7]

Once we see that social formations and memberships are not naturally given but are invented or imagined, we can see the bonds between us. These bonds are not ones of mutual affection or concern, not ones of nature, but are the creation of systems of discursive power and hegemony that tell us who we are and where we fit. This recognition in turn forces us to rethink common action. If common action is not (or not exclusively) jostling for one's (pregiven) interest against others who would deny it, what is it? If our group memberships are provisional because those groups are provisional entities/concepts, how do we know whom to work with?

Lesbians are involved in every struggle, sometimes on sides I would not choose. Before it is an identity, lesbianism is a characteristic of many diverse people. Audre Lorde's powerful response to the charge that black lesbians don't support black struggle is a documentation of her presence, a black lesbian presence, in all the struggles that supposedly did not involve gender or sexuality (Lorde 1988). Lesbians active in antiracist work, in work against violence against women or US imperialism or AIDS or for economic justice all remain lesbian, as do their Republican, antifeminist, or militarist sisters. All belie a monolithic politics of unitary subjectivity.

This is not news. However, it has historically been explained or prescribed on the basis of oppressions that share the same root and the same oppressor – white straight bourgeois men versus everybody else – and the false consciousness of those who deny the connections. Such arguments do not prepare us for the inevitable contradictions and conflicts among and within members of these various groups. A postmodernist coalitional politics can avoid this struggle by recognizing that such conflicts are inevitable, and that they are not cause for despair but grounds for continued rearticulation, new narratives of political structures and change. As a more modest politics, it reduces the invitation to despair and burnout that is such a chronic problem among the various opponents of the established order(s). In this project, the issue is not whom to work with, but how to work with them; or, it is both. If politics is a matter of negotiating identities and discourses as much as distribution of goods, then we cannot assume that the people we work with will remain the same (or that we will, for that matter).

transformatni

Queer – a coalitional identity?

"Queer" politics is often presented as this articulation of a coalitional identity. Queer theory and politics are products of the 1980s. This new identity had several sources. First, the feminist sex wars exhausted many lesbians and led them to seek new locations. Secondly, the rising demands of bisexuals for inclusion in gay and lesbian communities and organizations invited a new analysis of the relationship between politics and sexuality. Third, AIDS introduced new patterns of relationships between men and women and provided a basis for alliances. Lastly, the ascendancy of poststructuralism provided a theoretical terrain for queer theory in the academy.

"Queers" are on a path that follows a different geography than their older sisters and brothers, a postmodern landscape sculpted by performance art, by punk rock and its descendants, by Madonna and multiculturalism, and by Reagan and Bush. They are unafraid of camp, or of "roles" that do not mean what they once did but do not mean nothing. They have a sense of humor unlike that of "gays" or "lesbians." The 1993 March on Washington exemplified much of this: while the march was organized along "political" lines, issues of justice and equity and inclusion and dignity, the marchers were much more diverse and hilarious. "We're here, we're gay, can Bill come out and play?" in front of the White House has a very different tone from "hey

hey ho ho, homophobia's got to go!" I was raised on anger, but I was delighted in DC.

In a deeper way, though, "queers" have not transcended any of the challenges facing "lesbians" or "gays." There are several angles to this. First, who is queer? To many, "queer" is simply a new label for "lesbian and gay." Among these, there is a split between those who use "queer" simply as a convenient shorthand and those who imply a nationalist politics, who see lesbians and gays as a "people" with a shared history and purpose. Neither usage provides anything new and the nationalist vision recycles much that is better left to decompose. While the shorthand usage is a matter claiming a word that was used against us, the nationalist version of "queer" reanimates the problems of lesbian-feminism in its cultural feminist versions without resolving them. The conflicts within this supposedly naturally unified group are suppressed, and allies and enemies are defined a priori rather than through political experience.

For others, "queer" moves beyond lesbian and gay to encompass bisexuals, transgendered people, and other sexual minorities. This is the move toward a coalitional identity. In Lisa Duggan's words, this usage points toward a "new community" that is "unified only by a shared dissent from the dominant organization of sex and gender" (1992, 20). "Dissent from the dominant organization of sex and gender" does not however guarantee a feminist position. The feminist heritage of "lesbians" is crucial if queers are to avoid the pitfalls of "gays" (white male) politics. While Queer Nation chapters worked consciously at being nonsexist and nonracist, and castigated gay men for their sexism and racism, the later battles within chapters demonstrated that nirvana had not yet been achieved. Both of these understandings of queer, the reclaiming and the new identity, must be challenged to deny the colonization of lesbians and people of color that occurs within "gay" politics.

The tension between nationalism and its most thoroughgoing deconstruction lies latent in queerdom. Self-described queers include both those who see queerness as a cross-cultural and transhistorical "natural" identity or position, and those who use "queer" to designate a liminal position within the contingent sexual and gender frontiers of contemporary capitalist societies. This tension is not to be resolved by the ceding of one side to the other, but will remain a field of contestation. As a lesbian feminist, however, I can only fear nationalism. To the extent that queers become nationalist, they will ignore or lose patience with those among them who do not fit their idea of the nation. This dynamic in nationalism will always limit its political usefulness. The only fruitful nationalism I can imagine is one that has at its heart the idea of the nonnation – the nation of nonidentity, formed not by any shared attribute but by a conscious weaving of threads between tattered fabrics. And at that point, why speak of nations? Alliances are not nations, and need not be to be strong.

"Queer" does not guarantee a better alliance politics than "gay" or "lesbian" has. The larger notion of queer as encompassing all sexual minorities does not eliminate this problem, but reinscribes it in the heart of the queer. The alliance with (heterosexual or homosexual) sadomasochists, fetishists, pedophiles that is adumbrated in this usage does not enlarge the field of alliance, but simply shifts the privilege within it. When others are faced with a "nation" that they do not recognize or desire, they will simply leave. The hegemonic inscription of the queer as *the* sexual minority will then amount to an exclusionary colonization of those who refuse their membership.   *queer – universal category on the ground*

Character and coalition

In the end, identity politics will always be either a nationalist politics or a "practical politics of the open end" (Spivak 1991). Doing a better identity politics does not mean finding the best definition of our identities so as to eliminate problems of membership and goals, but means continual shuffling between the need for categories and the recognition of their incompleteness. No one can decide simply on the basis of identity who any of us will be able to work with. Simple versions of identity politics, in which we know who and what we are and we know who is trustworthy by their identifications, are inadequate. The contingency and multiplicity of agendas furthers this indeterminacy. Because lesbians, gays, and queers differ in their political aims among themselves as well as between groups, the ground for common action cannot be "identity" but must be shared commitments; it must be sympathy and affinity rather than identity. Sympathy and affinity need not be total to be real and effective. They do, however, require a self-consciousness about one's actions and allegiances that is often taken for granted in identity politics. If identity is not sufficient ground for trust or political agreement, but abstract principles in the manner of liberalism or Marxism are not sufficient either, then we need to get specific with one another about what we value and what we will do to realize that value.

identity as process

self-consciousness

recognition of values

Getting specific helps us to locate our allies at particular points, for particular struggles. Paying close attention to our particular social locations forces us to go beyond simple counting of the categories. Our lives are not lived as chunks; though we can certainly specify in some instances structural conditions and inequalities that produce results, most of the time we just live, all of our elements jostling together. Our identities are those jostling, shifting elements. Our politics must account for this. I may work with gay men because we are both targets of a larger hegemonic culture. When I do such work, I do not experience the euphoria of community. I am often downright disgusted. But it is necessary nonetheless, because heterosexism and homophobia structure my existence inescapably. When I work with women of other racial and/or ethnic identifications, I do so not out of "compassion" for them, or to assuage my guilt. I do so, first, because injustice is not segmentable, but spreads beyond garden borders laid down for it. I do so, second, because I value them in spite of my own racism. That value is not just the value of "difference," of the sort we see on the "ethnic days" in cities where groups gather to dance and sing and eat before returning to being Anglo. I value specific different voices because they intersect with my own, creating a world. There are other different voices that I do not value and do my best not to support: Nazis, white supremacists, antifeminists, corporate polluters, George Bush. And then there are people in neither camp; those who, while racist, sexist, classist, and heterosexist, share concerns and try to overcome their pasts and presents.

The question to ask about "allies," then, is not whether they are "really" allies, but how to *make* them allies. While identity politics has sometimes been framed in terms of identity checklists, a larger identity politics will ask instead about character. Identity politics, as a politics arising out of the specific oppressions faced by each of us, need not result in a politics shared only by others sharing those oppressions – indeed, it cannot, for that sharing will always be tested as we dwell together in the house of difference. The questions to ask are not whether we share a given position but whether we share a commitment to improve it, and whether we can commit to the pain of embarrassment and confrontation as we disagree. The question is whether we can *decide* to be allies, and whether we have the strength to follow through on that decision. Unless these questions are addressed, no theory and no identity will provide a satisfactory result. With positive answers to them, we can forge the bonds between specificities to create a fence against oppression. These very local links can provide the ground for the strength needed to address structures that currently appear insurmountable.

Thus the relevance to political theory of both ethics and of a certain

ethics + aesthetics

aesthetics of the self. Ethics, treated not as simple rules but as guidelines and starting points for choice, and aesthetics, as the conscious fashioning of character, are both required if politics is to change and produce anything of lasting value. If we fail to address questions of character, formulations of identity will never produce the changes we (any of us) seek. Character is not a static entity on which we will be judged by some distant god; character is one name for the processes of the self. Those processes are inseparable from the processes of politics.

Where will this character come from? From practice. Those looking for allies must begin by volunteering to become allies, developing a commitment to challenge racism in ourselves and in others. Middle-class and wealthy lesbians must work to learn about and support working-class and poor people's lives and struggles. Men who want to be allies must become knowledgeable and become willing to learn from women. And so on. Alliances are not a matter of harmony and univocity. The distinction between coalitions and alliances is not one of unity or even of durability (though I think there are reasons to expect greater durability from alliances), but of motive and purpose. Recognition of the publicity, the "inter esse" of interest, requires the self-extension of each person toward others. Awareness of others must be developed into a conscious commitment to the welfare of others, both in general and in each person we meet. This commitment is a form of love. It is a love of the world, a love of democracy, a love of others as inseparably part of the community within which we live. As an activity based on conscious commitment rather than a feeling, love can be chosen and it can be refused. Love need not entail self-negation, but it does require a willingness to "go under," to suffer the small deaths of humility and pain and self-examination. And as love does not come from others unless we offer it to them, so allies will develop as we ally ourselves with their causes. As we increasingly open our eyes and hearts, we will help to create those fences against oppression by modeling decency. Without decency and love, bringing us toward one another without requiring sameness, our rhetorical and heartfelt commitments to others will continually be frustrated in the face of ineluctable difference.

The awareness of the incompleteness of any narrative, of the instability of identities and of social topologies, is the opening from modern arrogance to such humility. It requires not only theoretical elegance and acuity, but profound interrogation and transformation of oneself. While not all arrogance is modern, surely the postmodern, "that which denies itself the solace of good forms, the consensus of a taste which would make it possible to share collectively the nostalgia for the unattainable"

(Lyotard 1984, 81), that which confronts the abyss of responsibility and choice, is inconsistent with arrogance of any sort. Faced with such an awareness, bereft of models that justify theoretical imperialism on anyone's part, we are forced to confront one another, to build a ground together instead of finding one and inviting others to sit on it.

Lesbians should not refuse the specificity and reality of lesbian experiences, nor should we reify it into an identity and history so stable that no one can speak to it besides other lesbians who agree on that particular description of their existence. Our politics, disappointingly enough, must consist of continued patient and impatient struggle with ourselves and those "within" and "without" our "communities" who seek to fix us (in the many senses of that term). We can afford neither simple assimilation into mainstream politics nor total withdrawal in search of the authentic community – or we must demand the right to both. We have to stand where we are, acknowledging the contradictions and forging the links between ourselves and other marginal citizens of the world, resisting the temptation to cloak crucial differences with the cloak of universality while also refusing to reify those differences into hardened identities that cannot be crossed. The promise of getting specific is the promise of theorizing, which is to say discussing and working on, the possibility of such a politics.

Notes

1. There is great ideological disparity even in these words. The "preference" language is liberal, implying a purely private desire along the lines of consumer choice. The "orientation" discourse is denser, aiming at suggesting an enduring, probably innate, facet of one's identity. I include both terms here because both have been used in lesbian identity politics, and the oscillation from one to the other continues even as "orientation" becomes the legal term of choice.
2. Edelman 1991. Approval ratings of George Bush were most striking: when asked in 1991 "Do you approve or disapprove of the way George Bush is handling his job as President?," the total ratio was 57 approve/40 disapprove, the ratio for "all women" was 54/42, that for gay men was 45/53, and that for lesbians was 32/60. When asked whether they considered themselves liberal, moderate, or conservative, the total was 18/46/33; gay men 47/41/9; lesbians 48/38/13. I have no explanation for the greater percentage of lesbian conservatives than gay male conservatives, but I do not know the margin of error in this sample; it does not strike me as a terribly great difference.
3. Robson 1992, 19; it should be noted that the division between outlaw and solid citizen here is not the same as the "good girl/bad girl" split of the 1980s

"sex wars." There, many of those who would be "outlaws" in Robson's sense because of their feminist agenda were "good girls" in their critique and/or rejection of sadomasochism and butch/femme. For a review of those debates, see Phelan 1989, ch. 6, and Vance 1984.

4. Jonasdottir 1988, 39–40. See also Balbus 1971; Connolly 1972; and Diamond and Hartsock 1981.

5. If the farmer does make such a decision, all hell will break loose in American politics. For the behavior of the national and state governments makes clear that they expect their citizens to construe their interest as narrowly as possible.

6. Anne Phillips makes this point about women's participation when she says that "the crucial requirement is for women's political presence: which is not to say that only women can speak on 'women's' issues, that women must speak only as a sex" (1991, 167).

7. For a discussion of social formations as historically specific and "imagined," see Anderson 1983. The most impressive example of personal recognition and exploration of these bonds by a white person remains Minnie Bruce Pratt's essay "Identity: Blood Skin Heart" (1984). Rather than discuss that work here, I recommend that every reader of this book drop everything and read it!

References

Anderson, Benedict. 1983. *Imagined Communities: Reflections on the Origins and Spread of Nationalism*. London: Verso.

Balbus, Isaac. 1971. "The Concept of Interest in Pluralist and Marxian Analysis." *Politics and Society*, 1 (2): 151–77.

Butler, Judith. 1990. *Gender Trouble: Feminism and the Subversion of Identity*. New York: Routledge.

Connolly, William E. 1972. "On 'Interests' in Politics." *Politics and Society*, 2 (4): 459–77.

Diamond, Irene, and Nancy Hartsock. 1981. "Beyond Interests in Politics: A Comment on Virginia Shapiro's 'When Are Interests Interesting? The Problem of Political Representation of Women.'" *American Political Science Review*, 75 (3): 717–23.

Duggan, Lisa. 1992. "Making It Perfectly Queer." *Socialist Review*, 22 (1): 11–29.

Edelman, Murray. 1991. "The Gay Vote, 1990: Preliminary Findings." Paper presented at annual meeting of American Political Science Association, August–September 1991, Washington, DC.

Foucault, Michel. 1989. "Friendship as a Way of Life," in *Foucault Live*. New York: Semiotext(e).

Fuss, Diana. 1989. *Essentially Speaking*. New York: Routledge.

Haraway, Donna. 1990. "A Manifesto for Cyborgs." In *Feminism/ Postmodernism*, ed. Linda Nicholson. New York and London: Routledge.

Jonasdottir, Anna G. 1988. "On the Concept of Interest, Women's Interests, and the Limitations of Interest Theory." In *The Political Interests of Gender*, ed. Kathleen B. Jones and Anna G. Jonasdottir. London and Newbury Park, Calif.: Sage.

Kirk, Marshall, and Hunter Madsen. 1989. *After the Ball: How America Will Conquer Its Fear and Hatred of Gays in the 90s*. New York: Penguin.

Lorde, Audre. 1982. *Zami: A New Spelling of My Name (A Biomythography)*. Freedom, Calif.: Crossing.

——— 1988. "I Am Your Sister: Black Women Organizing Across Sexualities." In *A Burst of Light*, ed. Audre Lorde. Ithaca, N. Y.: Firebrand Books.

Lowi, Theodore. 1979. *The End of Liberalism: The Second Republic of the United States*, 2nd ed. New York: W. W. Norton.

Lyotard, Jean-François. 1984. *The Postmodern Condition: A Report on Knowledge*. Minneapolis: University of Minnesota Press.

Madison, James. 1961. "Number 10." In *The Federalist Papers*, intro. Clinton Rossiter. New York: New American Library.

Phelan, Shane. 1989. *Identity Politics*. Philadelphia, Pa.: Temple University Press.

Phillips, Anne. 1991. *Engendering Democracy*. Cambridge, England: Polity Press.

Pratt, Minnie Bruce. 1984. "Identity: Blood Skin Heart." In *Yours in Struggle: Three Feminist Perspectives on Anti-Semitism and Racism*, ed. Minnie Bruce Pratt, Barbara Smith, and Elly Bulkin. Brooklyn, N.Y.: Long Haul Press.

Robson, Ruthann. 1992. *Lesbian (Out)law: Survival Under the Rule of Law*. Ithaca, N.Y.: Firebrand Books.

Spelman, Elizabeth V. 1988. *Inessential Woman: Problems of Exclusion in Feminist Thought*. Boston: Beacon.

Spivak, Gayatri Chakravorty. 1991. "The Practical Politics of the Open End." In *The Post-Colonial Critic: Interviews, Strategies, Dialogues*, ed. Sarah Harasym. New York and London: Routledge.

Vance, Carole. 1984. "Pleasure and Danger: Toward a Politics of Sexuality." In *Pleasure and Danger: Exploring Female Sexuality*, ed. Carole Vance. London: Routledge.

Walzer, Michael. 1983. *Spheres of Justice: A Defense of Pluralism and Equality*. New York: Basic Books.

13

Against the liberal state: ACT-UP and the emergence of postmodern politics

Stanley Aronowitz

I

The election of Rudolph Giuliani as New York city's first Republican mayor in more than twenty years challenged a number of political assumptions that had solidified into myths in the city's political culture. Among them, none was more significant than the idea (vigorously promoted by the person Giuliani defeated, Mayor David Dinkins) that, despite Staten Island and Queens's fabled conservatism, New York remained, indeed, a gorgeous mosaic of different ethnicities, races, and sexual orientations, the sum of which added up to one of the last liberal outposts in the midst of an increasingly rightward drift of the national polity. Even though Giuliani was a Republican and a militant champion of the now hegemonic doctrine that the chief role of government was to insure law and order by pursuing an unrelenting war on crime, his other political priorities were carefully disguised during the 1993 mayoral campaign as they had been in his unsuccessful bid of 1989. The political spin doctors assured us after his narrow victory over Dinkins – the city's first African-American mayor – that, beneath his conservative exterior, Giuliani was really a "Rockefeller" Republican, a designation that marked him as a softie, committed to the provision of social welfare and public goods even as he might be tough on crime. After all, who could deny that Rockefeller's administration of New York state government followed the broad pattern established by welfare liberalism during the 1930s and 1940s? Rockefeller's one great crime initiative, mandatory sentencing for drug dealers and drug users, and his order to brutally suppress the famous Attica uprising of 1969 were not, in any case, partisan political gestures. Indeed, by the 1970s organized skepticism about the criminal justice system had been dissipated by a series of media-manufactured crime waves built on the rapidly shifting racial and ethnic composition of large cities. No big city administration, whether Democratic or Republican, could afford to ignore the mounting public clamor for law and order. According to some, Giuliani was merely following a script written by most other big city mayors, including many Democrats.

Thus, for many, including some Giuliani supporters, it came as something of a surprise and, for liberals and the majority black and Latino communities, a calumny, that the new mayor fully intended to carry out at the municipal level many of the elements of the national conservative project to "downsize" government and privatize public goods. Among his plans none was more provocative than Giuliani's intention to abolish or otherwise shrink services to the homeless and to victims of AIDS. Shortly after his election victory, the press was informed that the mayor-elect would offer a plan to close a $2.5 billion budget gap by cutting municipal services: in the first place by eliminating 15,000 jobs; privatizing part of the vast municipal hospital system and paring such basic health services as pest control; selling the licenses of the municipal radio and TV stations; and, despite an official rate of youth unemployment of some 38 percent, reducing youth programs, including summer employment. As a visible sign of his serious intent to shrink the government's role in positively addressing social need, he would close some shelters for the homeless and eliminate the Department of Aids Services (DAS).

Having run as a law-and-order candidate, Giuliani pledged not to cut the uniformed employees of the police and fire departments, although sanitation would not be spared; in fact, he indicated that garbage collection might be privatized, that is, services to apartment dwellers and homeowners would be contracted out to private haulers, a measure that might not cut costs since most garbage collectors in the private sector were unionized. But it would make some free-market ideologues and large contributors among the hauling companies to Giuliani's campaign happy. Further, since the 60,000-strong teachers' union broke precedent by remaining "neutral" during the campaign (responding to its long-standing feud with the Dinkins administration), the new mayor rewarded this discretion by promising not to lay off teachers, although Board of Education administrative and clerical employees (who are represented by a union that formed one of the key elements of the Dinkins coalition) would face draconian reductions, a measure Giuliani trumpeted as a way to puncture the board's fabled bloated bureaucracy.

Within his first hundred days of elective office, the new mayor tossed many balls in the air. Faced with Armageddon, with scarcely a whimper, the union leadership of the 200,000 nonuniformed city workers conceded and averted a potentially embarrassing confrontation with the mayor by making a deal quickly. In order to allow union leaders to save face, Giuliani agreed to grant employees who elected to leave municipal employment modest lump-sum payments of up to $25,000, depending on length of service. But he made clear the administration's resolve to proceed with layoffs if the unions rejected these terms. With an 11 percent jobless rate in New York city (compared to an official national rate of 6 percent), many low-level employees had little chance of landing another job, but the much anticipated head-to-head battle between the conservative mayor and the liberal labor movement was averted by a compromise that reproduced some of the conditions of the 1975–76 fiscal crisis which had ultimately resulted in 50,000 layoffs, mostly of the working poor.

In the main, despite grumbling by African-American and Latino political leaders, Giuliani largely had his way, at least in his first months, except for his plan to sell the municipal radio and TV stations – which are listener-supported National Public Radio affiliates – and the plan to abolish the DAS. The management of the stations mobilized their considerable white middle-class membership to pledge more money to make up for anticipated lost revenue that would result from the city's withdrawal of some $1.7 million in subsidies. Given Giuliani's considerable backing among white liberals, who had been herded into his camp by their growing fear of crime and other signs of urban mayhem, the mayor backed down from his plan to sell off the stations' licenses without securing another spot on the FM dial for its classical music station. In the end, he agreed, unconditionally, to keep the license of the AM public affairs television and radio channels.

The leading AIDS activist movement, ACT-UP, swung into action against the proposed shutdown of the DAS. Activists staged a series of confrontations with the mayor: noisy demonstrations at public events, including some where the mayor was delivering speeches; a lie-in across the Brooklyn Bridge; deploying the more conventional tactics of letter-writing and rallies. After four months of press attention and disruptions promulgated by a small group of relentless activists, the city administration quietly dropped its proposal. When the new budget was finally issued in early May 1994, the DAS had been preserved. Where unions representing tens of thousands of municipal employees had failed, a relatively small, but highly vocal, social movement succeeded in staying the administration's hand.

ACT-UP's victory illustrates the relative decline of the number game in contemporary politics. ACT-UP neither represents most lesbian and gay voters who, in any case, were heavily in the Dinkins column, nor by itself has a "constituency" which could make a significant electoral difference. (At the nearly one-million-strong New York parade commemorating the twenty-fifth anniversary of the Stonewall confrontation, ACT-UP's alternative demonstration for AIDS action drew a comparatively small crowd of some six thousand.) Moreover, the establishment lesbian and gay organizations have been careful to maintain distance from ACT-UP's confrontational tactics and relatively uncompromising positions on several aspects of AIDS policy. As I want to argue, ACT-UP engages itself in the struggle for power but its capacity to win battles, enjoy influence in AIDS policy, and unsettle hegemonic political forces rests, in part, on the complexity of the contemporary political system in which majoritarian ideologies have lost some of their moral force because of the partial breakdown of the legitimacy of the liberal state (where "liberal" connotes not so much the dominance of political parties of modern social welfarism but a system where "representation" is considered an adequate measure of legitimate power).

The crisis of the United States is *overdetermined* by economic, political, and ideological developments: the loss of the state's sovereignty in the wake of the intensification of economic globalization which, concomitantly, has increased the power of international capital and the newer power centers – Germany, at the head of a new Western European alliance, and Japan – over many of the crucial decisions once made routinely by the US President and his administration. In effect, the US political system is faced with many of the same problems once reserved for Europe and developing countries. It must, for the first time in more than a hundred years, face the painful fact that its autonomy is severely constrained from without. From the Civil War until World War I, the goals and ideology of the executive branch were virtually identical to those of the decision-making sections of national financial capital and this identity was expressed openly by both partners. Between 1890 and 1912, the insurgent populist and socialist movements were able to force significant reforms on various states, a wave that resulted in the election of Woodrow Wilson's reform Democratic administration in 1912. Since Woodrow Wilson's presidency, the separation of economic from political power has become a leading tenet of a new ideology embraced by modern liberals and conservatives alike at the national level.

Yet, substantial sections of the electorate persist in disbelief. Only

✳ crisis of representative gov't

slightly more than half of the eligible voters cast ballots in the last
Presidential election, and this proportion represented a slight advance
over previous elections. At the state and local levels, the percentages
are much lower. While Ronald Reagan was elected by some 29 percent
of eligible voters in the 1984 election, many governors and mayors are
selected by even smaller proportions. Contrary to liberal explanations
asserting that the problem is voter "apathy," one might argue with
equal credibility that the United States suffers legitimation problems,
especially among economically and socially disaffected groups who
cannot see themselves in the processes of representative government.
We may observe similar dissatisfactions with the mainstream Catholic
and Protestant churches, even as membership and activism among
religious fundamentalists and formerly tiny sects has exploded. The
political parties, too, suffer from a palpable loss of activists, while
the insurgent Presidential campaign of Ross Perot in the 1992 election
succeeded in recruiting tens of thousands of volunteers.

The liberal state is losing its sovereignty, even though its sovereign
powers are insured by law which, among other rights, gives government the unconditional right to dispose of private property for public
purposes. In addition, while the legislature retains the legal right to
impose and differentiate the burden of taxes, "outside" influences such   *tax*
as political action committees, lobbies, and, perhaps equally powerfully,
the press and electronic media have effectively blocked and, in many
respects, reversed the progressive principle of distributing the tax burden
on the basis of the ability to pay.

To be sure, progressive taxation, a carry-over of Wilson's New Freedom and especially the wartime policies of the Roosevelt administration,
remains official doctrine to which, until recently, even the most rabid
conservatives were obliged to pay tribute. However, since World War
II, Democratic and Republican public officials have undermined progressive taxation by consistently enacting legislation that flattens the
proportion of tax to income between affluent and relatively hard-pressed
taxpayers. Many tax measures are regressive, such as tolls, lotteries,
and taxes on sales, fees, property, and road use, all of which fall
disproportionately on poor and lower middle-class people. And, in
the Clinton era, there is a new campaign to institute a "flat" income
tax which would merely fine-tune the Reagan–Bush tax "reforms" of
the 1980s.

I want to argue that ACT-UP is the quintessential social movement   *arg*
for the era of postmodern politics. In contrast to the leading premise
of modern politics, namely, that the legitimacy of the liberal state

is guaranteed by electoral majorities, ACT-UP tacitly challenges the *ethical* legitimacy of the majority – just as business interests have buried the majority interest in areas such as tax policy, national health care, and environmental protection. Although ACT-UP eschews doctrinal pronouncements, it insists on and seeks to impose a *substantive* rather than procedural criterion upon claims to representation. If the majority accepts or otherwise acquiesces to the institutionalized homophobia of the state and its apparatuses (including large sections of the church), citizens are under no obligation to obey the law and rules of conduct prescribed in its name. Although this gesture appears at first glance to follow Alisdair MacIntyre's call (1984) for a return to substantive justice in the mode of Aristotle's ethics, in the context of the canon of procedural rationality that governs modern politics, ACT-UP operates from "post" modern premises.

It may be claimed that Giuliani could afford to bow to ACT-UP's resistance because the financial stakes were much lower than the antici- pated savings on the wages and benefits for 15,000 employees. In any case, we may never know what effect labor union resistance might have had on the government's policies. What we do know is that the numbers game, the staple of modern electoral politics, may no longer regulate policy struggles and their outcomes (if it ever did), except in terms of the "bottom-line" issue of who may claim the right to rule. In terms of the pragmatics of governance, electoral majorities have little effect on the day-to-day political struggles which constitute what we mean by political power. Even Giuliani knew that, having won the election by a slim margin, he could not legitimately claim to have won a mandate for a determinate set of policies. Thus, he adapted the well-known Eastern European strategy of "shock" therapy to New York. He administered a torrent of changes to an unsuspecting public in the hope that the patient would be too stunned to offer resistance. In this respect, Giuliani's strategy paralleled that of economist Jeffrey Sachs, whose advice to the Polish reform government was to act swiftly to privatize state-owned enterprises and reduce welfare spending radically before the rest of the population had a chance to express its displeasure. In the subsequent Polish election the voters decisively rejected the policies of the privatizers and returned a reformed Communist Party to power. But, of course, the changes were by then sufficiently entrenched so that the new government was unable to renounce, let alone reverse, them.

In any case, postmodernity in our era of political rule consists, in a large measure, of the indeterminacy of the relation between electoral outcomes and public policy. Just as the Polish voters were largely unsuspecting about Sachs's prescriptions for their economy, what the US government actually does is the result of a series of struggles over discursive power, such as who sets the framework for the debate, how decisions are to be configured, what the constructed "public" perceives to be the case.[1]

For example, the influence of business interests on local tax, urban redevelopment, and social welfare policies is rooted not in the ability to deliver large quantities of votes, or even in the substantial campaign contributions real estate, banking, and other commercial groups bestow on both major political parties (although such a judgement would be rejected by those who favour conspiracy or economic determinist perspectives). The power of capital resides, principally, in the public perception that, in the absence of an alternative economic discourse and plan, corporations, such as those engaged in financial services, hold the economic strings; that they and the financial centers such as New York, Pittsburgh, Los Angeles, and not the production companies, are indispensible for the lifeblood of the cities. Almost everybody who counts in political terms accepts the idea that no fiscal program can be *perceived* to hurt business.

The consequences of anti-business public finance extend beyond general perceptions. As the New York fiscal crisis of 1976 demonstrates, public policy bears on such matters as the city's bond rating and, concomitantly, whether investors, notably the banks, pension and mutual funds, and insurance companies will purchase municipal bonds and at what interest rates to pay the city government's ongoing expenses. In 1975–76, labor unions and education, health, and social welfare organizations were informed that unless they agreed to substantial cuts in employment and *therefore* services, investors would undertake a capital strike against New York city (Lichten 1986). During this crisis, many were impressed by the simple formula that the business of government was, in the first place, business and that any violation of that principle risked disaster. Recall that during the previous thirty years the Democrats occupied city hall for all but eight of those years, so there was no question of an ideologically determined partisan contest over public finance. When faced with demands by a highly mobilized financial sector that the size of government be substantially reduced, the Democratic mayor obliged by proposing to lay off 50,000 city workers, a fifth of the labor force. The unions, which by the mid-1970s represented all of the city's manual and clerical employees and most nonsupervisory professionals, felt constrained to go along with the program, fearing the reaction of investors more than their own rank and file.

Since the Great Depression, successive New York municipal administrations have awarded tax abatements and other types of subsidies to
employers who threaten to remove plants and offices to greener union-
free and tax-free environments. In many of these cases, the spectre of
capital flight is enough to send even civic and labor organizations, not
to mention city officials, scurrying. Politicians have been intimidated by
the threat of job losses much more than the consequent withdrawal of
campaign funds from corporate political action committees, currently the
lifeblood of politicking in the United States. When business threatens to
relocate to the suburbs, rural areas, overseas, or, in the rare instances
when local government fails, for whatever reasons, to grant a lucrative
package of tax breaks and subsidies, the news inevitably gets around,
especially to the media. Politicians hasten to accommodate business
demands lest they be accused of impoverishing their city or town.

Despite the democratic palaver that regularly litters the linguistic
landscape, public debate about probusiness government policies at
the local level remains a rare occurrence, even when by granting
concessions, the government inevitably shifts the tax burden to small
business and the working class. Under these circumstances, services such
as education, health, and transportation suffer from consequent budget
cuts since the main source of local revenue – taxes on real property – falls
disproportionately on small holders. Since the devastation of the cities
by deindustrializing capital flight in the 1970s and 1980s, many municipal
administrations have become little more than adjuncts of the remaining
corporations. The assumption is that when large employers threaten to
move, political opposition to granting them concessions must collapse.
At the same time, if these concessions result in substantial reduction
of tax revenues to pay for programs such as AIDS services, the role of
concessions in preserving jobs takes precedence.

Thus, the fight to save city services, in the wake of the consequent
narrowing local tax base resulting from business migration and massive government concessions to those that remain, takes a distinctly
postmodern turn. Rather than being fought *primarily* at the ballot
box which in the eyes of most activists is stuffed by the de facto
one-party system, the battle must be joined in the new public sphere:
the visual images emanating from TV's 11 o'clock news of intransigent
protesters conducting in-your-face politics, street actions that embarrass
public officials through exposure, and other disruptions. Publicity is the
movement's crucial strategic weapon, embarrassment its major tactic.
ACT-UP's tacit strategy is to force on public officials, church, and
business leaders their most horrific nightmare: exposure by means of

actions that signify disrespect. By presenting itself as an "out-of-control" intransigent melange of queers and misfits, it reveals a capacity to opt out of what is expected of a "responsible" civic organization: to play by the rules. From the perspective of the establishment's code, to refuse these rules is to engage in the politics of *terror*.

In this respect, ACT-UP figuratively highjacks the rituals of respectability. When in 1991 it disrupted the cardinal's conduct of a High Service at Saint Patrick's Cathedral, it demonstrated a militancy which even the most radical civil rights and anti-war demonstrators had carefully avoided in the 1960s and early 1970s, despite ACT-UP's debt to the philosophy and politics of civil disobedience. As with all who hold up substantive justice to the vagaries of the procedurality of the liberal state, the AIDS movement has been charged with violating the fundamental freedoms of its adversaries by disrupting the most sacred rituals of the Catholic faith, and with destroying the ability of public figures to engage, with security, in dispassionate public discourse.[2]

Despite the growing number of openly gay and lesbian public officials, most AIDS activists take little comfort from these gains, at least in the face of the spreading AIDS and homophobia epidemic. In the long tradition of radical movements – anarchists, communists, feminists, and militant pacifists – ACT-UP may be regarded as the latest tribune of the idea that the grievances of the oppressed cannot be submitted for adjudication to the oppressor without factoring in a moral equivalent of power. Put another way, the presence of openly gay public officials or civic leaders is inadequate to *represent* the needs of those afflicted with AIDS, especially under conditions where determined and, more to the point principled, opponents exercise equal or greater force.[3]

For example, ACT-UP is no match for (perhaps) the leading opponent of rights for gays and lesbians, the Catholic church, either with respect to institutional power (not the least of which manifestations is the church's moral and doctrinal hold on sitting legislators and other public officials who are among its parishioners), or with respect to its status as an electoral force. Like the active core of pro-abortion activist women who are practicing Catholics, the Catholics in ACT-UP are in a unique position to understand how formidable is the church as a political influence and how daunting is the task of undermining this influence in the larger public sphere. Given the lopsided power equation, ACT-UP has effectively played the postmodern concatenation of outrageous confrontation with adroit media politics to help level the playing field.[4] Likewise, as we shall see, the movement has played the institutional game by a combination

of inside negotiation and outside agitation: as a moving target it is hard
to ensnare.

II

What ACT-UP has grasped during its decade-long existence is that the
styles appropriate to modernist political combat *do not apply* to issues
of sexuality and its vicissitudes. (The question here is whether they
still apply to any other kinds of struggles.) Having determined that the
political arena is suffused with homophobic responses to the urgency
of the AIDS epidemic, of which benign neglect and determined denial
constitute perhaps the most egregious manifestations, the pressure on
elected officials to soft-pedal public funding of AIDS research and
care programs precludes AIDS becoming a major political priority by
bureaucratic means.

For these reasons the movement has disdained relying primarily on
legislative and electoral niceties.[5] The fight to win publicly financed
AIDS services such as outpatient care, hospital care, and hospices, and
to expand research has tacitly elided the rules of prevailing definitions
of political "reason." That is, AIDS activists have refused to accept the
necessity of subordinating the urgent need for services to overarching
conceptions of economic rationality or political expediency in which
private interests are considered prior to the provision of public goods.
Nor do they accept the liberal politician's need to placate homophobic
and racist opposition to providing extensive care and expanding research
as a reasonable barrier to moving swiftly to provide what is needed.

ACT-UP's working assumption is that the prevailing economic and
political rationality is a mask for homophobia, a judgement that prompts
the movement to ignore or otherwise deride appeals to fiscal responsibility. Like its attitude toward civil virtue, ACT-UP shows little or no
respect for the problems of the money managers. In contrast, steeped
in the presupposition that fiscal austerity corresponds to the given
economic "facts," other movements and organizations such as labor
unions, health advocacy groups – among them the American Cancer
Society and the American Heart Association, whose constituents are
at least as victimized by scarce resources for research and care as those
endangered by, or suffering from, AIDS – have generally gone along
with cuts despite trepidation, because, at the level of policy if not
individual belief, they accept as credible the doctrine that expanded
health care and other social needs depend on private sector growth.
This perception is, of course, simply another way of expressing the

utter subordination of the remnants of the liberal welfare coalition to the exigencies of "free-market" economic policy. Its naïveté consists not so much in the tie to economics, but in the belief that if the resources were available for social spending, there would be no ideological barriers to more bountiful resources to deal with dread diseases, unemployment, hunger, and homelessness.[6]

To this ideological passivity one may add the degree to which nearly all erstwhile social movements have been integrated into the Democratic Party as "pressure groups," a transformation that constrains both their power base and their organizational configuration. From democratic anarchy, the internal life of the movements tends to become *normalized* in two ways: by adopting variants of Robert's Rules of Order and other means of bureaucratic management, and by entering the "contract state."[7] As metaphor, Robert's Rules assures orderly meetings and "rational" decision making, while the emergence of an organizational bureaucracy to replace the more or less anarchic and free-wheeling "movement" decision process, in which *all* members have a voice, facilitates its integration into the state system as one of the apparatuses of control.

One of the key mechanisms for transforming social movements from independent adversaries of the state to collaborators is the *service contract*. In the 1960s, under pressure from the federal requirement to dispense services with the "maximum feasible participation" of the recipients of these services, especially the poor, state and local governments contracted out large chunks of service delivery to community-based organizations (CBOs) and maintained a relatively small central staff to provide oversight, chiefly of fiscal responsibility. For example, New York city contracts some AIDS services to the Gay Men's Health Crisis (GMHC) and other locally based groups rather than reserving administration and delivery to itself. GMHC is perhaps only the most prominent of a series of once-militant groups which find themselves caught in the contradictions of the welfare state. Having been formed initially to fight for state and private support for AIDS services for an alarmingly growing community of HIV-infected gay men, it gradually, and somewhat reluctantly, became a health provider and its "movement" character receded in favor of service delivery and public policy "advocacy." By the late 1980s GMHC had become an adjunct of state and local governments seeking to enhance their own legitimacy among the now considerable "out of the closet" gay and lesbian community. On the one hand, with the rise of identity politics in the gay and lesbian community, GMHC may have been perceived as a more reliable advocate and sympathetic provider than the city. On the other hand, like antipoverty groups and other community organizations since the 1960s, it had been effectively demobilized by these relationships.

The predicament of GMHC signifies the complexity of the relationships between social movements and the political/administrative system of power. Can they or any other social movement maintain autonomy in the wake of the crumbling of the service-delivery capacity of governments which, understandably, seems to cry out for intervention by "community" groups to assure that victims actually get help? The evolution of GMHC helps explain the emergence of ACT-UP as the "outside" bad cop in AIDS crisis politics. Since the terms of becoming a de facto agent of government are increasingly rigid in the wake of numerous media-hyped examples of welfare fraud, the politics of management replaces the politics of protest for most of these erstwhile movements.

Under these conditions, the movement is often seriously constrained from taking direct action to reverse budget cuts, and wage a public fight for expanded funding and services. In time, many of the movements, now reformed as organizations, acquire elaborate staffs to lobby for grants and other funds, write and manage grants, as well as administer and deliver services. Specialists are employed in all of these areas and, even if the organization retains a membership, the expert bureaucracy tends to become its life-blood.

What, beyond creative protest and organized disrespect, distinguishes ACT-UP from traditional liberal organizations and advocacy groups? I believe the answer may be found in its different conception of *citizenship* emanating from its "ultra-democratic" style of organization which tacitly opposes traditional statist notions of "leadership."[8] The key point is this: for "good" historical reasons determined by the discourse of responsible public behavior, most social movements and advocacy groups dedicated to welfare and other aspects of social justice have subsumed their notions of citizenship under the general interest signified by the exigencies of the liberal state. Unions, groups devoted to expanding education and health services, and civil rights organizations, for example, may express their interests in forms such as legislative pressure, collective bargaining, and the like but, at the end of the day, their exercise of popular citizenship which may be best materialized in forms such as shared decision making, is constrained by the tacit rule that loyalty to the rules of representation governs political action. The advocate petitions the legislature and the executive for redress; the social movement demands, by direct action, shared power because it does not trust the canon of procedural democracy.

In a time of economic stagnation and decline, deregulation, and fiscal austerity, the *universal* interest is said to be identical with a weakened public sector. Fueled by service functions, the social movement-turned-organization's bureaucracy, members of which are frequently recruited from the ranks of government because of their expertise in "government relations" including grants acquisition, take a larger role in policy formation, even if they remain formally subject to membership review and consent. Or, as in the case of the crisis of the New York municipally owned media enterprises, many organizations have accepted the principle of voluntarism and a skewed conception of self-help as the moral equivalent of public responsibility.

For example, saving New York's public radio and TV stations was achieved by accepting the terms imposed by the Giuliani administration. What had increasingly been de facto privatization, after the concept of preponderant listener-sponsorship replaced municipal control twenty years ago, became de jure. In the future, the largely upper middle-class audience for the classical top forty offered by the FM station and for a refined version of talk radio on the AM band will pay more for their entertainment and for their social and political enlightenment. "Public" radio connotes little more than commercial-free programming except for the week-long quarterly public fund drives. Like the high deductibles many Americans are forced to accept in order to maintain their health insurance, or the ever-rising tolls to pay for urban highways, as listener-sponsored radio loses its government subsidy the price of even the shell of independence retained by these stations will be borne by its constituents or it will pass into the annals of nostalgia, together with old union songs and memories of the "movement."

Similarly, even though cancer and heart disease remain the leading killers in the United States, public funds continue to dry up for research and treatment. Consequently, a larger portion of the costs of dealing with these diseases is borne by users and corporate givers in the forms of prepaid health insurance plans, and private charitable contributions extracted, in the main, from employees during special corporate-sponsored fund drives.

And, of course, the pharmaceutical industry has stepped up its collaboration with university-sponsored research. In return for financial support for research many, if not most, scientists engaged in medical research have agreed to sell or otherwise transfer the patents for their discoveries to drug, genetic engineering, and other private companies.

As a result, and despite vehement denials by providers, access to knowledge as well as full treatment for these diseases remains restricted. Secrecy, a prime characteristic of the emerging national security state, is being replicated in the scientific community, which has a tradition of shared open knowledge.[9]

The efforts of advocacy groups to win federal and local support for care and research have been successful only in periods of relative national affluence. For the last twenty years, under the austerity regimes begun by the Nixon administration, raised to the level of a virtue by the Reagan and Bush administrations, but fostered by two Democratic administrations as well, advocates have experienced increasing difficulty obtaining enough funds to meet the burgeoning demand resulting from the veritable cancer epidemic that has afflicted the country.

ACT-UP is fairly unique among social movements, including those of mainstream feminism and racial justice insofar as it has rejected the economic determinist framework of contemporary political discourse, insisting that the AIDS epidemic, rather than fiscal constraint, *is* the definition of the crisis. The movement flourishes on its refusal of conventional definitions of responsible social and political behavior whose underpinning is loyalty to the state and to the business priorities that increasingly drive its policies. I will argue in the next section that this turn away from the rules of conventional political action within the liberal state results not from an explicit radical antistatist ideology such as that which has motivated earlier anarchist movements such as the Industrial Workers of the World (but not the socialist and communist parties which were supremely statist), but from radical democratic practices which are inspired by the early radical feminist movement and the civil rights movement, each of which perfected in-your-face politics.

With some exceptions, ACT-UP has rejected the core practices of modernist politics – centralized, bureaucratic control over decision making – which, in many social movements, have subverted their ostensible political intention. The practical effect of this rejection is that control over ACT-UP's policy is displaced from a putative center occupied by a swollen bureaucracy to autonomous voluntary committees which frequently vigorously disagree with each other, but are unable to veto the proposals of those with whom they disagree. Put another way, precisely because ACT-UP has no significant service function and hence no bureaucracy and, perhaps more important, no overarching political ideology, it has been able to mitigate, if not entirely avoid, the contradiction between opposition and integration that inheres in the underlying organizational logic of liberal movements and groups. Once sanctioned by a vote of the organization's membership assembly, the committee acts according to its own deliberations; the membership retains power over expenditures from the treasury over $1,000, a prerogative that retains a vestige of oversight. In turn, many committees raise their own money, in part to maintain their independence.

III

After a century of struggle, in the late nineteenth century Western labor and social democratic movements overcame the determined opposition of the liberal bourgeoisie to working-class (male) participation in government. In Europe, citizenship was attendant upon winning the vote – first for males regardless of property, and then for women. Although the property qualification for white male suffrage was removed prior to the industrializing era of US capitalism in the 1820s and 1830s, women were excluded from the vote until 1920, and restrictive racial criteria remained in force until the late 1960s. But even though white male workers were able to vote, until the New Deal, their alliance with the Democratic Party was both fragile and fickle. Many in the labor movement distrusted the political process and preferred to express their interests through direct action rather than the ballot, and others were determined advocates of socialist and labor parties which, until the late 1920s, claimed the adherence of many activists, including a considerable minority of rank-and-file unionists (Weinstein 1975; Lasch 1968).

In Europe, workers and their unions formed and supported labor and socialist parties which, by the end of World War II, had, under pressure from the newly emergent communist countries and mass disillusionment with liberal capitalism's capitulation to fascism, succeeded in bringing into existence welfare states that provided health care, pensions, and other basic services. Although the welfare state may be viewed as a concession to a potentially insurgent, even revolutionary, workers' movement, it succeeded in persuading the working class to stake its future on the liberal state.

No less militant than their European counterparts, US workers exacted similar gains from a reluctant Roosevelt administration and the Democratic Party to whom, after experimenting in various third party and antiparty strategies, they eventually gave electoral support, at least until the early 1970s (Weinstein 1968). This loyalty persisted from the late 1930s until the mid-1960s when a number of influences conjoined to produce a political transformation of major proportion: the intense pressure of the civil rights movement for social and economic equality, the anti-working-class bias of much of the new left, a massive shift in the tax burden to the working class, and economic stagnation which witnessed the renewal of periodic economic recessions. Buffeted by these changes many, if not a majority, of white male workers turned to the right and began the long march, at least in national elections, into the Republican Party, a trend which continues to this day. Since the 1980s, despite its attempt to head off these near-fatal defections by joining the trek away from modern liberalism as it had been defined by the Keynesian welfare state, the Democratic Party has become a minority party at the national level. Despite maintaining a fairly large tent under which feminists, blacks, and Latinos, labor unions and intellectuals coalesced, Democratic Presidential candidates after 1968 won only 40 percent of the vote in two-party elections. In fact, Bill Clinton attracted only 43 percent, and was victorious only because the two conservative candidates split some 57 percent of the remainder. Nevertheless, the Democratic Party retained its hold on Congress and most state capitals only by pledging allegiance to the free market and to the corporate-sponsored political action committees which have rewarded various Democratic as well as Republican legislators with generous contributions, even as it struggled to keep together the broad coalition which had, since Woodrow Wilson's victory in 1912, sustained the electoral viability of the party.

In retrospect the great achievement of the New Deal was to have brought the working class into the fold of liberal/welfare capitalism through the mechanisms of state-directed collective bargaining and other regulatory measures and making a place for the labor leadership at high Democratic Party councils. Although integration was not accomplished without altering the relationship between party, class, and nation, the price (social security, minimum wages, union rights) was not deemed too steep in a post-Depression era of apparently boundless growth.

Economic globalization ushered in an era of disarticulation characterized by deregulation, sharp reductions in welfare-state expenditures abetted by the eclipse of liberal ideology, and, more recently, the changes attendant upon the end of the Cold War, leading to reductions in the military budget, among other consequences. To the extent that military expenditures are linked to requirements of warfare, and may be seen as perhaps the government's most extensive form of economic intervention, including the provision of social welfare in the form of income, education, housing, and other benefits to millions of people, and also as a premier employment- and capital-generating program, the reductions are a further blow to the welfare commitments of the liberal state.

While it is both premature and excessive to claim that we are witnessing the beginning of the end of the era of state economic interventionism (after all, the federal budget is still almost $1.5 trillion) one cannot fail to observe radical shifts in the chief functions of government, and the relationship of citizens to a seriously weakened national state. Although the term "national security state" predates the current era, having been coined to describe US government policies during the rapid military build-up of the Johnson and Reagan administrations, we can observe, in the guise of the quest for personal security in the face of an increasingly dangerous world, the triumph of law-and-order ideology and, particularly, the near-hegemony of retributive justice. In this respect, the law-and-order imperative is not only a response to the changing racial and ethnic composition of cities or the rise in violent crime, but also a symptom of the shared sense that the environment has become more perilous, that human action is fraught with increased risk.[10]

Poll data show that Americans are increasingly reluctant to become involved in risky foreign policy adventures such as those manifested in the early 1990s: Bosnia, Somalia, Haiti, and Rwanda. Under intense conservative pressure we cannot avoid the risk entailed by seeking power over our own environment. Fighting crime intensifies even as it allays many of the fears that seem out of control on other fronts. In fact, "retributive" has largely replaced the adjective "social" in the very definition of justice. Perpetrator and victim, once technical terms of police work have, under the disseminating power of television and popular film, become commonplace in ordinary conversation. The "victim" is no longer defined chiefly in socioeconomic connotations or in terms of discrimination on the basis of race, sexual orientation, or gender, for example. Now, victimization means simply those individuals who have been mugged, raped, or killed by *perps*. In the conservative conception of justice, redressing the harm caused by violent criminals by sending them to prison or to the gas chamber/electric chair is coincident with its definition. In the process, the invocation of crime is *always* preceded by the modifier *violent*.

Thus, when an employer fails to provide healthful and safe working conditions and, as a result, workplace accidents rise; when women suffer employment discrimination or something other than aggressive physical sexual harassment on the job; when African-Americans are subject to hate speech; or when those afflicted with AIDS are victimized by the "benign" neglect of governments, invocations by activists and intellectuals of these "crimes" of negligence are dismissed as instances of political correctness. "Real" crime appears on the police blotter and happens exclusively to individuals.

For the Giuliani administration and many other big-city governments the charge that they are transforming themselves into a police state is by no means an extremist epithet. The new conservatism waxes proud of its pared-down mission to mete out swift and sure justice against those who would tear at the "social fabric" of the community by preying on its unprotected citizens. Although not lacking compassion for the sick and the lame (while at the same time condemning these categories to near penury in social Darwinist terms), conservatism vigorously denies government a crucial role in providing them with more than the most minimal level of subsistence.

Compassion may itself be a substitute for justice. As Hannah Arendt reminds us, compassion always already signifies inequality. The compassionate intend not justice, for justice might disrupt current power arrangements (1965, 74–85). Rather, the concern evinced by those in power for victims of AIDS, handicap, poverty, and other social diseases may be the occasion for a black-tie charity dinner, even as the charity diners cut public funds to the bone. Surely conservatives believe that the middle class can fend for itself when it comes to education and health. In the case of modern conservative administrations, this faith in privatization and voluntarism extends to the provision of pure water. While not (yet) renouncing its responsibility to provide water that is relatively free of toxins and harmful bacteria, conservatives have been so emboldened as to declare the commodification of water, if not air, a perfectly defensible position in a free (market) economy. (In this respect, perhaps the most significant distinction between New York's former Democratic governor, Mario Cuomo, and its Republican mayor is that the former still believes in environmental protection. In contrast, Giuliani has declared recycling to be a luxury incompatible with the higher aims of privatization and budget-balancing, an economy which could, in time, reduce New York's water quality to the level of the rest of the country.)

Needless to say, while the law-and-order doctrine has been with us for many years before the current crisis of the modernist liberal state, it increasingly occupies center stage. In this sense the postmodern state exhibits two contrary tendencies: its lumbering bureaucracies are under attack for being redundant in a time when the state does less, except in criminal detention and prosecution (misnamed criminal "justice"); at the same time, as its security functions proliferate, the police commissioner becomes, as much as the mayor, the central governmental figure: dialing 911, the emergency number, is the most effective way to reach city hall.

This is the vortex in which ACT-UP's practice of "no respect" plays itself out. Unwilling to follow the pattern established by the old modernist movements to fret, compromise, and ultimately disappear from the public fray, a choice which, despite their proliferating advocacy functions, tacitly accepts the new definition of the state as minimalist, ACT-UP nevertheless rejects the prevailing definition that citizens should be loyal to repressive civilization. Nor, on the other side, can the AIDS movement afford to adopt a contemporary version of Marcuse's pure refusal, according to which the notion of citizenship has itself been sundered by the authority of executive powers and any participation in the affairs of the state is tantamount to complicity. Faced with the AIDS epidemic, to focus on self-help as some have done is to foreclose hope, except for the relatively small number of its victims who can be made more comfortable in their cline. Thus, entering into intense dialogue with the liberal state is a strategy born of the insight that the remedial strategies of noblesse oblige, self-help, and voluntarism are no match for an epidemic. Thus, ACT-UP chose to fight for the provision of solid, institutionalized tax-levy money to pay for publicly administered services.

The dilemma of AIDS activists is that they must struggle within as well as against the remnants of the liberal state, asserting citizenship but avoiding giving their loyalty to its current definition. This strategy entails a process of constant testing of the liberal state's capacity to respond to every form of oppositional intervention, from engaging in protest, to offering alternative policy proposals, to negotiating and monitoring their implementation. For it is increasingly evident that legislative or administrative mandates are no assurance that a given policy will be put into effect. It is not only a question of institutional homophobia but of its fiscal variant, austerity. The budgets of many agencies charged with responsibility for dealing with AIDS were cut to the bone during the 1980s and early 1990s but not (yet) restored to operational strength during the Clinton administration. For this reason no serious social movement can afford to remain entirely on the outside of the policy framework of the provision of health, education, and other social services, an imperative, as I have previously noted, which produces severe conflicts *within the movement*. It cannot be a movement in "radical chains" in, but not of, society. It must enter society as a player, but try to retain its adversarial position. Few movements have been able or willing to walk this tight-rope. ACT-UP's frequent crises are produced by the strain of this journey. As Gilbert Elbaz (1993) has shown, contrary to widespread perception, ACT-UP is not principally a protest movement of the usual type, seeking more resources to fight AIDS on terms dictated by the scientific and technological establishment; nor is it an "interest group" with a limited agenda. It has concentrated its energies on sexually transmitted AIDS and avoided forming alliances with black and Latino communities where the AIDS epidemic has taken different forms. Nor has ACT-UP joined coalitions to fight for broader aims such as, for instance, universal health care. One of Elbaz's central arguments is that New York ACT-UP is at once two movements: a cultural movement of (primarily) gay activists seeking a democratic *community* within which their identity may be freely expressed; and an organization of heterosexual and homosexual men and women dedicated to addressing the AIDS crisis through direct action, independent research, and policy interventions.

ACT-UP's radical democratic pluralism has led to important innovations in the style and scope of social movement activity. Perhaps most significant has been its ability to intervene in science policy. Confronting the Food and Drug Administration's (FDA) slow approval process that regulates the pace of introduction of new drugs on the market, the movement has been able to speed up the process, now by confrontational tactics, now by carefully wrought arguments delivered at agency and legislative hearings.

Even more dramatic, members of an ACT-UP committee were able to offer an affirmative research program that partially altered the priorities of the key federal medical research institution, the National Institutes of Health (NIH). While *Science* and other journals of medical and scientific research consistently conceal ACT-UP's role in deciding such policy questions – such as budgeting for research and whether new vaccine trials and approvals should be accelerated – and present the debates as *internal* to the scientific community, say, between the federal Environmental Protection Administration (EPA), FDA, and NIH's Centers for Disease Control, there is no question that ACT-UP has made important interventions chiefly through direct action at these agency headquarters as well as through critiques and testimony before Congressional committees and scientific conferences.

The hubris of AIDS activists has been to set its face against the conventional view that scientific knowledge is the intellectual property of the professional/business/scientific community but instead has insisted that as "laypersons" they have the right and, perhaps more to the point, the capacity to participate in making crucial policy decisions. Armed with the ideology that science is independent of state and private intervention, scientists and science administrators at first vehemently tried to deny activists access to information and a place at the negotiating table. ACT-UP had to overcome more than homophobic prejudice; it was obliged to challenge the neutrality of science. In the process, and for many against their own predilections to accept the sacredness of scientific knowledge, it had to address a whole range of questions that bear on the applicability of democratic participation: elitism, professionalism, expertise – in short, the contradiction between the power/knowledge model and that of grass-roots democratic citizenship.

Even though a crucial part of its strategy entailed winning over a critical mass of scientists to recognize the urgency of the AIDS epidemic, the energy for change came from the movement, not chiefly from the scientific circles whose priorities often elided the AIDS epidemic both by not recognizing it and by invoking fiscal austerity after being forced to recognize the epidemic.

IV

ACT-UP's extraordinary history may be distinguished from all previous health movements by several crucial features: it is a movement of and by the victims, not merely for them. It was born in the struggle against the decision of the Gay Men's Health Crisis, the oldest AIDS advocacy organization, to become an arm of the state and, specifically, the refusal of a critical group of activists to define the AIDS crisis in terms of issues of service provision rather than that of sexual politics. ACT-UP's organizational style may be described as one of *radical democracy* as opposed to the liberal service/advocacy modes characteristic of the rest of the health movement. When, by marginalizing and otherwise excluding dissonant voices, ACT-UP exhibited some of the authoritarian characteristics of the liberal organizations, it experienced some fairly profound splits, especially the formation of two women's AIDS activist groups, the larger of which was the Women's Health Action Movement (WHAM). Although these groups were disaffected from ACT-UP's sexist practices, they departed neither from its organizational model nor from its reliance on direct action as a strategic principle behind which lay a largely unarticulated critique of the liberal state and its model of subordination, accommodation, and incremental change.

That ACT-UP has experienced deep fissures should come as no

surprise because it is, at the end of the day, not exempt from the enormous pressures of what may be described as the politics of "risk." In a moment in which the environment is increasingly unstable – a fact which makes folly of the strategy of playing by the rules – ACT-UP has to define an internal/external boundary in order to secure its own position. The internal is the community of activists, but particularly gay men, and those afflicted with AIDS. The external is coterminous with the environment within which the group exists. Consequently, it would be surprising if ACT-UP did not develop an us/them mentality, which in this case placed women on the outside. In the wake of the breakup of the old progressivist hegemonies there is simply no available worldview to hold different factions together within a single framework. After all, as a movement principally of and for gay men, which has disdained the messy ideological debates which would have had to accompany a significant address to gender, class, and race issues, its relationship to male patriarchal politics is ambiguous but nevertheless complicit. What is remarkable is that its model – the tactical arsenal which it largely borrowed from the militant wing of the civil rights and antiwar movements – has succeeded in remaining a fairly coherent alternative within the lesbian and gay movement and, more generally, in the wider sphere of sexual politics of which anti-abortion activism is an unwelcome adherent. The key issue is whether the presuppositions of ACT-UP's interventions will spread more widely to form oppositions in other spheres.

V

In the May 23, 1994, issue of *New Republic*, John Judis purports to detect, after years of retreat and decline, a new insurgency in the labor movement at the grass roots. Although he acknowledges the advanced sclerotic state of the AFL-CIO top leadership, he adduces evidence of some recently won strikes among miners, teamsters, and airline employees as well as new organizing efforts. The major strike activity may be ascribed to successful efforts to stem the employer offensive on past gains. What impresses, for example, is a Service Employees Union Project, *Janitors for Justice*, an organizing drive among Washington-area janitors. In a departure from the traditional modern union strategy of organizing workers in a particular firm for the purpose of gaining a union contract the SEIU, following the earlier example of the farm workers' effort of the 1970s, have focused on recruiting janitors regardless of whether their employers are under union contract or whether the union has enough support to demand collective bargaining status.

It is too early to tell whether these sporadic instances of labor insurgency signify the possibility – let alone the imminence – of the transformation of the unions from a series of bureaucratic fiefdoms and insurance companies into a revived social movement. Such an eventuality would presuppose that at least a considerable fraction of workers, as well as rank-and-file and middle-level unionists, recognize themselves as a distinct social group, but that alliances should be built with the likes of ACT-UP, feminists, and race and ethnic activists rather than the liberal establishment and the state, even though in the last three decades these movements have seen little reason to ally with a hostile trade union establishment.

If ACT-UP's major thesis is right, that the moment is passed for liberal hegemony, this modernist program has been, for better or worse, profoundly displaced. The conditions for modern liberal hegemony and for the interventionist state led by a political directorate capable, simultaneously, of popular mobilization and influence among and over fairly large segments of corporate capital, no longer obtains. Moreover, the limits of the national state as a vehicle for the achievement of social justice are all too apparent in an era when it has been weakened, perhaps mortally, by the emergence of a global *metastate* which increasingly demands of the national state that it shed more and more of its welfare functions.

Of course, the appearance of a postmodern politics may be ascribed to a multiplicity of developments that signify a major shift in the cultural and intellectual presuppositions of political life. Chief among these is that the category of "reason" proposed by modernity as an unimpeachable standard against which politics and culture may be measured has become a contested category. Recall that for the Enlightenment there was only one science, that of the ratio, and the determination of truth was reserved to those qualified to judge it. Although modernity never succeeded in making politics into a science, it claims the theoretical possibility that a polity of individuals may be formed which obey rules, largely procedural, that relegate the disposition of common resources to technical solutions.

The postmodern polity is defined precisely by the fact that it recognizes no universal and reductionist principle that governs resource allocations. The new social movements must act *as if* the government is a relatively autonomous system and that the disposition of public funds, for example, is always subject to partisan evaluation of the relative merits of specific proposals. In this "*as if* understanding," neither legislatures nor courts may be relied upon to adjudicate difference since only the dead are neutral. Thus, there are no "higher" powers to replace religion, invested with the right to override the judgement of those most directly affected by a given harm. Consequently, in the postmodern turn, under conditions of imposed scarcity, there is no uncontestable way to evaluate the relative merits of providing funds for cancer research and treatment in comparison to AIDS.

Under these circumstances, ACT-UP as a practitioner of postmodern politics remains remorseless in the pursuit of its own ends and is constitutionally skeptical of the priorities set by official bodies. Since these bodies are deemed both institutionally homophobic and bureaucratically repressive no presumption of unencumbrance may be made concerning their social policies. Needless to say, it was these assumptions that drove some in ACT-UP to examine the most hallowed of discourses, science, hallowed because notwithstanding Nietzsche's aphoristic declaration about the death of God, it was natural science which quickly assumed the mantle of the deity. Whereas most social movements and civil organizations in the health field are constrained by their wholehearted acceptance of the algorithms of modern science and the results of research medicine, ACT-UP has asked questions of AIDS science, including those of *verification*, considered to be the heart of scientific verisimilitude, and backs up its claims for changes with rule-breaking public demonstrations. No greater threat to modern claims that scientific decisions conform to the canons of reason could be posed. For ACT-UP insists upon its own passion against the presumption of dispassion explicit in scientific method.

Of course, ACT-UP's decision to build a non-institution with only a minimum apparatus, and to disdain the formation of bureaucracies to sustain its organization during periods of ebbing activity is fraught with the same weaknesses that have befallen previous movements. The anti-institutional bias of Students for a Democratic Society, the Student Non-Violent Coordinating Committee, the radical wing of the civil rights movement, and the groups of early radical feminism such as Redstockings and New York Radical Women, steadfastly resisted insistent demands *from within* that they stabilize their organizations, join coalitions, and form electoral parties. In the face of the almost-inevitable tendency of activists to burn out, form factions, and undergo splits these movements disappeared; what remained of the broader movements were the mainstream organizations: the National Organization for Women, the National Association for the

Advancement of Colored People, and the National Student Association.

The wager of postmodern social movements is that they can maintain their strength by hewing to the thin line between oppositional independence to and troubled participation in the institutions of state policy, if not the legislative and executive branches of government. More to the point, ACT-UP is a movement without utopias and bereft of illusions, and in consequence has eschewed ideological flags, thus abandoning the core religiosity that has sustained the historical opposition. This wager is crucial for any possible postmodern politics. Will the pattern of co-optation, of which the integration of GMHC is only the most recent example in a long line of modernist victories, prevail? Or is informed skepticism enough to sustain the passion for caring which has propeled the AIDS movement?

Notes

1. Foucault 1984. But we don't need Foucault to tell us what every politician, in and out of government, knows in her/his gut. Control the agenda and you've won half the battle. The other half is to rule everything else out of order.
2. This is perhaps the most controversial aspect of ACT-UP's approach to public authority. Contrary to the invocations by, say, Jürgen Habermas and Hannah Arendt to create a public sphere in which discussion between rational actors may resolve differences, the movement has, without acknowledgement, adopted Marcuse's doctrine of repressive tolerance. According to this view, in a grossly unequal power situation, the oppressed have no obligation to observe discursive decorum. Needless to say, the authoritarian implications – on both sides of this debate – are yet to be debated fully.
3. The question concerning representation is among the perennial issues in political theory, at least since Machiavelli beseeched the Prince to heed his subjects' will and, despite his arbitrary power, to build a base among them. As soon as the "subjects" can articulate their own will, political authority contrives to homogenize difference in the service of stability. ACT-UP's contribution to political theory, one that foreshadowed the emergence of what has become known in the 1990s as "identity" politics, is to assert the impossibility of representative authority when mandates are secured by ignoring and otherwise subverting real difference.
4. The element of surprise is among ACT-UP's most potent weapons. But when the unexpected becomes a stock-in-trade of political combat, may we speak of the routinization of outrage?
5. But New York ACT-UP has pressed for new laws to ban discrimination against AIDS victims in employment, housing, etc., and has entered the

budget debate in New York and nationally, without relying on legislation to solve the problems it raises.

6. Recall how the peace movement and many liberals expected that the end of the Cold War resulting from the collapse of the Soviet Union and Eastern European communist states would likely produce a "peace dividend." Instead, under pressure from the tax revolt, the slow erosion of the military establishment has become the occasion for a massive campaign to reduce the size of government and to privatize its services.

7. Nieburg 1965 is the pioneering study of the proliferation of the contract state and its consequences for democratic politics after World War II.

8. The most extensive discussions of citizenship in modern political theory are the works of Hannah Arendt; see especially "What is Authority?" and "What is Freedom" in *Between Past and Future* (1993); also see Lefort 1988.

9. Needless to say, among the most significant developments in the recent history of liberal states is the part played by secrecy, not only in the conduct of foreign policy or so-called national security, but also important "domestic issues." As these words are written, three public interest organizations have threatened a civil suit against the Clinton White House's task force on health care because its planning processes were conducted *in camera*. The plaintiffs contend that such activities must be subject to public scrutiny.

10. For a discussion of the issue of risk in contemporary politics see Zolo 1992, 60–62. In this book, under the rubric of *complexity* Zolo addresses directly the problem of achieving political trust and political legitimacy in an environment marked by instability and fear. He notes, without approbation, that under these conditions, from the perspective of oligarchic power, democracy appears to be an increasingly unwarranted risk.

References

Arendt, Hannah. 1965. *On Revolution*. New York: Viking Press.

1993a. "What is Authority?" In *Between Past and Future*. New York: Penguin.

1993b. "What is Freedom?" In *Between Past and Future*. New York: Penguin.

Elbaz, Gilbert. 1993. *New York ACT-UP*. Ph.D dissertation, City University of New York.

Foucault, Michel. 1984. *Power/Knowledge*. New York: Vintage Books.

Lasch, Christopher. 1968. *The Agony of the American Left*. New York: Vintage Books.

Lefort, Claude. 1988. "On Freedom." In *Democracy and Political Theory*. Minneapolis: University of Minnesota Press.

Lichten, Eric. 1986. *Class, Power, and Austerity: The New York City Fiscal Crisis*. South Hadley, Mass.: Bergin and Garvey.

MacIntyre, Alisdair. 1984. *After Virtue*. South Bend, Ind.: University of Notre Dame Press.

Nieburg, H. L. 1965. *In the Name of Science*. New York: Quadrangle Books.

Weinstein, James. 1968. *The Corporate Ideal in the Liberal State, 1900–1918*. Boston: Beacon Press.

　　1975. *Ambiguous Legacy: The Left in American Politics*. New York: Franklin Watts.

Zolo, Danilo. 1992. *Democracy and Complexity: A Minimalist Approach.* Minneapolis: University of Minnesota Press.

14

Democracies of pleasure: thoughts on the goals of radical sexual politics

R. W. Connell   Q- Why call this 'PoMo'?

Sexual liberation

The idea of sexual liberation that emerged from the new left of the 1960s (with sources going back to avant-garde intellectuals at the turn of the century) has been heavily criticized, sometimes for good reasons and sometimes for bad. It has, however, continued to influence the radical politics and social movements that have emerged since: women's liberation, gay liberation, a variety of countercultural and youth movements, the movement for "safe sex" in response to AIDS, queer politics, and others. As Marcuse (1969) suggested a quarter-century ago, these issues are a measure of the depth of the radical project.

Some currents of radicalism have remained in the trap into which Marcuse's own theorizing fell, a trap contained even in the language of "sexual liberation." Marcuse was seduced by Freud's scientific poetry, by the reification of desire in psychoanalytic theory. ("The id" in English translations is "das Es" in German, literally "the it," virtually The Thing from the Black Lagoon of the unconscious. One imagines the Instincts writhing and weaving in the depths, wailing to be free.)

Sartre's (1958) critique of the reification of libido in psychoanalytic theory is devastating. The conception of libido in need of release is based on a category-mistake about human action. We act sexually, we become sexual, but we are not constituted from the start as sexual beings. We are not driven, and we cannot act so as to liberate what is in process of being constituted. The goal of radical politics, therefore, cannot be the "liberation of sexuality" from social constraint. We can no more liberate libido than we can liberate the square root of minus one. There is no Thing there to liberate.

Sex is fluid.

But in that case, what is radical about radical sexual politics? Reiche

384

(1970), in the German student movement of the 1960s, observed how a politics of sexual freedom by itself amounted to a "perpetual puberty." The women of the new left came to see how the unconditional claim for sexual freedom privileged the sexuality of the most powerful, i.e., heterosexual men; and that was a founding moment of contemporary feminism (Segal 1983).

It seems that a similar problem is emerging in contemporary radical theory in the rich capitalist countries. The emphasis on sexuality as performance, on the adoption of shifting sexual identities, on the multiplicity of positions in discourse and possibilities of signification, defines sexual politics as a kind of play. This approach is stimulating for the players, and it does involve a certain personal risk to simulate being queer in the streets, if the streets are patrolled by homophobes.

It does not necessarily involve much more – in the sense of a politics capable of getting rid of the homophobia. Indeed, absorption in the game, on the part of players who are greatly privileged in global terms, might be considered the semiotic equivalent of what Marcuse (1964) called "repressive desublimation" – as we might now call it, getting lost in sexual cyberspace.

Contemporary sexual politics does have radical potential, and radical achievement. For instance, the remaking of sexual culture in urban gay communities in the face of AIDS is a remarkable example of collective self-management in the face of oppression (for documentation of this process, see Kippax et al. 1993). To sustain and widen that kind of achievement, it is important to find ways of reformulating the radical potential of sexual politics and thus rethinking its goals. Tools for the job can be found in debates about the nature of sexuality, and especially in the emerging analysis of structure in sexual social relations.

Sexual social relations

Sexuality, in something like its modern sense, became an issue for the European intelligentsia through the work of Darwin, whose evolutionary theory both naturalized an issue formerly the domain of theology and morals, and problematized it. The early texts of sexology accepted the premise of the biological constitution of sexuality and applied it to humans. The twentieth-century landmarks of sexology, the work of Kinsey and Masters and Johnson, fall in this tradition but also mark its exhaustion (the story is told in Connell and Dowsett 1993).

The scientific discourse of sexology was often scandalous – Kinsey was abused as violently as Freud had been – but in truth its assumptions were widely shared. Conservative ideology typically places sex at the boundary of the social, representing what is irrational or animal in human life. Readings of sexuality as natural, or at any rate beyond the social, have also been made by the left, providing a theoretical base for resistance from homophile politics at the turn of the century to cultural feminism in the 1970s.

The intellectual program of nativist sexology has nevertheless been exhausted, and since the 1970s the cutting edge of sexology has been in research on the social construction of sexuality. North American research, epitomized by Gagnon and Simon (1974), emphasized that sexual behavior was learned behavior, and set out to trace the cultural scripts by which its learning was guided. European research, epitomized by Foucault (1980), emphasized the cultural processes involved in the definition of sexuality itself and in the constitution of sexual categories.

Social constructionism has displaced scientific nativism, not as an alternative explanation of exactly the same object, but because it has brought into view a wider object of knowledge. This includes the social practices and relations in which bodily processes occur, mostly written out of positivist sexology. Social constructionism insists that sexuality is historical, and this idea has been scandalous to people who correctly take sexuality to be about bodies, but wrongly assume bodies to be outside history. Bodily processes are drawn into social relations. A sociology of the body has now developed (Turner 1984, Glassner 1988) which explores the wide variety of ways in which this happens: through fashion, sport, body culture, etc. The bodily processes of sexuality are thus shaped by social relations which occur in history.

This principle was accepted by critical theorists from Reich and Marcuse to Foucault, but only in connection with social relations constituted outside of sexuality – specifically, class relations. Here Foucault remained on the same ground as the Marxism he rejected. The power active in power/knowledge, in the discursive constitution of "sexuality," is precisely a class power, the power of a professional and property-owning bourgeoisie. Foucault is right in thinking class power does invest sexuality; but there is more to the social process than that.

Here we run up against one limit of social theories of sexuality. Another concerns the way in which social constructionism paradoxically relies on biology to define that-which-is-being-constructed. Treating the body as an object of social process makes it difficult to distinguish the construction of sexuality from any other process of social scripting or control. As Vance puts it:

to the extent that social construction theory grants that sexual acts, identities and even desire are mediated by cultural and historical factors, the object of the study – sexuality – becomes evanescent and threatens to disappear.

(1989, 22)

Understandably, the result is likely to be an appeal back to nativism. Hence, in part, the revival of "essentialist" views in lesbian and gay studies (Stein 1990).

The logical limit of the social constructionist tendency is a purely semiotic view of sexuality, concerning itself only with discourse and subject positions in discourse. Here, indeed, the problem disappears. Bodies are present as surfaces on which discursive meanings are inscribed (the language, if taken literally, is reminiscent of the machine in Kafka's (1961) story "In the Penal Settlement"). The politics of sexuality consists of the contestation of meanings and representations.

This definition evacuates, rather than resolves, problems about bodies; which are certainly surfaces to be written on, but are also busy growing, aging, reproducing, getting sick, feeding well or badly, getting aroused or turned off, and so on. All these are social processes, and all are hard to separate from sexual practice and sexual signification.

To take good account of bodily experience and bodily process we do not need to retreat from social analyses of sexuality. Rather we need an advance to a more thorough and comprehensive social analysis. The bases of such a theory are readily to hand. The new left, feminism, and gay liberation between them opened up a range of issues not just about the social construction of sexuality but also about the sexual construction of society, about the relations constituted through sexual practice.

I will call these "sexual social relations," following the pioneering analysis of personal life and its structural contexts by the British group that called itself the Red Collective (1978). As the Red Collective argued, there are systematic relationships between the sexual relationships between people. That is to say, there is a social structure in sexuality. In this structure personal practice encounters organized limits and organized enablements. Of the many ways in which this could be illustrated, perhaps the most striking is the ordering of sexuality through the gender of object choice – heterosexuality and homosexuality, considered not as opposites but as a couple.

As the hegemonic position of heterosexuality illustrates, the structuring of sexuality may make the enablement of some groups' practice the condition of limitation on others'. In this case the structure requires inequality and gives rise to oppression, as Rubin (1984) argues. This defines a sexual politics, not reducible to any other form of politics, arising within a specific structure of social relationships.

To name "sexual social relations" is not to imagine a separate sphere of life which one enters like walking through a door. It is to identify a logic of practice, a course which social action may take in any of the settings in which practice does occur. Research on the sexual dimension of life in offices and factories, which Hearn and Parkin (1987) call "organization sexuality," together with the political mobilization around sexual harassment, make it abundantly clear that sexual politics is not confined to special settings.

Several logically different forms of politics are generated within contemporary sexual social relations. The first is the kind explored by Rubin, arising from the "speciation" of sexualities within a hierarchy of power or legitimacy. A legitimate form of sexuality is defined, and other forms are declared to be perverted, deviant, sinful, degenerate, etc. Those people who engage in stigmatized sexual practice are oppressed through the hierarchy of sexualities, whatever their social position in other respects. Oppression of gays by straights, and resistance through the formation of a sexual subculture, is the paradigm for this kind of politics. A striking feature of current sexual politics is the way other stigmatized groups are now following this path.

Second is the constitution of inequalities through sexual practice itself. The most familiar cases are within heterosexuality, where the gendered object-choice brings into play the structure of gender inequalities. Research on marital rape (Russell 1982), for instance, shows sexual violence by husbands occurring in a continuum of coercion, intimidation, claims of ownership, claims of right, claims of need, economic pressure, persuasion, and customary interpretations of marriage.

In both kinds of politics the relations of power extend beyond particular families or neighborhoods. The institutions that define sexual ideology on a society-wide scale are involved in the struggle of interests: the church, the mass media, the school system.

The state is also deeply involved. Governments attempt population policies directly regulating sexuality, and public health measures which often bear on sexual practice. A current example is the attempt to change sexual practice through AIDS-prevention advertising campaigns. The "regulation of desire," as Kinsman (1987) put it in his Canadian study, is a persistent feature of state policy.

Beyond this again are global processes that regulate and reconstruct sexual practice. If we look at them historically their political character is inescapable: violent appropriation of bodies, social disruption, and indeed mass death. Colonial occupation commonly meant the taking of indigenous women for the sexual service of settlers, the occupation force being mainly men. In Australia, as in the United States, aboriginal children were liable to be seized from their parents to be "civilized" in missions, boarding schools, or white foster homes. Venereal disease followed the flag: European sailors were the vector for the spread of syphilis as well as Christianity around the globe.

The coercive sexuality of the colonial frontier is now eerily replayed in the postcolonial global market, with the growth of sex tourism. An extreme disparity of wealth allows businessmen and tourists visiting destinations like Thailand to command sexual services hard to get elsewhere, the most important being condom-free penetration. The current result is a high level of sexually transmitted disease in the prostitute workforce and a looming AIDS disaster (Bonacci 1992).

The third dimension of sexual politics concerns how the practice of one person or group becomes constraint and enablement for another. In Sartre's analysis of this problem (1976), the underlying condition for structural antagonism is material scarcity – not natural scarcity but historically produced scarcity.

The argument seems apt for sexuality, where scarcity is a familiar condition and is socially produced. A compound of prohibitions, the incest taboo, was central in Freud's analysis of the making of personalities. A sense of their total weight fueled both Freud's and Reich's critiques of modern civilization. And this sense was eventually taken over into the agenda of "sexual liberation."

As the politics of liberation implied, scarcity is not inherent in sexual practice. Indeed one of the most striking things about sexuality is its social amplification, the way in which an increase of pleasure for one partner need not decrease, but may increase the pleasure of the other. Stepping outside the Western discourse of sexuality, Ram (1991) notes how the very language in which sexual matters are spoken of among the Mukkuvar people of south India makes women's sexuality inseparable from questions of auspiciousness and fertility. The denial of plenitude marks the operation of repressive power in sexual intercourse, where one partner "takes" pleasure from the other.

There is, then, a contradiction between the social production of plenitude and the social denials of its possibility. In this sense sexual politics, while taking quite specific forms, is not fundamentally different from the other kinds of politics which shape human possibilities and the creation of collective futures.

Democracies of pleasure

To understand sexuality neither as nature nor discourse, but as a sphere of social practices that constitute social relations, helps clarify the goal of sexual politics. As I have argued, the goal cannot be the "liberation of sexuality" from social constraint. The only thing that can be liberated is people. It is meaningful to speak of "sexual liberation" where oppression is accomplished in the sexual social relations between groups of people. What "liberation" then means is that the oppressed gain power over their own lives, power that was formerly exercised by other groups. Where there is a deeply entrenched, long-established pattern of power and control, its overthrow is a revolutionary process. Literally, not metaphorically, revolutionary. It requires the overthrow of institutions, it depends on mass action, and it points to a profoundly altered social order.

That a real revolution is involved was perfectly clear to women's liberation and gay liberation activists and theorists around 1970, and is exactly what has been lost in the evolution of theory since. The early formulas of sexual liberation, which drew their model of power and revolution from a bookish Marxism, were implausible. But they had a sound understanding of the depth of change involved.

The goal of this process is not the abolition of the social structuring of sexuality, but the democratization of the social relations involved – in the terms I have been using, the democratization of sexual social relations. This means a search for equality and empowerment across the whole social terrain of body-reflexive practices relating to erotic pleasure and reproduction.

As we have seen, these social relations have a macro-structure, and are the field of operation of large-scale institutions. The goal of democratization necessarily embraces these, as well as the face-to-face interactions more normally thought of as the sites of sexuality. The agenda must address states, markets, media. To reapply Abraham Lincoln's principle, we cannot settle for a sexual world half-slave and half-free.

Democratizing the social relations of sexuality is, in principle, no more mysterious than democratizing any other complex of social relations and social practices. It involves equalizing resources, creating means of shared decision making, and making sure the process continues into the future.

"Equalizing resources" is a mild phrase for an enormous project. In much of the world, sexual social relations are constructed in conditions of dire inequality, from the Jakarta prostitutes interviewed by Murray (1991) to the London teenagers interviewed by Lees (1986). In both these cases their disempowerment as women, and the social empowerment of men, is fundamental in the making of sexuality.

Empowerment requires not only material equality, but cultural resources, notably knowledge and social respect. The lack of respect, for Lees's adolescent girls, shapes their sexuality under the threat of discrediting as "slags" – and behind that, the threat of violence. Contesting violence against women (Dobash and Dobash 1992), and violence against gays (McMaster 1991), is an essential part of a democratic agenda in sexuality.

To speak of "shared decision making" is to invoke the classical conception of democracy, direct rule by the citizens – not its contemporary caricature, parliamentary plutocracy. It is necessary to have organized ways of taking control over the social processes constituting sexuality, as a joint project of all those affected by them – the "citizens" of the sexual republic concerned.

This project may sound abstruse, but is concrete enough in a situation like AIDS prevention or contraception. Making decisions about someone else's life by fucking them is a process that has to be under their control, through disclosure and negotiation. Everything Habermas has said about power producing systematically distorted communication (Pusey 1987) becomes relevant here. Truth matters; and truthfulness can only be tested in a process under democratic control.

"Making sure the process continues" is part of what distinguishes a democratic enterprise from a personal claim. Action in the present involves caring for others, including others still to come. This argument gets into sticky issues about claims to represent other people and their interests, a prime target in postmodern criticism of the traditional left. The criticism of vanguard claims to represent the common interest is perfectly valid – it goes back before postmodernism (Bakunin 1971 [1872]). It does not imply, however, that everyone should shrink back and make claims only about themselves. To make any claim about oppression or exclusion is to make a claim of justice, which requires consideration of the impersonal structure of power, and the interests of the least advantaged whoever they are.

For these interests to be served over the long term requires an educational agenda, only the haziest beginnings of which are visible in sex education in the schools and adult education for AIDS prevention. Both enterprises operate under severe constraint; a considerable struggle would be required to turn them into resources for a democratic reconstruction of sexuality.

It is also necessary to think about what kinds of political organization might have the continuity to be a resource for others beyond the immediate participants. We cannot depend on commercial mass media to hand down political experience to new generations. (They do that, of course – in their own fashion, as entertainment and cautionary tales.)

Some difficulties

What replaced the rhetoric of revolution, as the new left faded from the scene, was the idea of individual rights to sexual expression or sexual pleasure. In the United States especially this became the language of mainstream feminism in campaigns for the Equal Rights Amendment, abortion rights, equal opportunity in employment, the right to be free of pornography and sexual harassment, etc. It also became the language of gay activism, in campaigns for civil rights and antidiscrimination laws.

The idea of an individual right to choose one's sexual partners and practices fits easily into the structure of US law and political discourse, and certain protections have been won this way. The 1993 struggle over the right of gays to serve in the US military is a striking illustration of how far this shift has gone. The last thing that the gay liberationists of 1970 wanted was to be part of imperialism's apparatus of violence.

But to treat one's body as a private possession (the basis of the discourse of sexual rights within a capitalist society) is to refuse the issue of inequality between owners. The arguments work as if the body were everyone's only possession, so far as sexual practices are concerned.

But this assertion is patently untrue. Major inequalities impinge on sexuality: hence prostitution, straight and gay; hence the economic pressure on women to marry. The scale of these inequalities can be seen in the dynamics of sex tourism, and in the statistics of men's and women's income. Claims of rights are vulnerable to counterclaims of rights based on other people's possession of their bodies. It is difficult to see that a sexual politics based on concepts of individual rights can be more than defensive in the long run. Yet this is the leading form that sexual politics currently takes.

A politics of rights has, even in defensive mode, provided some protection for the growth of sexual subcultures, and this poses the second difficulty I want to raise. What happens when the sexual practice itself centers on power?

It is a striking feature of sexuality that erotic interest can attach to the structure that governs sexual practice. The distinction of femininity from masculinity is itself cathected, which is why the ambiguities in gender-bending are disturbing and culturally powerful (Garber 1992), not just muddy. Power relations too can be cathected, and often are, judging from how frequently sexual fantasies include force – either coercing or being coerced.

The political issue is sharply posed by the "leatherfolk" (Thompson 1991) who go beyond fantasy to practice: whose sexual pleasure is sado-masochistic and whose sexual practice involves enacting master/slave relationships and deploying symbols of power and domination – whips, boots, black leather, body piercing, chains. Not much democracy in view. And these are the "sexual outlaws" who, more than anyone else, have kept alive the radical rejection of convention, the demand for pleasure and expression on one's own terms, that marked the impulse towards sexual liberation.

SM theorists, themselves bothered about this issue, have developed the idea that the leather community's practice involves an exchange of power. Someone who is "top" in one interaction may be "bottom" in the next; the bottom in any case sets the parameters of a sexual scene and conditionally entrusts the top with power. Thus, though power is celebrated, it also circulates.

This argument works for the immediate relationship, but does not deal with the wider significance of the power symbolism. Sexual sub-cultures are not hermetically sealed; playing games with slavery and swastikas, for instance, is not an innocent pursuit in terms of race. Nor is the circulation free and equal, either in SM fantasy or in practice.

At the same time, the subculture's theorists have a strong point that what matters most is not what formulas sexual practice starts with, but what it makes of them. Human practice is transformative; the materials of a patriarchal culture can be transformed by being used in new ways. There are feminist reappropriations of fashion (Chapkis 1986), gay reworkings of masculine styles (Humphries 1985), and so on.

Sexuality, always refractory, bounces off the conventions of the social order that is being rejected. The argument that transgressive sexuality is inherently subversive is not convincing. But transgressive sexuality can be a component of the move "towards a more colorful revolution" if, as Chapkis argues for the politics of appearance, it is embedded in a vigorous politics of equality.

In conclusion

To treat sexuality as a realm of democratic social politics feels awkward. We do not have a comfortable, familiar, or even fashionable language for doing this. We have to push against some well-established habits of thought and some familiar radical positions, as I have indicated in the case of "rights."

The notion that there should be some kind of collective responsibility in sexual practice has been established in gay community action in response to AIDS, but does not exist at all as a project in hetero-sexuality. What exists instead is a repressive discourse of "community standards," a demand for respectability not responsibility – and a radical impulse toward transgression.

The massive irresponsibility in the dominant ideology is shown by the dismal state of AIDS education in schools. Real respect for the interests of children in the face of a lethal epidemic would by now have produced – ten years after public recognition of the epidemic – a vigorous, explicit, no-holds-barred curriculum on sexuality as a universal part of schooling.

The cultural authority of hegemonic heterosexuality remains the limit to radical sexual politics at present. Hegemonic heterosexuality is not a static system of sexual practice. Its repertoire expands (e.g., the addition of oral-genital sex), and new contexts of practice are created (e.g., new forms of prostitution). Hegemonic heterosexuality is capable of being modernized and absorbing some of the impulses of sexual radicalism.

A striking example can be found as early as the mid-1970s in Marabel Morgan's book *The Total Woman*. Within a framework of evangelical religion and self-help psychology, the author advises an audience of middle-class housewives about how to spice up their marriages and hold onto their husbands by eroticizing everyday life. Bubble baths, make-up, candlelight, and perfume figure heavily. Some of the techniques are things of beauty:

For an experiment I put on pink baby-doll pajamas and white boots after my bubble-bath. I must admit that I looked foolish and felt even more so. When I opened the door that night to greet Charlie, I was unprepared for his reaction. My quiet, reserved, nonexcitable husband took one look, dropped his briefcase on the doorstep, and chased me around the dining-room table.

(Morgan 1975, 94)

Morgan draws on the sexual enthusiasm of the liberation movements, but utterly reverses the social message: assuming, indeed promoting, complete dependence of the wife on the husband's earnings, and subordination to the husband's authority. The wife becomes an erotic doormat. According to the publisher, two million copies circulated.

Comedy, doubtless; but two million is a lot. Hegemonic heterosexuality can be reinforced by eroticism as well as contested. It is the program of social equality that defines the radicalism of sexual politics.

References

Bakunin, Michael. 1971 [1872]. "The International and Karl Marx." In *Bakunin on Anarchy*, ed. S. Dolgoff, 287–320. London: George Allen and Unwin.

Bonacci, Mark A. 1992. *Senseless Casualties: The AIDS Crisis in Asia.* Washington D.C.: International Voluntary Services/Asia Resource Center.

Chapkis, Wendy. 1986. *Beauty Secrets: Women and the Politics of Appearance*. Boston: South End Press.

Connell, R. W., and G. W. Dowsett. 1993. "The Unclean Motion of the Generative Parts: Frameworks in Western Thought on Sexuality." In *Rethinking Sex*, ed. R. W. Connell and G. W. Dowsett, 49–75. Philadelphia: Temple University Press.

Dobash, R. Emerson, and Russell P. Dobash. 1992. *Women, Violence and Social Change*. London: Routledge.

Foucault, Michel. 1980. *The History of Sexuality: Vol. I. An Introduction*. New York: Vintage.

Gagnon, John H., and William Simon. 1974. *Sexual Conduct: The Social Sources of Human Sexuality*. London: Hutchinson.

Garber, Marjorie. 1992. *Vested Interests: Cross-Dressing and Cultural Anxiety*. New York: Routledge.

Glassner, Barry. 1988. *Bodies: Why We Look the Way We Do (And How We Feel About It)*. New York: Putnam.

Hearn, Jeff, and Wendy Parkin. 1987. *"Sex" at "Work": The Power and Paradox of Organization Sexuality*. Brighton: Wheatsheaf.

Humphries, Martin. 1985. "Gay Machismo." In *The Sexuality of Men*, ed. Andy Metcalf and Martin Humphries, 70–85. London: Pluto.

Kafka, Franz. 1961. "In the Penal Settlement." In *Metamorphosis and Other Stories*, 167–99. Harmondsworth: Penguin.

Kinsman, Gary. 1987. *The Regulation of Desire: Sexuality in Canada.* Montreal: Black Rose Books.

Kippax, Susan, R. W. Connell, G. W. Dowsett, and June Crawford. 1993. *Sustaining Safe Sex: Gay Communities Respond to AIDS*. London: Falmer.

Lees, Sue. 1986. *Losing Out: Sexuality and Adolescent Girls*. London: Hutchinson.

McMaster, David. 1991. *One Does Not Stir Without the "Other": Homophobia, Masculinity, and Intention*. Honors Research Essay, Macquarie University, Sydney.

Marcuse, Herbert. 1964. *One-Dimensional Man: Studies in the Ideology of Advanced Industrial Society*. Boston: Beacon Press.

——— 1969. *An Essay on Liberation*. Boston: Beacon Press.

Morgan, Marabel. 1975. *The Total Woman*. London: Hodder and Stoughton [first published 1973].

Murray, Alison J. 1991. *No Money, No Honey: A Study of Street Traders and Prostitutes in Jakarta*. Singapore: Oxford University Press.

Pusey, Michael. 1987. *Jürgen Habermas*. Chichester and London: Ellis Horwood/Tavistock.

Ram, Kalpana. 1991. *Mukkuvar Women: Gender, Hegemony, and Capitalist Transformation in a South Indian Fishing Community*. Sydney: Allen and Unwin.

Red Collective. 1978. *The Politics of Sexuality in Capitalism*. London: Red Collective/Publications Distribution Cooperative.

Reiche, Reimut. 1970. *Sexuality and Class Struggle*. London: NLB.

Rubin, Gayle. 1984. "Thinking Sex: Notes for a Radical Theory of the Politics of Sexuality." In *Pleasure and Danger: Exploring Female Sexuality*, ed. Carole S. Vanie, 267–319. Melbourne: Routledge and Kegan Paul.

Russell, Diana E. H. 1982. *Rape in Marriage*. New York: Macmillan.

Sartre, Jean-Paul. 1958. *Being and Nothingness: An Essay on Phenomenological Ontology*. London: Methuen.

——— 1976. *Critique of Dialectical Reason: Vol. I, Theory of Practical Ensembles*. London: NLB.

Segal, Lynne. 1983. "Smash the Family? Recalling the 1960s." In *What Is To Be Done about the Family?*, ed. Lynne Segal, 25–64. London: Penguin/Socialist Society.

Stein, Edward, ed. 1990. *Forms of Desire: Sexual Orientation and the Social Constructionist Controversy*. New York: Garland.

Thompson, Mark, ed. 1991. *Leatherfolk: Radical Sex, People, Politics, and Practice*. Boston: Alyson.

Turner, Bryan S. 1984. *The Body and Society*. Oxford: Basil Blackwell.

Vance, Carole S. 1989. "Social Construction Theory: Problems in the History of Sexuality." In *Homosexuality, Which Homosexuality?* ed. Dennis Altman, et al., 13–34. London: GMP and Amsterdam: Uitgeverij An Dekker/Schorer.